THE
RAVEN'S CHILD

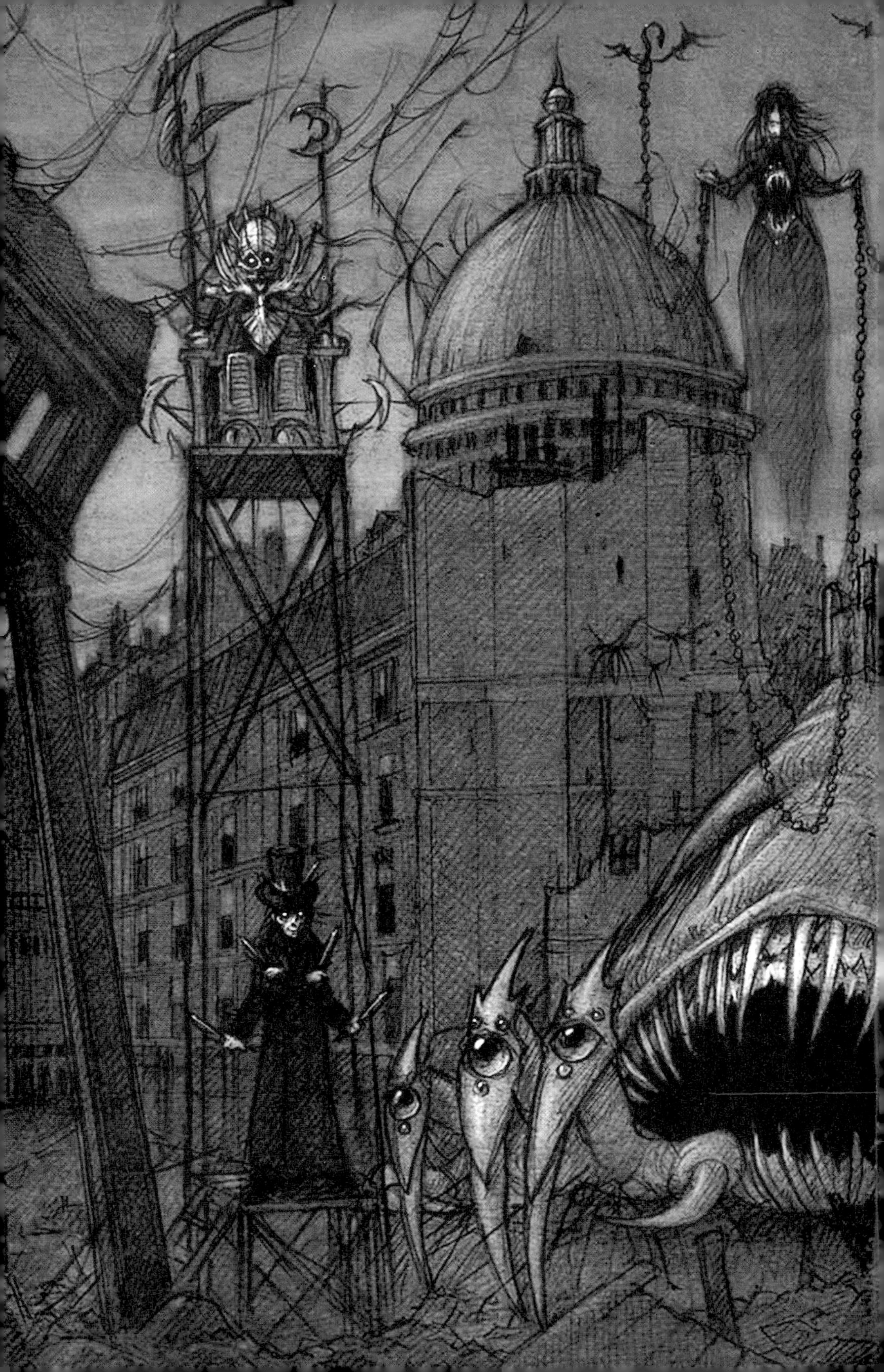

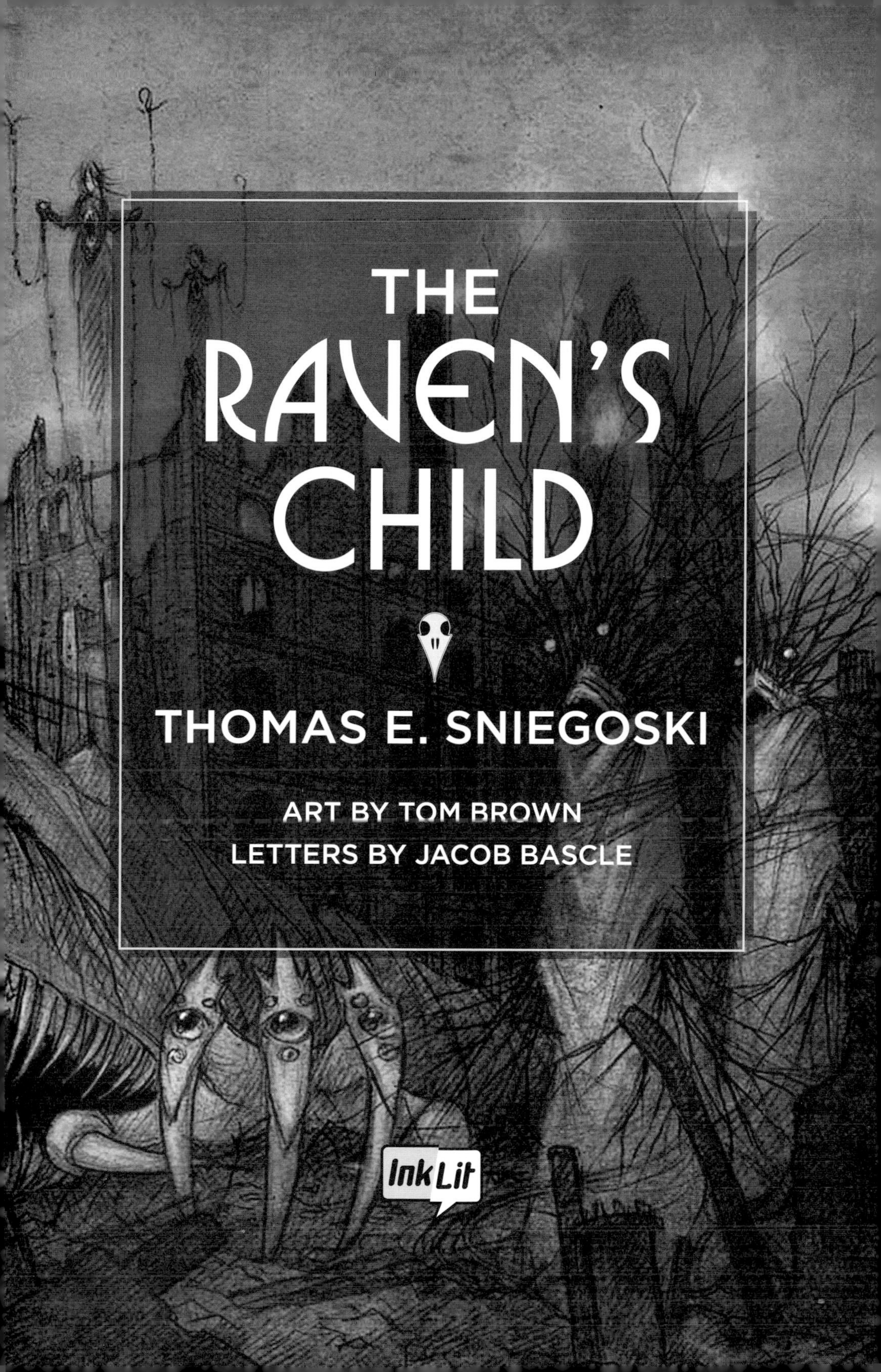

THE RAVEN'S CHILD

THOMAS E. SNIEGOSKI

ART BY TOM BROWN

LETTERS BY JACOB BASCLE

InkLit

InkLit

An imprint of Penguin Random House LLC
375 Hudson Street, New York, New York 10014

This book is an original publication of Penguin Random House LLC.

For more information, visit penguin.com.

Library of Congress Cataloging-in-Publication Data

Sniegoski, Tom.
The Raven's child / Thomas E. Sniegoski.
pages ; cm
ISBN 978-0-425-27907-6 (paperback)
I. Title.
PS3619.N537R38 2015
813'.6—dc23
2015005830

PUBLISHING HISTORY
InkLit trade paperback edition / August 2015

PRINTED IN THE UNITED STATES OF AMERICA

10 9 8 7 6 5 4 3 2 1

Cover art by Tom Brown.
Cover design by Jason Gill.

Penguin
Random
House

FOR DAVID KRAUS
best friend, brother, King of Monster Island
This one is for you.

August 10, 1963–January 12, 2013

ACKNOWLEDGMENTS

Thomas E. Sniegoski: As always, thanks and love to the enduring LeeAnne—my wife and partner in crime—and to Kirby for showing me the ways of being a monster.

Special thanks are also due to Christopher Golden, Mike Mignola, Eric Powell, Jeff Smith, Jack Kirby, Mom Sniegoski, Frank Cho, Pam Daley, Tom and Nimue Brown, Pete Donaldson, Kate Schafer Testerman, the incredible Rich Johnson, and Tim Cole and the murderous Throng down at Cole's Comics in Lynn, Massachusetts. Turn on anything, you'll get it.

Tom Brown: Firstly, gratitude and love to Nimue Brown, without whom I could not have possibly completed the art for this book and maintained what little sanity I possess (which is not a great deal, but I treasure it all the more for that). Secondly, my thanks to Walter Sickert & the Army of Broken Toys. Their music powered me through the tough patches. It was fuel for the soul. Thirdly, vast and boundless thanks to Mr. Thomas Sniegoski for his friendship and for including me in this epic adventure. I have been keen to work with him for years and am so very glad to have had this opportunity at last. Fourthly (is that a word?) but hardly last in importance, my thanks to our editor, Rich Johnson, whose calm professionalism and sharp eye have made this both a fantastic experience and a better book.

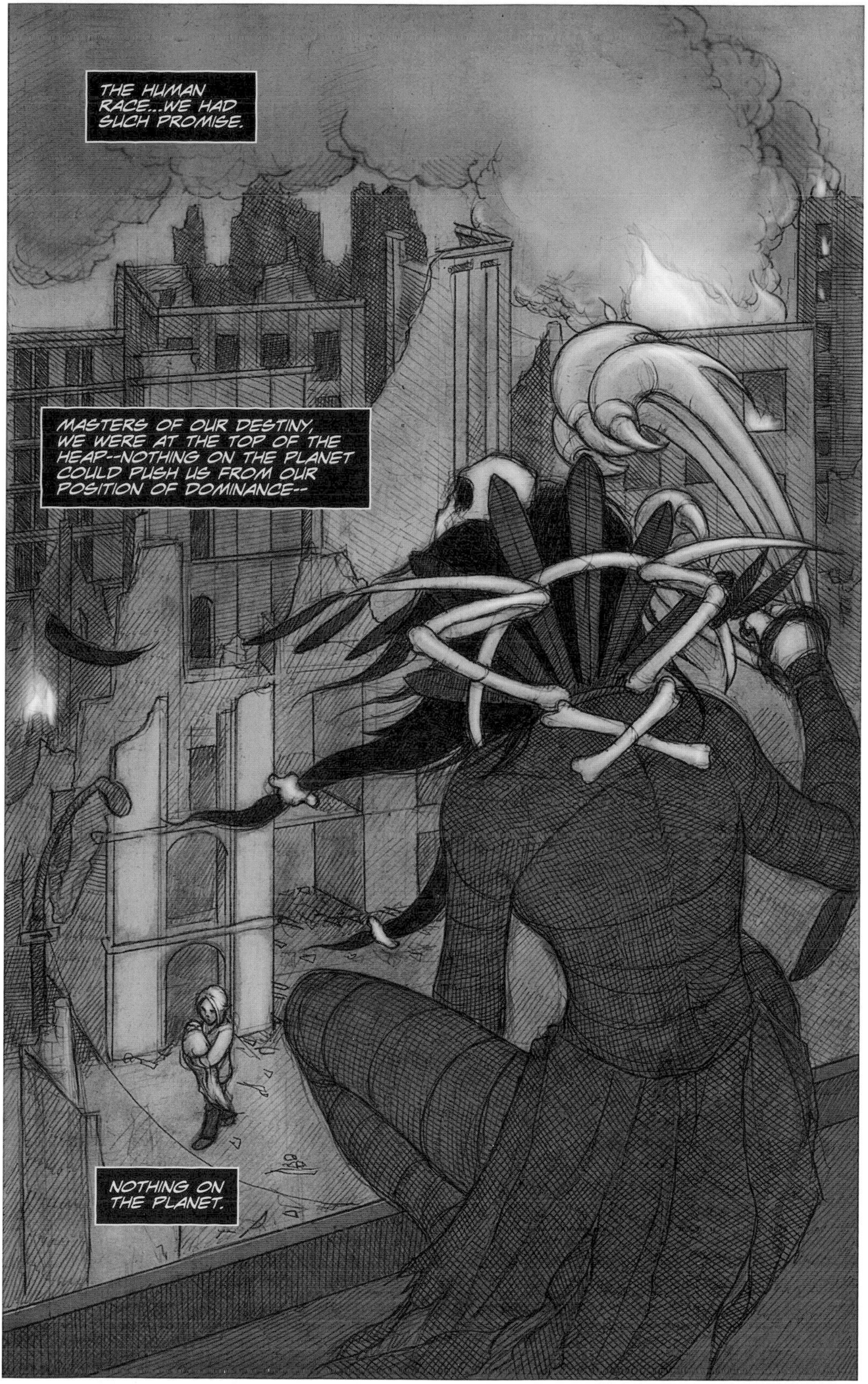
THE HUMAN RACE...WE HAD SUCH PROMISE.
MASTERS OF OUR DESTINY, WE WERE AT THE TOP OF THE HEAP--NOTHING ON THE PLANET COULD PUSH US FROM OUR POSITION OF DOMINANCE--
NOTHING ON THE PLANET.

GHHAAAA

SHHHHH, NOW. WE'LL BE AT THE SHELTER SOON ENOUGH, AND YOU CAN MAKE ALL THE NOISE YOU WANT.

BUT FOR NOW, SHHHHHH!

NO ONE KNEW WHERE THE THRONG CAME FROM... IT WASN'T FROM HERE, I CAN TELL YOU THAT.

OH, YESSSSSSS.

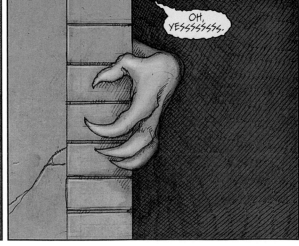

IT WAS ONLY A FEW SHORT MONTHS BEFORE WE LOST OUR TOP-DOG STATUS. THE MONSTERS SUDDENLY RULED THE NIGHT AND THERE WASN'T ANYTHING WE COULD DO ABOUT IT.

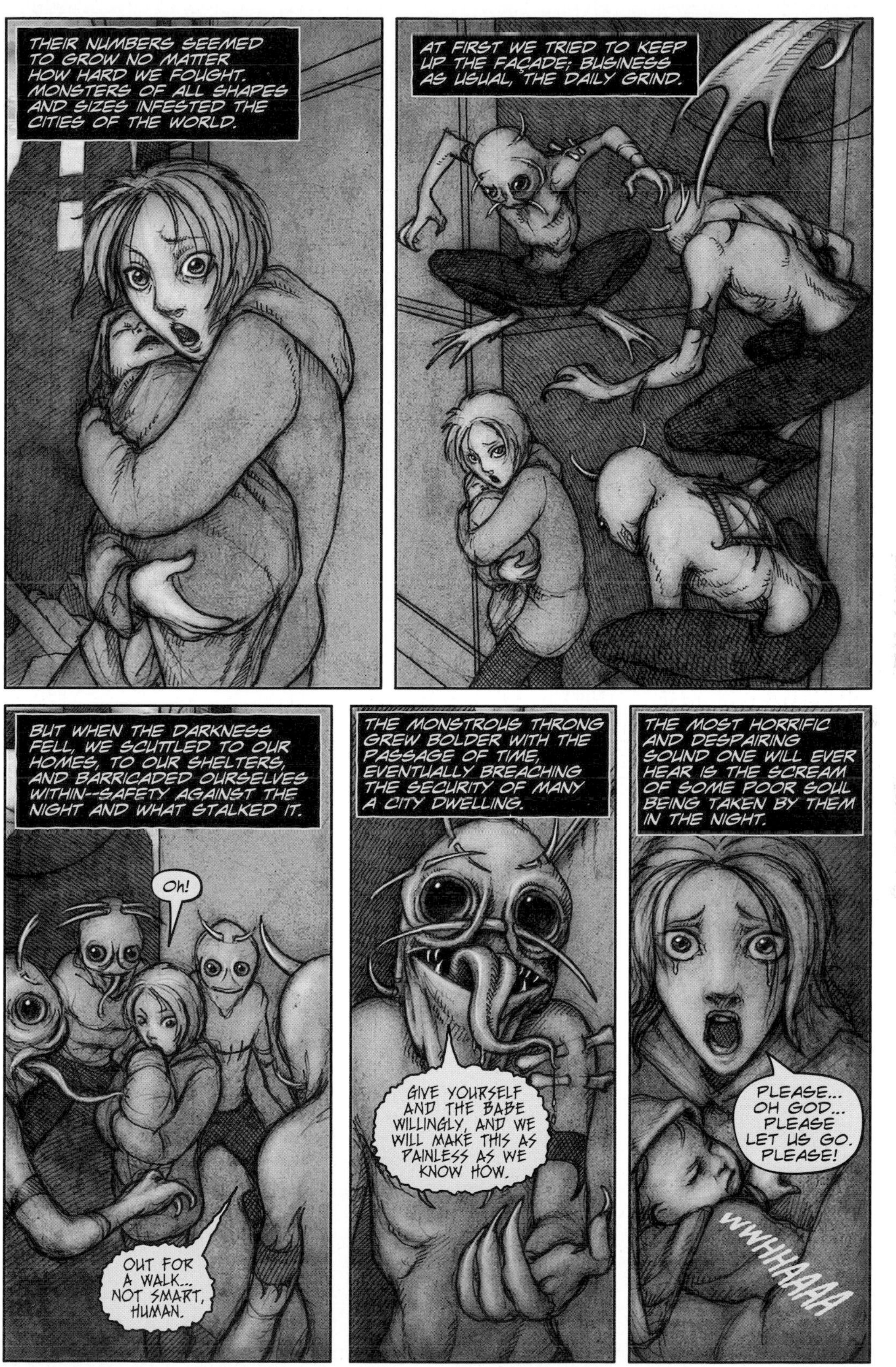
THEIR NUMBERS SEEMED TO GROW NO MATTER HOW HARD WE FOUGHT. MONSTERS OF ALL SHAPES AND SIZES INFESTED THE CITIES OF THE WORLD.
AT FIRST WE TRIED TO KEEP UP THE FAÇADE; BUSINESS AS USUAL, THE DAILY GRIND.
BUT WHEN THE DARKNESS FELL, WE SCUTTLED TO OUR HOMES, TO OUR SHELTERS, AND BARRICADED OURSELVES WITHIN--SAFETY AGAINST THE NIGHT AND WHAT STALKED IT.
Oh!
OUT FOR A WALK... NOT SMART, HUMAN.
THE MONSTROUS THRONG GREW BOLDER WITH THE PASSAGE OF TIME, EVENTUALLY BREACHING THE SECURITY OF MANY A CITY DWELLING.
GIVE YOURSELF AND THE BABE WILLINGLY, AND WE WILL MAKE THIS AS PAINLESS AS WE KNOW HOW.
THE MOST HORRIFIC AND DESPAIRING SOUND ONE WILL EVER HEAR IS THE SCREAM OF SOME POOR SOUL BEING TAKEN BY THEM IN THE NIGHT.
PLEASE... OH GOD... PLEASE LET US GO. PLEASE!
WWHHAAAA

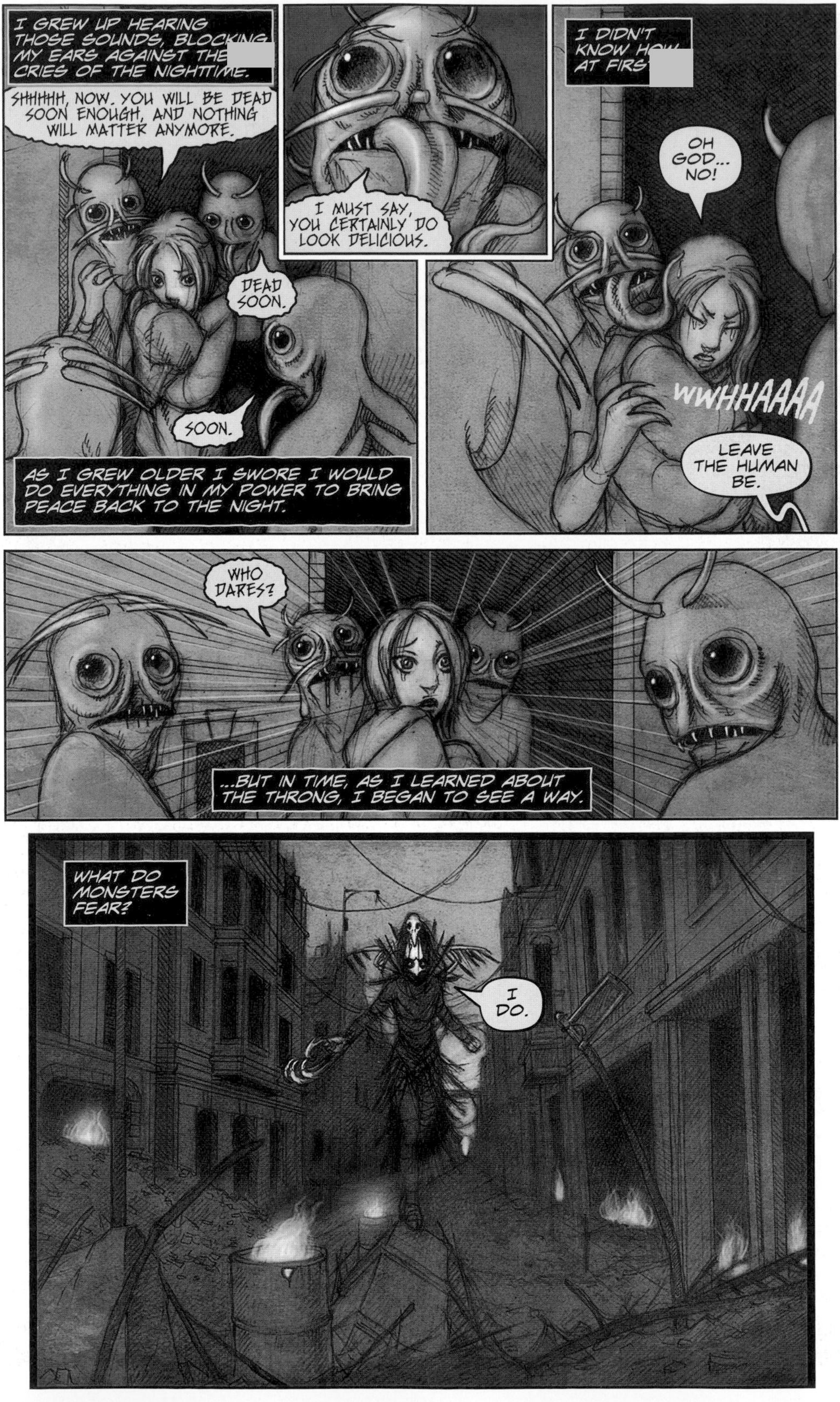
I GREW UP HEARING THOSE SOUNDS, BLOCKING MY EARS AGAINST THE CRIES OF THE NIGHTTIME.
SHHHHH, NOW. YOU WILL BE DEAD SOON ENOUGH, AND NOTHING WILL MATTER ANYMORE.
DEAD SOON.
SOON.
AS I GREW OLDER I SWORE I WOULD DO EVERYTHING IN MY POWER TO BRING PEACE BACK TO THE NIGHT.
I MUST SAY, YOU CERTAINLY DO LOOK DELICIOUS.
I DIDN'T KNOW HOW AT FIRS
OH GOD... NO!
WWHHAAAA
LEAVE THE HUMAN BE.
WHO DARES?
...BUT IN TIME, AS I LEARNED ABOUT THE THRONG, I BEGAN TO SEE A WAY.
WHAT DO MONSTERS FEAR?
I DO.

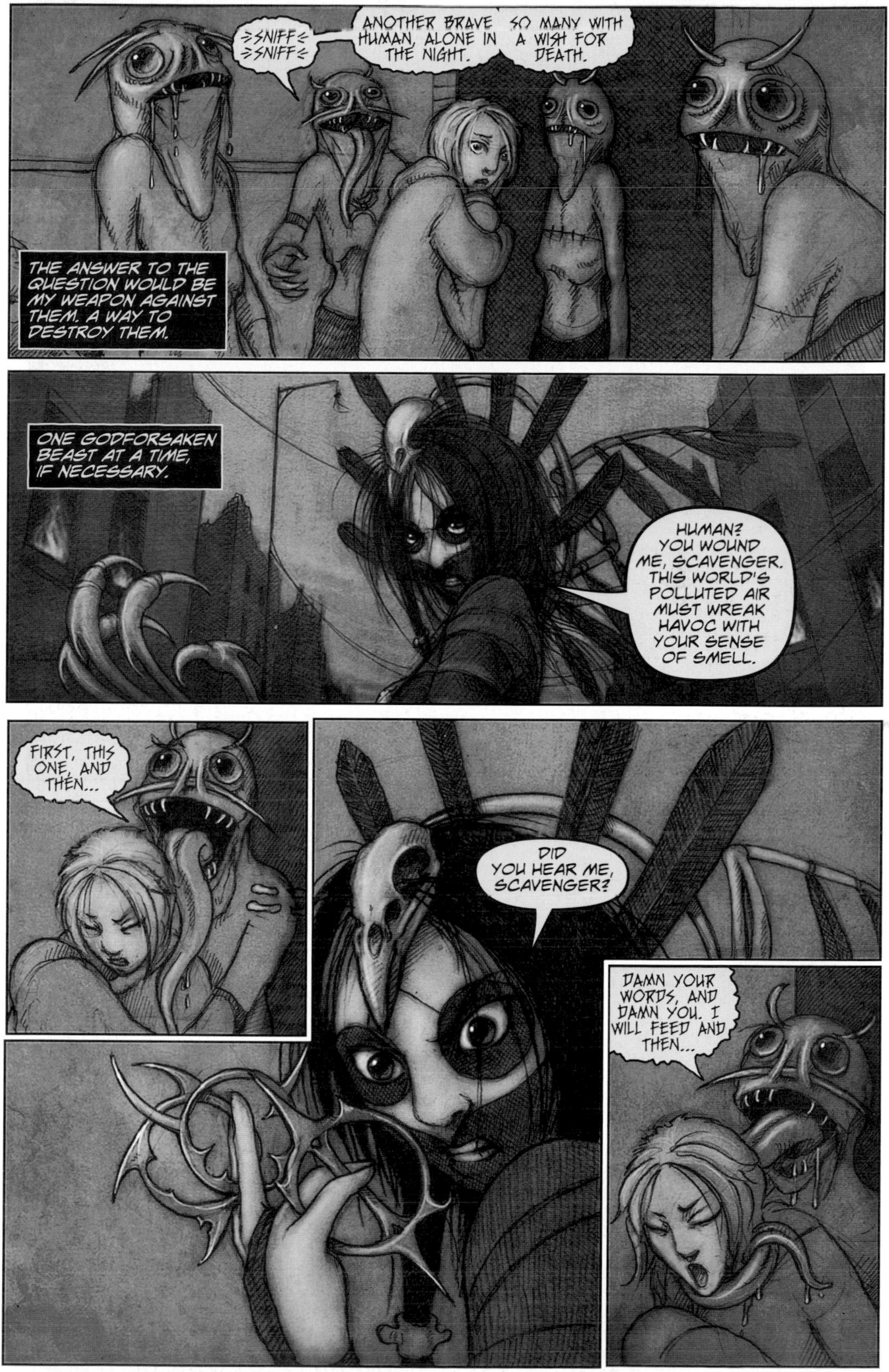

>SNIFF< >SNIFF<
ANOTHER BRAVE HUMAN, ALONE IN THE NIGHT.
SO MANY WITH A WISH FOR DEATH.
THE ANSWER TO THE QUESTION WOULD BE MY WEAPON AGAINST THEM. A WAY TO DESTROY THEM.
ONE GODFORSAKEN BEAST AT A TIME, IF NECESSARY.
HUMAN? YOU WOUND ME, SCAVENGER. THIS WORLD'S POLLUTED AIR MUST WREAK HAVOC WITH YOUR SENSE OF SMELL.
FIRST, THIS ONE, AND THEN...
DID YOU HEAR ME, SCAVENGER?
DAMN YOUR WORDS, AND DAMN YOU. I WILL FEED AND THEN...

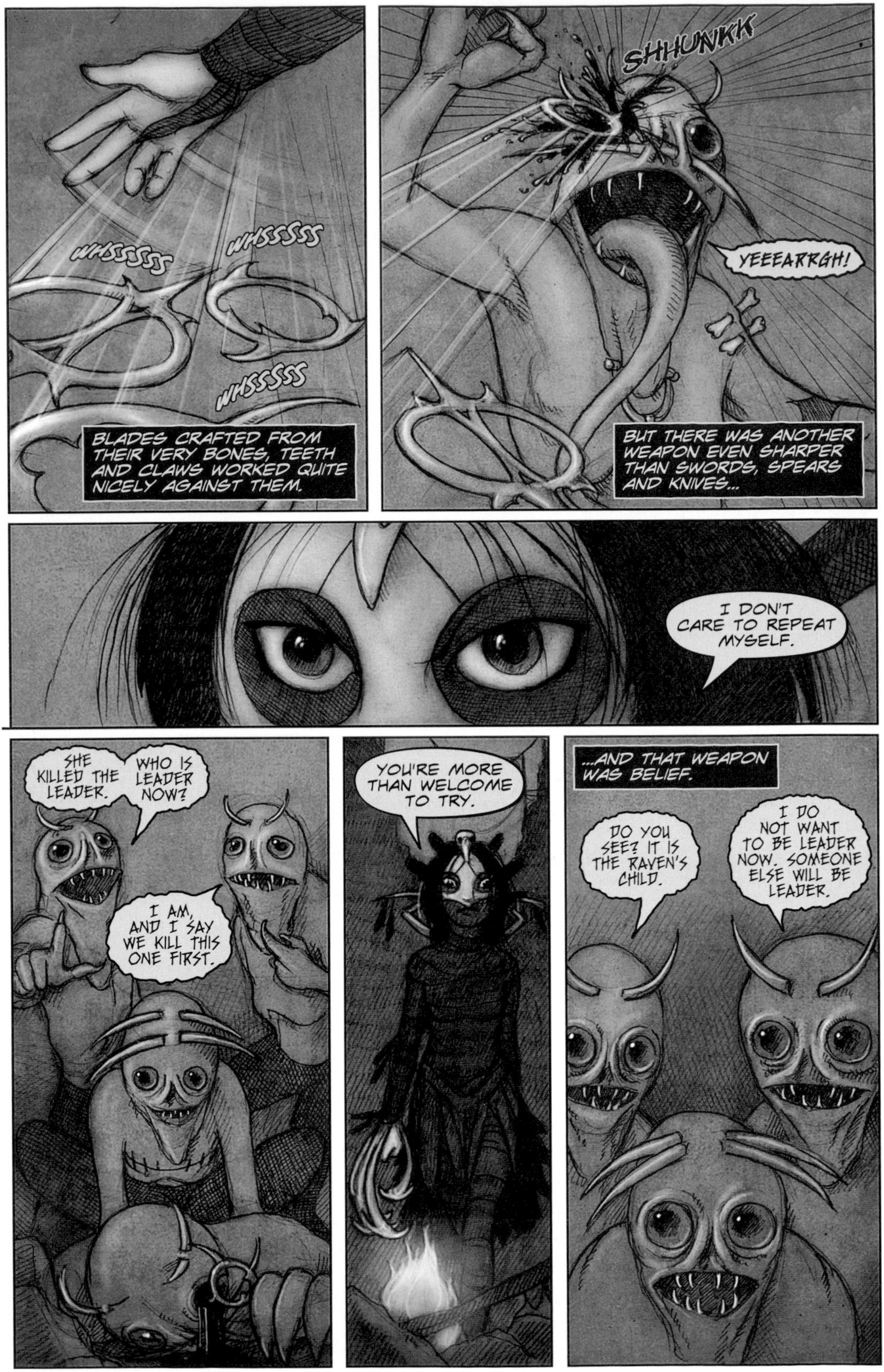
WHSSSSSS
WHSSSSSS
WHSSSSSS
BLADES CRAFTED FROM THEIR VERY BONES, TEETH AND CLAWS WORKED QUITE NICELY AGAINST THEM.
SHHUNKK
YEEEARRGH!
BUT THERE WAS ANOTHER WEAPON EVEN SHARPER THAN SWORDS, SPEARS AND KNIVES...
I DON'T CARE TO REPEAT MYSELF.
SHE KILLED THE LEADER.
WHO IS LEADER NOW?
I AM, AND I SAY WE KILL THIS ONE FIRST.
YOU'RE MORE THAN WELCOME TO TRY.
...AND THAT WEAPON WAS BELIEF.
DO YOU SEE? IT IS THE RAVEN'S CHILD.
I DO NOT WANT TO BE LEADER NOW. SOMEONE ELSE WILL BE LEADER.

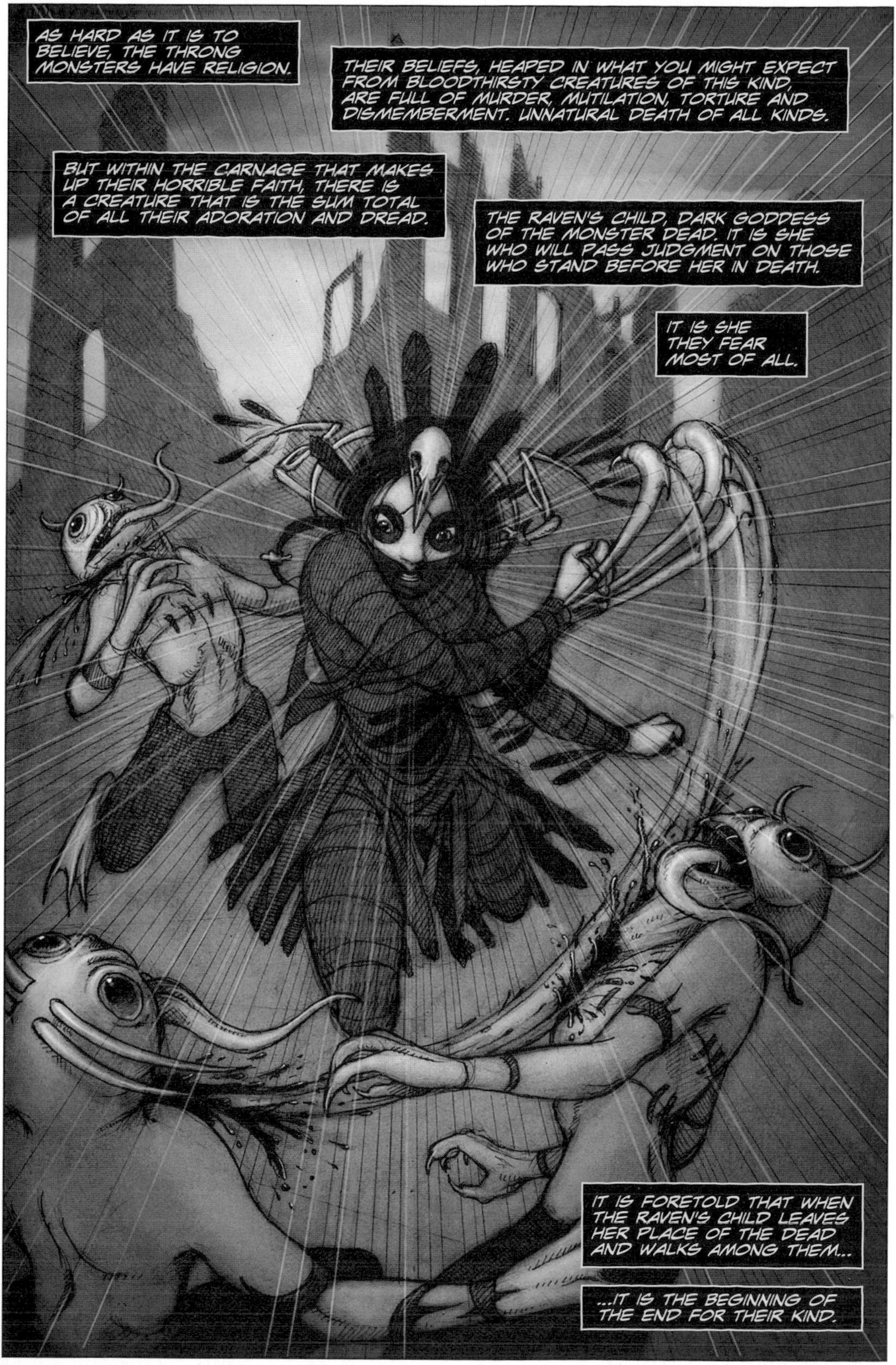
AS HARD AS IT IS TO BELIEVE, THE THRONG MONSTERS HAVE RELIGION.
THEIR BELIEFS, HEAPED IN WHAT YOU MIGHT EXPECT FROM BLOODTHIRSTY CREATURES OF THIS KIND, ARE FULL OF MURDER, MUTILATION, TORTURE AND DISMEMBERMENT. UNNATURAL DEATH OF ALL KINDS.
BUT WITHIN THE CARNAGE THAT MAKES UP THEIR HORRIBLE FAITH, THERE IS A CREATURE THAT IS THE SUM TOTAL OF ALL THEIR ADORATION AND DREAD.
THE RAVEN'S CHILD, DARK GODDESS OF THE MONSTER DEAD. IT IS SHE WHO WILL PASS JUDGMENT ON THOSE WHO STAND BEFORE HER IN DEATH.
IT IS SHE THEY FEAR MOST OF ALL.
IT IS FORETOLD THAT WHEN THE RAVEN'S CHILD LEAVES HER PLACE OF THE DEAD AND WALKS AMONG THEM...
...IT IS THE BEGINNING OF THE END FOR THEIR KIND.

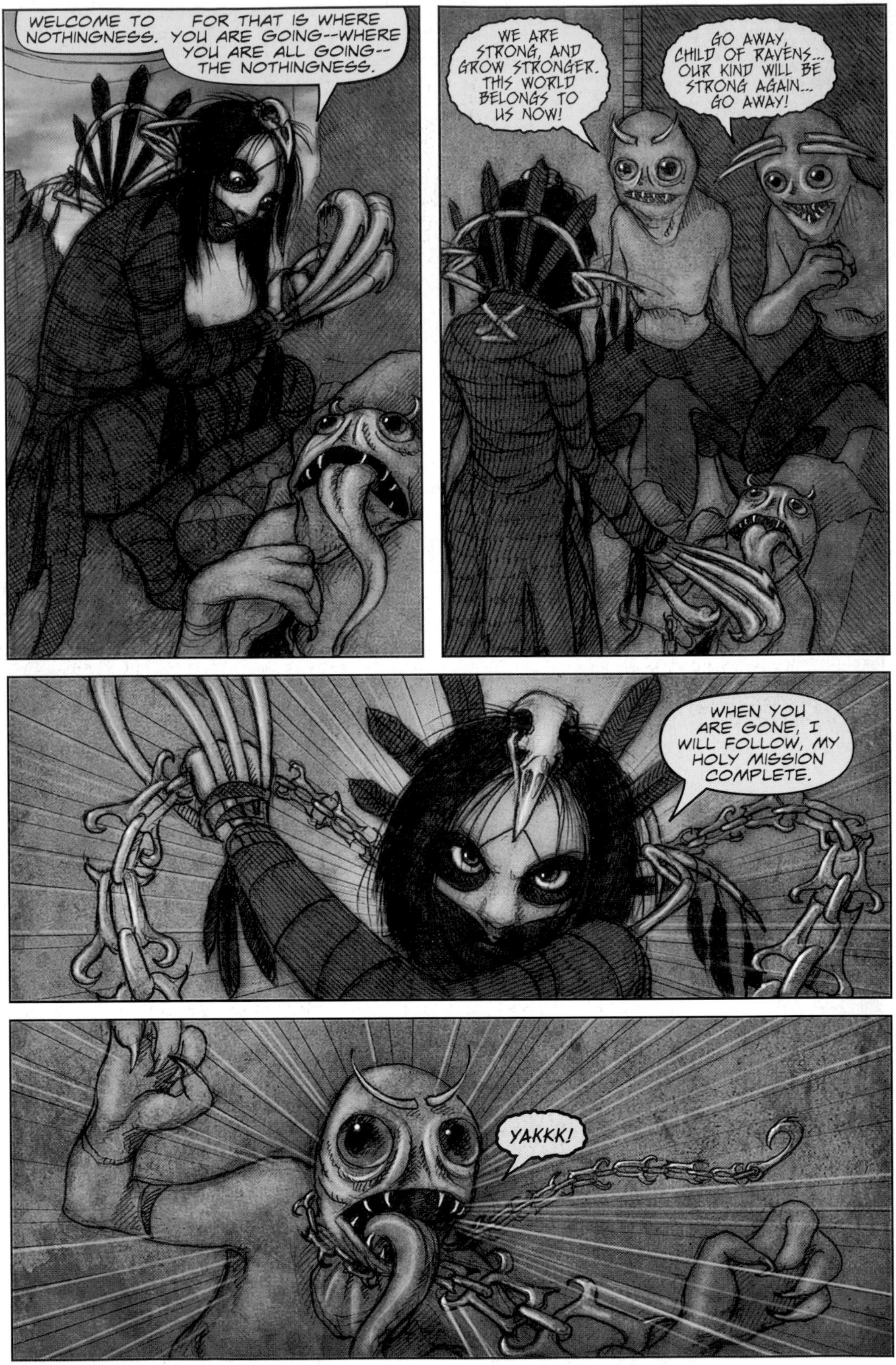
WELCOME TO NOTHINGNESS.
FOR THAT IS WHERE YOU ARE GOING--WHERE YOU ARE ALL GOING-- THE NOTHINGNESS.
WE ARE STRONG, AND GROW STRONGER. THIS WORLD BELONGS TO US NOW!
GO AWAY, CHILD OF RAVENS... OUR KIND WILL BE STRONG AGAIN... GO AWAY!
WHEN YOU ARE GONE, I WILL FOLLOW, MY HOLY MISSION COMPLETE.
YAKKK!

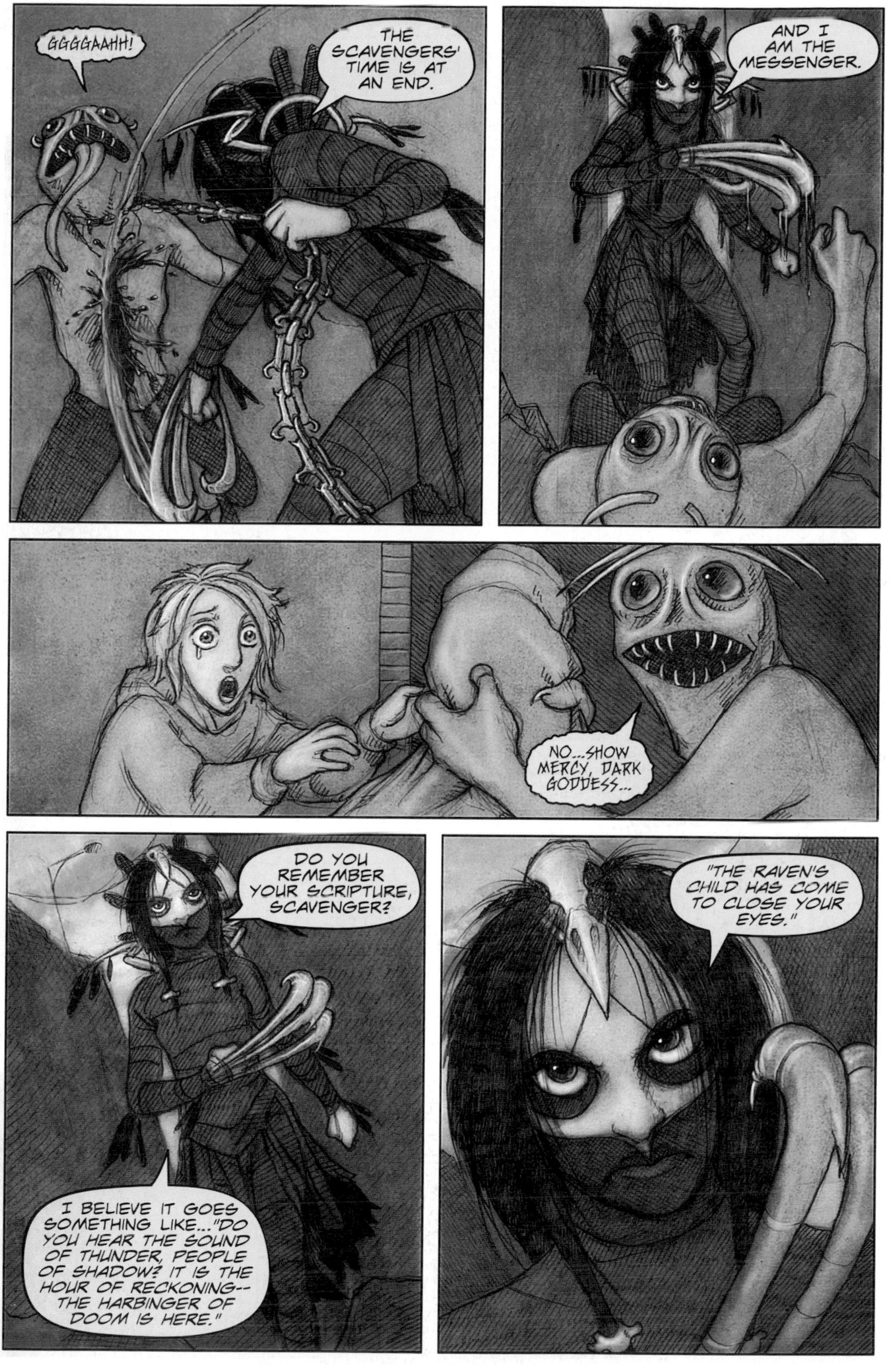
GGGGAAHH!
THE SCAVENGERS' TIME IS AT AN END.
AND I AM THE MESSENGER.
NO...SHOW MERCY, DARK GODDESS...
DO YOU REMEMBER YOUR SCRIPTURE, SCAVENGER?
I BELIEVE IT GOES SOMETHING LIKE..."DO YOU HEAR THE SOUND OF THUNDER, PEOPLE OF SHADOW? IT IS THE HOUR OF RECKONING--THE HARBINGER OF DOOM IS HERE."
"THE RAVEN'S CHILD HAS COME TO CLOSE YOUR EYES."

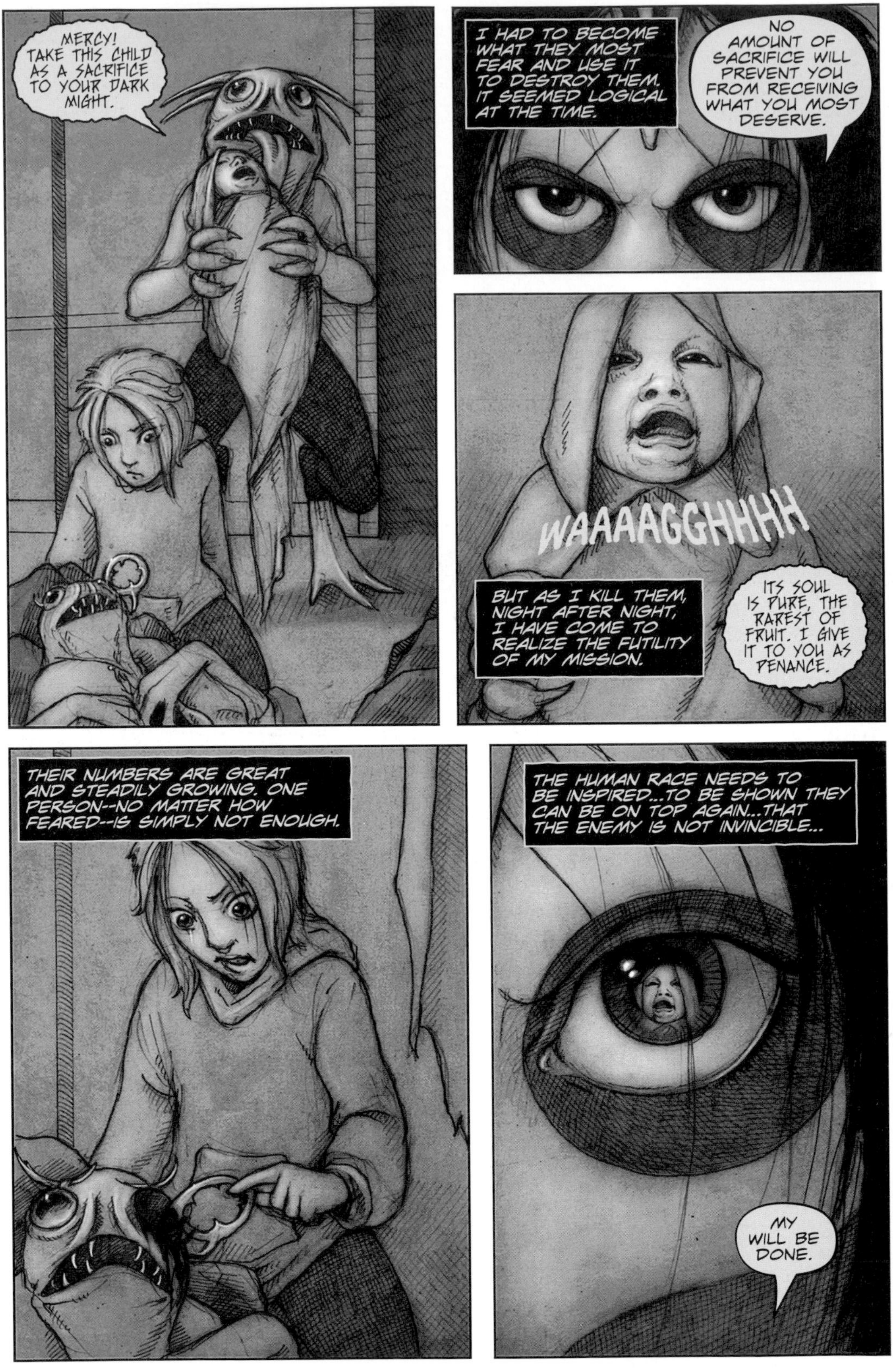
MERCY! TAKE THIS CHILD AS A SACRIFICE TO YOUR DARK MIGHT.
I HAD TO BECOME WHAT THEY MOST FEAR AND USE IT TO DESTROY THEM. IT SEEMED LOGICAL AT THE TIME.
NO AMOUNT OF SACRIFICE WILL PREVENT YOU FROM RECEIVING WHAT YOU MOST DESERVE.
WAAAAGGHHHH
BUT AS I KILL THEM, NIGHT AFTER NIGHT, I HAVE COME TO REALIZE THE FUTILITY OF MY MISSION.
ITS SOUL IS PURE, THE RAREST OF FRUIT. I GIVE IT TO YOU AS PENANCE.
THEIR NUMBERS ARE GREAT AND STEADILY GROWING. ONE PERSON--NO MATTER HOW FEARED--IS SIMPLY NOT ENOUGH.
THE HUMAN RACE NEEDS TO BE INSPIRED...TO BE SHOWN THEY CAN BE ON TOP AGAIN...THAT THE ENEMY IS NOT INVINCIBLE...
MY WILL BE DONE.

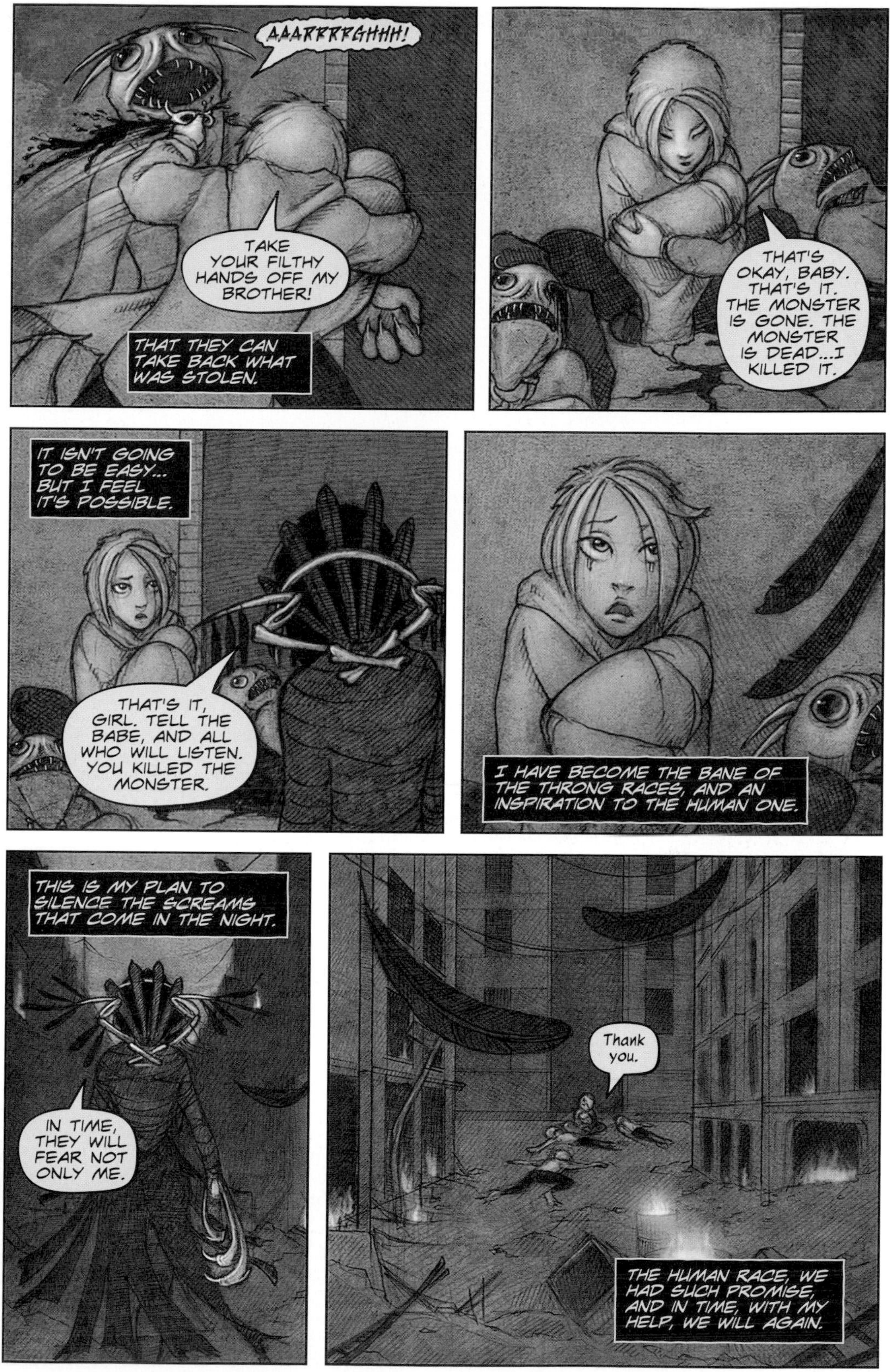
AAARRRRGHHH!
TAKE YOUR FILTHY HANDS OFF MY BROTHER!
THAT THEY CAN TAKE BACK WHAT WAS STOLEN.
THAT'S OKAY, BABY. THAT'S IT. THE MONSTER IS GONE. THE MONSTER IS DEAD...I KILLED IT.
IT ISN'T GOING TO BE EASY... BUT I FEEL IT'S POSSIBLE.
THAT'S IT, GIRL. TELL THE BABE, AND ALL WHO WILL LISTEN. YOU KILLED THE MONSTER.
I HAVE BECOME THE BANE OF THE THRONG RACES, AND AN INSPIRATION TO THE HUMAN ONE.
THIS IS MY PLAN TO SILENCE THE SCREAMS THAT COME IN THE NIGHT.
IN TIME, THEY WILL FEAR NOT ONLY ME.
Thank you.
THE HUMAN RACE, WE HAD SUCH PROMISE, AND IN TIME, WITH MY HELP, WE WILL AGAIN.

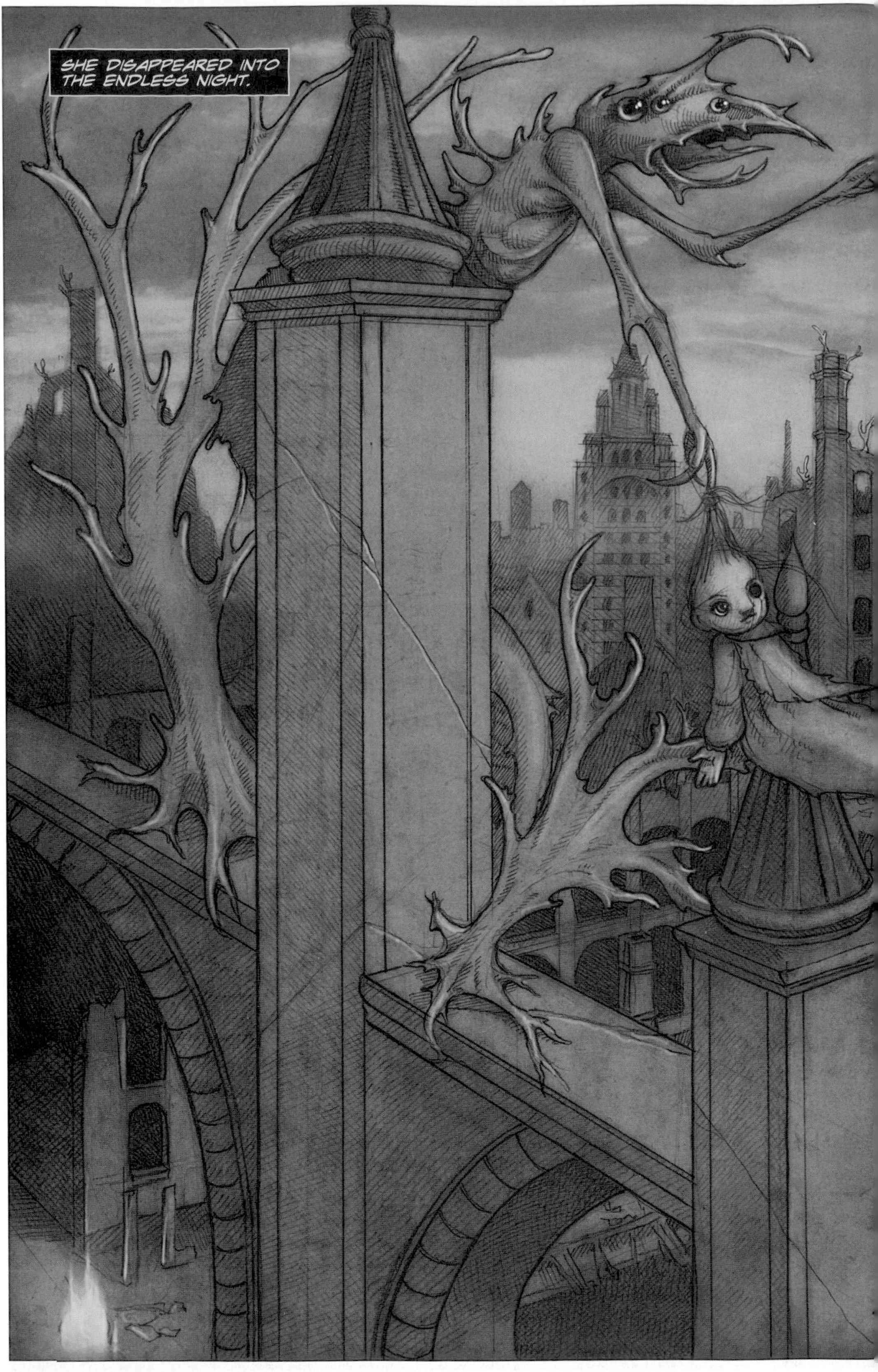
SHE DISAPPEARED INTO THE ENDLESS NIGHT.

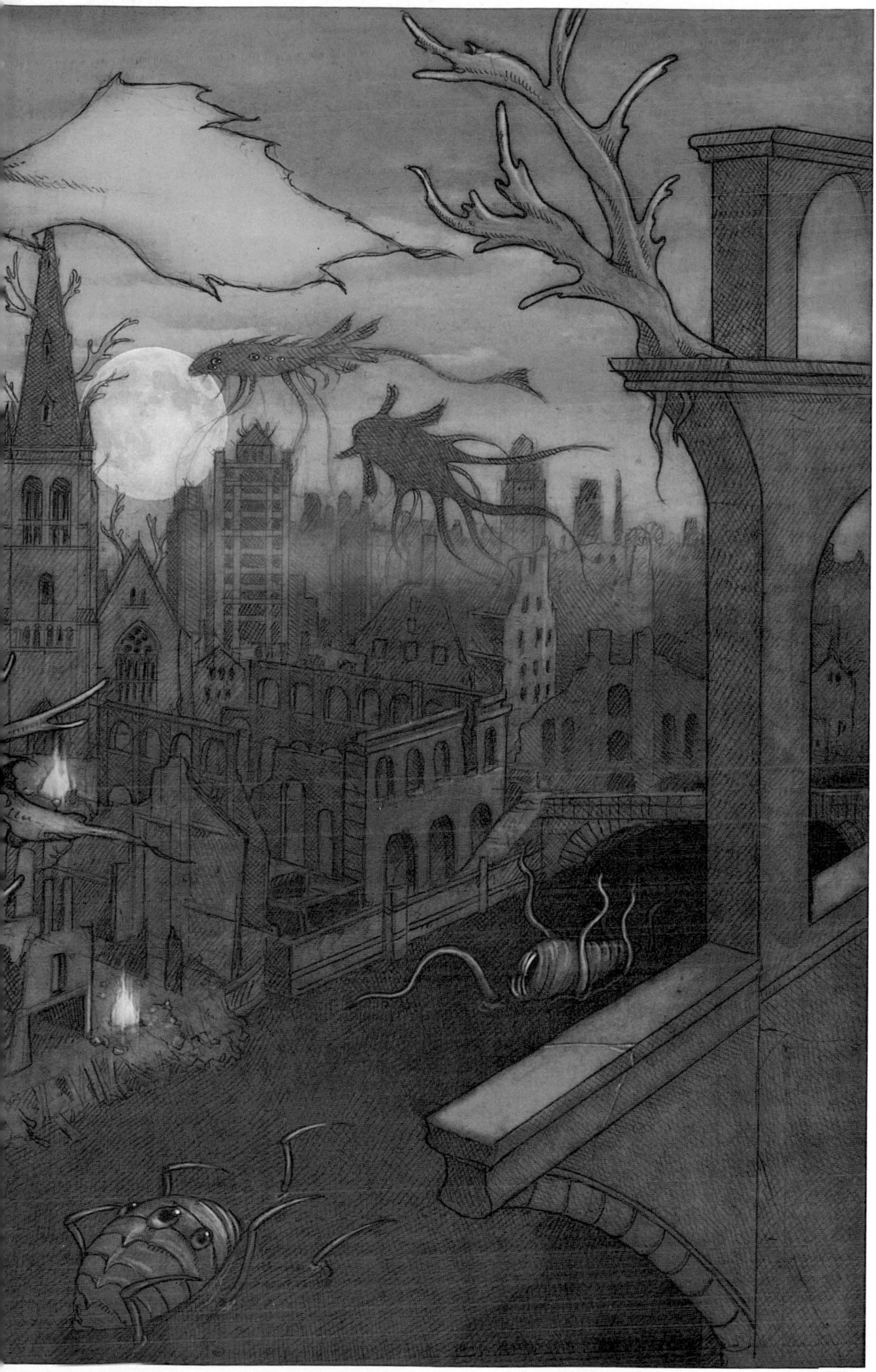

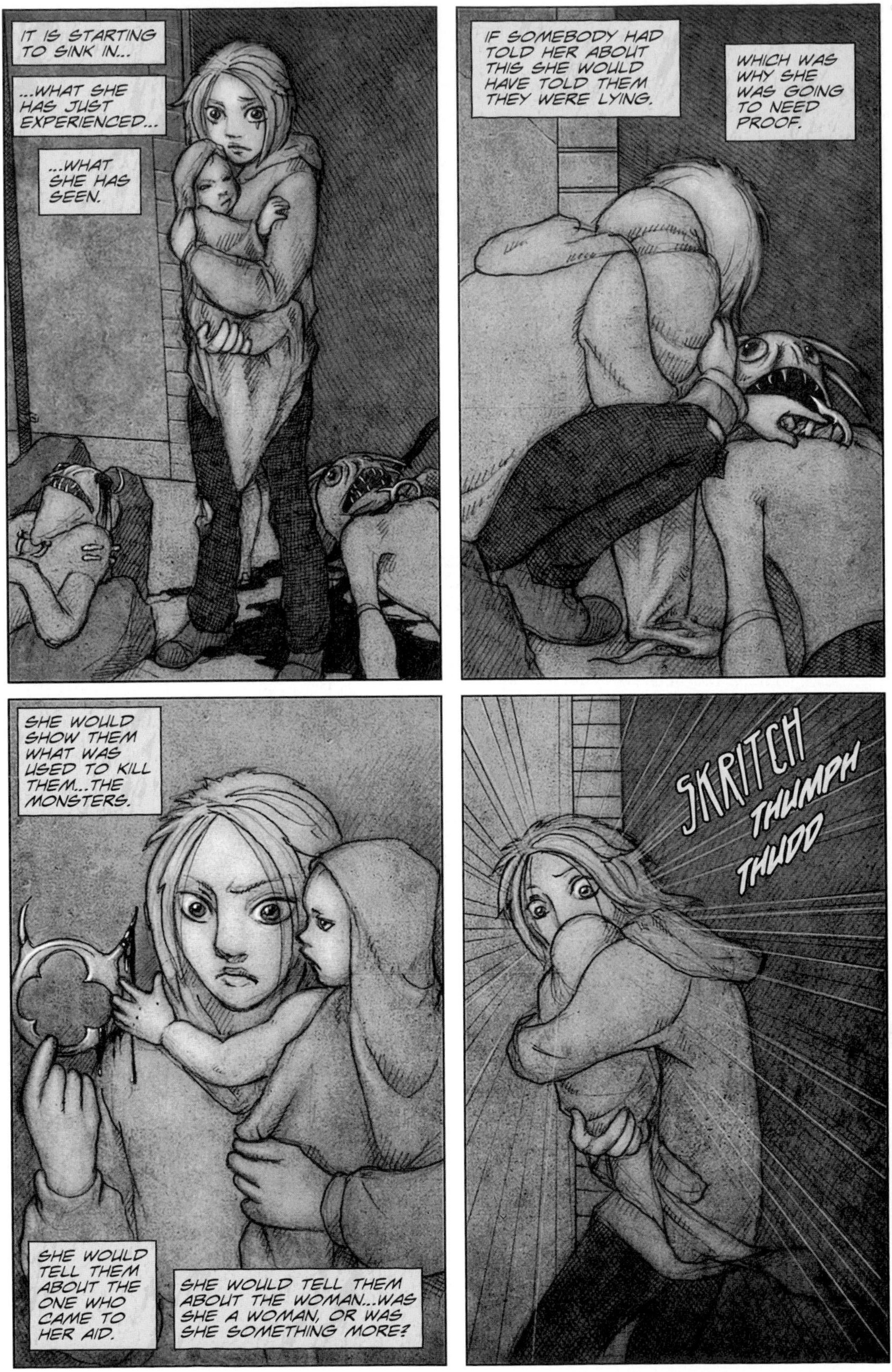
IT IS STARTING TO SINK IN...
...WHAT SHE HAS JUST EXPERIENCED...
...WHAT SHE HAS SEEN.
IF SOMEBODY HAD TOLD HER ABOUT THIS SHE WOULD HAVE TOLD THEM THEY WERE LYING.
WHICH WAS WHY SHE WAS GOING TO NEED PROOF.
SHE WOULD SHOW THEM WHAT WAS USED TO KILL THEM...THE MONSTERS.
SHE WOULD TELL THEM ABOUT THE ONE WHO CAME TO HER AID.
SHE WOULD TELL THEM ABOUT THE WOMAN...WAS SHE A WOMAN, OR WAS SHE SOMETHING MORE?
SKRITCH
THUMPH
THUDD

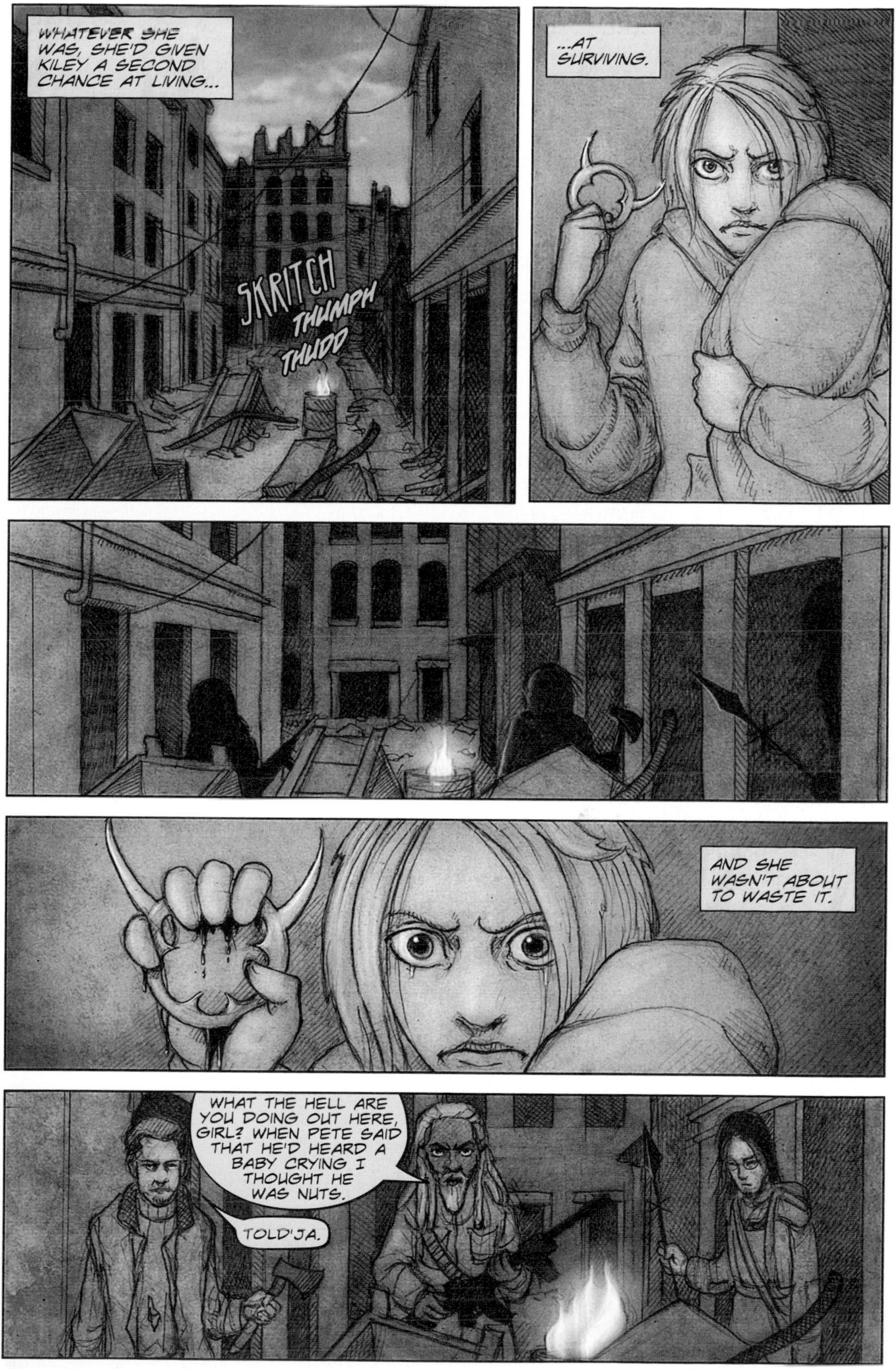
WHATEVER SHE WAS, SHE'D GIVEN KILEY A SECOND CHANCE AT LIVING...
SKRITCH
THUMPH
THUDD
...AT SURVIVING.
AND SHE WASN'T ABOUT TO WASTE IT.
WHAT THE HELL ARE YOU DOING OUT HERE, GIRL? WHEN PETE SAID THAT HE'D HEARD A BABY CRYING I THOUGHT HE WAS NUTS.
TOLD'JA.

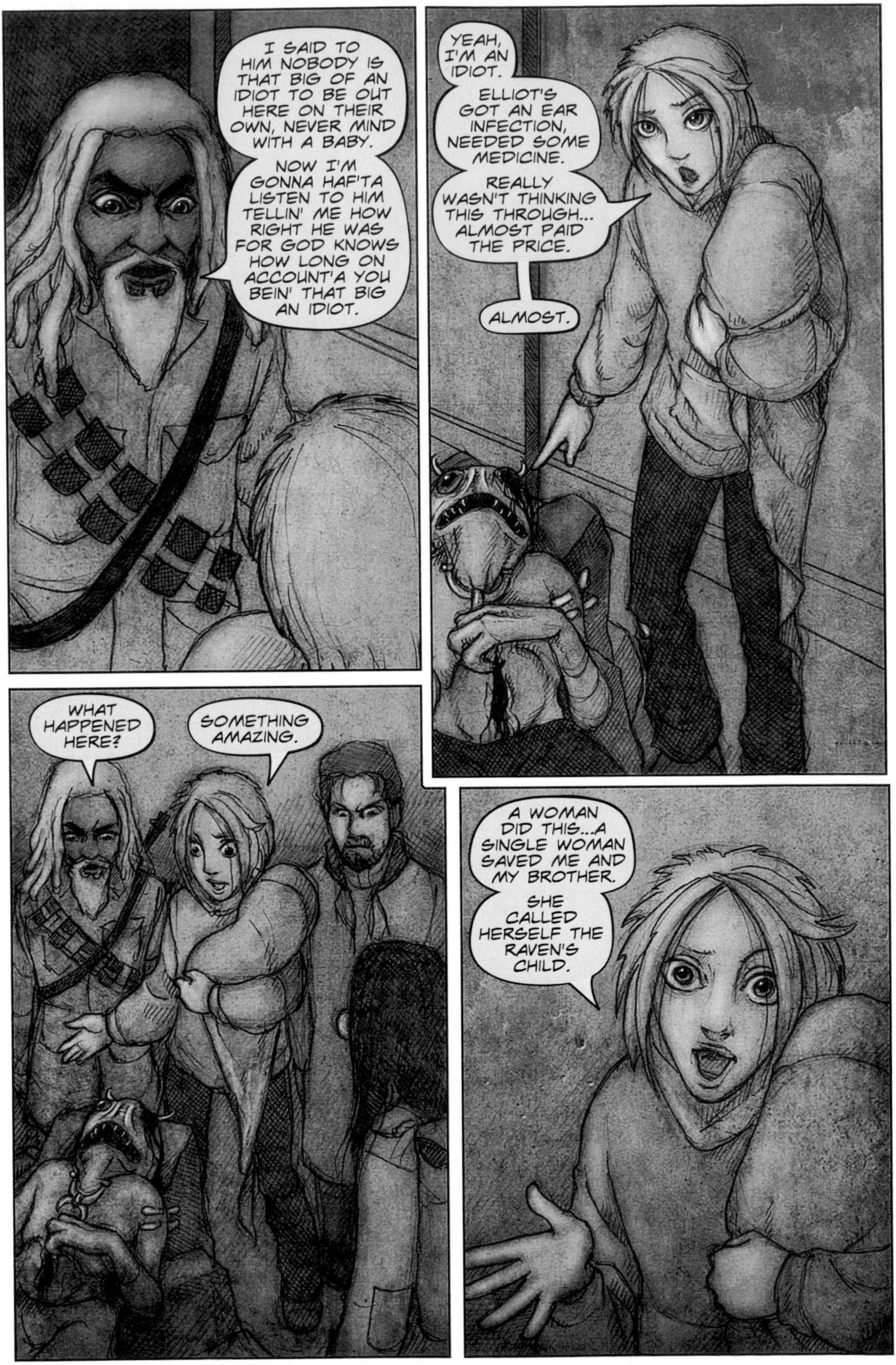
I SAID TO HIM NOBODY IS THAT BIG OF AN IDIOT TO BE OUT HERE ON THEIR OWN, NEVER MIND WITH A BABY.
NOW I'M GONNA HAF'TA LISTEN TO HIM TELLIN' ME HOW RIGHT HE WAS FOR GOD KNOWS HOW LONG ON ACCOUNT'A YOU BEIN' THAT BIG AN IDIOT.
YEAH, I'M AN IDIOT.
ELLIOT'S GOT AN EAR INFECTION, NEEDED SOME MEDICINE.
REALLY WASN'T THINKING THIS THROUGH... ALMOST PAID THE PRICE.
ALMOST.
WHAT HAPPENED HERE?
SOMETHING AMAZING.
A WOMAN DID THIS...A SINGLE WOMAN SAVED ME AND MY BROTHER.
SHE CALLED HERSELF THE RAVEN'S CHILD.

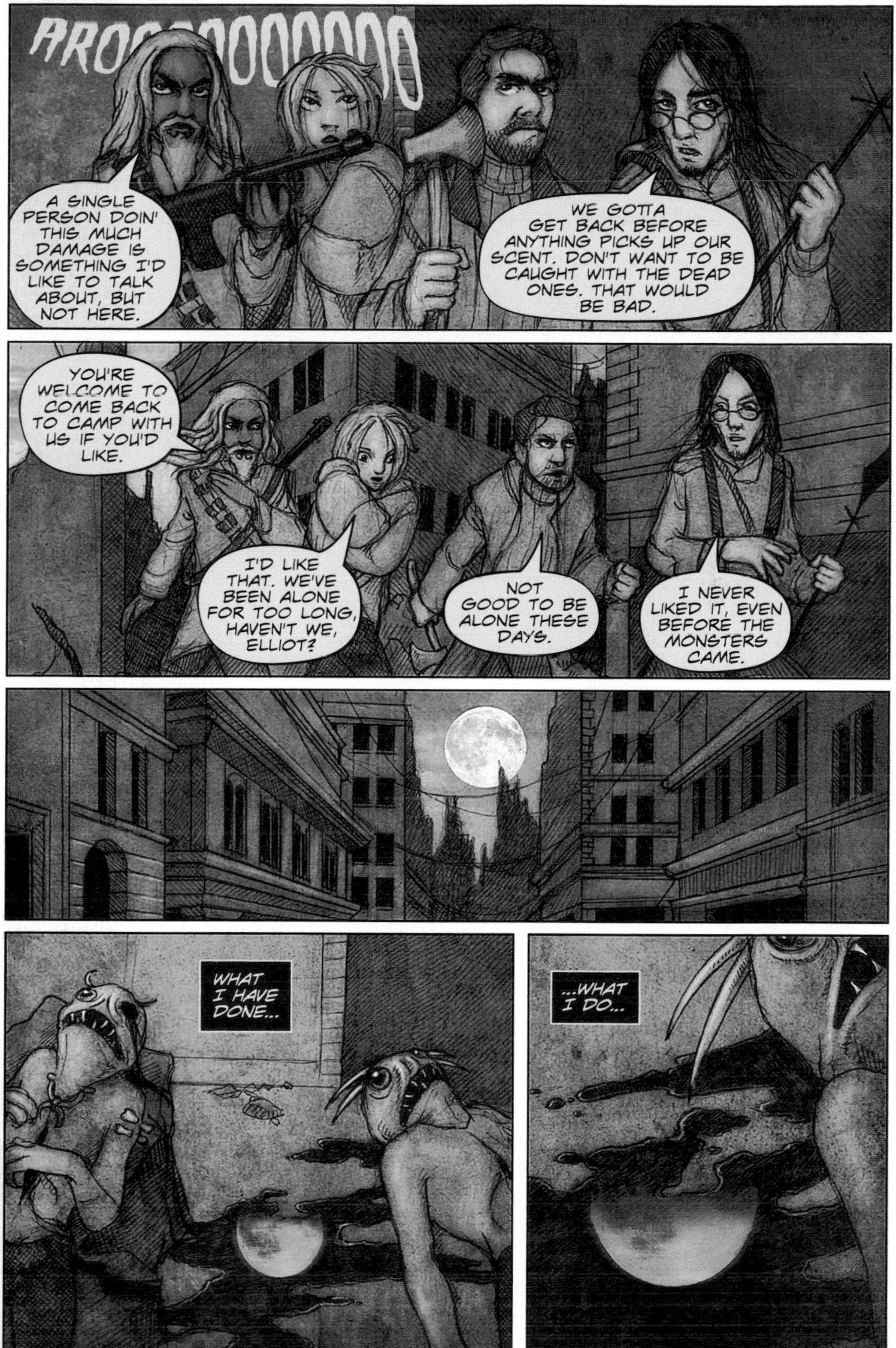
AROOOOOOOOOO
A SINGLE PERSON DOIN' THIS MUCH DAMAGE IS SOMETHING I'D LIKE TO TALK ABOUT, BUT NOT HERE.
WE GOTTA GET BACK BEFORE ANYTHING PICKS UP OUR SCENT. DON'T WANT TO BE CAUGHT WITH THE DEAD ONES. THAT WOULD BE BAD.
YOU'RE WELCOME TO COME BACK TO CAMP WITH US IF YOU'D LIKE.
I'D LIKE THAT. WE'VE BEEN ALONE FOR TOO LONG, HAVEN'T WE, ELLIOT?
NOT GOOD TO BE ALONE THESE DAYS.
I NEVER LIKED IT, EVEN BEFORE THE MONSTERS CAME.
WHAT I HAVE DONE...
...WHAT I DO...

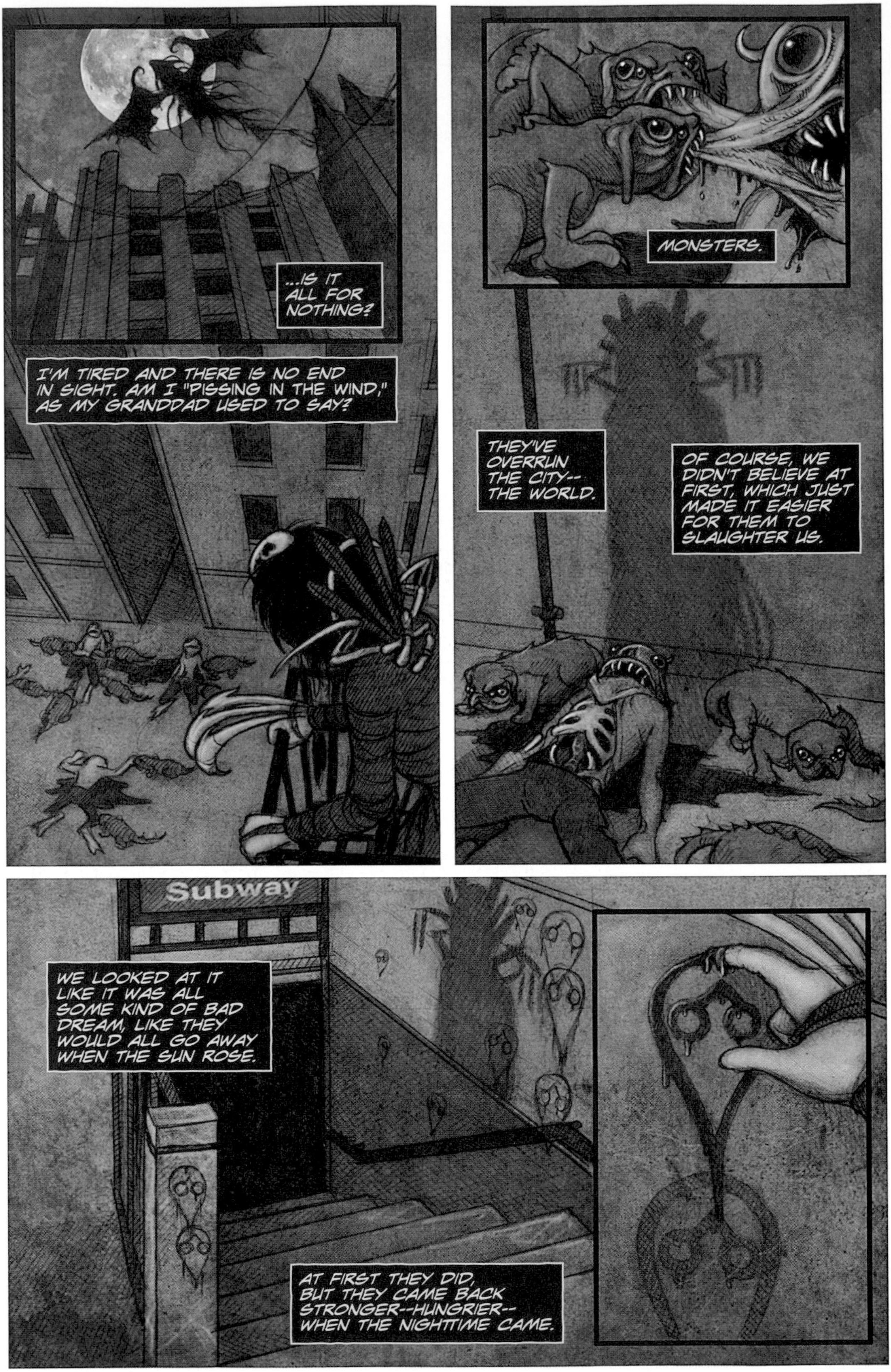
...IS IT ALL FOR NOTHING?
I'M TIRED AND THERE IS NO END IN SIGHT. AM I "PISSING IN THE WIND," AS MY GRANDDAD USED TO SAY?
MONSTERS.
THEY'VE OVERRUN THE CITY-- THE WORLD.
OF COURSE, WE DIDN'T BELIEVE AT FIRST, WHICH JUST MADE IT EASIER FOR THEM TO SLAUGHTER US.
Subway
WE LOOKED AT IT LIKE IT WAS ALL SOME KIND OF BAD DREAM, LIKE THEY WOULD ALL GO AWAY WHEN THE SUN ROSE.
AT FIRST THEY DID, BUT THEY CAME BACK STRONGER--HUNGRIER-- WHEN THE NIGHTTIME CAME.

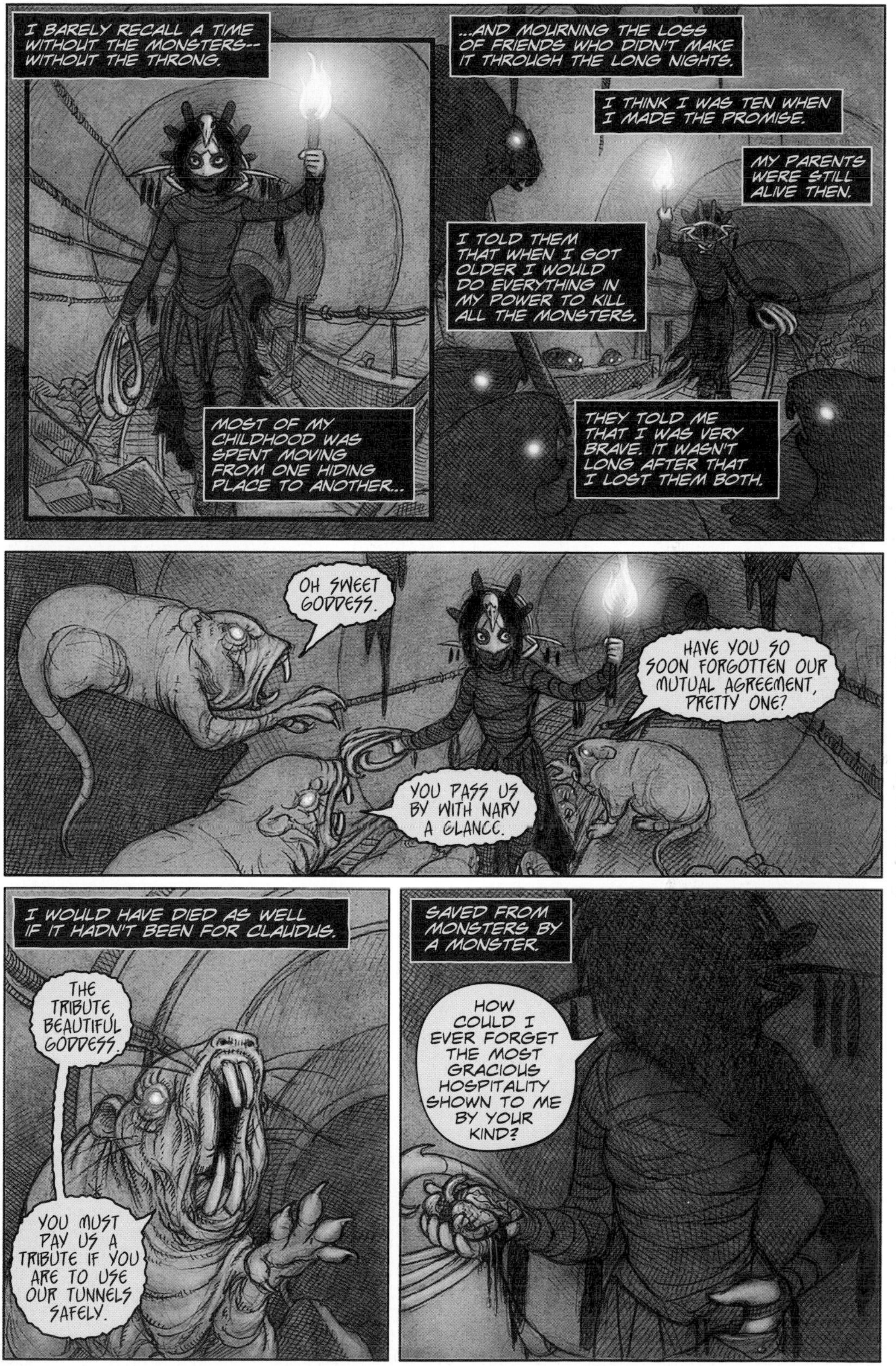
I BARELY RECALL A TIME WITHOUT THE MONSTERS-- WITHOUT THE THRONG.
MOST OF MY CHILDHOOD WAS SPENT MOVING FROM ONE HIDING PLACE TO ANOTHER...
...AND MOURNING THE LOSS OF FRIENDS WHO DIDN'T MAKE IT THROUGH THE LONG NIGHTS.
I THINK I WAS TEN WHEN I MADE THE PROMISE.
MY PARENTS WERE STILL ALIVE THEN.
I TOLD THEM THAT WHEN I GOT OLDER I WOULD DO EVERYTHING IN MY POWER TO KILL ALL THE MONSTERS.
THEY TOLD ME THAT I WAS VERY BRAVE. IT WASN'T LONG AFTER THAT I LOST THEM BOTH.
OH SWEET GODDESS.
HAVE YOU SO SOON FORGOTTEN OUR MUTUAL AGREEMENT, PRETTY ONE?
YOU PASS US BY WITH NARY A GLANCE.
I WOULD HAVE DIED AS WELL IF IT HADN'T BEEN FOR CLAUDUS.
THE TRIBUTE, BEAUTIFUL GODDESS.
YOU MUST PAY US A TRIBUTE IF YOU ARE TO USE OUR TUNNELS SAFELY.
SAVED FROM MONSTERS BY A MONSTER.
HOW COULD I EVER FORGET THE MOST GRACIOUS HOSPITALITY SHOWN TO ME BY YOUR KIND?

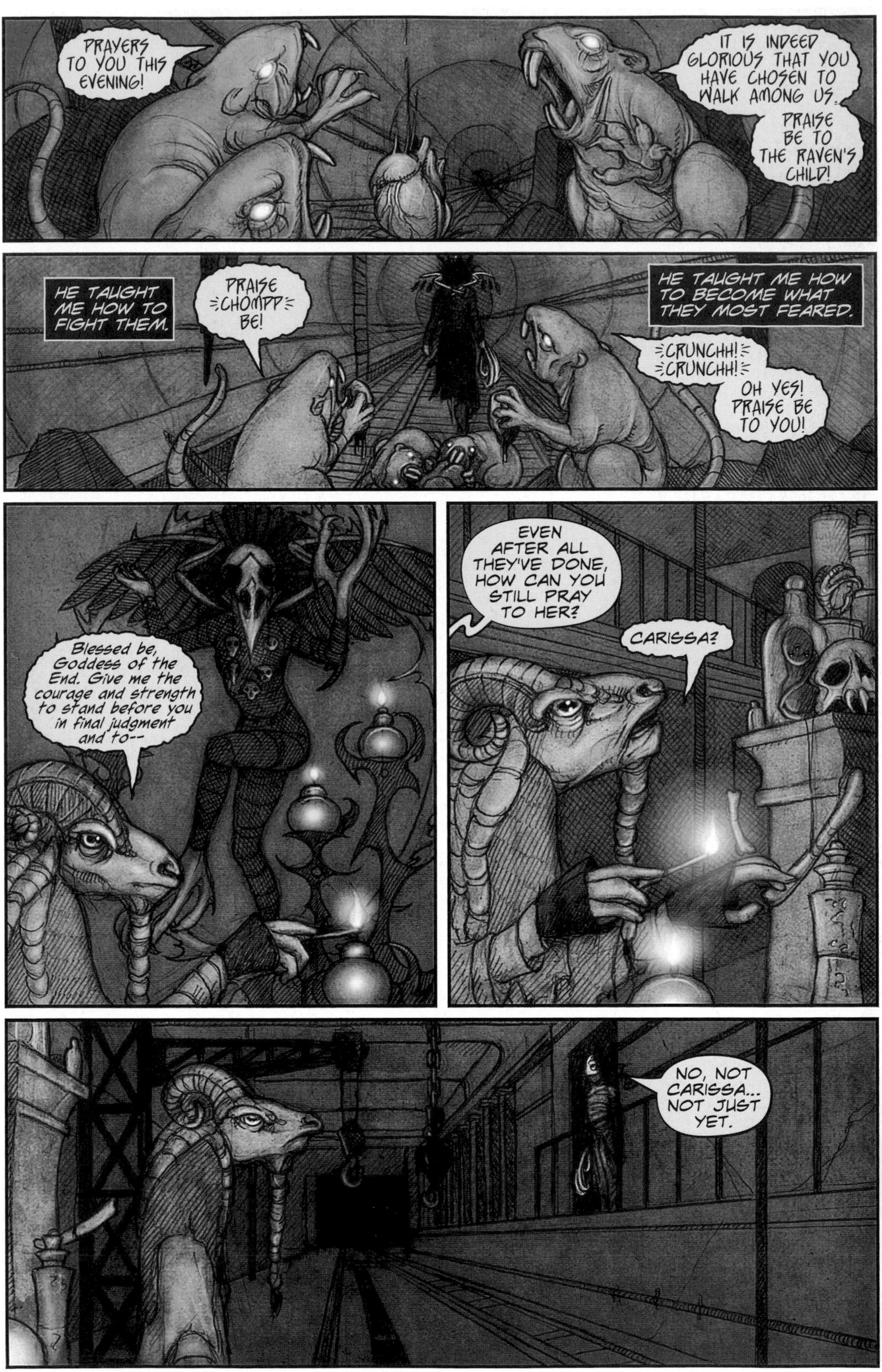
PRAYERS TO YOU THIS EVENING!
IT IS INDEED GLORIOUS THAT YOU HAVE CHOSEN TO WALK AMONG US.
PRAISE BE TO THE RAVEN'S CHILD!
HE TAUGHT ME HOW TO FIGHT THEM.
PRAISE CHOMPP BE!
HE TAUGHT ME HOW TO BECOME WHAT THEY MOST FEARED.
CRUNCHH! CRUNCHH!
OH YES! PRAISE BE TO YOU!
Blessed be, Goddess of the End. Give me the courage and strength to stand before you in final judgment and to--
EVEN AFTER ALL THEY'VE DONE, HOW CAN YOU STILL PRAY TO HER?
CARISSA?
NO, NOT CARISSA... NOT JUST YET.

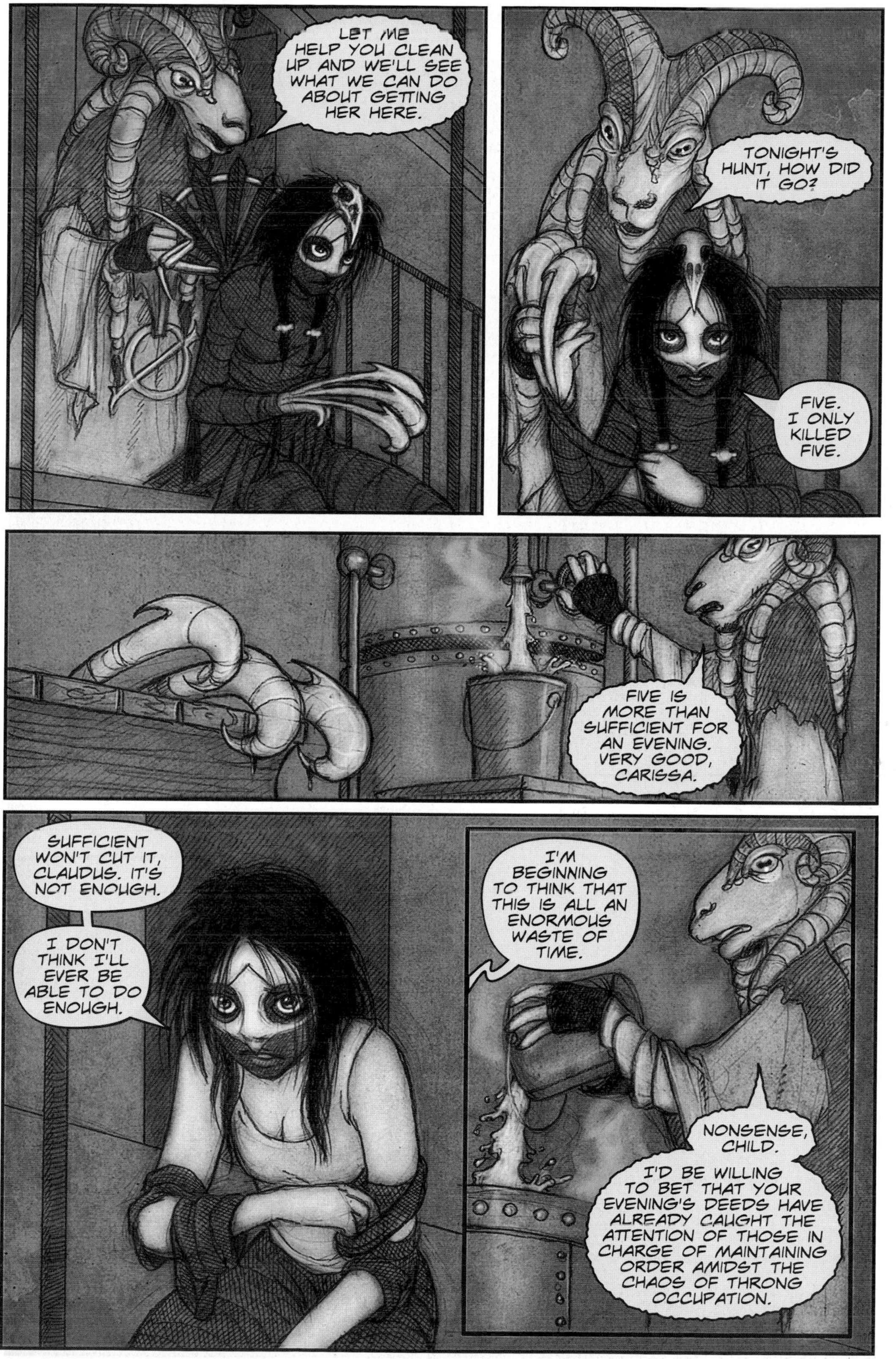
LET ME HELP YOU CLEAN UP AND WE'LL SEE WHAT WE CAN DO ABOUT GETTING HER HERE.
TONIGHT'S HUNT, HOW DID IT GO?
FIVE. I ONLY KILLED FIVE.
FIVE IS MORE THAN SUFFICIENT FOR AN EVENING. VERY GOOD, CARISSA.
SUFFICIENT WON'T CUT IT, CLAUDUS. IT'S NOT ENOUGH.
I DON'T THINK I'LL EVER BE ABLE TO DO ENOUGH.
I'M BEGINNING TO THINK THAT THIS IS ALL AN ENORMOUS WASTE OF TIME.
NONSENSE, CHILD.
I'D BE WILLING TO BET THAT YOUR EVENING'S DEEDS HAVE ALREADY CAUGHT THE ATTENTION OF THOSE IN CHARGE OF MAINTAINING ORDER AMIDST THE CHAOS OF THRONG OCCUPATION.

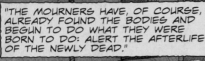

"THE MOURNERS HAVE, OF COURSE, ALREADY FOUND THE BODIES AND BEGUN TO DO WHAT THEY WERE BORN TO DO: ALERT THE AFTERLIFE OF THE NEWLY DEAD."

ARRROOCCOOOOO

ARRROOOOOOOOO

"THIS HAS MOST LIKELY DRAWN THE ATTENTION OF THE AUTHORITIES."

"A MAGISTRATE OF THE LAW WILL GO ABOUT HIS BUSINESS, EXAMINING THE SCENE OF THE DISTURBANCE--OF THE VICTIMS--TO DETERMINE THE EXTENT TO WHICH MONSTER LAW HAS BEEN BROKEN."

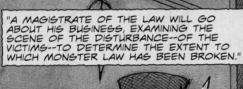

"AND THE SYMBOL--DID YOU LEAVE IT WHERE IT COULD BE NOTICED?"

"OF COURSE, YOU DID."

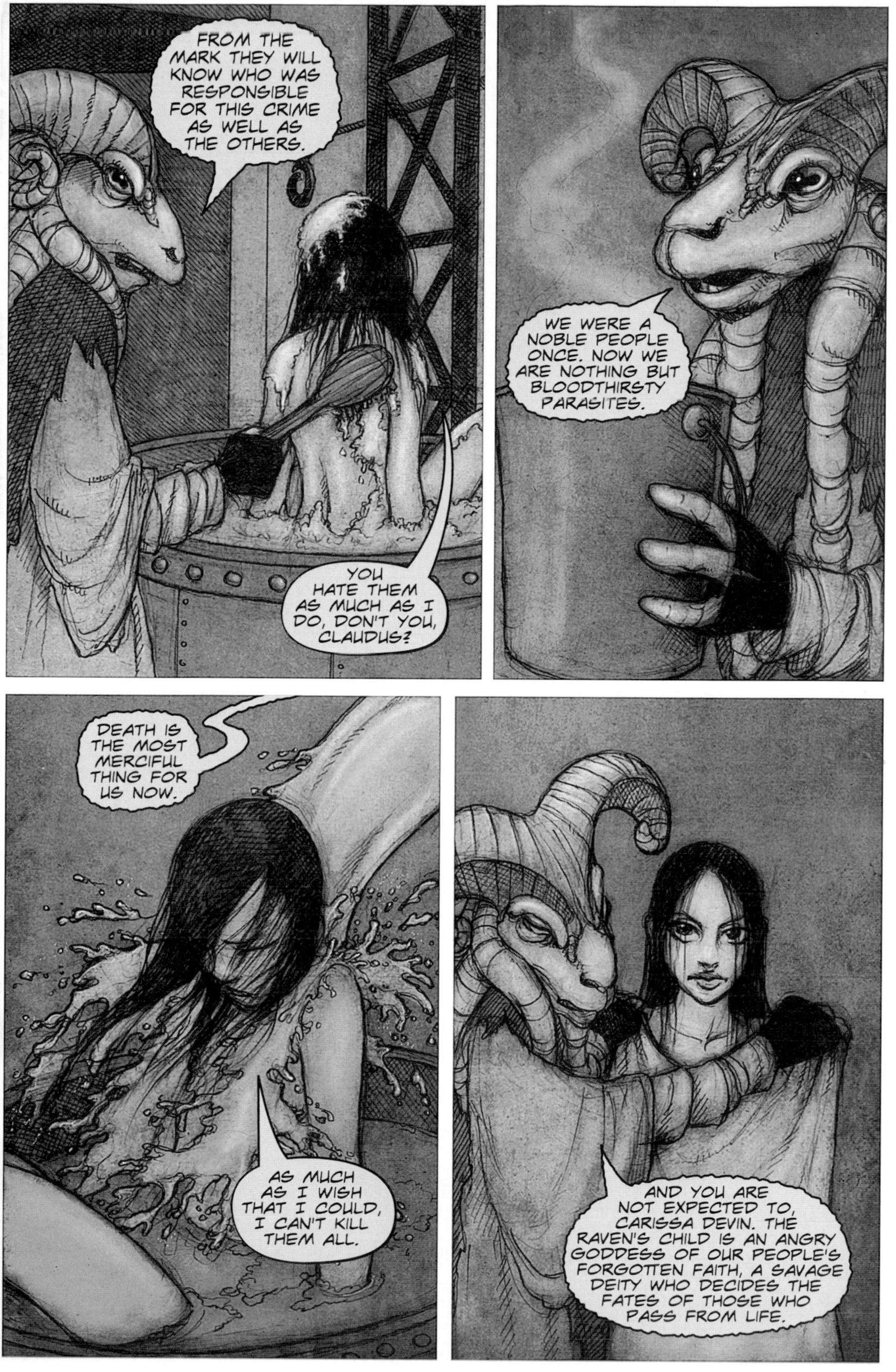
FROM THE MARK THEY WILL KNOW WHO WAS RESPONSIBLE FOR THIS CRIME AS WELL AS THE OTHERS.
YOU HATE THEM AS MUCH AS I DO, DON'T YOU, CLAUDUS?
WE WERE A NOBLE PEOPLE ONCE. NOW WE ARE NOTHING BUT BLOODTHIRSTY PARASITES.
DEATH IS THE MOST MERCIFUL THING FOR US NOW.
AS MUCH AS I WISH THAT I COULD, I CAN'T KILL THEM ALL.
AND YOU ARE NOT EXPECTED TO, CARISSA DEVIN. THE RAVEN'S CHILD IS AN ANGRY GODDESS OF OUR PEOPLE'S FORGOTTEN FAITH, A SAVAGE DEITY WHO DECIDES THE FATES OF THOSE WHO PASS FROM LIFE.

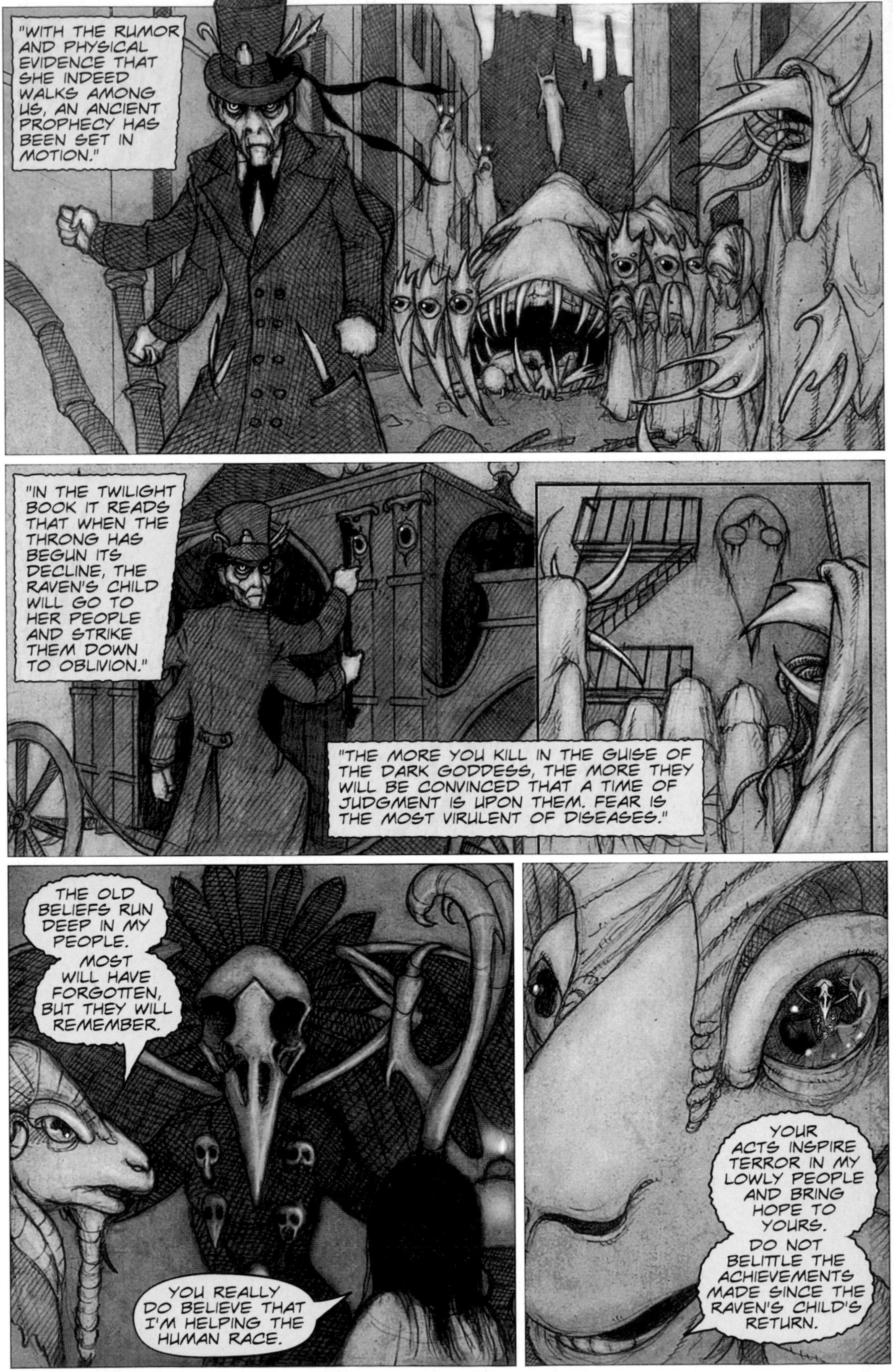
"WITH THE RUMOR AND PHYSICAL EVIDENCE THAT SHE INDEED WALKS AMONG US, AN ANCIENT PROPHECY HAS BEEN SET IN MOTION."
"IN THE TWILIGHT BOOK IT READS THAT WHEN THE THRONG HAS BEGUN ITS DECLINE, THE RAVEN'S CHILD WILL GO TO HER PEOPLE AND STRIKE THEM DOWN TO OBLIVION."
"THE MORE YOU KILL IN THE GUISE OF THE DARK GODDESS, THE MORE THEY WILL BE CONVINCED THAT A TIME OF JUDGMENT IS UPON THEM. FEAR IS THE MOST VIRULENT OF DISEASES."
THE OLD BELIEFS RUN DEEP IN MY PEOPLE.
MOST WILL HAVE FORGOTTEN, BUT THEY WILL REMEMBER.
YOU REALLY DO BELIEVE THAT I'M HELPING THE HUMAN RACE.
YOUR ACTS INSPIRE TERROR IN MY LOWLY PEOPLE AND BRING HOPE TO YOURS.
DO NOT BELITTLE THE ACHIEVEMENTS MADE SINCE THE RAVEN'S CHILD'S RETURN.

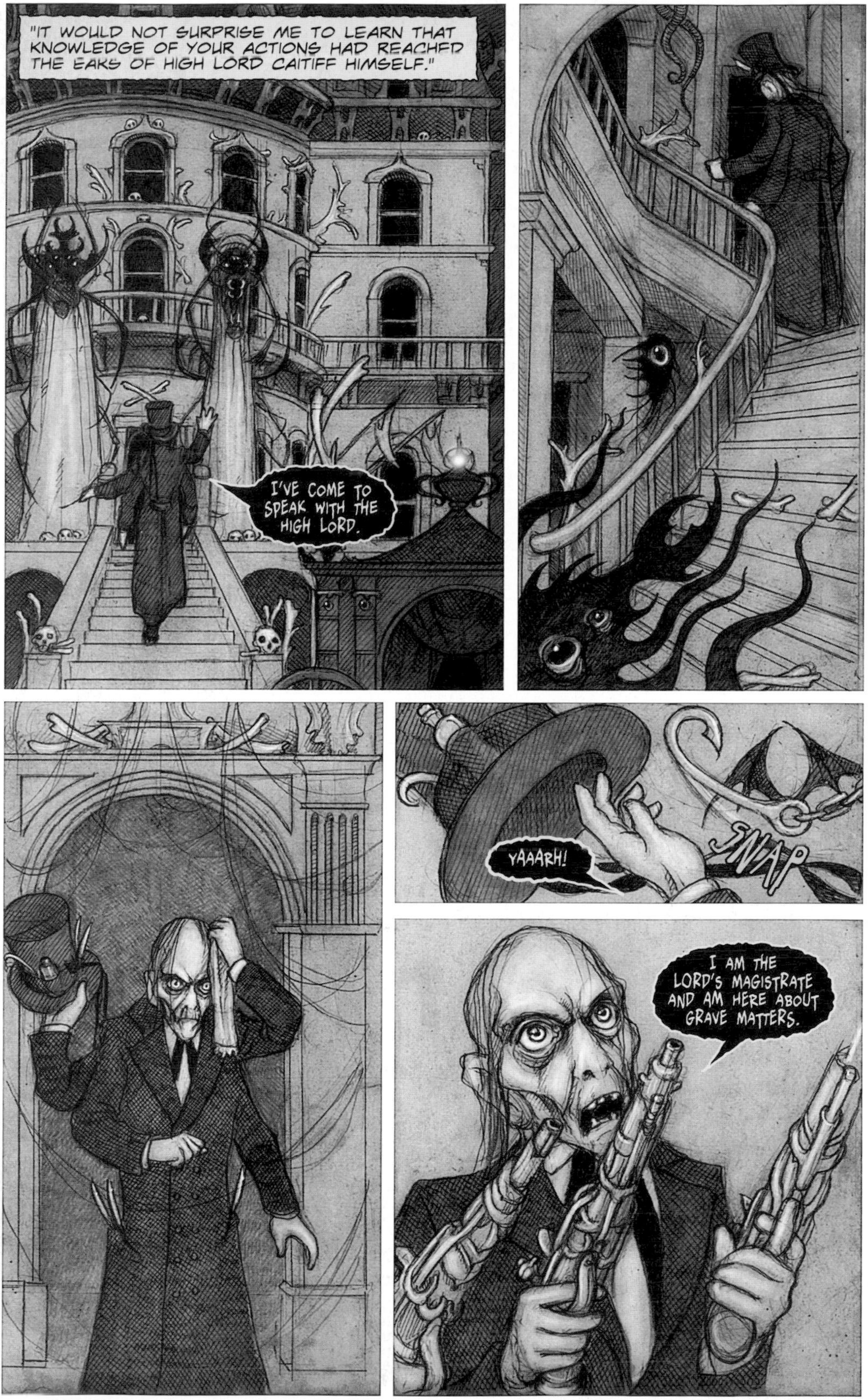
"IT WOULD NOT SURPRISE ME TO LEARN THAT KNOWLEDGE OF YOUR ACTIONS HAD REACHED THE EARS OF HIGH LORD CAITIFF HIMSELF."
I'VE COME TO SPEAK WITH THE HIGH LORD.
YAAARH!
SNAP
I AM THE LORD'S MAGISTRATE AND AM HERE ABOUT GRAVE MATTERS.

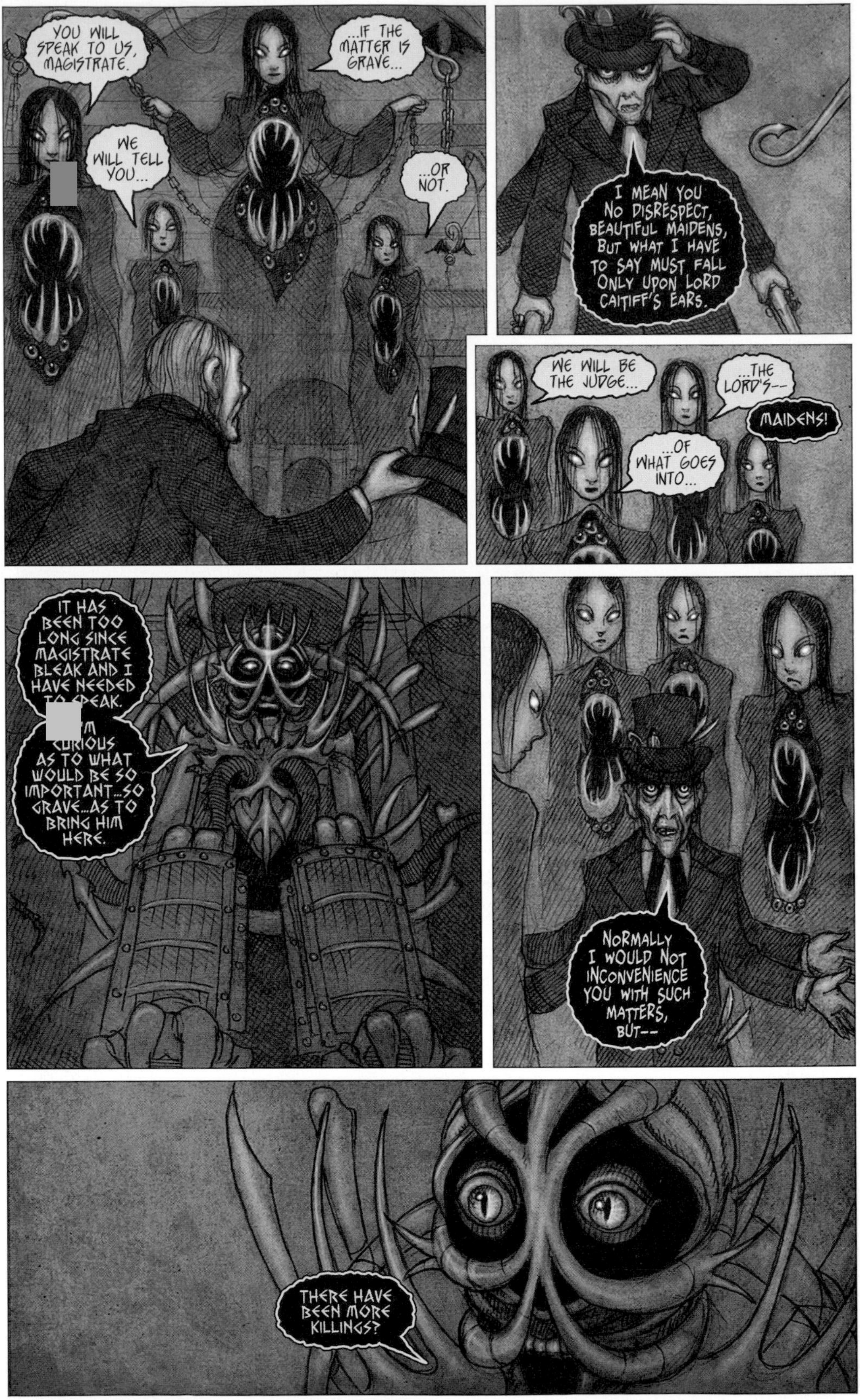

YOU WILL SPEAK TO US, MAGISTRATE.
...IF THE MATTER IS GRAVE...
WE WILL TELL YOU...
...OR NOT.
I MEAN YOU NO DISRESPECT, BEAUTIFUL MAIDENS, BUT WHAT I HAVE TO SAY MUST FALL ONLY UPON LORD CAITIFF'S EARS.
WE WILL BE THE JUDGE...
...OF WHAT GOES INTO...
...THE LORD'S--
MAIDENS!
IT HAS BEEN TOO LONG SINCE MAGISTRATE BLEAK AND I HAVE NEEDED TO SPEAK.
'M CURIOUS AS TO WHAT WOULD BE SO IMPORTANT...SO GRAVE...AS TO BRING HIM HERE.
NORMALLY I WOULD NOT INCONVENIENCE YOU WITH SUCH MATTERS, BUT--
THERE HAVE BEEN MORE KILLINGS?

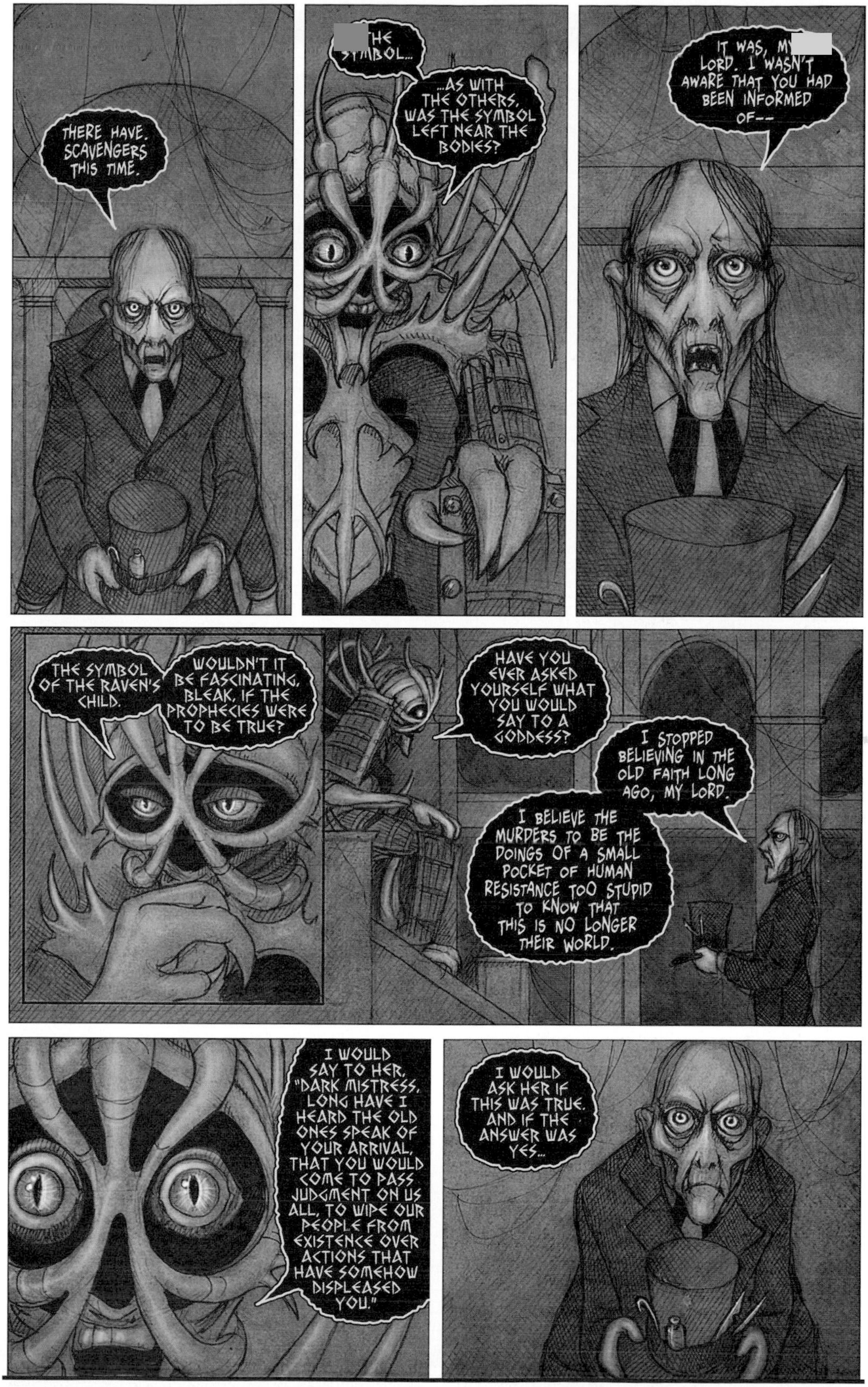
THERE HAVE. SCAVENGERS THIS TIME.
THE SYMBOL...
...AS WITH THE OTHERS, WAS THE SYMBOL LEFT NEAR THE BODIES?
IT WAS, MY
LORD. I WASN'T AWARE THAT YOU HAD BEEN INFORMED OF--
THE SYMBOL OF THE RAVEN'S CHILD.
WOULDN'T IT BE FASCINATING, BLEAK, IF THE PROPHECIES WERE TO BE TRUE?
HAVE YOU EVER ASKED YOURSELF WHAT YOU WOULD SAY TO A GODDESS?
I STOPPED BELIEVING IN THE OLD FAITH LONG AGO, MY LORD.
I BELIEVE THE MURDERS TO BE THE DOINGS OF A SMALL POCKET OF HUMAN RESISTANCE TOO STUPID TO KNOW THAT THIS IS NO LONGER THEIR WORLD.
I WOULD SAY TO HER, "DARK MISTRESS, LONG HAVE I HEARD THE OLD ONES SPEAK OF YOUR ARRIVAL, THAT YOU WOULD COME TO PASS JUDGMENT ON US ALL, TO WIPE OUR PEOPLE FROM EXISTENCE OVER ACTIONS THAT HAVE SOMEHOW DISPLEASED YOU."
I WOULD ASK HER IF THIS WAS TRUE. AND IF THE ANSWER WAS YES...

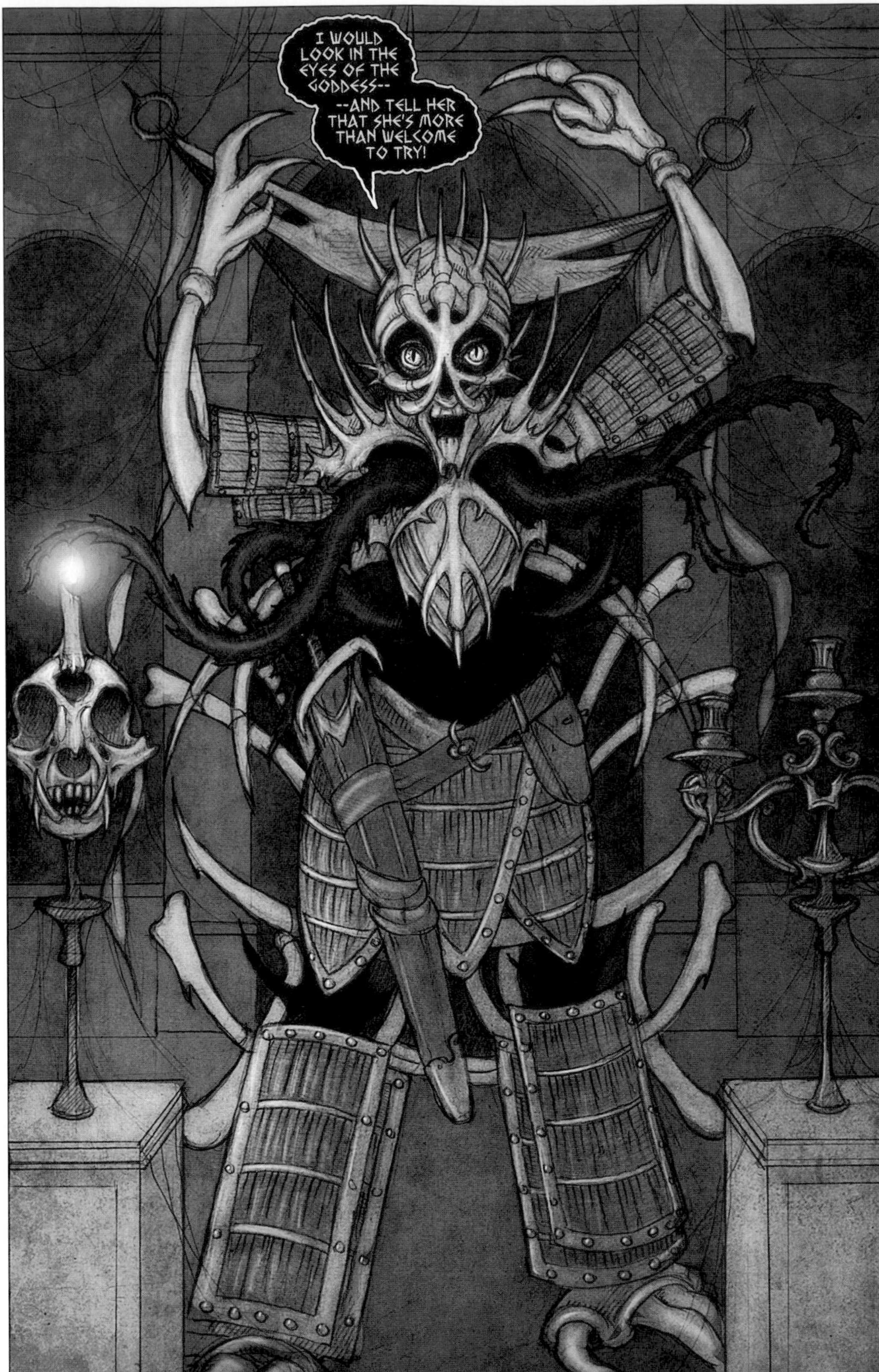
I WOULD LOOK IN THE EYES OF THE GODDESS--
--AND TELL HER THAT SHE'S MORE THAN WELCOME TO TRY!

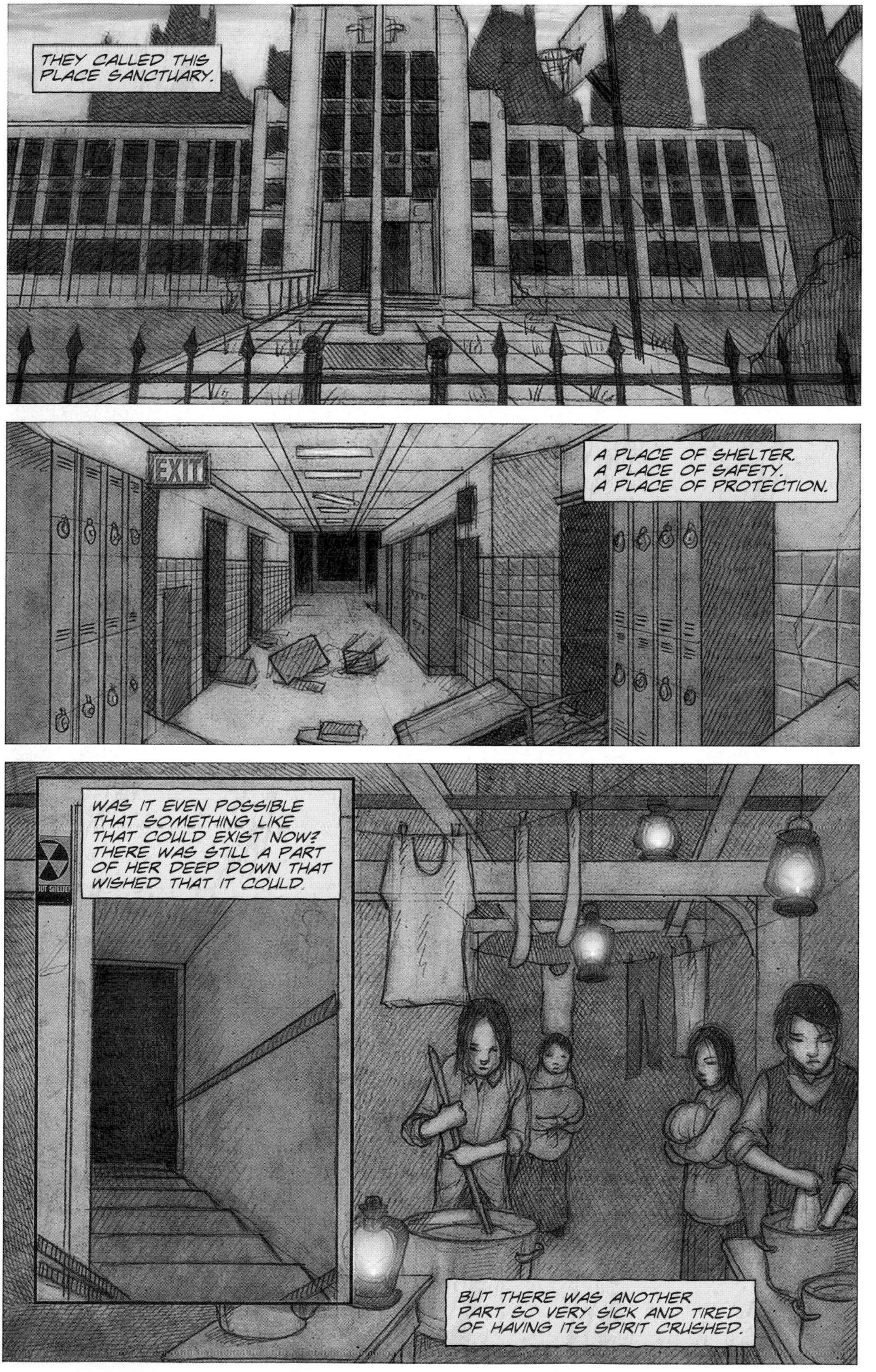
THEY CALLED THIS PLACE SANCTUARY.
A PLACE OF SHELTER. A PLACE OF SAFETY. A PLACE OF PROTECTION.
WAS IT EVEN POSSIBLE THAT SOMETHING LIKE THAT COULD EXIST NOW? THERE WAS STILL A PART OF HER DEEP DOWN THAT WISHED THAT IT COULD.
BUT THERE WAS ANOTHER PART SO VERY SICK AND TIRED OF HAVING ITS SPIRIT CRUSHED.

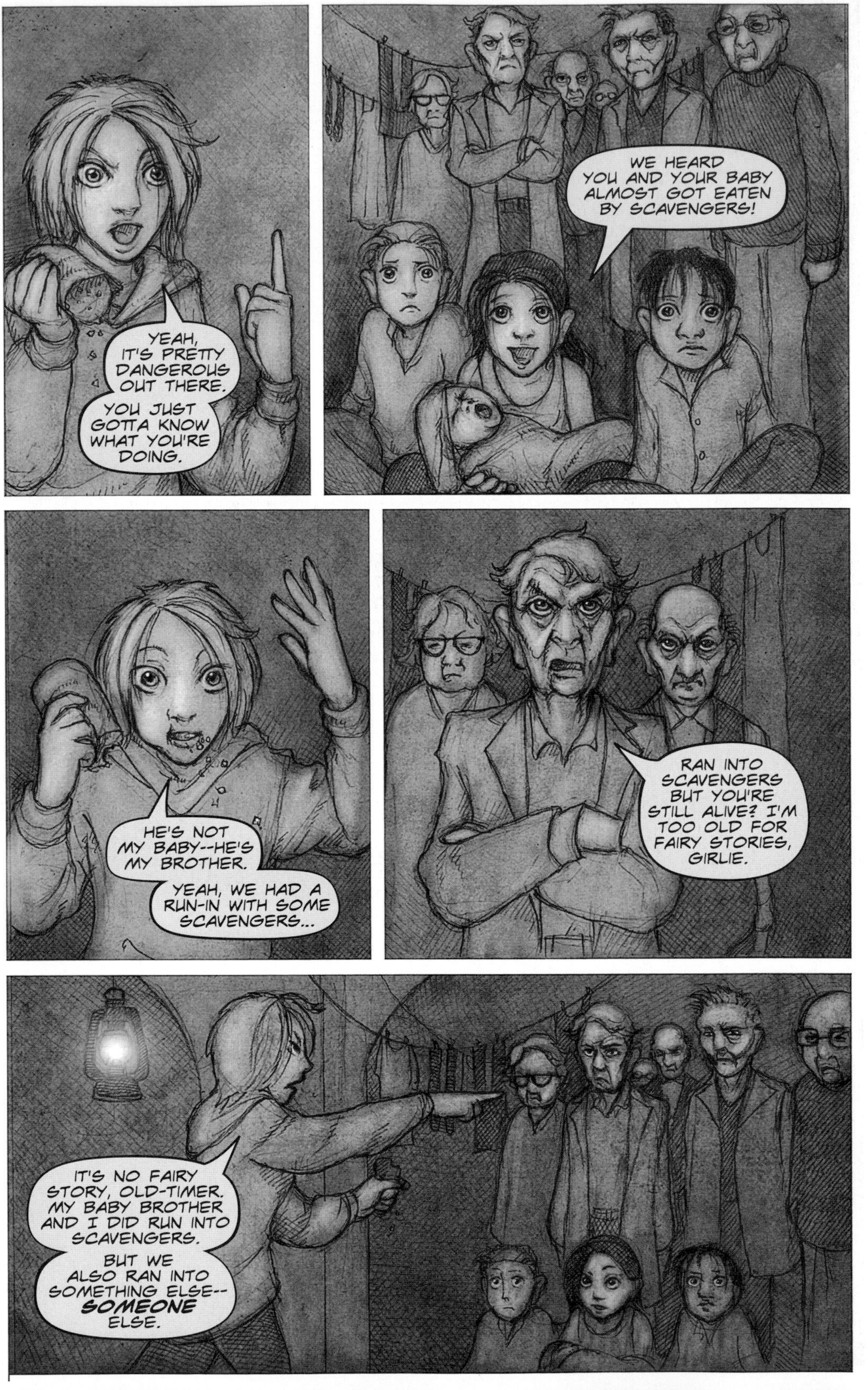
YEAH, IT'S PRETTY DANGEROUS OUT THERE.
YOU JUST GOTTA KNOW WHAT YOU'RE DOING.
WE HEARD YOU AND YOUR BABY ALMOST GOT EATEN BY SCAVENGERS!
HE'S NOT MY BABY--HE'S MY BROTHER.
YEAH, WE HAD A RUN-IN WITH SOME SCAVENGERS...
RAN INTO SCAVENGERS BUT YOU'RE STILL ALIVE? I'M TOO OLD FOR FAIRY STORIES, GIRLIE.
IT'S NO FAIRY STORY, OLD-TIMER. MY BABY BROTHER AND I DID RUN INTO SCAVENGERS.
BUT WE ALSO RAN INTO SOMETHING ELSE-- SOMEONE ELSE.

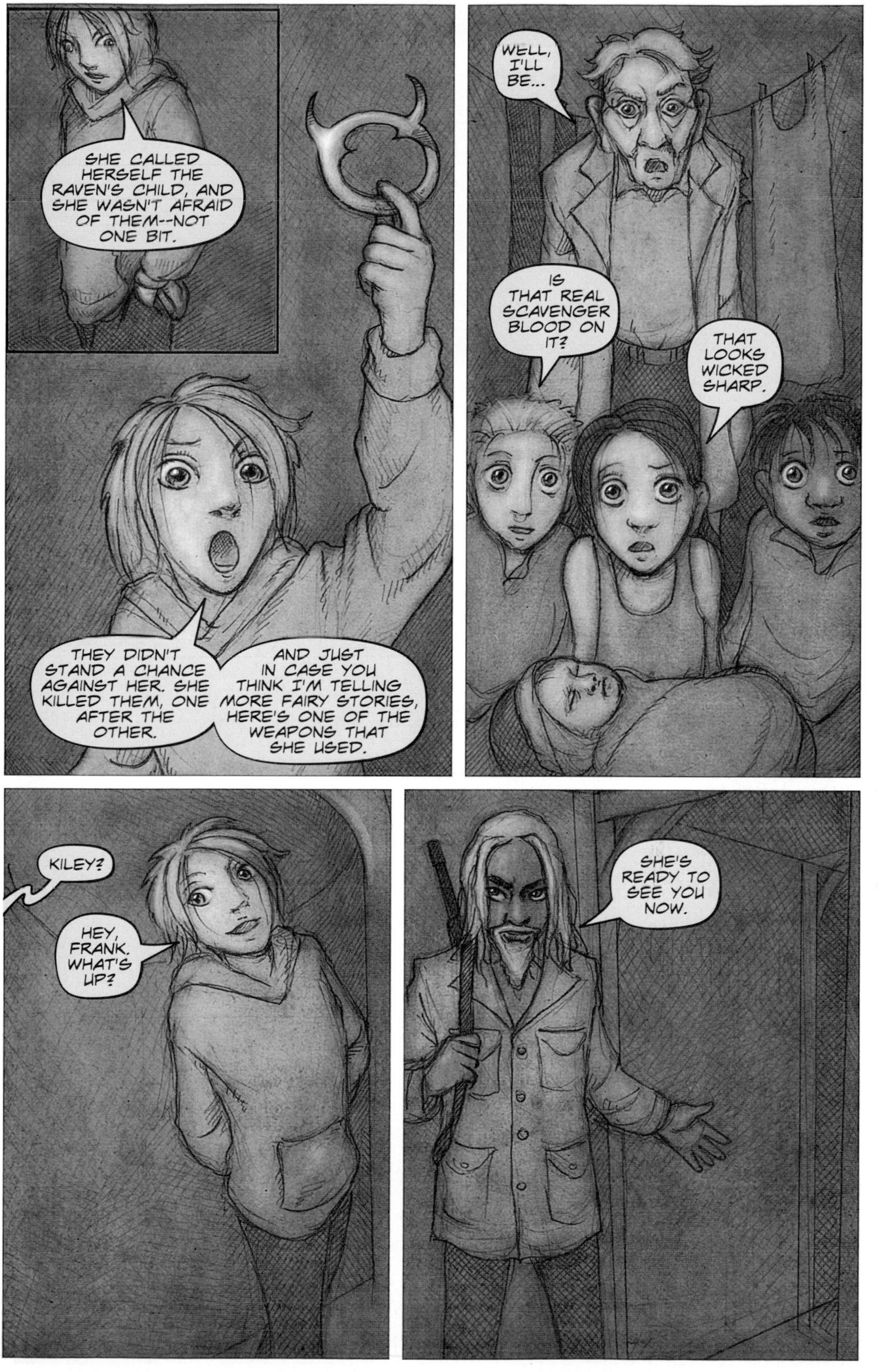
SHE CALLED HERSELF THE RAVEN'S CHILD, AND SHE WASN'T AFRAID OF THEM--NOT ONE BIT.
THEY DIDN'T STAND A CHANCE AGAINST HER. SHE KILLED THEM, ONE AFTER THE OTHER.
AND JUST IN CASE YOU THINK I'M TELLING MORE FAIRY STORIES, HERE'S ONE OF THE WEAPONS THAT SHE USED.
WELL, I'LL BE...
IS THAT REAL SCAVENGER BLOOD ON IT?
THAT LOOKS WICKED SHARP.
KILEY?
HEY, FRANK. WHAT'S UP?
SHE'S READY TO SEE YOU NOW.

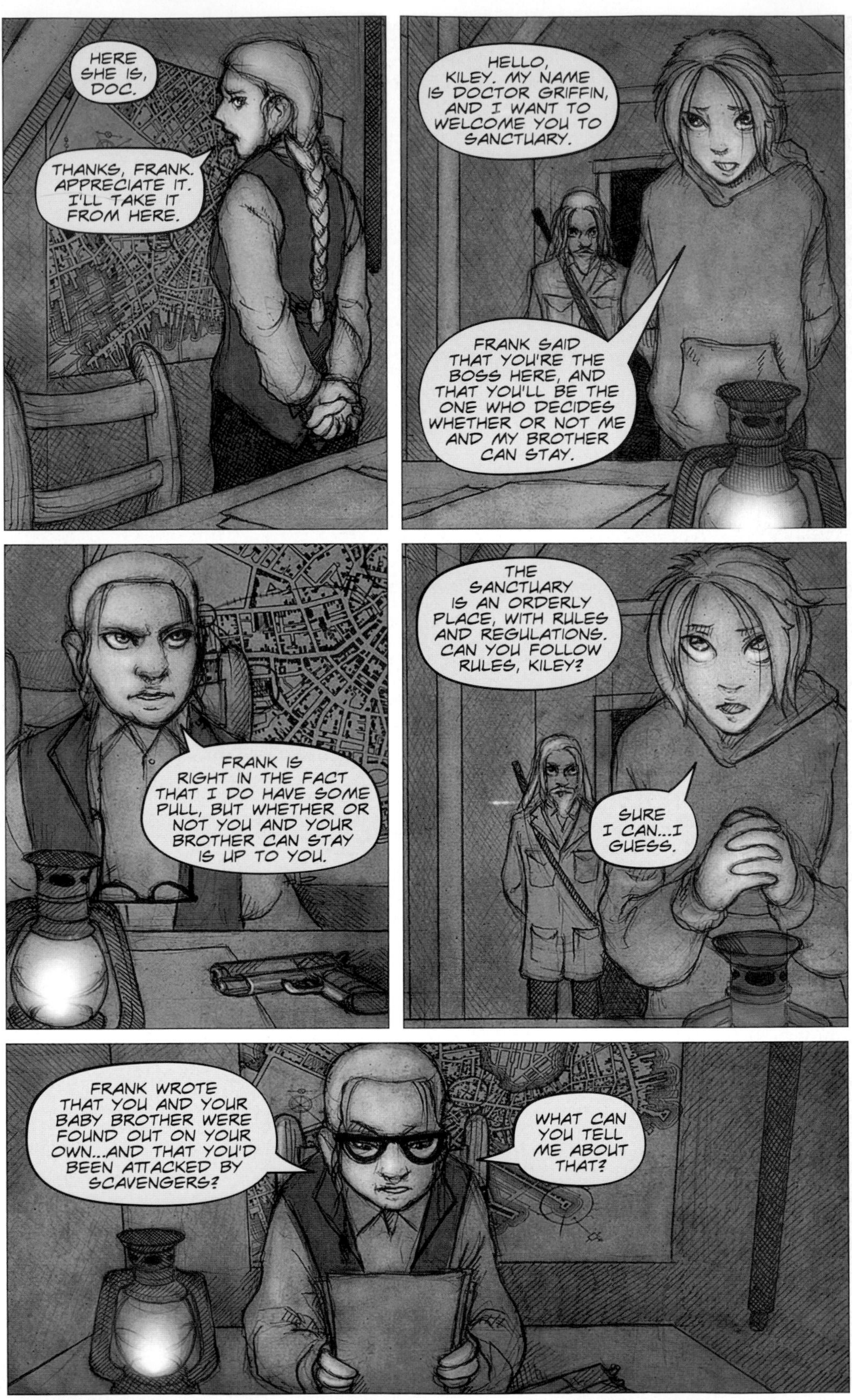
HERE SHE IS, DOC.
THANKS, FRANK. APPRECIATE IT. I'LL TAKE IT FROM HERE.
HELLO, KILEY. MY NAME IS DOCTOR GRIFFIN, AND I WANT TO WELCOME YOU TO SANCTUARY.
FRANK SAID THAT YOU'RE THE BOSS HERE, AND THAT YOU'LL BE THE ONE WHO DECIDES WHETHER OR NOT ME AND MY BROTHER CAN STAY.
FRANK IS RIGHT IN THE FACT THAT I DO HAVE SOME PULL, BUT WHETHER OR NOT YOU AND YOUR BROTHER CAN STAY IS UP TO YOU.
THE SANCTUARY IS AN ORDERLY PLACE, WITH RULES AND REGULATIONS. CAN YOU FOLLOW RULES, KILEY?
SURE I CAN...I GUESS.
FRANK WROTE THAT YOU AND YOUR BABY BROTHER WERE FOUND OUT ON YOUR OWN...AND THAT YOU'D BEEN ATTACKED BY SCAVENGERS?
WHAT CAN YOU TELL ME ABOUT THAT?

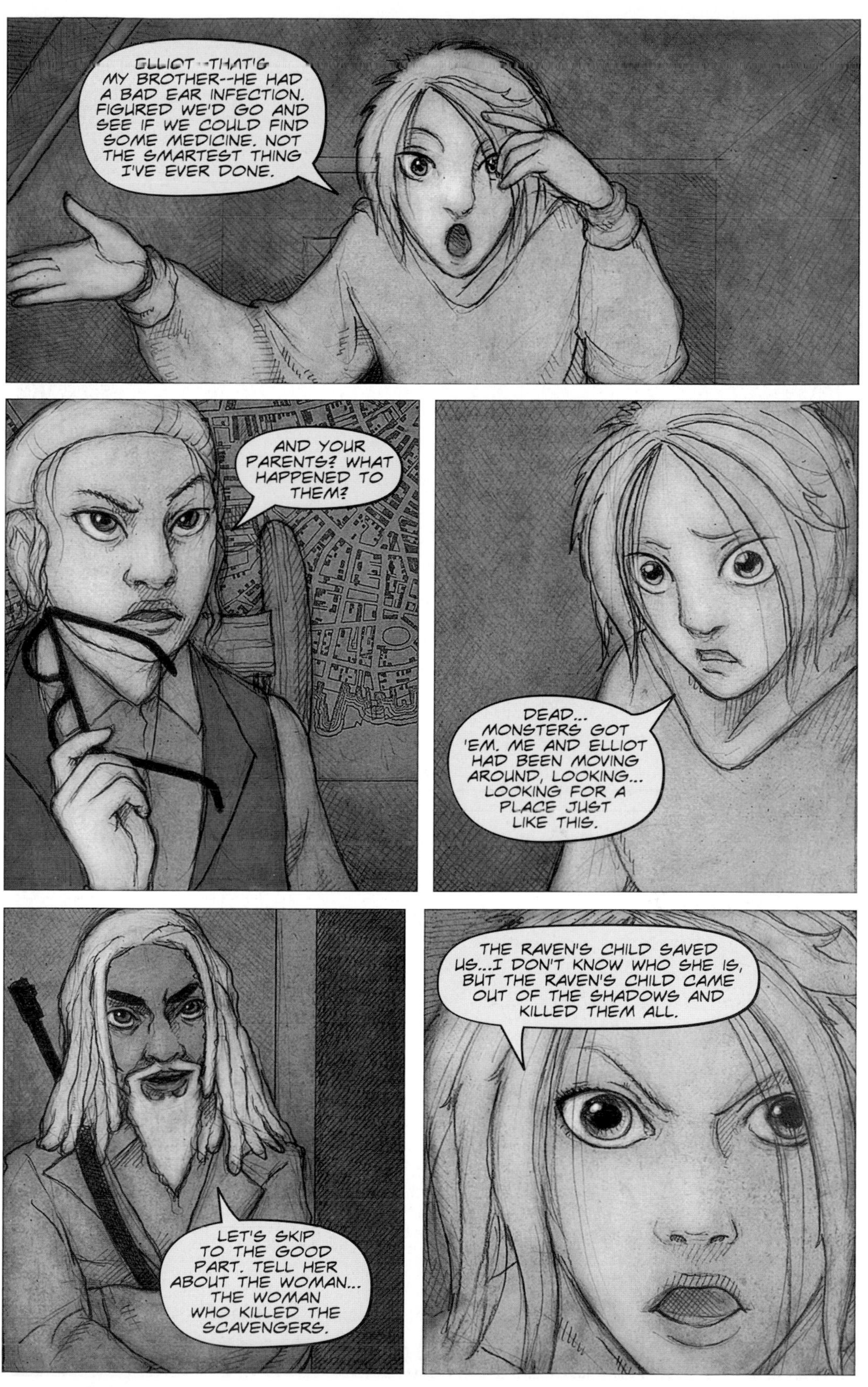
ELLIOT--THAT'S MY BROTHER--HE HAD A BAD EAR INFECTION. FIGURED WE'D GO AND SEE IF WE COULD FIND SOME MEDICINE. NOT THE SMARTEST THING I'VE EVER DONE.
AND YOUR PARENTS? WHAT HAPPENED TO THEM?
DEAD... MONSTERS GOT 'EM. ME AND ELLIOT HAD BEEN MOVING AROUND, LOOKING... LOOKING FOR A PLACE JUST LIKE THIS.
LET'S SKIP TO THE GOOD PART. TELL HER ABOUT THE WOMAN... THE WOMAN WHO KILLED THE SCAVENGERS.
THE RAVEN'S CHILD SAVED US...I DON'T KNOW WHO SHE IS, BUT THE RAVEN'S CHILD CAME OUT OF THE SHADOWS AND KILLED THEM ALL.

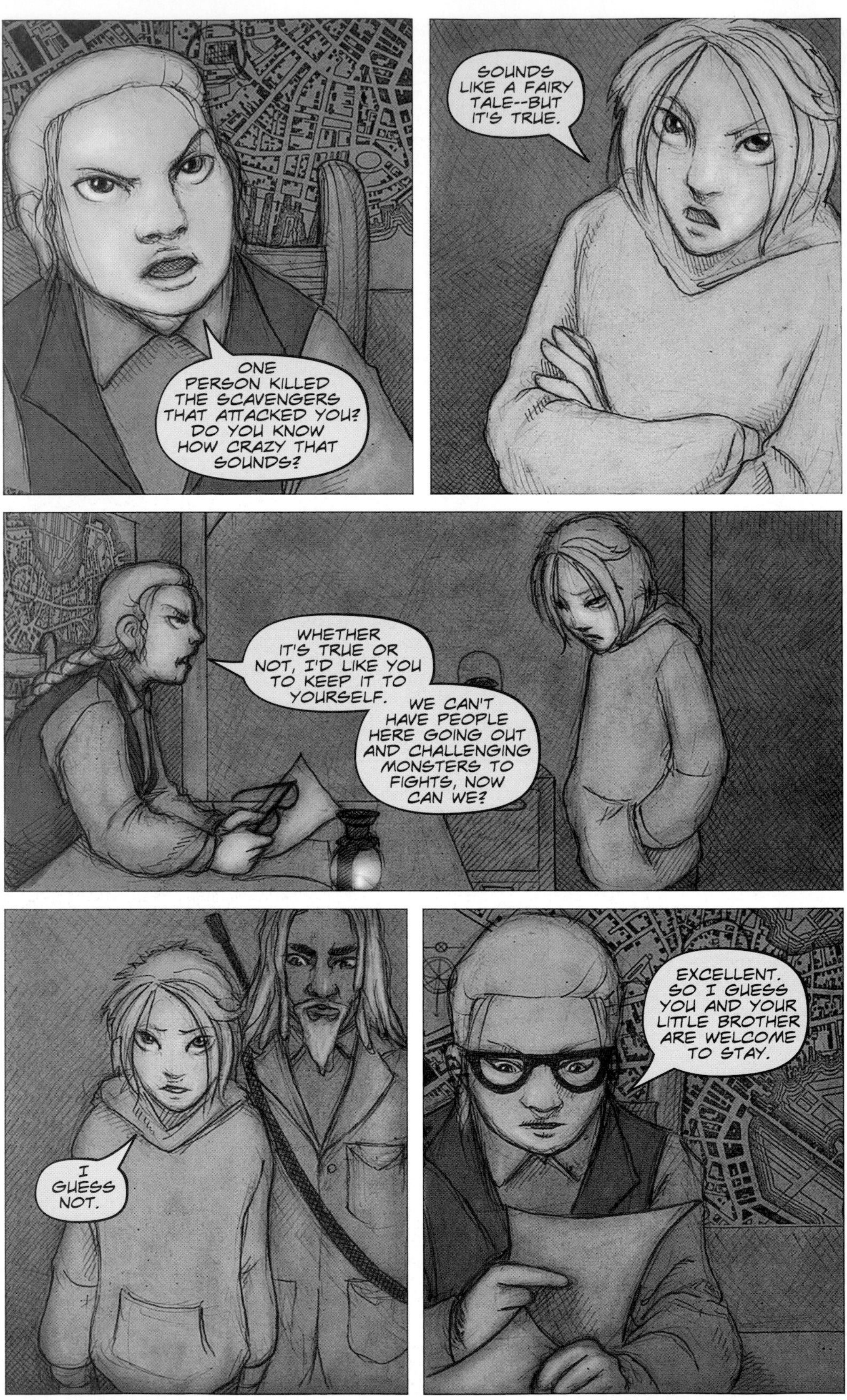
ONE PERSON KILLED THE SCAVENGERS THAT ATTACKED YOU? DO YOU KNOW HOW CRAZY THAT SOUNDS?
SOUNDS LIKE A FAIRY TALE--BUT IT'S TRUE.
WHETHER IT'S TRUE OR NOT, I'D LIKE YOU TO KEEP IT TO YOURSELF.
WE CAN'T HAVE PEOPLE HERE GOING OUT AND CHALLENGING MONSTERS TO FIGHTS, NOW CAN WE?
I GUESS NOT.
EXCELLENT. SO I GUESS YOU AND YOUR LITTLE BROTHER ARE WELCOME TO STAY.

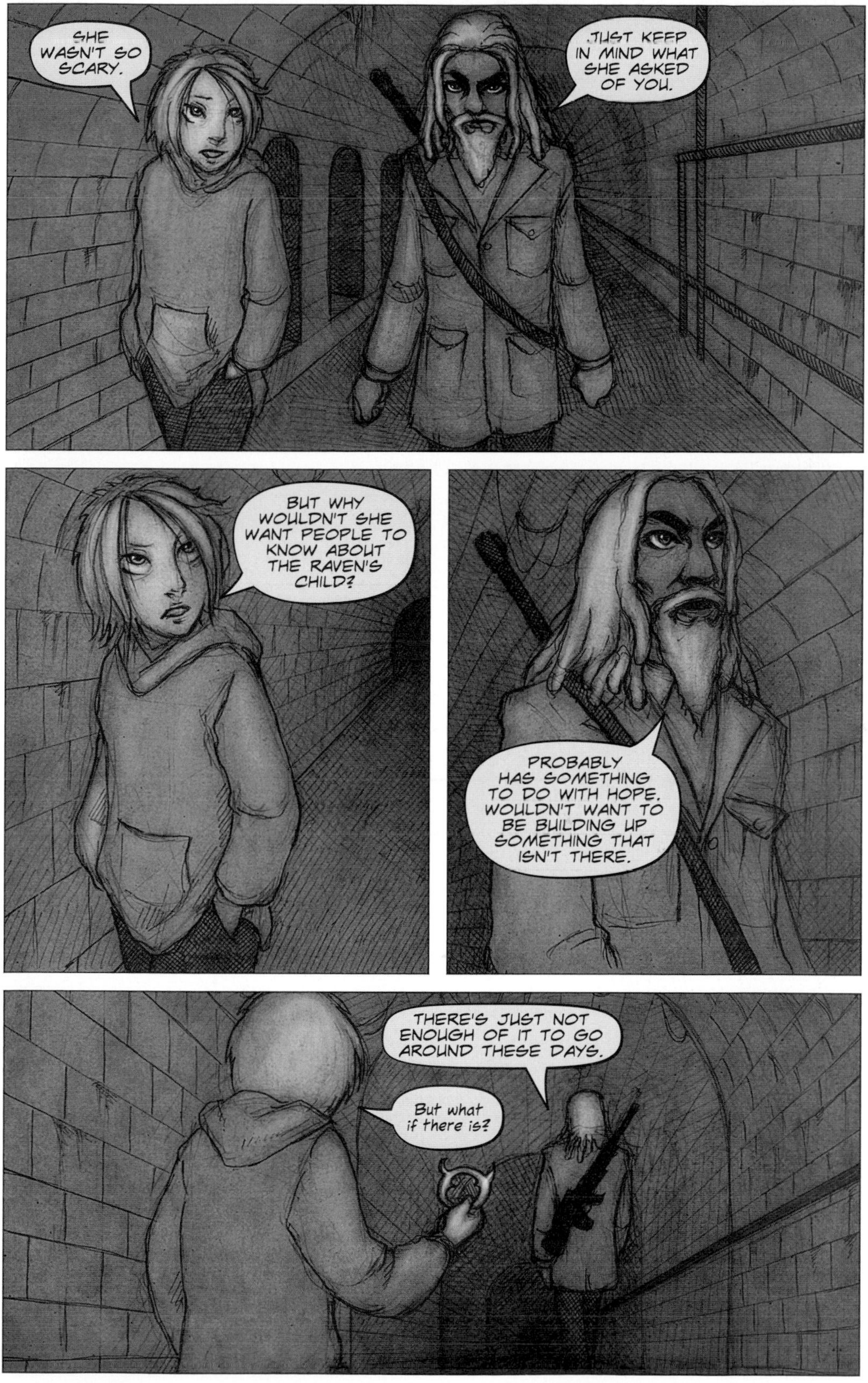
SHE WASN'T SO SCARY.
JUST KEEP IN MIND WHAT SHE ASKED OF YOU.
BUT WHY WOULDN'T SHE WANT PEOPLE TO KNOW ABOUT THE RAVEN'S CHILD?
PROBABLY HAS SOMETHING TO DO WITH HOPE. WOULDN'T WANT TO BE BUILDING UP SOMETHING THAT ISN'T THERE.
THERE'S JUST NOT ENOUGH OF IT TO GO AROUND THESE DAYS.
But what if there is?

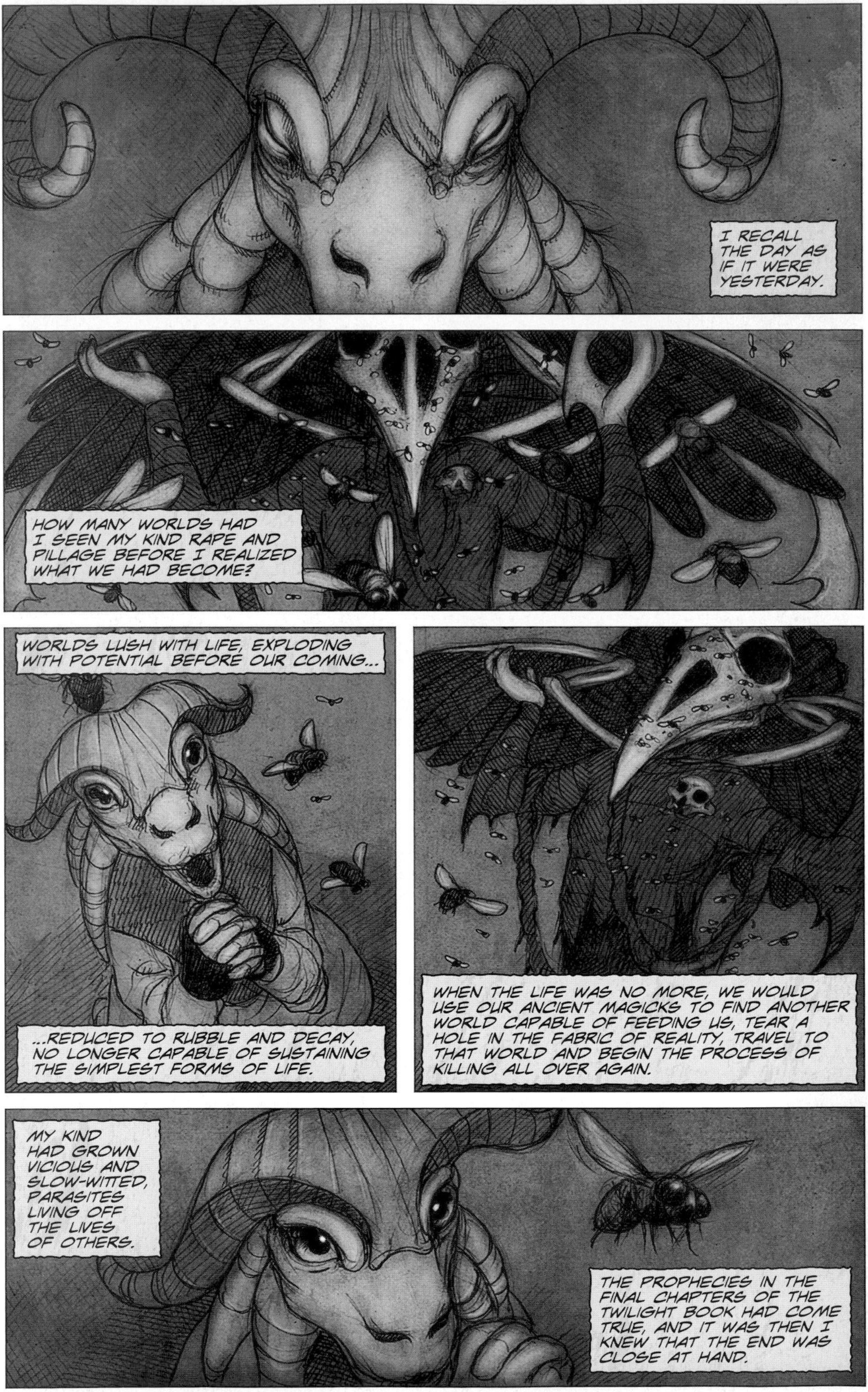
I RECALL THE DAY AS IF IT WERE YESTERDAY.
HOW MANY WORLDS HAD I SEEN MY KIND RAPE AND PILLAGE BEFORE I REALIZED WHAT WE HAD BECOME?
WORLDS LUSH WITH LIFE, EXPLODING WITH POTENTIAL BEFORE OUR COMING...
...REDUCED TO RUBBLE AND DECAY, NO LONGER CAPABLE OF SUSTAINING THE SIMPLEST FORMS OF LIFE.
WHEN THE LIFE WAS NO MORE, WE WOULD USE OUR ANCIENT MAGICKS TO FIND ANOTHER WORLD CAPABLE OF FEEDING US, TEAR A HOLE IN THE FABRIC OF REALITY, TRAVEL TO THAT WORLD AND BEGIN THE PROCESS OF KILLING ALL OVER AGAIN.
MY KIND HAD GROWN VICIOUS AND SLOW-WITTED, PARASITES LIVING OFF THE LIVES OF OTHERS.
THE PROPHECIES IN THE FINAL CHAPTERS OF THE TWILIGHT BOOK HAD COME TRUE, AND IT WAS THEN I KNEW THAT THE END WAS CLOSE AT HAND.

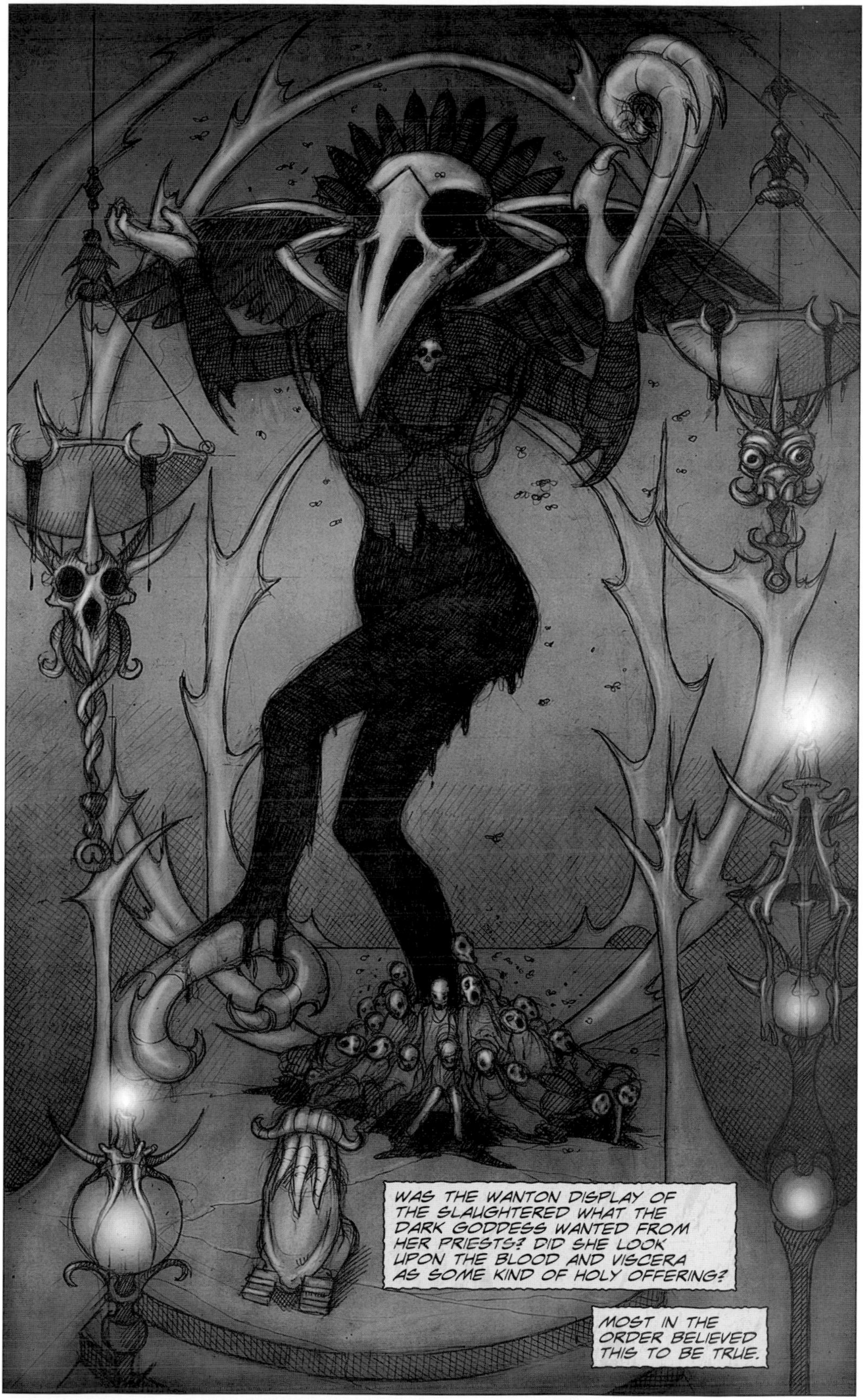
WAS THE WANTON DISPLAY OF THE SLAUGHTERED WHAT THE DARK GODDESS WANTED FROM HER PRIESTS? DID SHE LOOK UPON THE BLOOD AND VISCERA AS SOME KIND OF HOLY OFFERING?
MOST IN THE ORDER BELIEVED THIS TO BE TRUE.

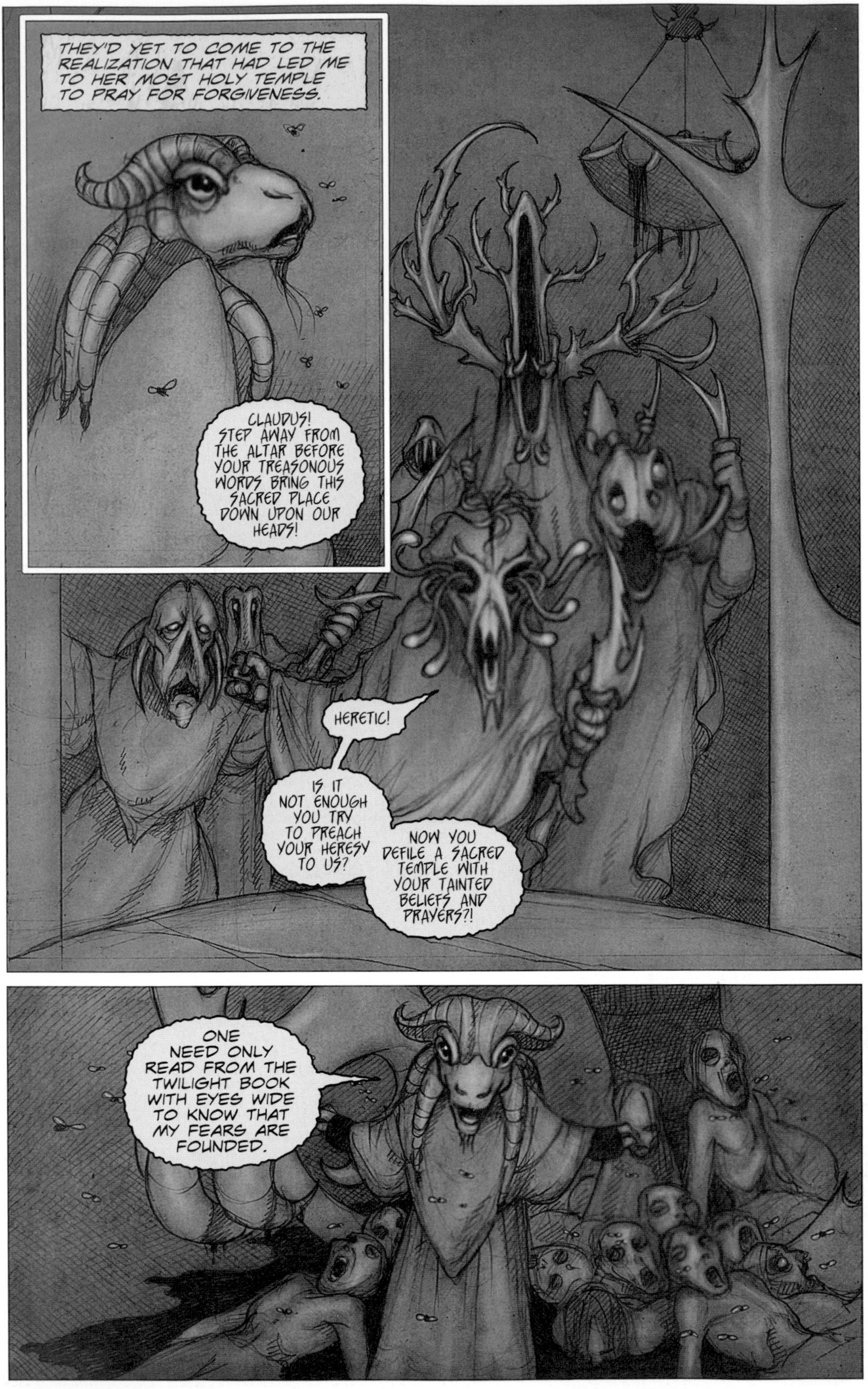
THEY'D YET TO COME TO THE REALIZATION THAT HAD LED ME TO HER MOST HOLY TEMPLE TO PRAY FOR FORGIVENESS.
CLAUDUS! STEP AWAY FROM THE ALTAR BEFORE YOUR TREASONOUS WORDS BRING THIS SACRED PLACE DOWN UPON OUR HEADS!
HERETIC!
IS IT NOT ENOUGH YOU TRY TO PREACH YOUR HERESY TO US?
NOW YOU DEFILE A SACRED TEMPLE WITH YOUR TAINTED BELIEFS AND PRAYERS?!
ONE NEED ONLY READ FROM THE TWILIGHT BOOK WITH EYES WIDE TO KNOW THAT MY FEARS ARE FOUNDED.

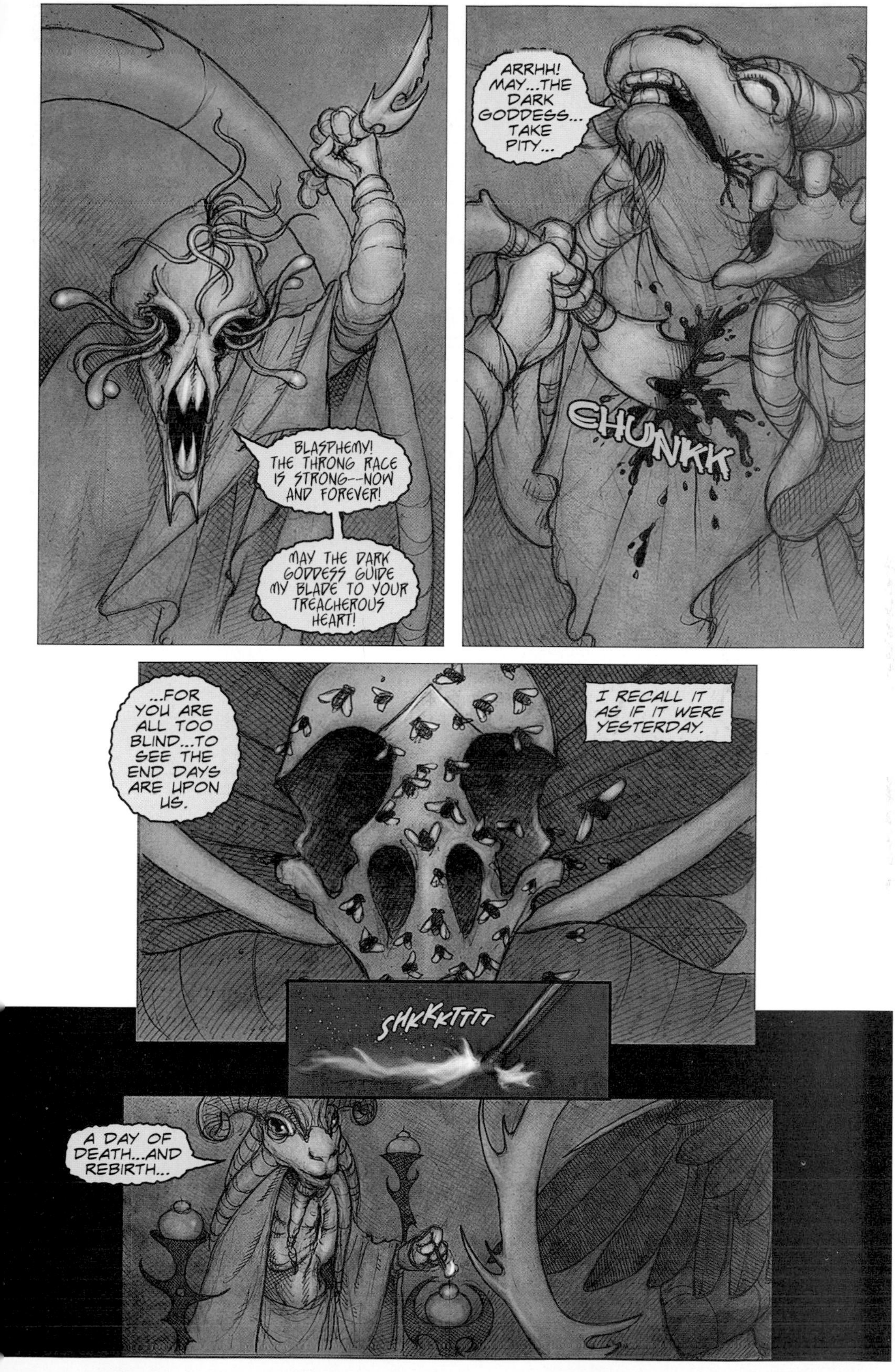
BLASPHEMY! THE THRONG RACE IS STRONG--NOW AND FOREVER!
MAY THE DARK GODDESS GUIDE MY BLADE TO YOUR TREACHEROUS HEART!
ARRHH! MAY...THE DARK GODDESS... TAKE PITY...
CHUNKK
...FOR YOU ARE ALL TOO BLIND...TO SEE THE END DAYS ARE UPON US.
I RECALL IT AS IF IT WERE YESTERDAY.
SHKKKTTTT
A DAY OF DEATH...AND REBIRTH...

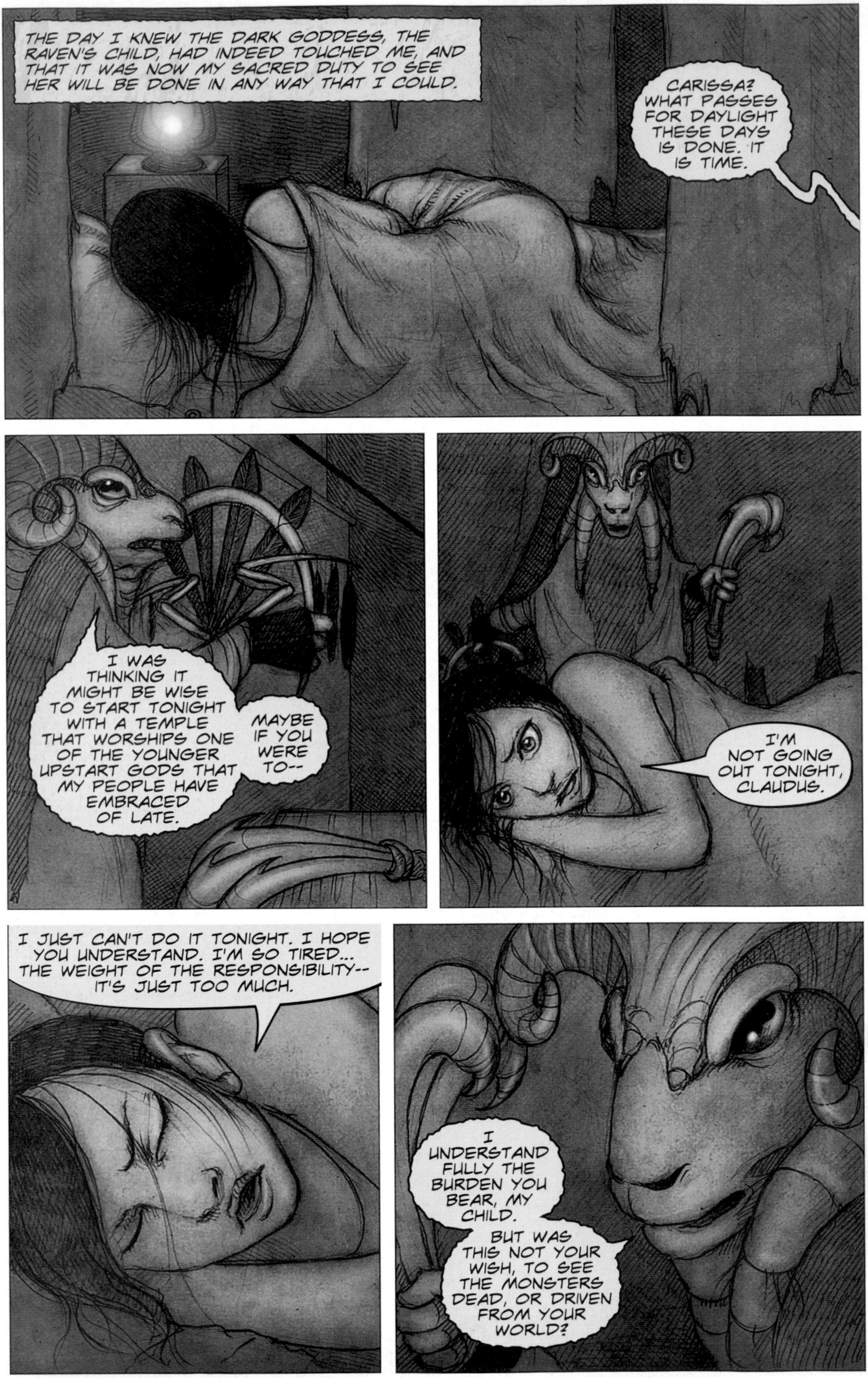
THE DAY I KNEW THE DARK GODDESS, THE RAVEN'S CHILD, HAD INDEED TOUCHED ME, AND THAT IT WAS NOW MY SACRED DUTY TO SEE HER WILL BE DONE IN ANY WAY THAT I COULD.
CARISSA? WHAT PASSES FOR DAYLIGHT THESE DAYS IS DONE. IT IS TIME.
I WAS THINKING IT MIGHT BE WISE TO START TONIGHT WITH A TEMPLE THAT WORSHIPS ONE OF THE YOUNGER UPSTART GODS THAT MY PEOPLE HAVE EMBRACED OF LATE.
MAYBE IF YOU WERE TO--
I'M NOT GOING OUT TONIGHT, CLAUDUS.
I JUST CAN'T DO IT TONIGHT. I HOPE YOU UNDERSTAND. I'M SO TIRED... THE WEIGHT OF THE RESPONSIBILITY-- IT'S JUST TOO MUCH.
I UNDERSTAND FULLY THE BURDEN YOU BEAR, MY CHILD.
BUT WAS THIS NOT YOUR WISH, TO SEE THE MONSTERS DEAD, OR DRIVEN FROM YOUR WORLD?

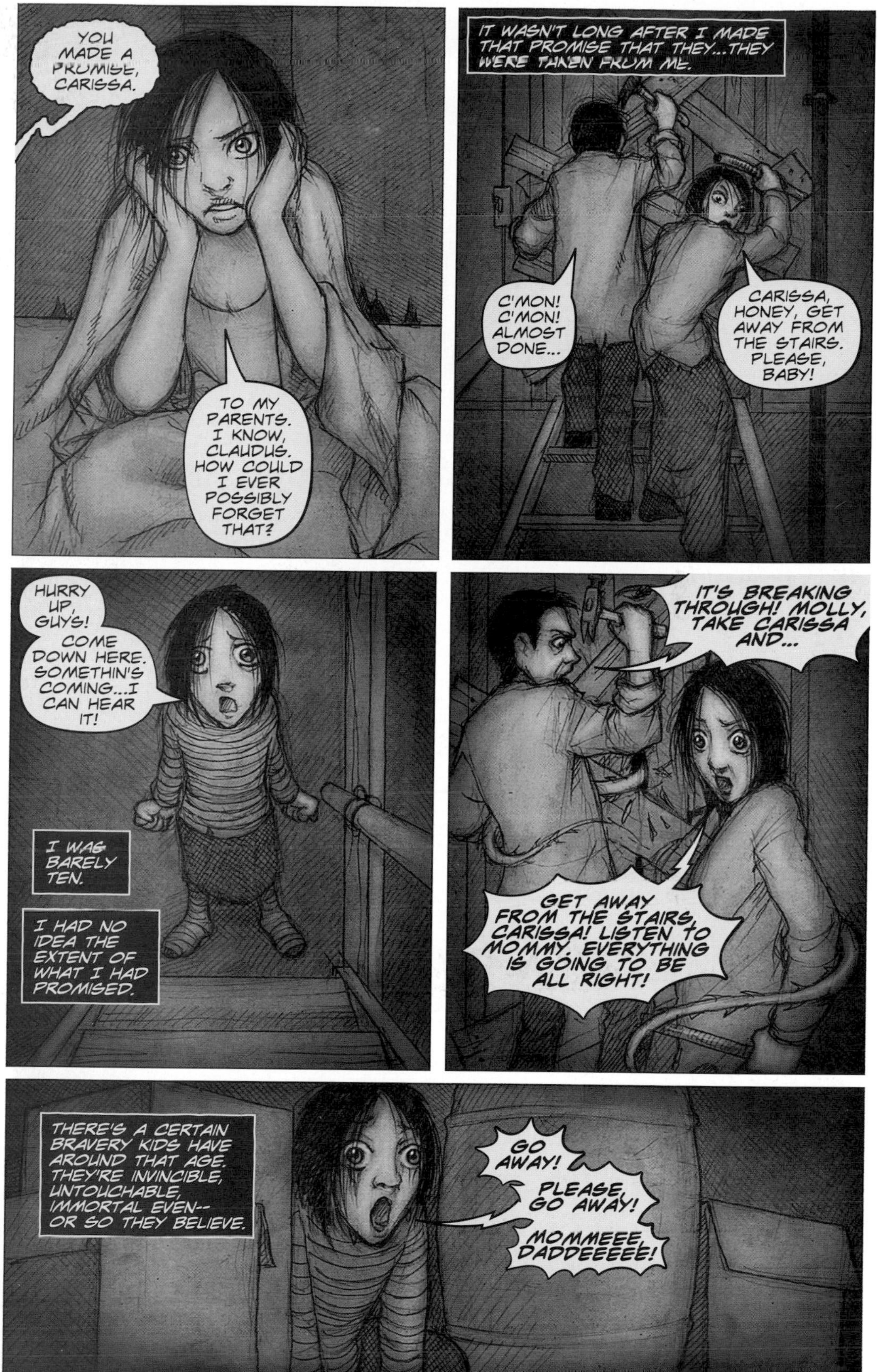
YOU MADE A PROMISE, CARISSA.
TO MY PARENTS. I KNOW, CLAUDUS. HOW COULD I EVER POSSIBLY FORGET THAT?
IT WASN'T LONG AFTER I MADE THAT PROMISE THAT THEY...THEY WERE TAKEN FROM ME.
C'MON! C'MON! ALMOST DONE...
CARISSA, HONEY, GET AWAY FROM THE STAIRS. PLEASE, BABY!
HURRY UP, GUYS!
COME DOWN HERE. SOMETHIN'S COMING...I CAN HEAR IT!
I WAS BARELY TEN.
I HAD NO IDEA THE EXTENT OF WHAT I HAD PROMISED.
IT'S BREAKING THROUGH! MOLLY, TAKE CARISSA AND...
GET AWAY FROM THE STAIRS, CARISSA! LISTEN TO MOMMY. EVERYTHING IS GOING TO BE ALL RIGHT!
THERE'S A CERTAIN BRAVERY KIDS HAVE AROUND THAT AGE. THEY'RE INVINCIBLE, UNTOUCHABLE, IMMORTAL EVEN-- OR SO THEY BELIEVE.
GO AWAY!
PLEASE, GO AWAY!
MOMMEEE, DADDEEEEEE!

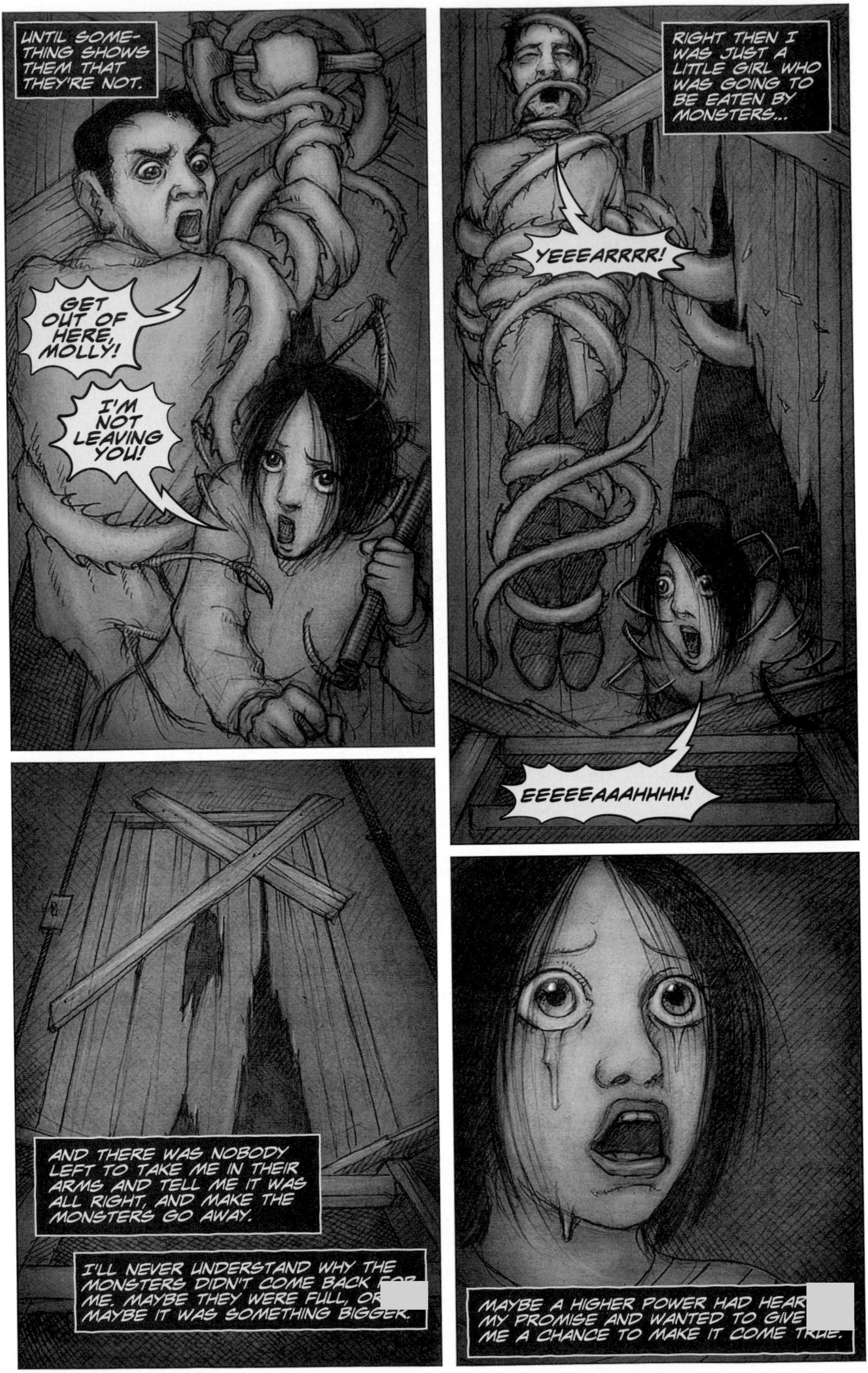
UNTIL SOMETHING SHOWS THEM THAT THEY'RE NOT.
GET OUT OF HERE, MOLLY!
I'M NOT LEAVING YOU!
RIGHT THEN I WAS JUST A LITTLE GIRL WHO WAS GOING TO BE EATEN BY MONSTERS...
YEEEARRRR!
EEEEEAAAHHHH!
AND THERE WAS NOBODY LEFT TO TAKE ME IN THEIR ARMS AND TELL ME IT WAS ALL RIGHT, AND MAKE THE MONSTERS GO AWAY.
I'LL NEVER UNDERSTAND WHY THE MONSTERS DIDN'T COME BACK FOR ME. MAYBE THEY WERE FULL, OR MAYBE IT WAS SOMETHING BIGGER.
MAYBE A HIGHER POWER HAD HEAR MY PROMISE AND WANTED TO GIVE ME A CHANCE TO MAKE IT COME TRUE.

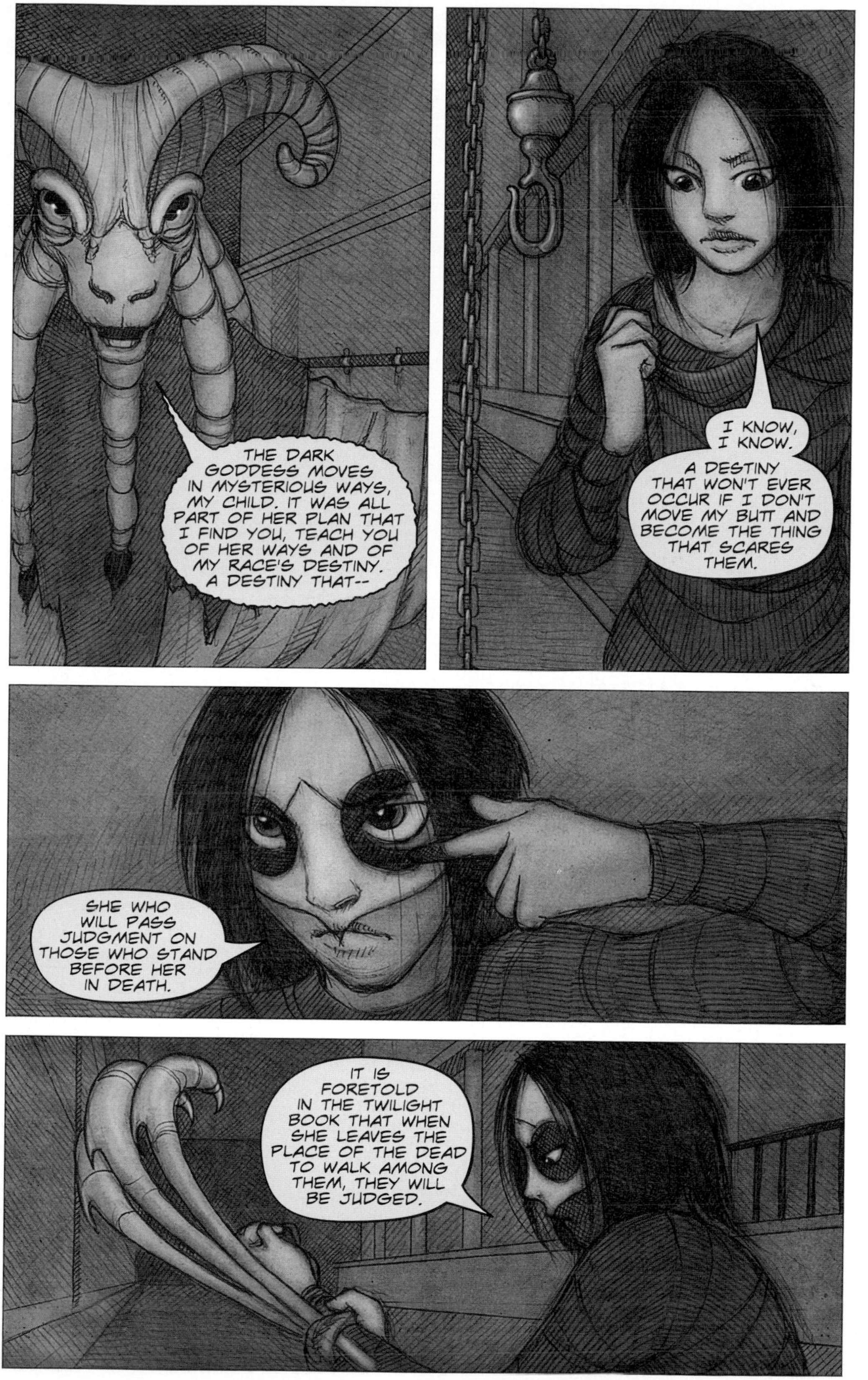
THE DARK GODDESS MOVES IN MYSTERIOUS WAYS, MY CHILD. IT WAS ALL PART OF HER PLAN THAT I FIND YOU, TEACH YOU OF HER WAYS AND OF MY RACE'S DESTINY. A DESTINY THAT--
I KNOW, I KNOW.
A DESTINY THAT WON'T EVER OCCUR IF I DON'T MOVE MY BUTT AND BECOME THE THING THAT SCARES THEM.
SHE WHO WILL PASS JUDGMENT ON THOSE WHO STAND BEFORE HER IN DEATH.
IT IS FORETOLD IN THE TWILIGHT BOOK THAT WHEN SHE LEAVES THE PLACE OF THE DEAD TO WALK AMONG THEM, THEY WILL BE JUDGED.

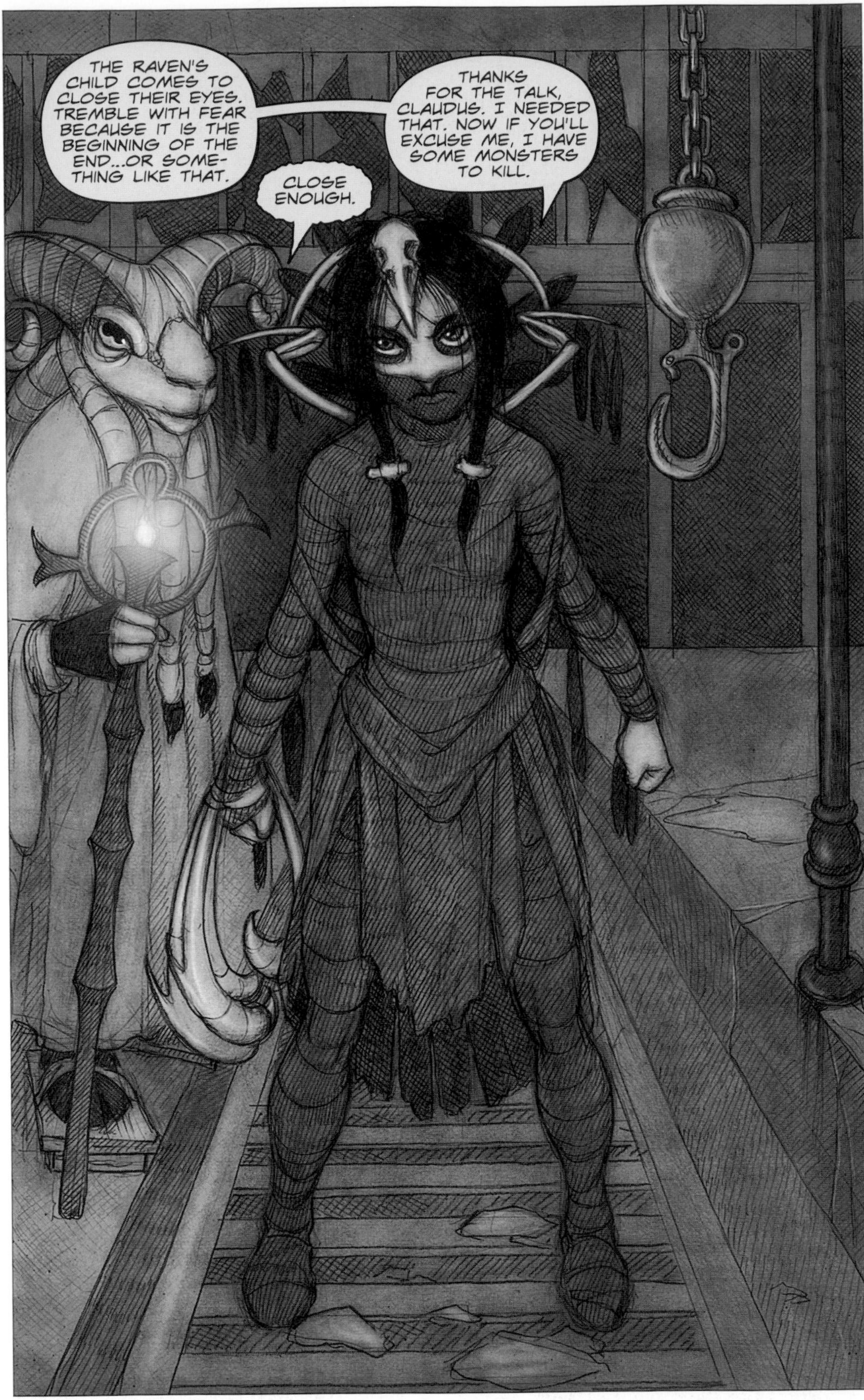
THE RAVEN'S CHILD COMES TO CLOSE THEIR EYES. TREMBLE WITH FEAR BECAUSE IT IS THE BEGINNING OF THE END...OR SOMETHING LIKE THAT.
CLOSE ENOUGH.
THANKS FOR THE TALK, CLAUDUS. I NEEDED THAT. NOW IF YOU'LL EXCUSE ME, I HAVE SOME MONSTERS TO KILL.

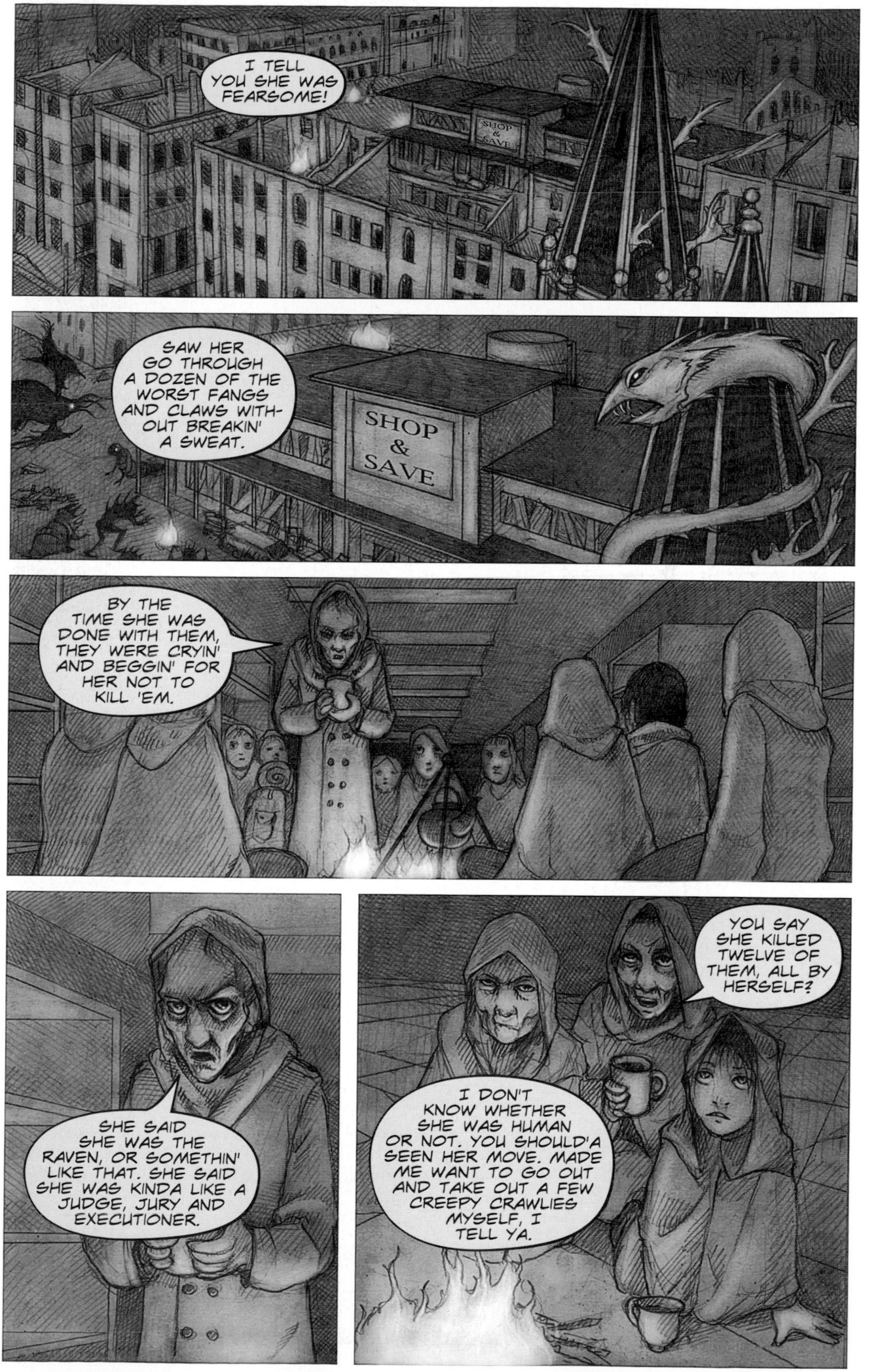
I TELL YOU SHE WAS FEARSOME!
SHOP & SAVE
SAW HER GO THROUGH A DOZEN OF THE WORST FANGS AND CLAWS WITH-OUT BREAKIN' A SWEAT.
SHOP & SAVE
BY THE TIME SHE WAS DONE WITH THEM, THEY WERE CRYIN' AND BEGGIN' FOR HER NOT TO KILL 'EM.
SHE SAID SHE WAS THE RAVEN, OR SOMETHIN' LIKE THAT. SHE SAID SHE WAS KINDA LIKE A JUDGE, JURY AND EXECUTIONER.
YOU SAY SHE KILLED TWELVE OF THEM, ALL BY HERSELF?
I DON'T KNOW WHETHER SHE WAS HUMAN OR NOT. YOU SHOULD'A SEEN HER MOVE. MADE ME WANT TO GO OUT AND TAKE OUT A FEW CREEPY CRAWLIES MYSELF, I TELL YA.

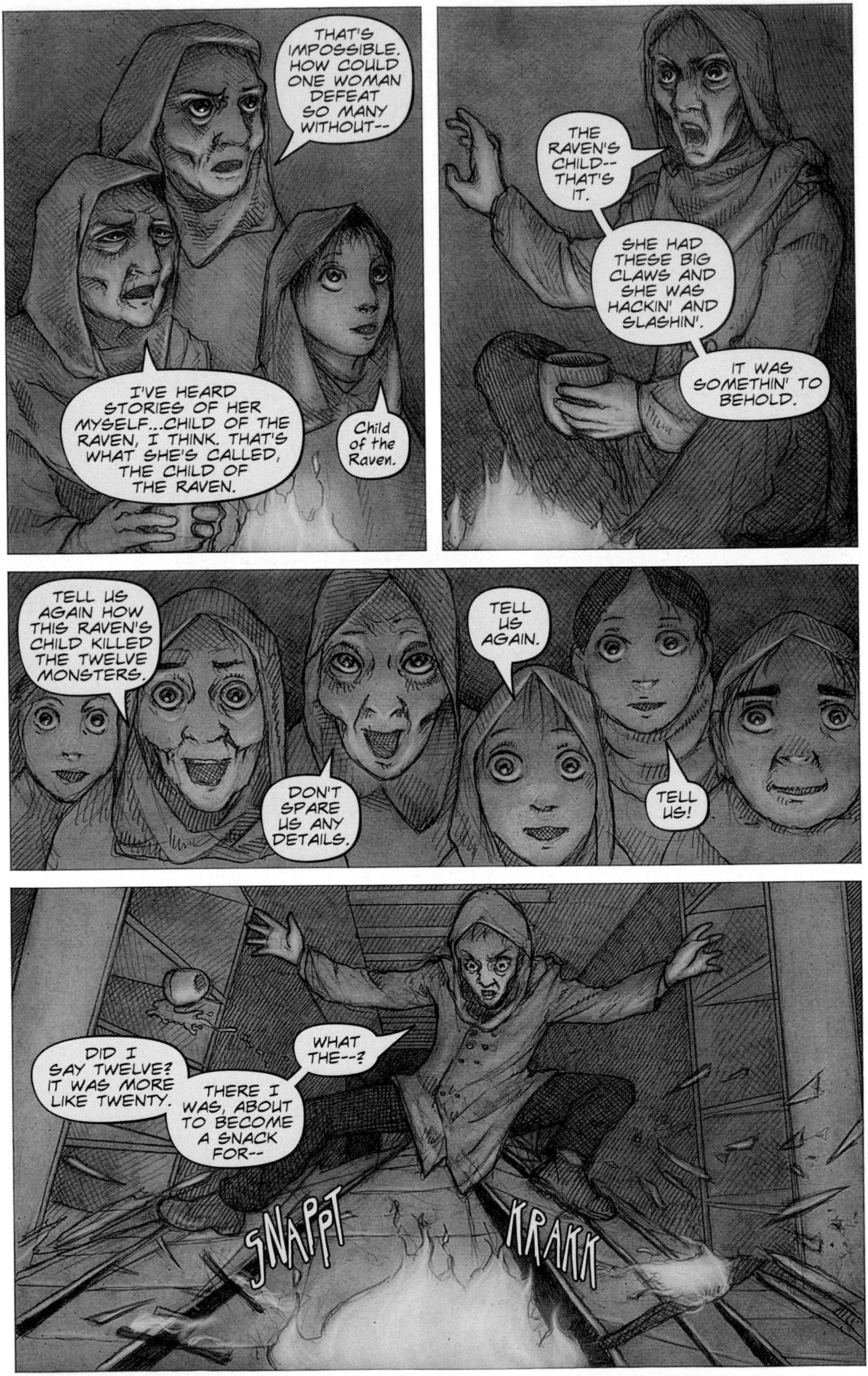
THAT'S IMPOSSIBLE. HOW COULD ONE WOMAN DEFEAT SO MANY WITHOUT--
I'VE HEARD STORIES OF HER MYSELF...CHILD OF THE RAVEN, I THINK. THAT'S WHAT SHE'S CALLED, THE CHILD OF THE RAVEN.
Child of the Raven.
THE RAVEN'S CHILD-- THAT'S IT.
SHE HAD THESE BIG CLAWS AND SHE WAS HACKIN' AND SLASHIN'.
IT WAS SOMETHIN' TO BEHOLD.
TELL US AGAIN HOW THIS RAVEN'S CHILD KILLED THE TWELVE MONSTERS.
DON'T SPARE US ANY DETAILS.
TELL US AGAIN.
TELL US!
DID I SAY TWELVE? IT WAS MORE LIKE TWENTY.
THERE I WAS, ABOUT TO BECOME A SNACK FOR--
WHAT THE--?
SNAPPT
KRAKK

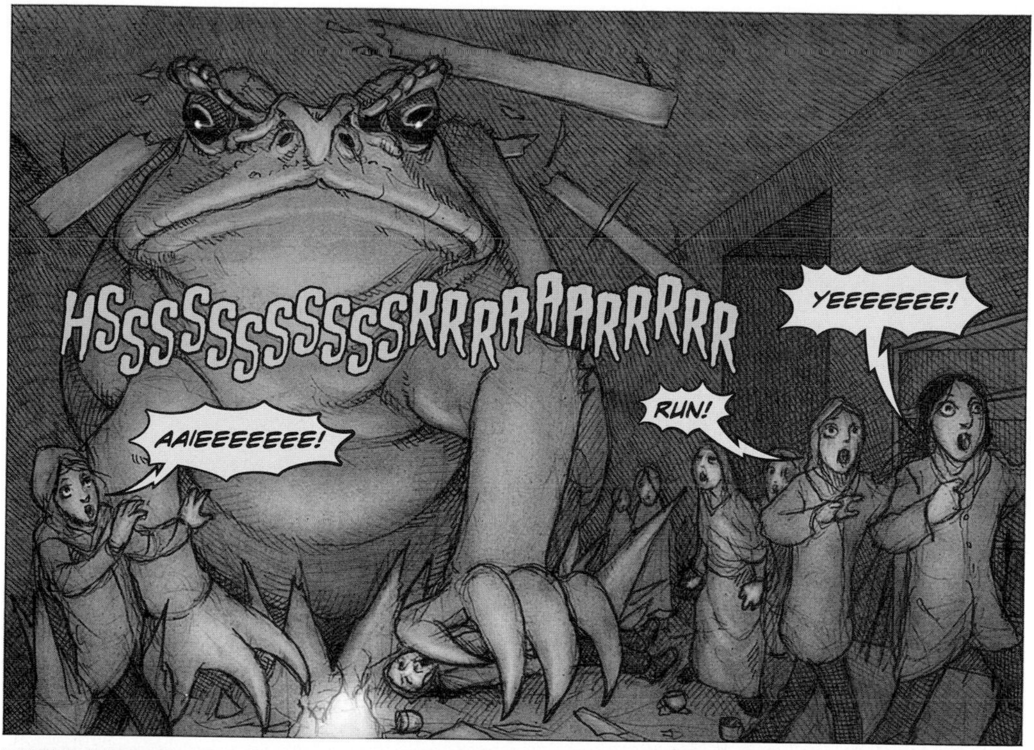
HSSSSSSSSSSSRRRAAARRRRR
AAIEEEEEEE!
RUN!
YEEEEEEE!

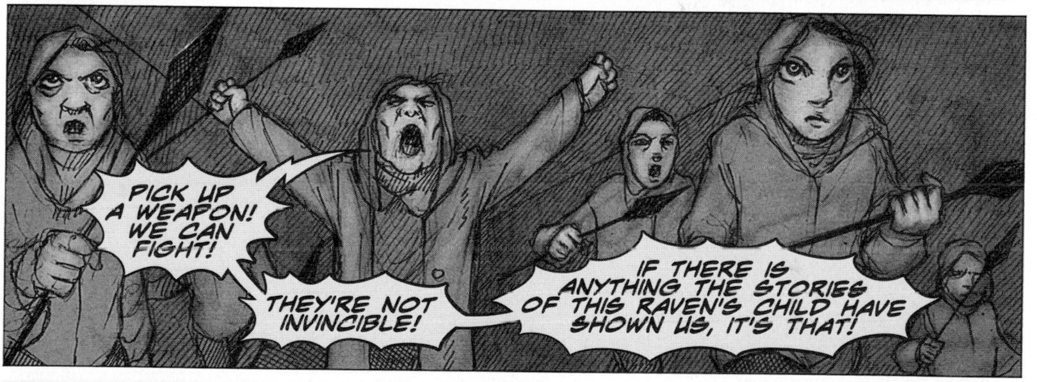
PICK UP A WEAPON! WE CAN FIGHT!
THEY'RE NOT INVINCIBLE!
IF THERE IS ANYTHING THE STORIES OF THIS RAVEN'S CHILD HAVE SHOWN US, IT'S THAT!

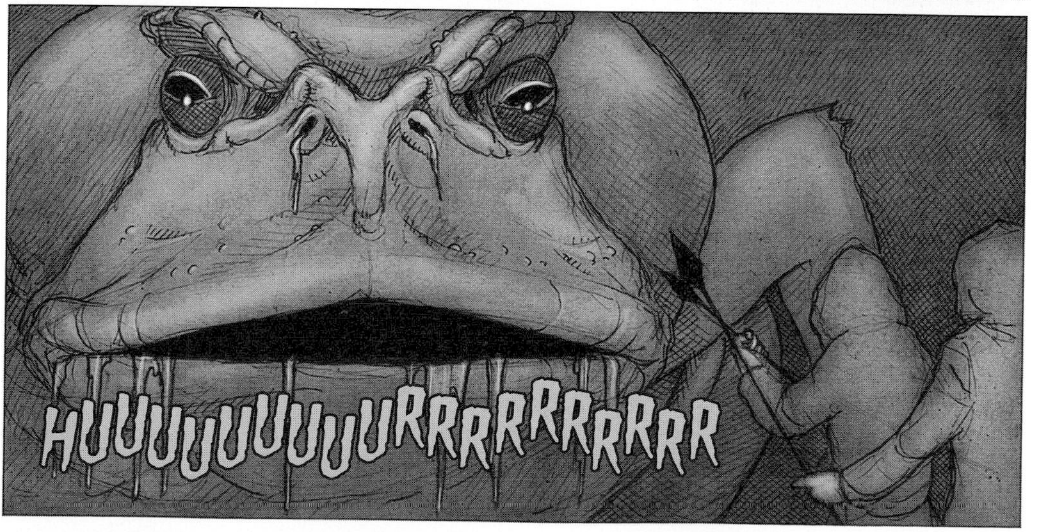
HUUUUUUUUURRRRRRRRRR

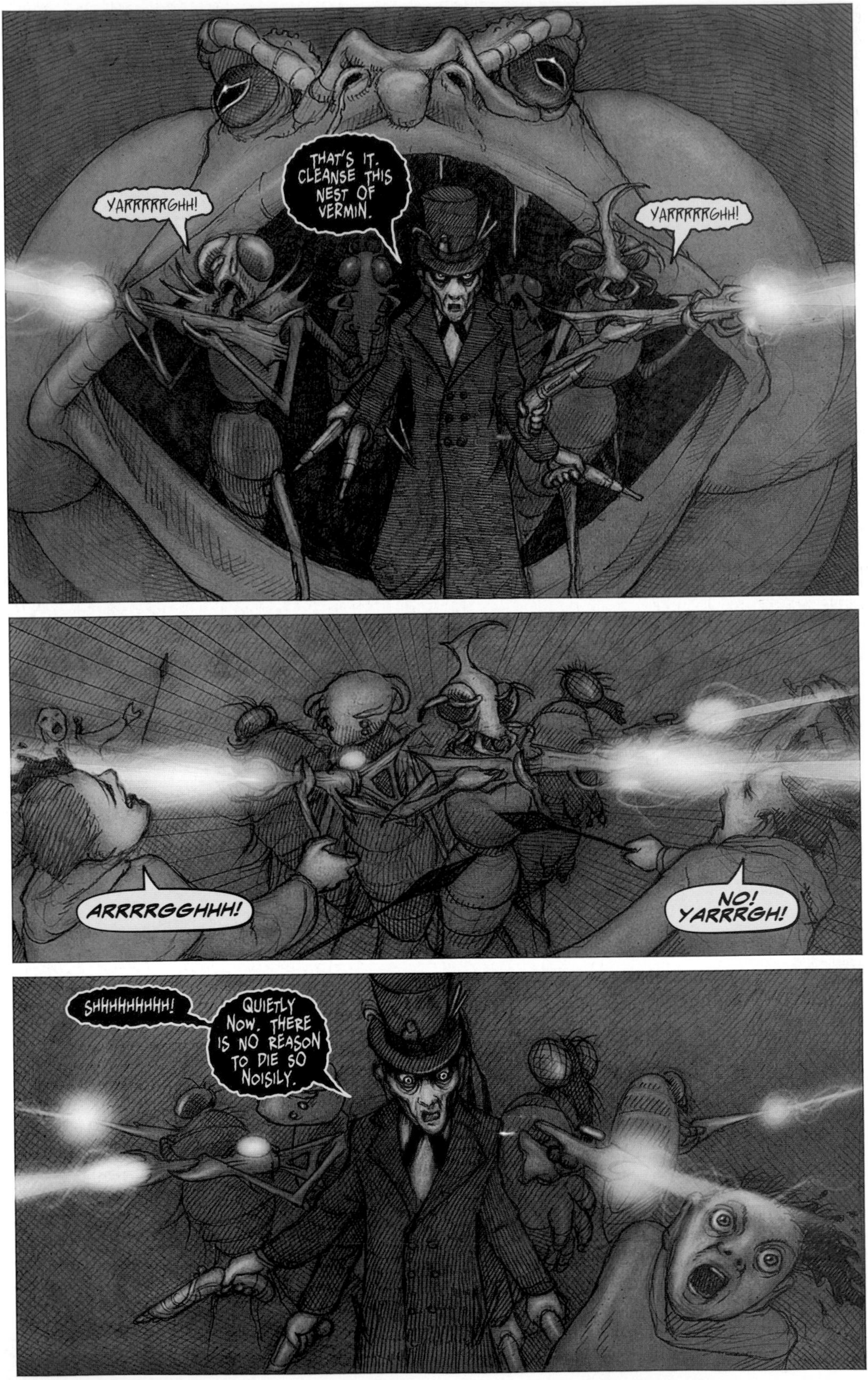
YARRRRRGHH!
THAT'S IT. CLEANSE THIS NEST OF VERMIN.
YARRRRRGHH!
ARRRRGGHHH!
NO! YARRRGH!
SHHHHHHHHH!
QUIETLY NOW. THERE IS NO REASON TO DIE SO NOISILY.

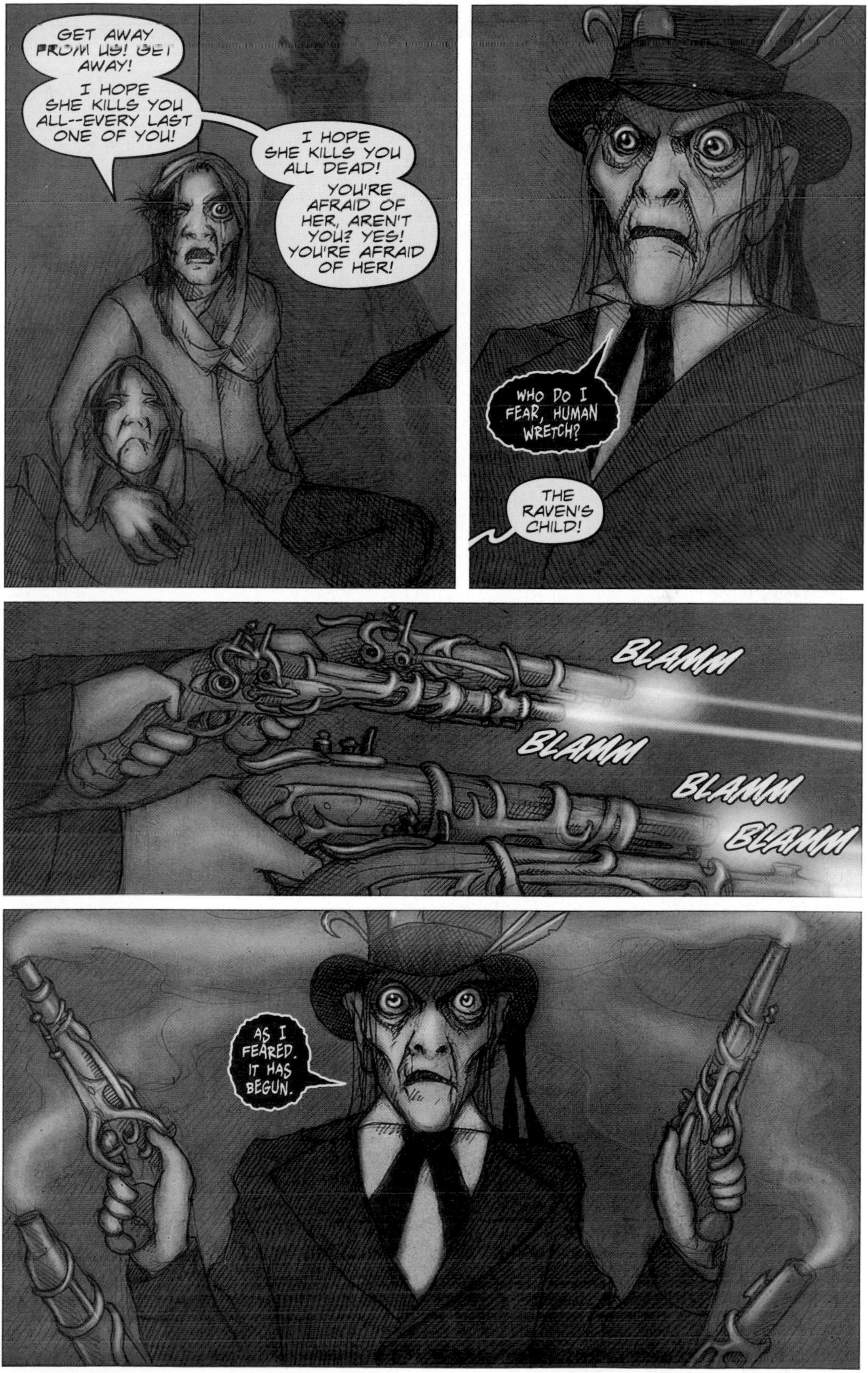
GET AWAY FROM US! GET AWAY!
I HOPE SHE KILLS YOU ALL--EVERY LAST ONE OF YOU!
I HOPE SHE KILLS YOU ALL DEAD!
YOU'RE AFRAID OF HER, AREN'T YOU? YES! YOU'RE AFRAID OF HER!
WHO DO I FEAR, HUMAN WRETCH?
THE RAVEN'S CHILD!
BLAMM
BLAMM
BLAMM
BLAMM
AS I FEARED. IT HAS BEGUN.

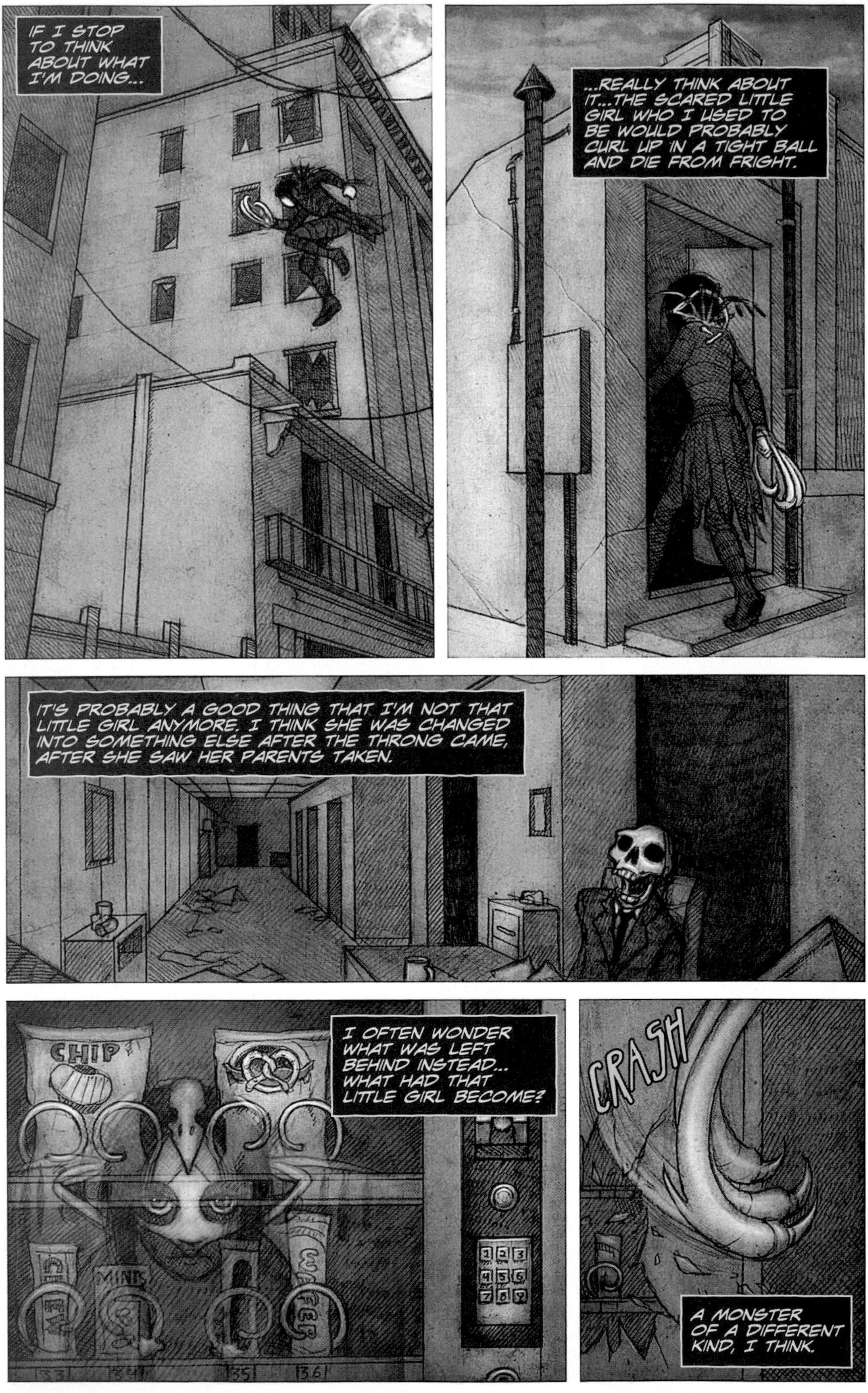
IF I STOP TO THINK ABOUT WHAT I'M DOING...
...REALLY THINK ABOUT IT...THE SCARED LITTLE GIRL WHO I USED TO BE WOULD PROBABLY CURL UP IN A TIGHT BALL AND DIE FROM FRIGHT.
IT'S PROBABLY A GOOD THING THAT I'M NOT THAT LITTLE GIRL ANYMORE. I THINK SHE WAS CHANGED INTO SOMETHING ELSE AFTER THE THRONG CAME, AFTER SHE SAW HER PARENTS TAKEN.
CHIP
MINTS
I OFTEN WONDER WHAT WAS LEFT BEHIND INSTEAD... WHAT HAD THAT LITTLE GIRL BECOME?
CRASH
A MONSTER OF A DIFFERENT KIND, I THINK.

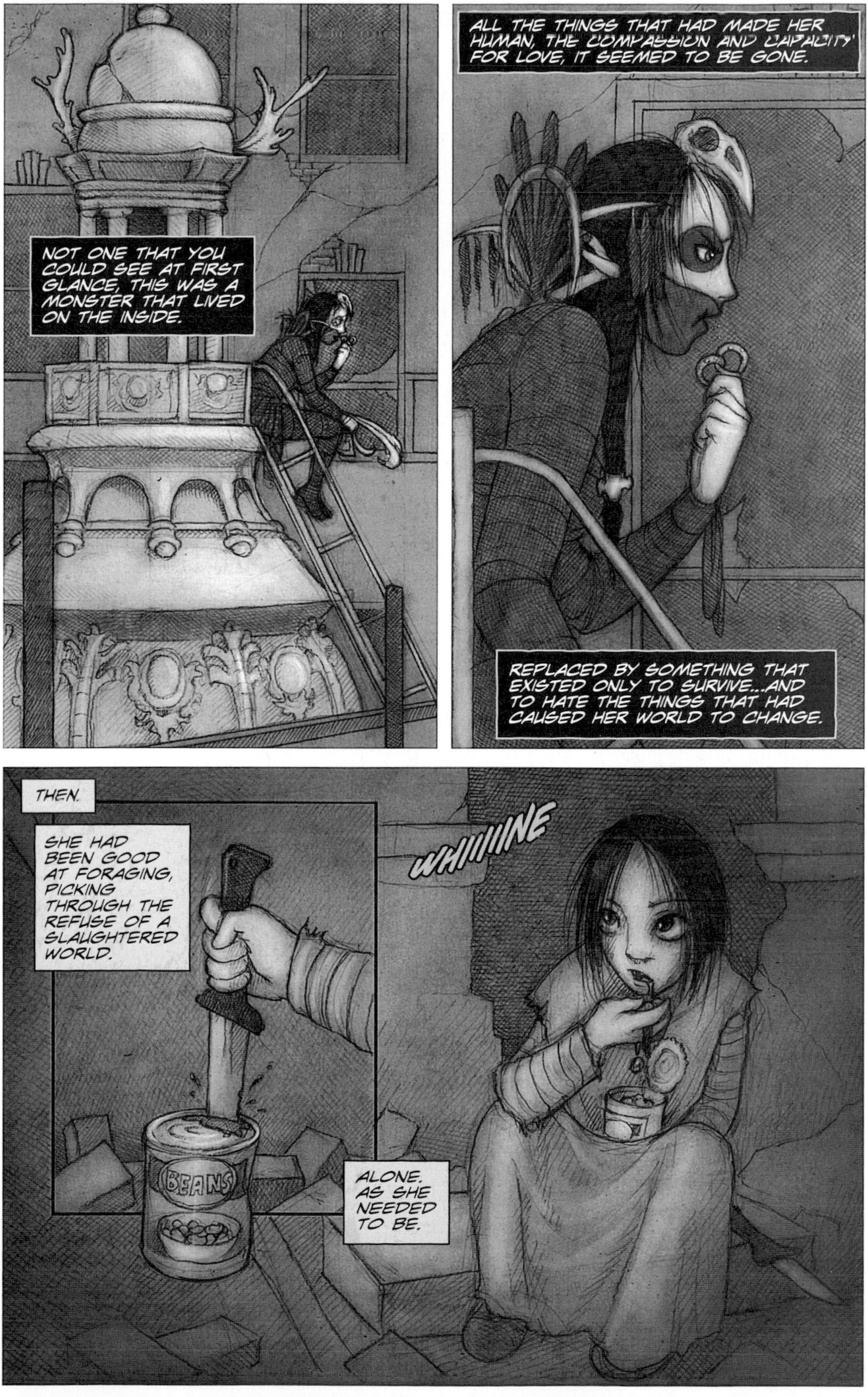
NOT ONE THAT YOU COULD SEE AT FIRST GLANCE, THIS WAS A MONSTER THAT LIVED ON THE INSIDE.
ALL THE THINGS THAT HAD MADE HER HUMAN, THE COMPASSION AND CAPACITY FOR LOVE, IT SEEMED TO BE GONE.
REPLACED BY SOMETHING THAT EXISTED ONLY TO SURVIVE...AND TO HATE THE THINGS THAT HAD CAUSED HER WORLD TO CHANGE.
THEN.
SHE HAD BEEN GOOD AT FORAGING, PICKING THROUGH THE REFUSE OF A SLAUGHTERED WORLD.
BEANS
WHIIIIINE
ALONE. AS SHE NEEDED TO BE.

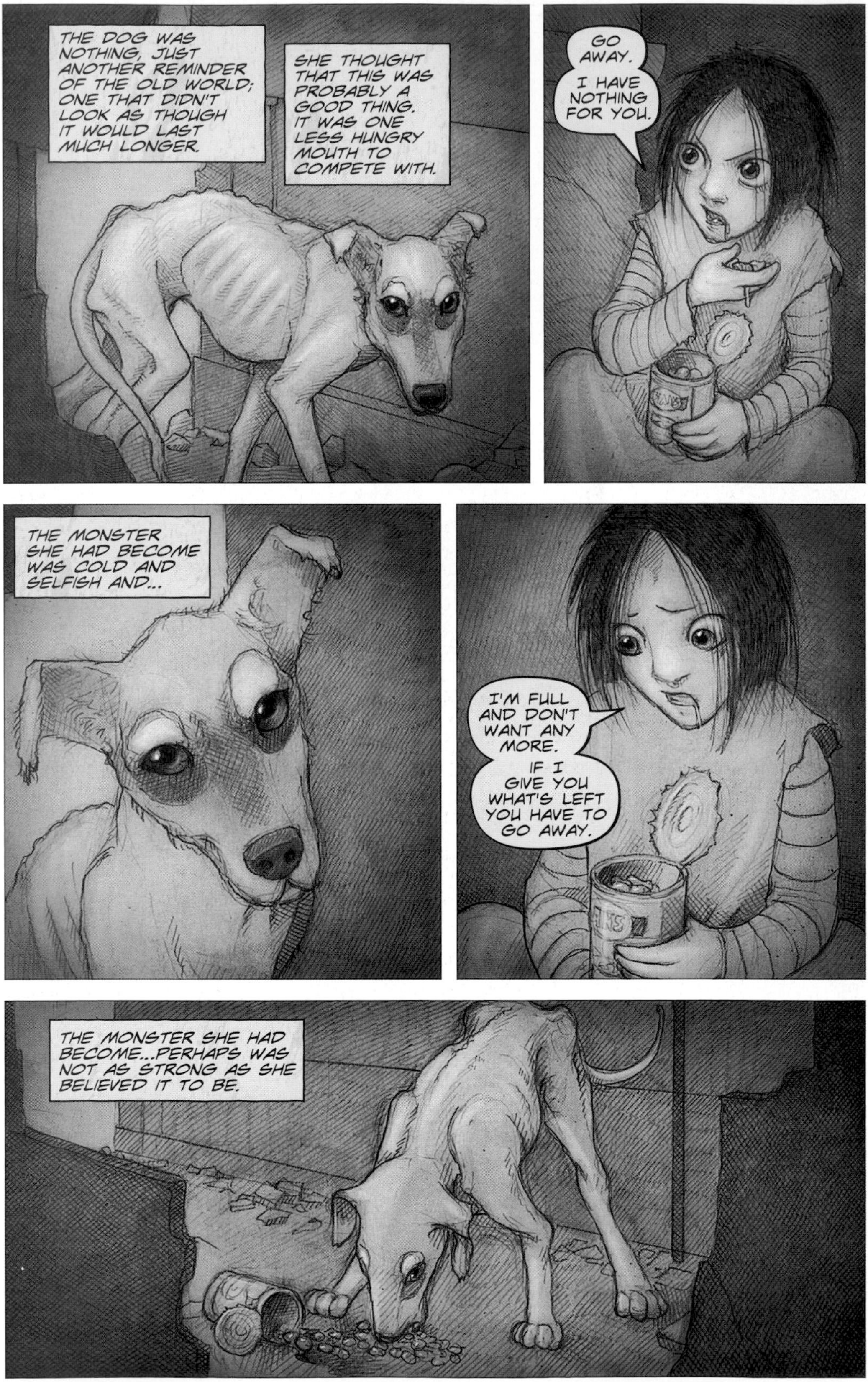
THE DOG WAS NOTHING, JUST ANOTHER REMINDER OF THE OLD WORLD; ONE THAT DIDN'T LOOK AS THOUGH IT WOULD LAST MUCH LONGER.
SHE THOUGHT THAT THIS WAS PROBABLY A GOOD THING. IT WAS ONE LESS HUNGRY MOUTH TO COMPETE WITH.
GO AWAY.
I HAVE NOTHING FOR YOU.
THE MONSTER SHE HAD BECOME WAS COLD AND SELFISH AND...
I'M FULL AND DON'T WANT ANY MORE.
IF I GIVE YOU WHAT'S LEFT YOU HAVE TO GO AWAY.
THE MONSTER SHE HAD BECOME...PERHAPS WAS NOT AS STRONG AS SHE BELIEVED IT TO BE.

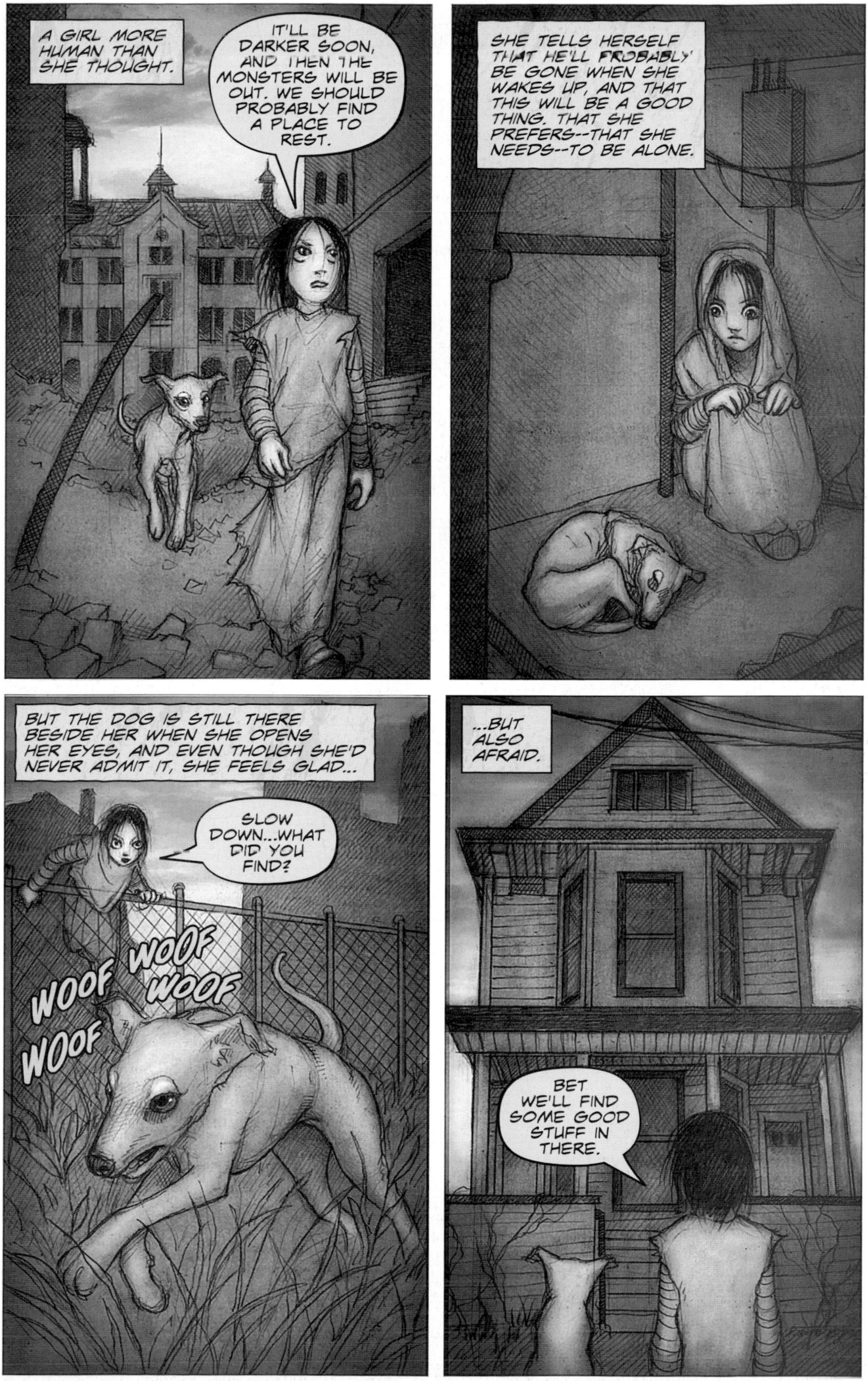
A GIRL MORE HUMAN THAN SHE THOUGHT.
IT'LL BE DARKER SOON, AND THEN THE MONSTERS WILL BE OUT. WE SHOULD PROBABLY FIND A PLACE TO REST.
SHE TELLS HERSELF THAT HE'LL PROBABLY BE GONE WHEN SHE WAKES UP, AND THAT THIS WILL BE A GOOD THING. THAT SHE PREFERS--THAT SHE NEEDS--TO BE ALONE.
BUT THE DOG IS STILL THERE BESIDE HER WHEN SHE OPENS HER EYES, AND EVEN THOUGH SHE'D NEVER ADMIT IT, SHE FEELS GLAD...
SLOW DOWN...WHAT DID YOU FIND?
WOOF WOOF WOOF WOOF
...BUT ALSO AFRAID.
BET WE'LL FIND SOME GOOD STUFF IN THERE.

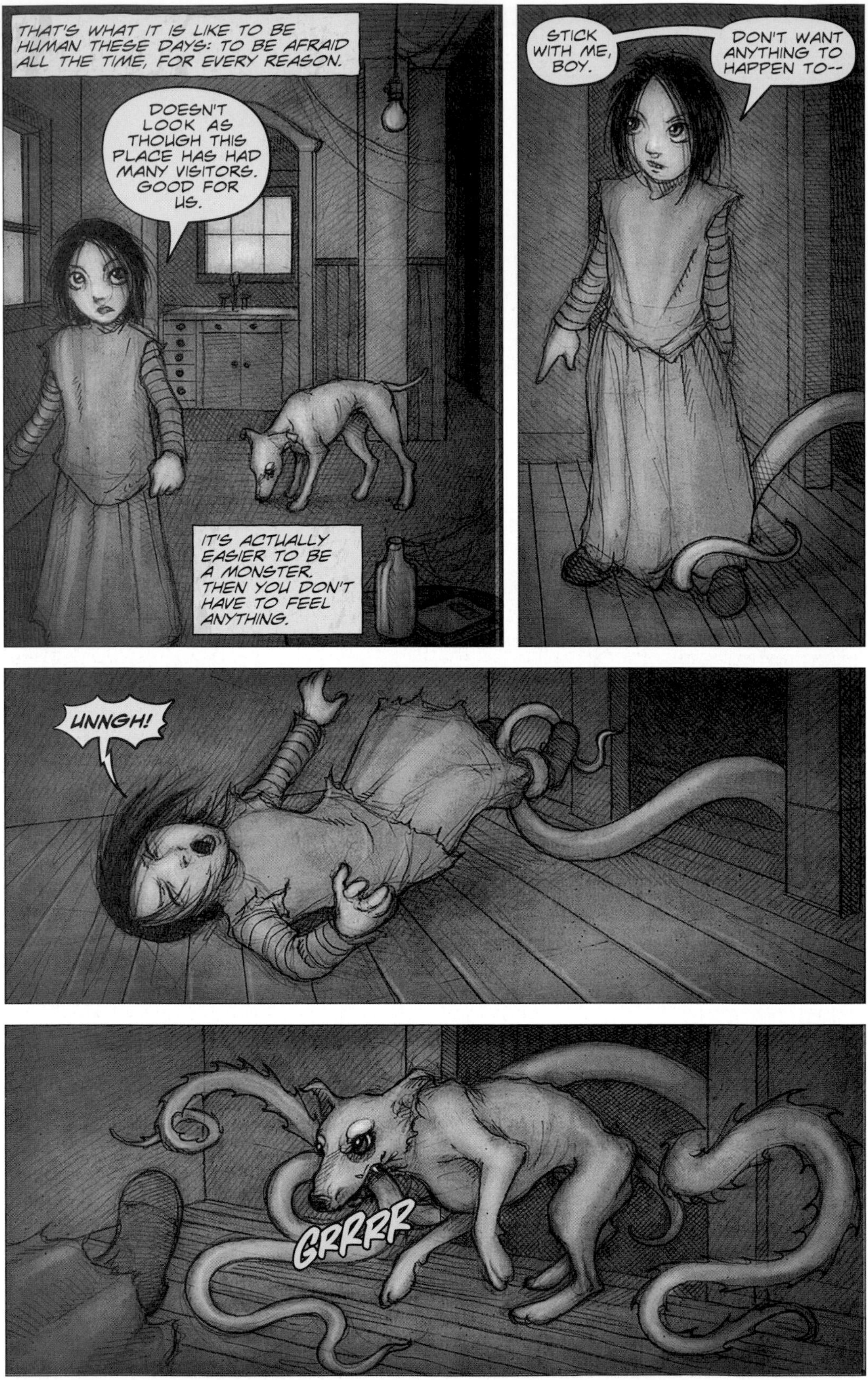
THAT'S WHAT IT IS LIKE TO BE HUMAN THESE DAYS: TO BE AFRAID ALL THE TIME, FOR EVERY REASON.
DOESN'T LOOK AS THOUGH THIS PLACE HAS HAD MANY VISITORS. GOOD FOR US.
IT'S ACTUALLY EASIER TO BE A MONSTER. THEN YOU DON'T HAVE TO FEEL ANYTHING.
STICK WITH ME, BOY.
DON'T WANT ANYTHING TO HAPPEN TO--
UNNGH!
GRRRR

NO!

IT WAS LIKE THE MONSTER THAT SHE THOUGHT SHE'D BECOME WAS THERE AND PUNISHING HER...

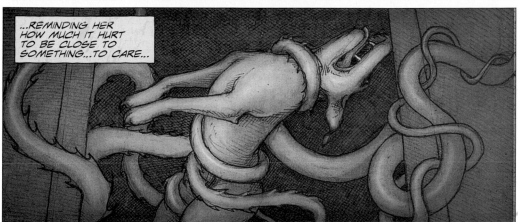

...REMINDING HER HOW MUCH IT HURT TO BE CLOSE TO SOMETHING...TO CARE...

...TO BE HUMAN.

NOW.

YOU'D THINK AFTER THAT I WOULD HAVE LEARNED.

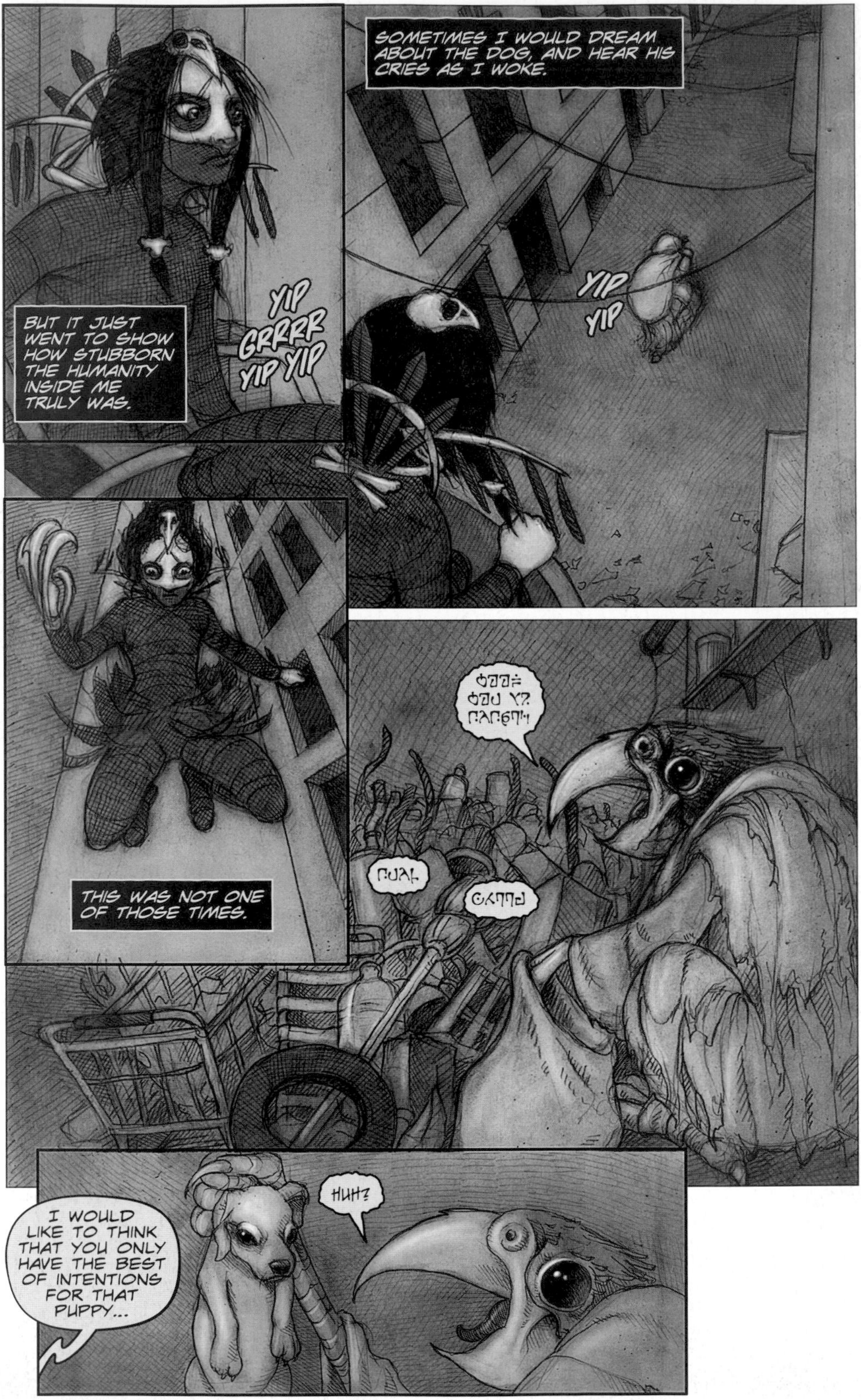

SOMETIMES I WOULD DREAM ABOUT THE DOG, AND HEAR HIS CRIES AS I WOKE.
BUT IT JUST WENT TO SHOW HOW STUBBORN THE HUMANITY INSIDE ME TRULY WAS.
YIP GRRRR YIP YIP
YIP YIP
THIS WAS NOT ONE OF THOSE TIMES.
HUH?
I WOULD LIKE TO THINK THAT YOU ONLY HAVE THE BEST OF INTENTIONS FOR THAT PUPPY...

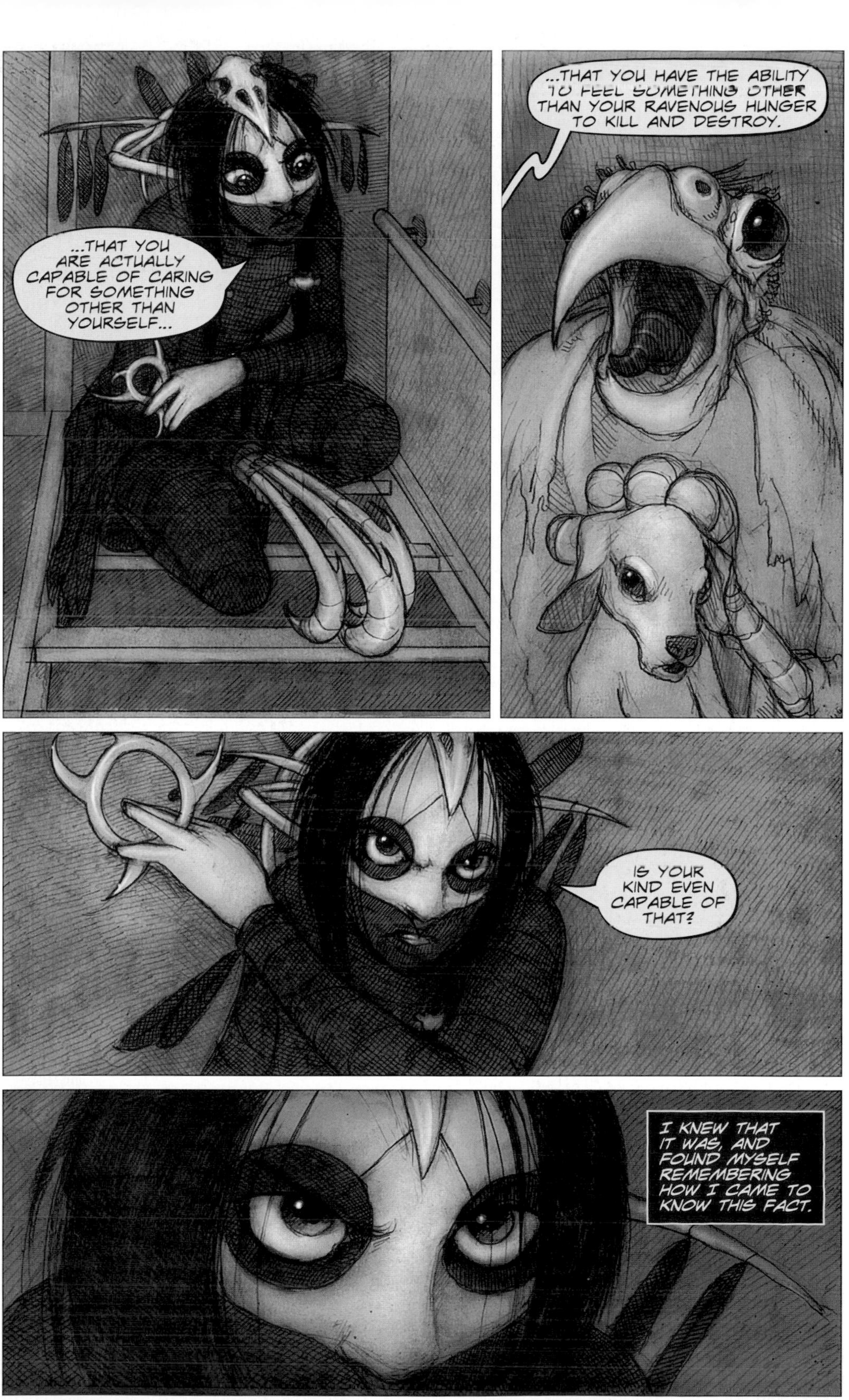
...THAT YOU ARE ACTUALLY CAPABLE OF CARING FOR SOMETHING OTHER THAN YOURSELF...
...THAT YOU HAVE THE ABILITY TO FEEL SOMETHING OTHER THAN YOUR RAVENOUS HUNGER TO KILL AND DESTROY.
IS YOUR KIND EVEN CAPABLE OF THAT?
I KNEW THAT IT WAS, AND FOUND MYSELF REMEMBERING HOW I CAME TO KNOW THIS FACT.

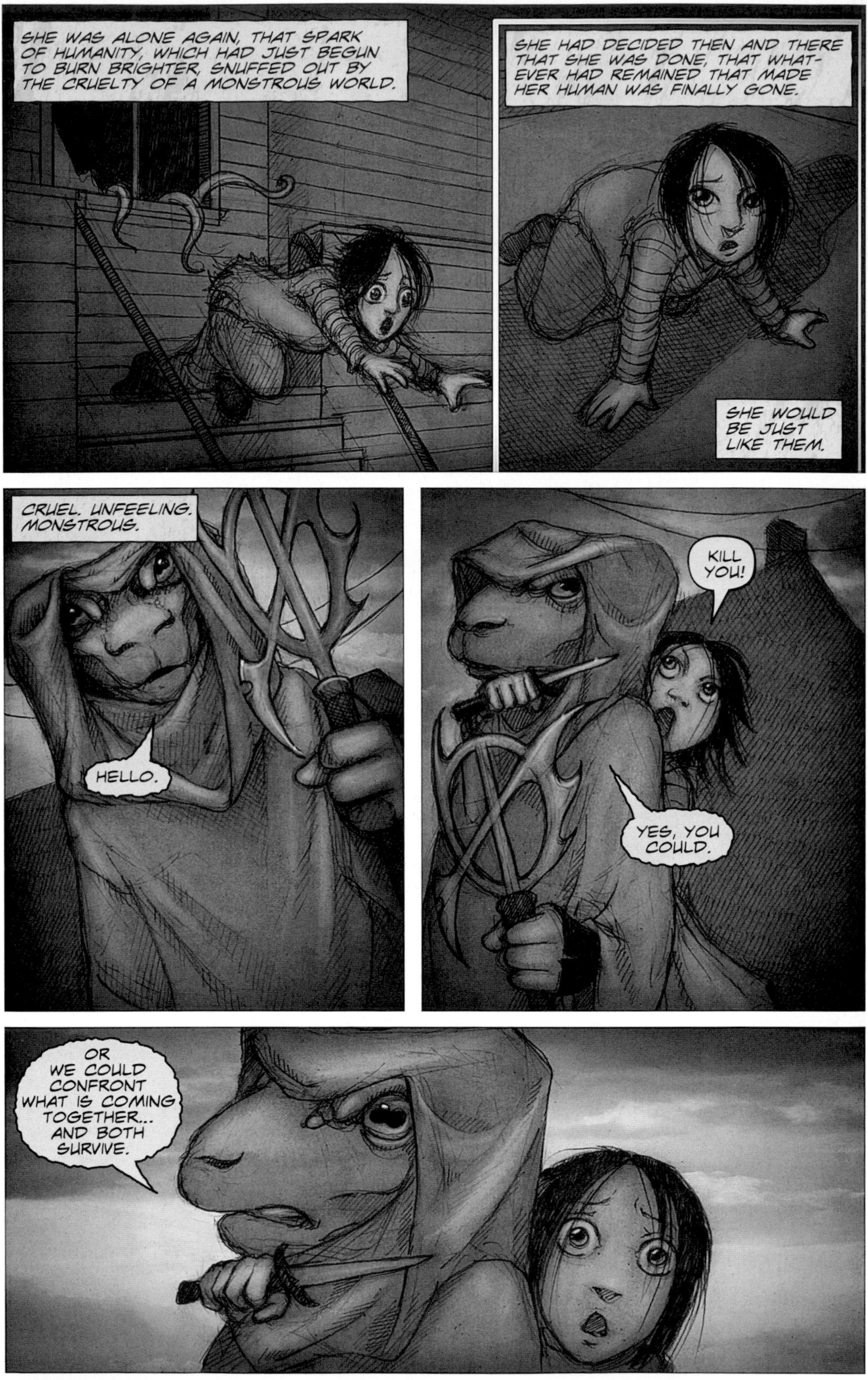
SHE WAS ALONE AGAIN, THAT SPARK OF HUMANITY, WHICH HAD JUST BEGUN TO BURN BRIGHTER, SNUFFED OUT BY THE CRUELTY OF A MONSTROUS WORLD.
SHE HAD DECIDED THEN AND THERE THAT SHE WAS DONE, THAT WHATEVER HAD REMAINED THAT MADE HER HUMAN WAS FINALLY GONE.
SHE WOULD BE JUST LIKE THEM.
CRUEL. UNFEELING. MONSTROUS.
HELLO.
KILL YOU!
YES, YOU COULD.
OR WE COULD CONFRONT WHAT IS COMING TOGETHER... AND BOTH SURVIVE.

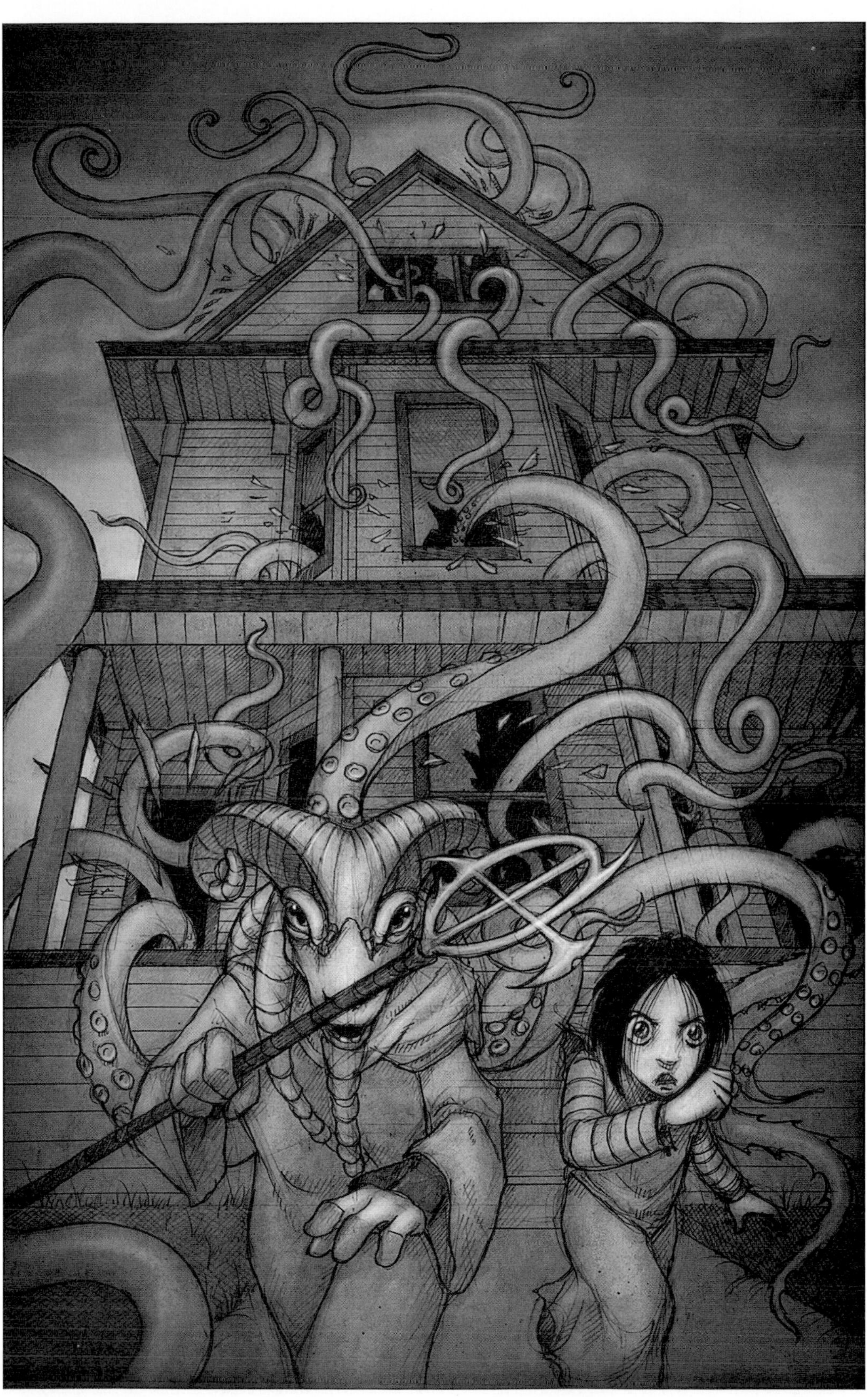

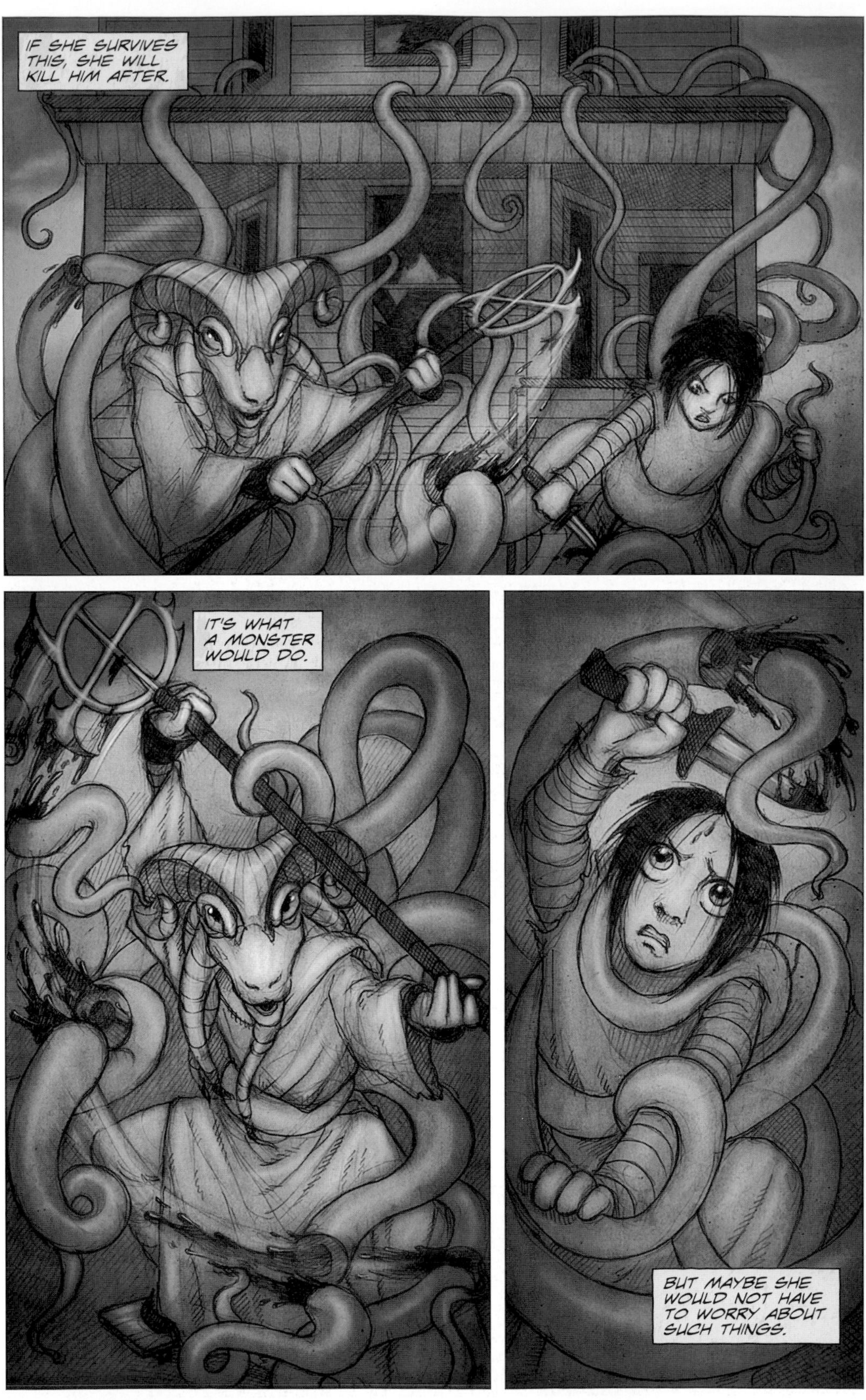
IF SHE SURVIVES THIS, SHE WILL KILL HIM AFTER.
IT'S WHAT A MONSTER WOULD DO.
BUT MAYBE SHE WOULD NOT HAVE TO WORRY ABOUT SUCH THINGS.

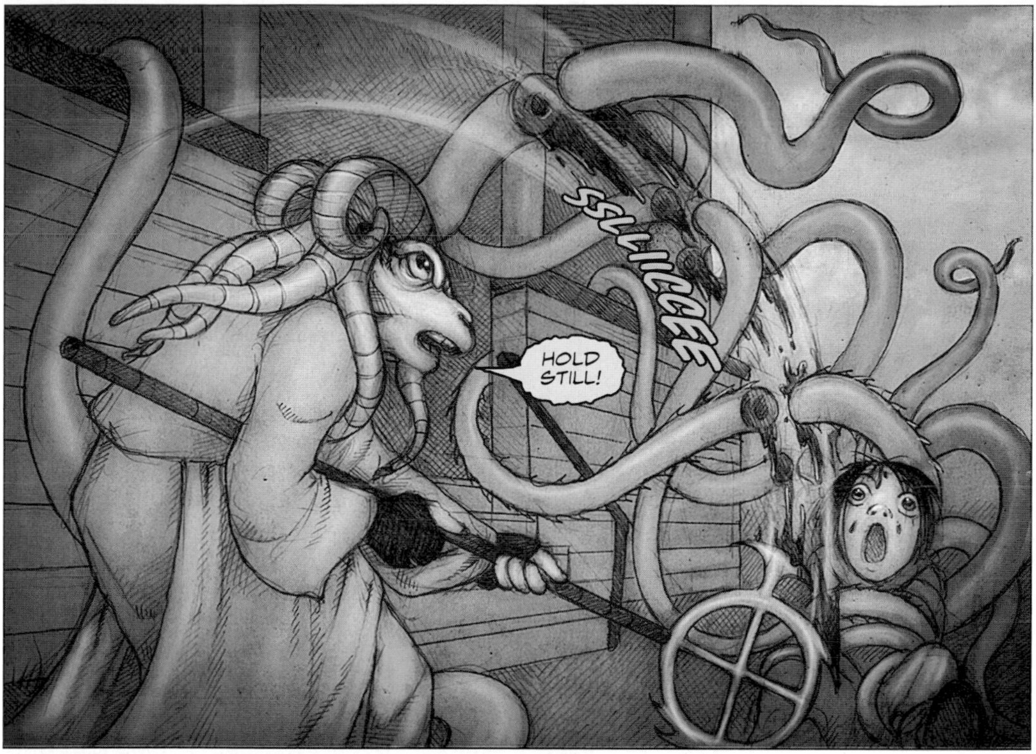
SSLLICCEE
HOLD STILL!

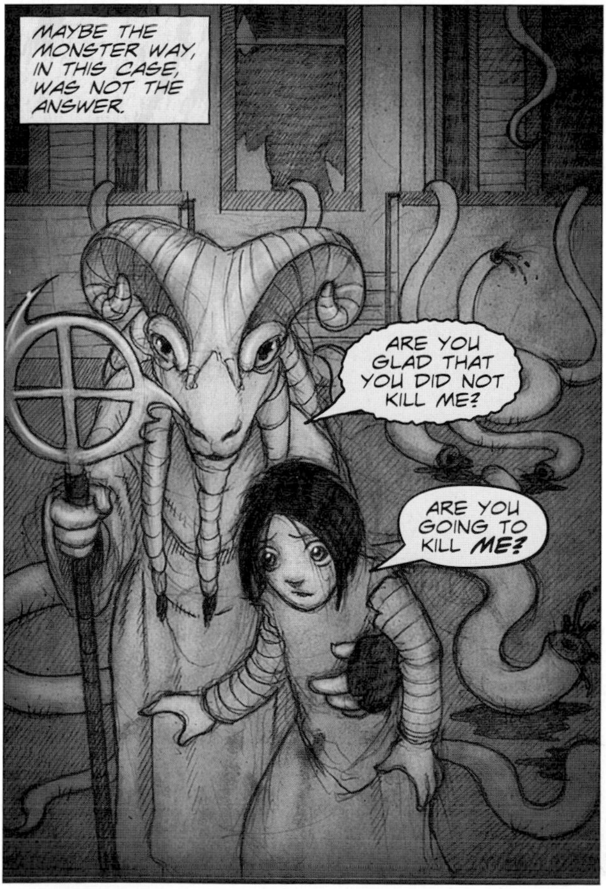
MAYBE THE MONSTER WAY, IN THIS CASE, WAS NOT THE ANSWER.
ARE YOU GLAD THAT YOU DID NOT KILL ME?
ARE YOU GOING TO KILL ME?

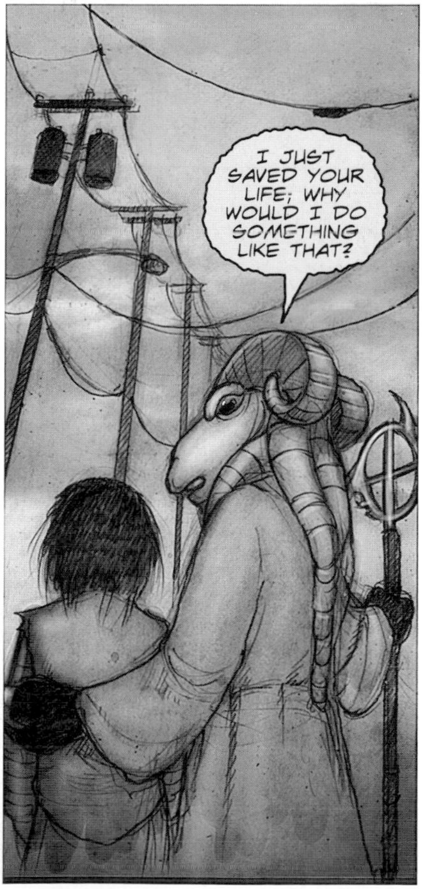
I JUST SAVED YOUR LIFE; WHY WOULD I DO SOMETHING LIKE THAT?

NOW.
IT WAS THE BEGINNING OF A NEW RELATIONSHIP...
YIP YIP YIP
...OF A NEW UNDERSTANDING.
PERHAPS YOU DO UNDERSTAND.
NOT ALL OF THE MONSTERS...WERE MONSTERS. SOME WERE JUST LIKE ME...
...JUST TRYING TO SURVIVE.
IF YOU DO, THEN YOU KNOW WHO I AM--WHAT I AM.
I SPARE YOUR LIVES SO THAT YOU WILL TELL THEM.

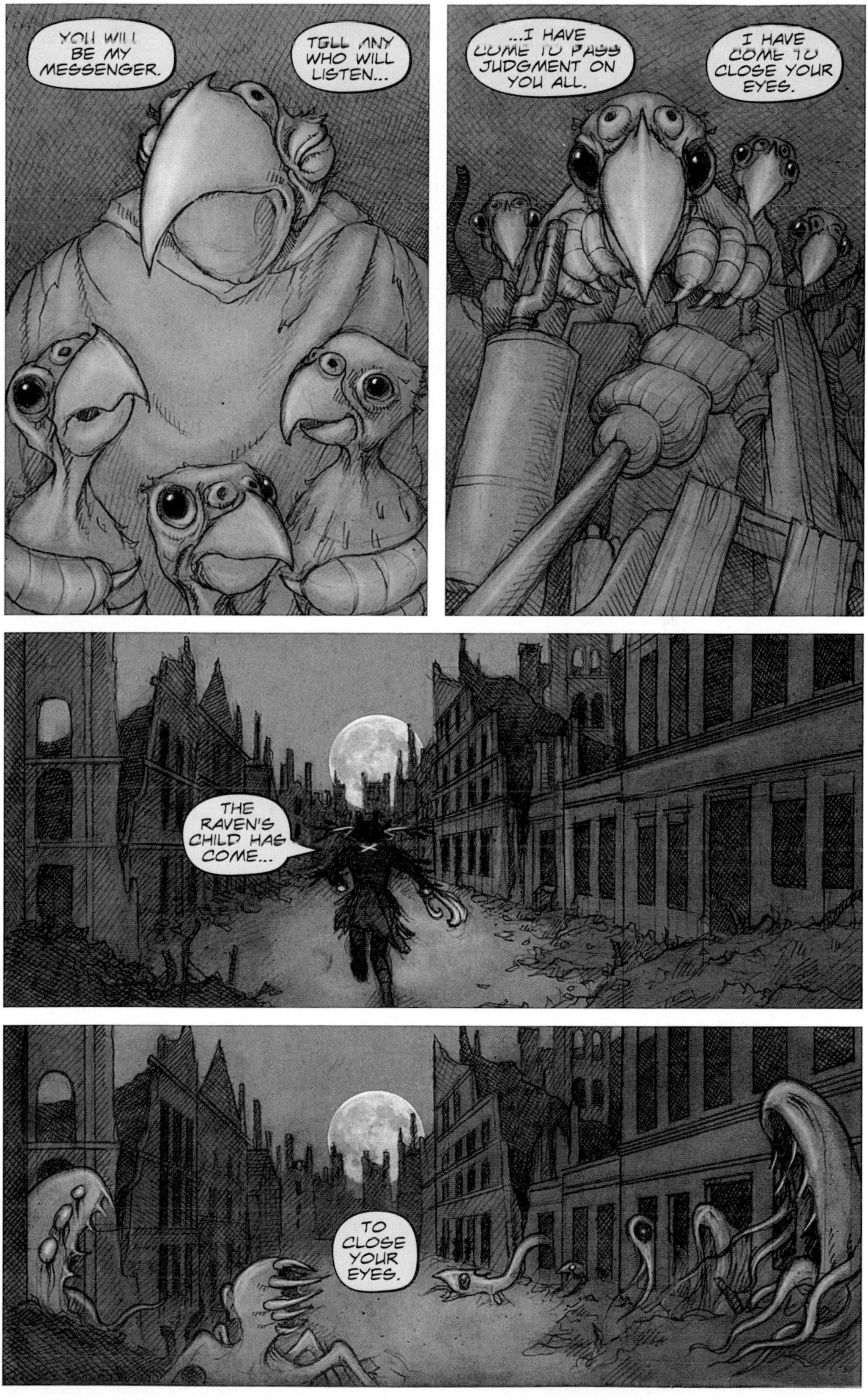
YOU WILL BE MY MESSENGER.
TELL ANY WHO WILL LISTEN...
...I HAVE COME TO PASS JUDGMENT ON YOU ALL.
I HAVE COME TO CLOSE YOUR EYES.
THE RAVEN'S CHILD HAS COME...
TO CLOSE YOUR EYES.

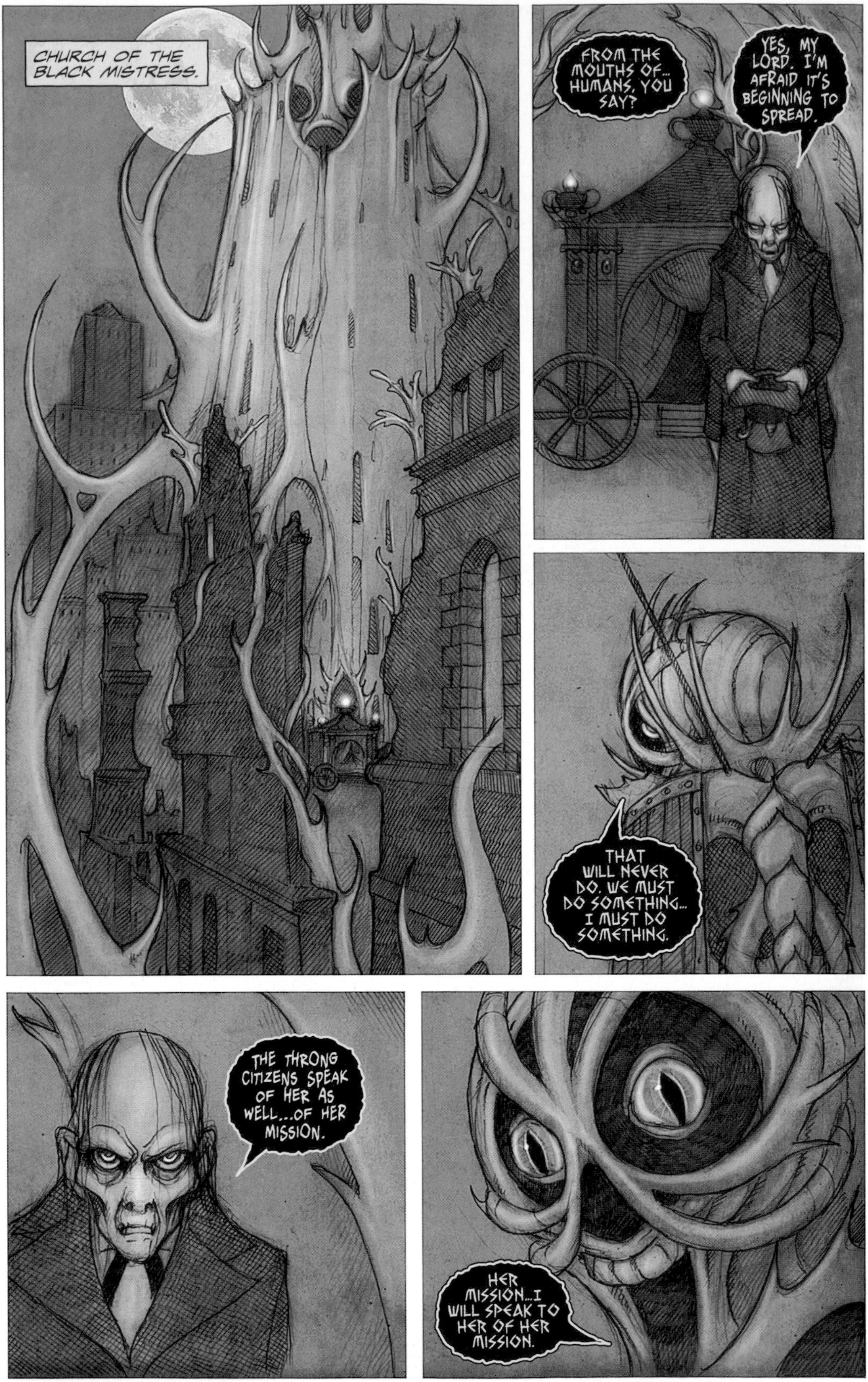
CHURCH OF THE BLACK MISTRESS.
FROM THE MOUTHS OF... HUMANS, YOU SAY?
YES, MY LORD. I'M AFRAID IT'S BEGINNING TO SPREAD.
THAT WILL NEVER DO. WE MUST DO SOMETHING... I MUST DO SOMETHING.
THE THRONG CITIZENS SPEAK OF HER AS WELL...OF HER MISSION.
HER MISSION...I WILL SPEAK TO HER OF HER MISSION.

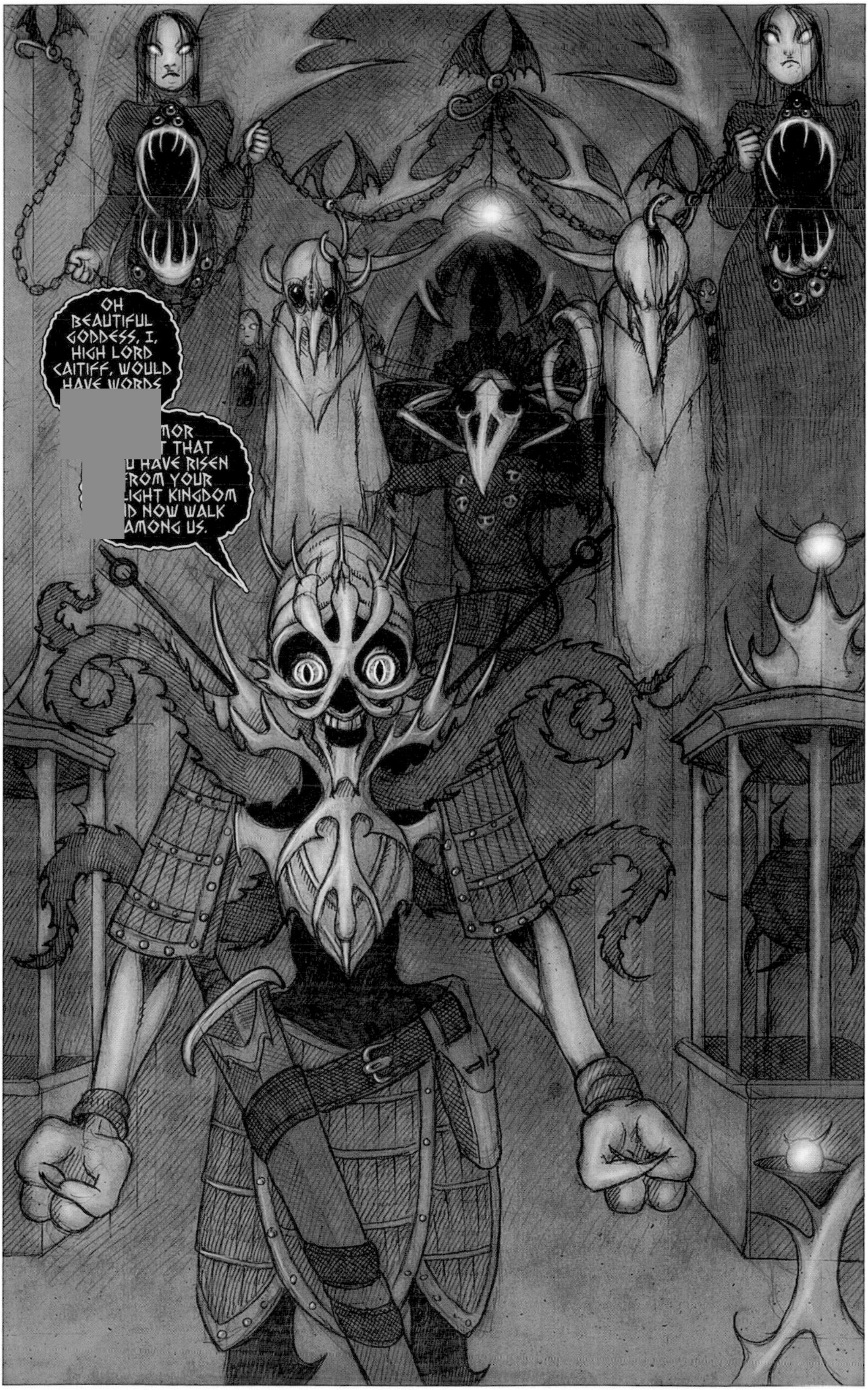
OH BEAUTIFUL GODDESS, I, HIGH LORD CAITIFF, WOULD HAVE WORDS
[redacted]MOR [redacted]T THAT [redacted]U HAVE RISEN [redacted]FROM YOUR [redacted]LIGHT KINGDOM [redacted]ID NOW WALK [redacted]AMONG US.

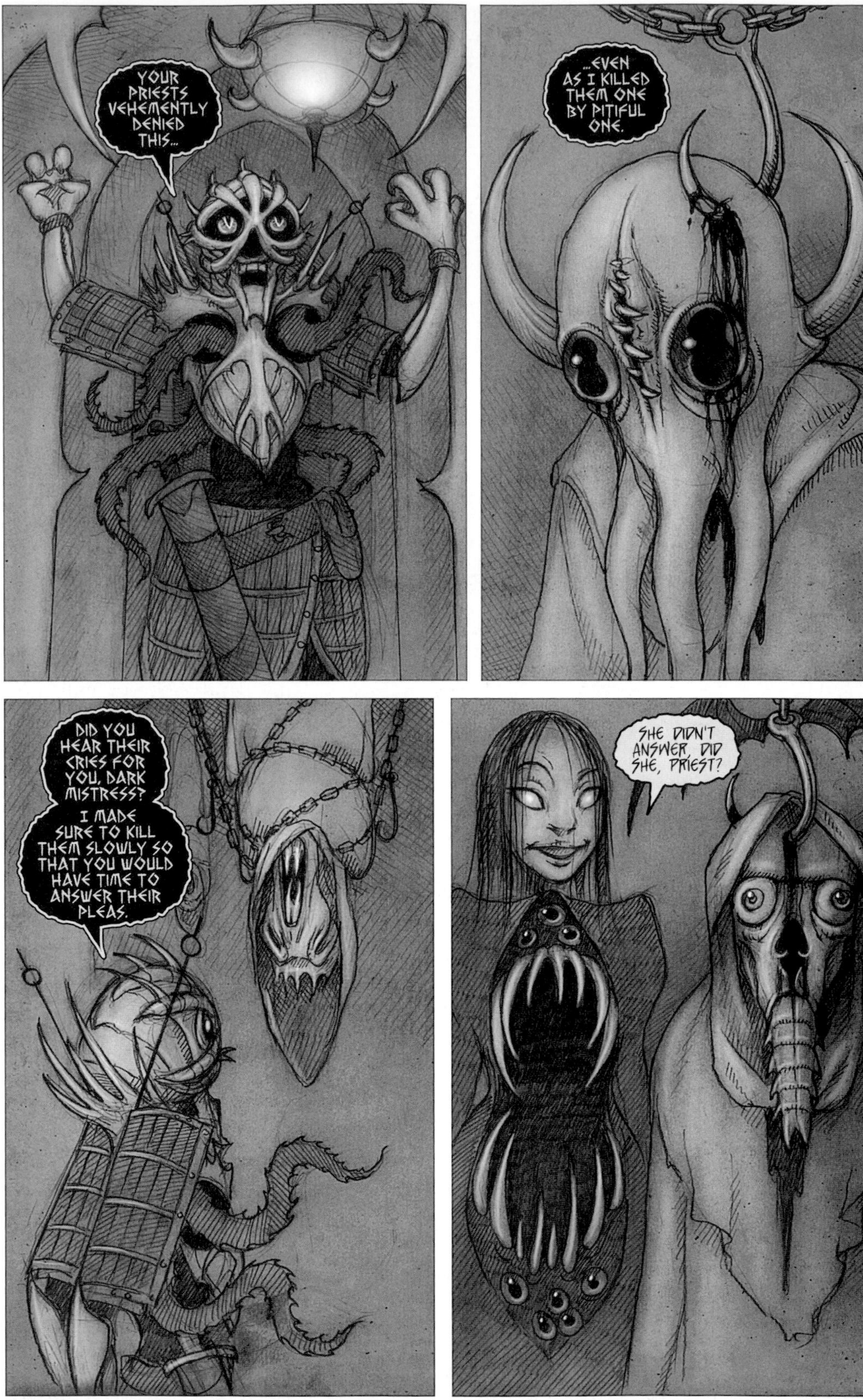
YOUR PRIESTS VEHEMENTLY DENIED THIS...
...EVEN AS I KILLED THEM ONE BY PITIFUL ONE.
DID YOU HEAR THEIR CRIES FOR YOU, DARK MISTRESS?
I MADE SURE TO KILL THEM SLOWLY SO THAT YOU WOULD HAVE TIME TO ANSWER THEIR PLEAS.
SHE DIDN'T ANSWER, DID SHE, PRIEST?

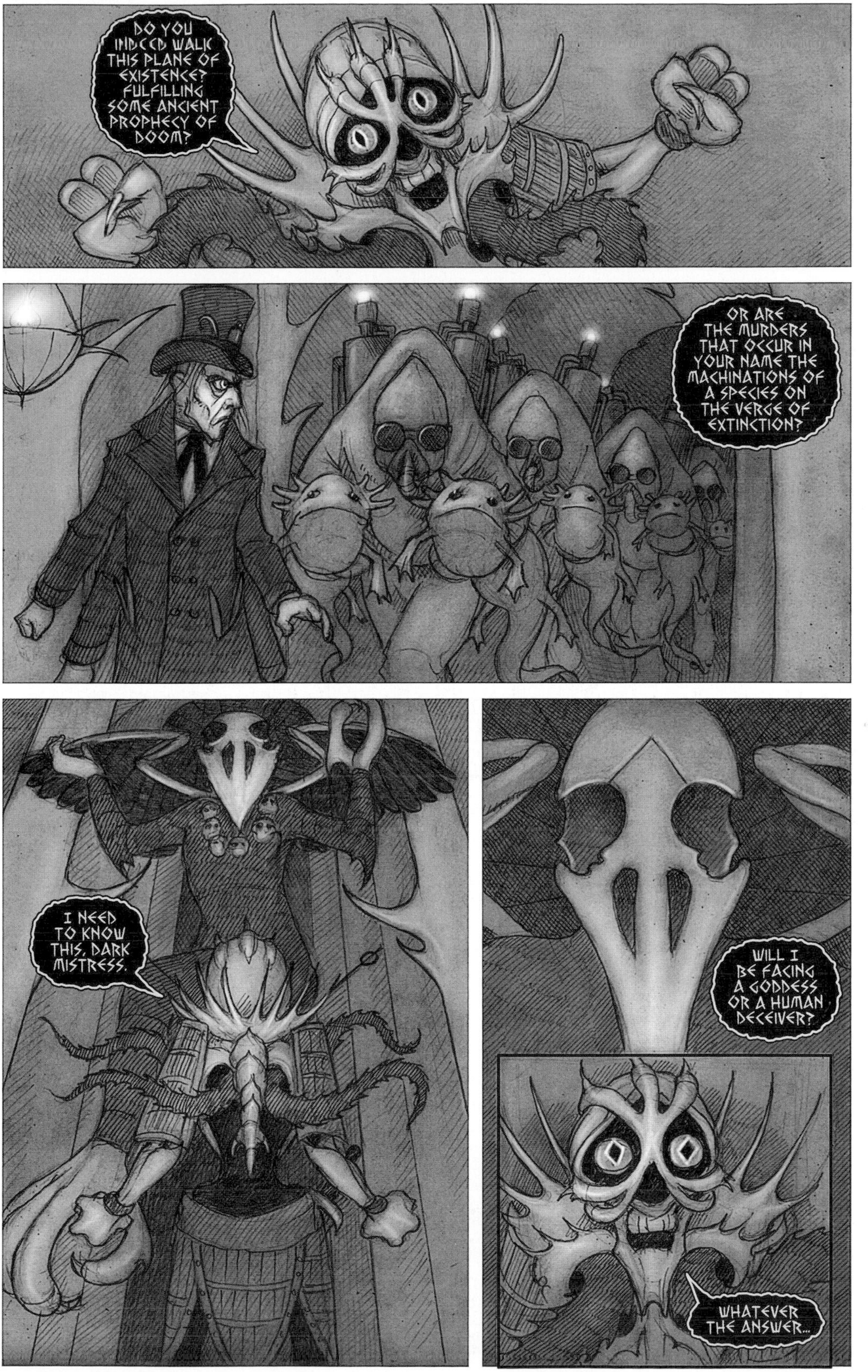
DO YOU INDEED WALK THIS PLANE OF EXISTENCE? FULFILLING SOME ANCIENT PROPHECY OF DOOM?
OR ARE THE MURDERS THAT OCCUR IN YOUR NAME THE MACHINATIONS OF A SPECIES ON THE VERGE OF EXTINCTION?
I NEED TO KNOW THIS, DARK MISTRESS.
WILL I BE FACING A GODDESS OR A HUMAN DECEIVER?
WHATEVER THE ANSWER...

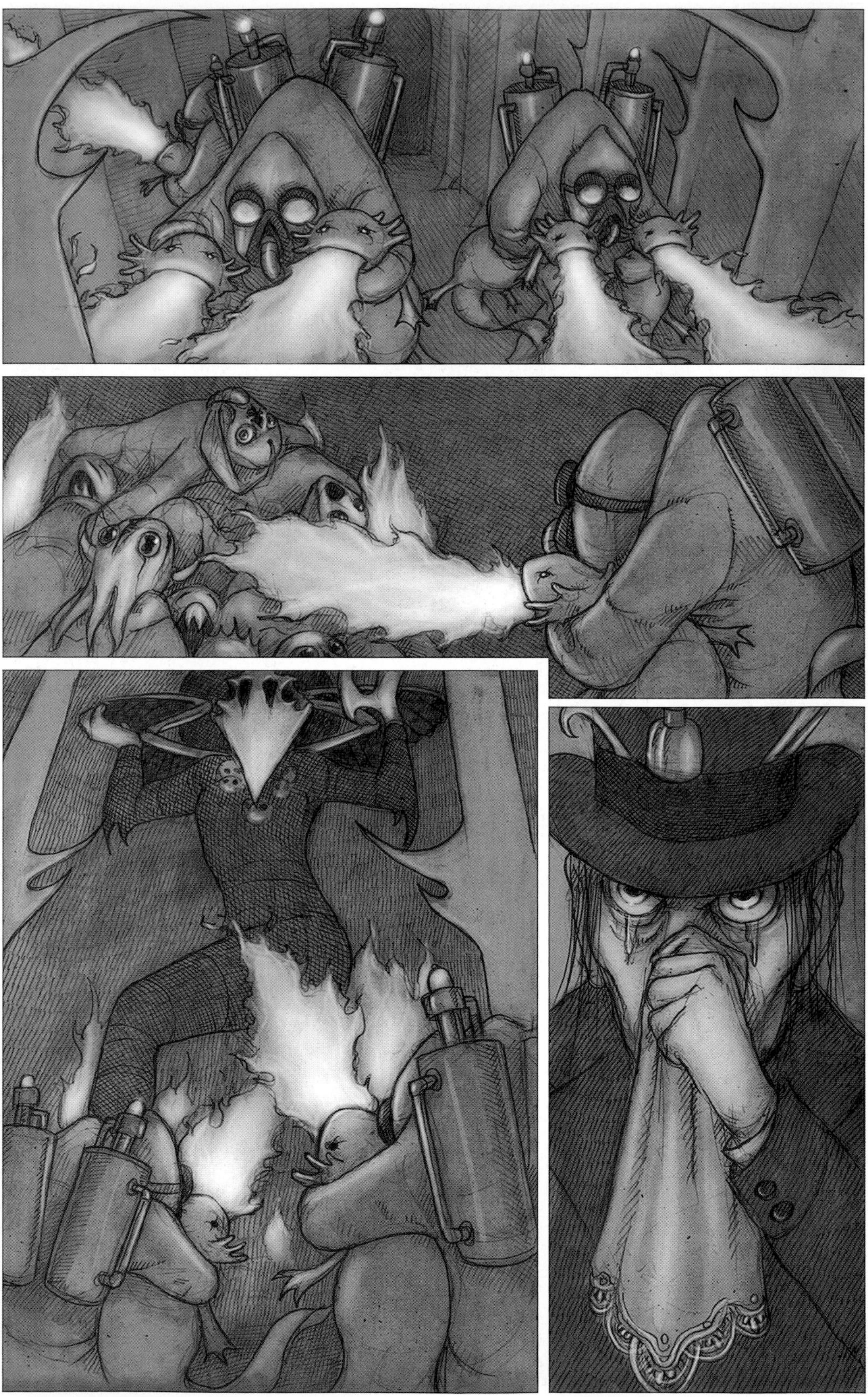

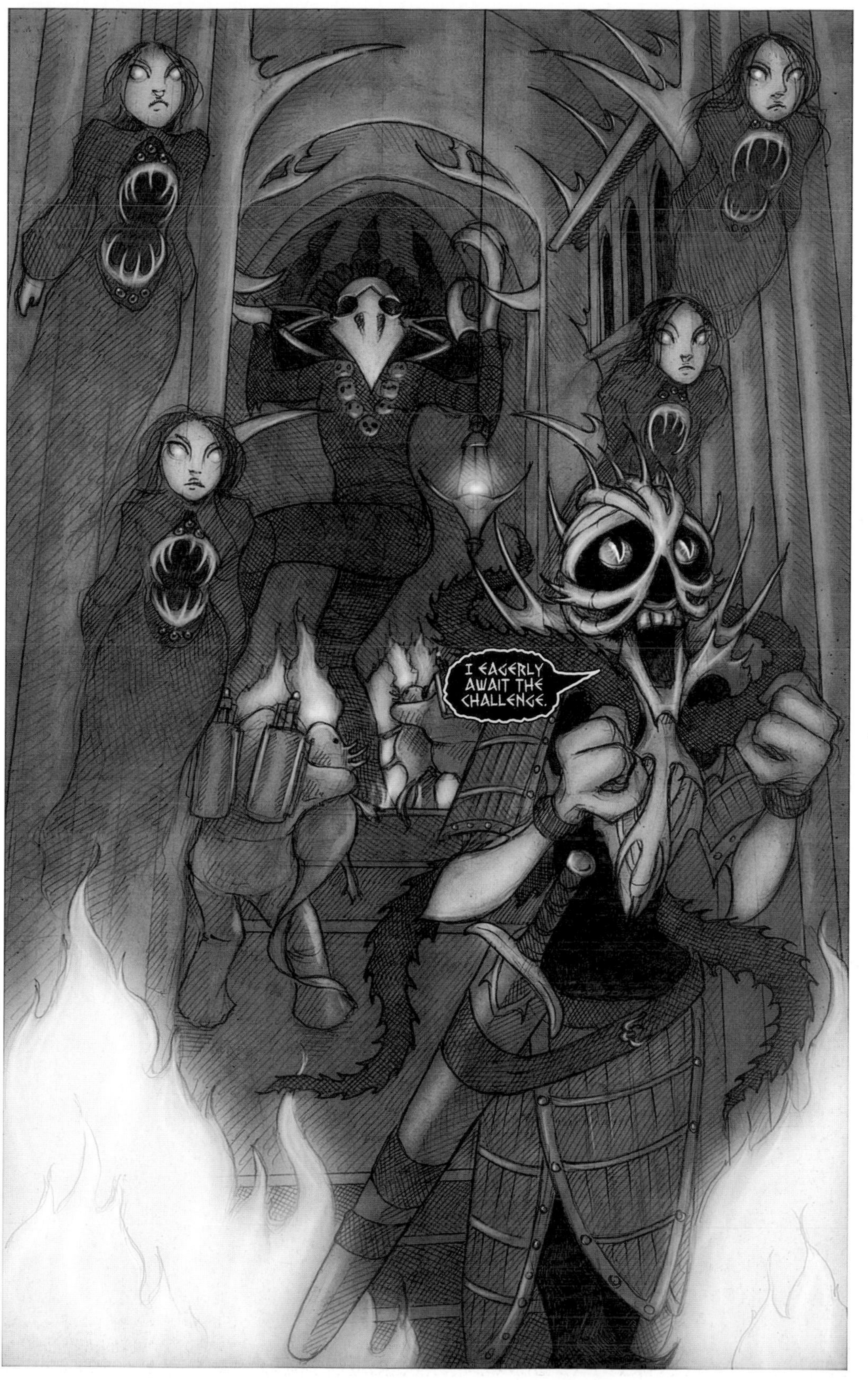
I EAGERLY AWAIT THE CHALLENGE.

THERE REALLY ISN'T NIGHTTIME ANYMORE.

THERE ARE JUST SOME TIMES THAT ARE DARKER THAN OTHERS.

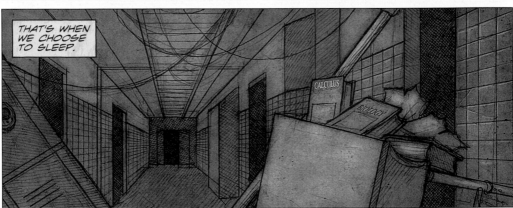

THAT'S WHEN WE CHOOSE TO SLEEP.

SOME DOING IT BETTER THAN OTHERS, WITH ONE EYE OPEN, JUST IN CASE.

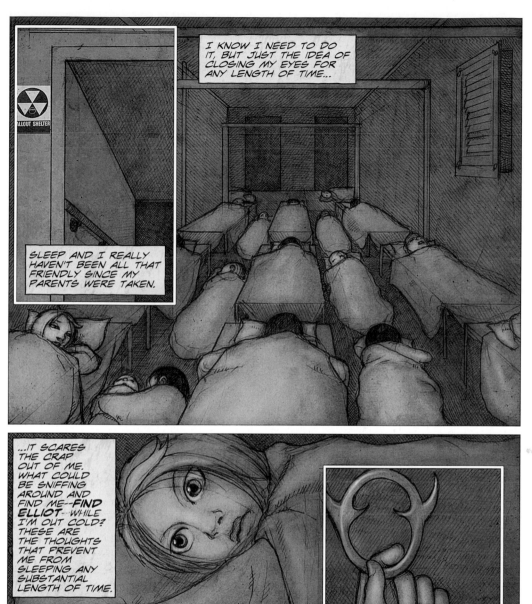

I KNOW I NEED TO DO IT, BUT JUST THE IDEA OF CLOSING MY EYES FOR ANY LENGTH OF TIME...

FALLOUT SHELTER

SLEEP AND I REALLY HAVEN'T BEEN ALL THAT FRIENDLY SINCE MY PARENTS WERE TAKEN.

...IT SCARES THE CRAP OUT OF ME. WHAT COULD BE SNIFFING AROUND AND FIND ME--**FIND ELLIOT**--WHILE I'M OUT COLD? THESE ARE THE THOUGHTS THAT PREVENT ME FROM SLEEPING ANY SUBSTANTIAL LENGTH OF TIME.

BUT LATELY, WHILE I'M LYING THERE AWAKE, I'VE BEEN THINKING ABOUT OTHER THINGS...

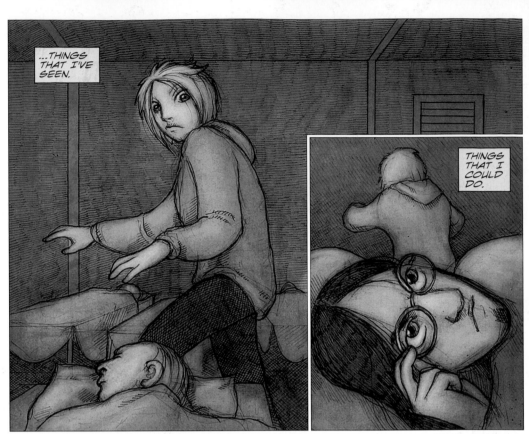

...THINGS THAT I'VE SEEN.

THINGS THAT I COULD DO.

I JUST HAVE TO BE BRAVE ENOUGH TO DO THEM.

HEY!

WHAT THE HELL DO YOU THINK YOU'RE DOING? ARE YOU CRAZY OR SOMETHING?

I THINK WE ALL HAVE TO BE A LITTLE CRAZY TO SURVIVE IN THIS WORLD. IT'S THE ONES WHO AREN'T WHO DON'T MAKE IT.

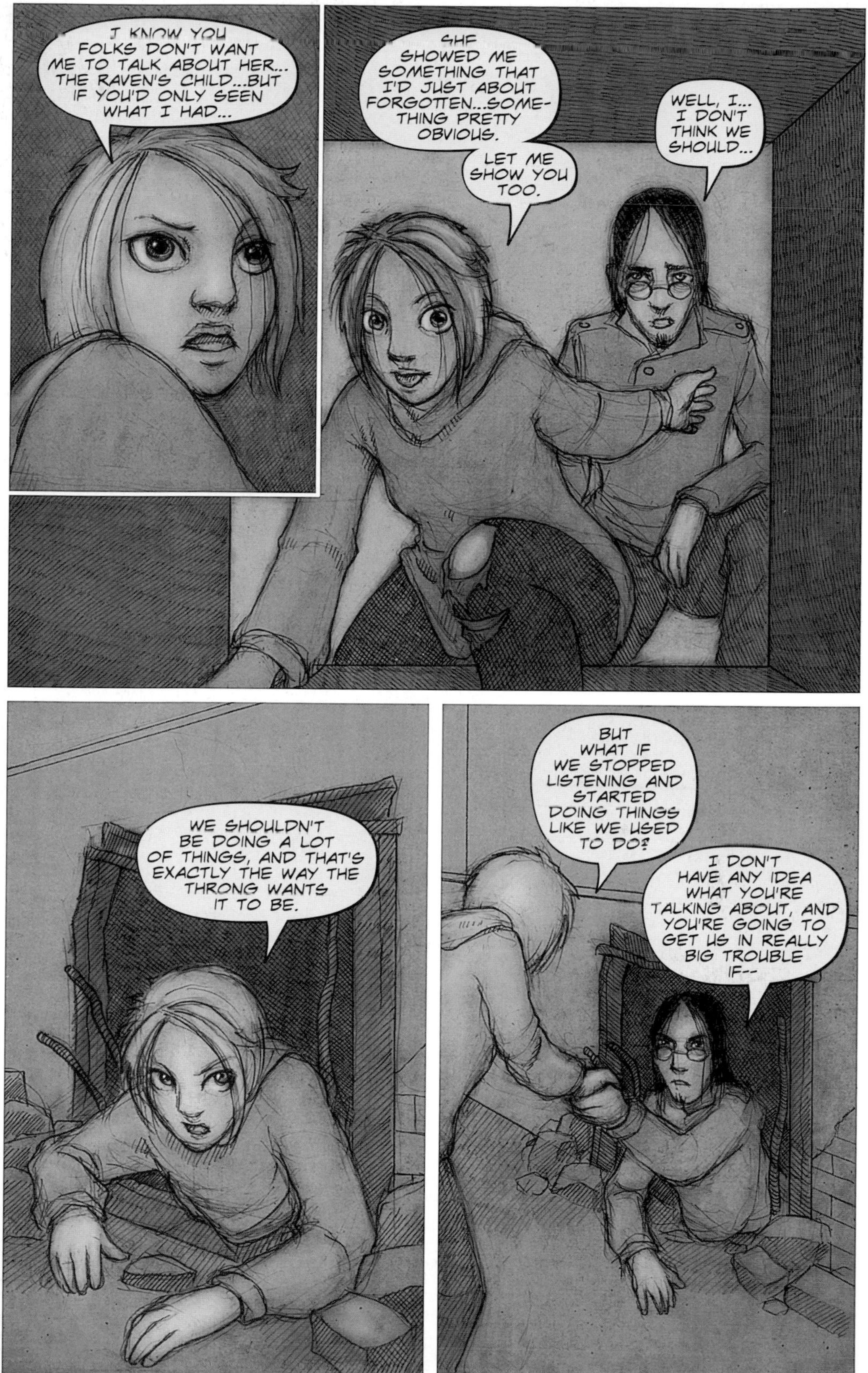
I KNOW YOU FOLKS DON'T WANT ME TO TALK ABOUT HER... THE RAVEN'S CHILD...BUT IF YOU'D ONLY SEEN WHAT I HAD...
SHE SHOWED ME SOMETHING THAT I'D JUST ABOUT FORGOTTEN...SOMETHING PRETTY OBVIOUS.
LET ME SHOW YOU TOO.
WELL, I... I DON'T THINK WE SHOULD...
WE SHOULDN'T BE DOING A LOT OF THINGS, AND THAT'S EXACTLY THE WAY THE THRONG WANTS IT TO BE.
BUT WHAT IF WE STOPPED LISTENING AND STARTED DOING THINGS LIKE WE USED TO DO?
I DON'T HAVE ANY IDEA WHAT YOU'RE TALKING ABOUT, AND YOU'RE GOING TO GET US IN REALLY BIG TROUBLE IF--

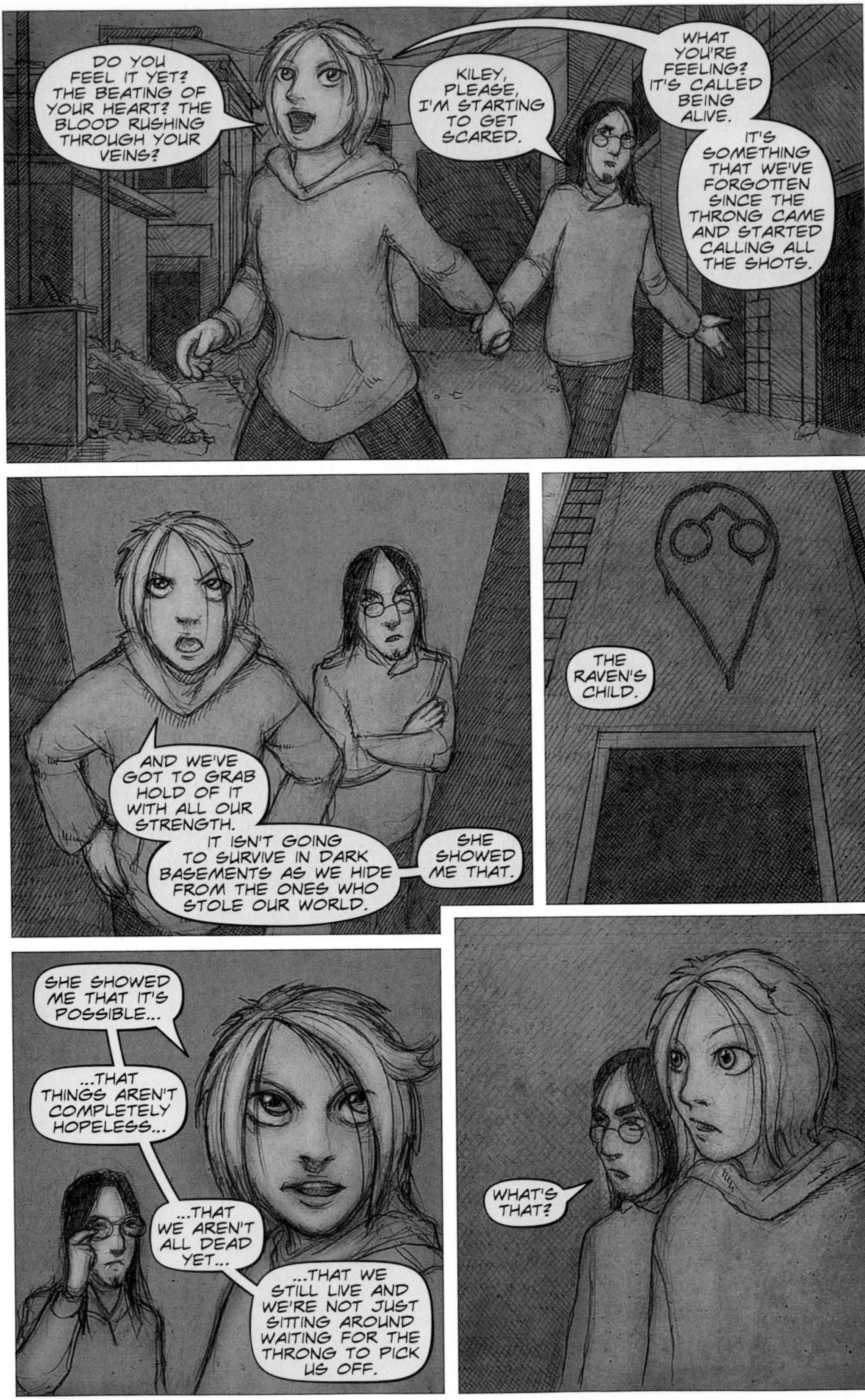
DO YOU FEEL IT YET? THE BEATING OF YOUR HEART? THE BLOOD RUSHING THROUGH YOUR VEINS?
KILEY, PLEASE, I'M STARTING TO GET SCARED.
WHAT YOU'RE FEELING? IT'S CALLED BEING ALIVE.
IT'S SOMETHING THAT WE'VE FORGOTTEN SINCE THE THRONG CAME AND STARTED CALLING ALL THE SHOTS.
AND WE'VE GOT TO GRAB HOLD OF IT WITH ALL OUR STRENGTH.
IT ISN'T GOING TO SURVIVE IN DARK BASEMENTS AS WE HIDE FROM THE ONES WHO STOLE OUR WORLD.
SHE SHOWED ME THAT.
THE RAVEN'S CHILD.
SHE SHOWED ME THAT IT'S POSSIBLE...
...THAT THINGS AREN'T COMPLETELY HOPELESS...
...THAT WE AREN'T ALL DEAD YET...
...THAT WE STILL LIVE AND WE'RE NOT JUST SITTING AROUND WAITING FOR THE THRONG TO PICK US OFF.
WHAT'S THAT?

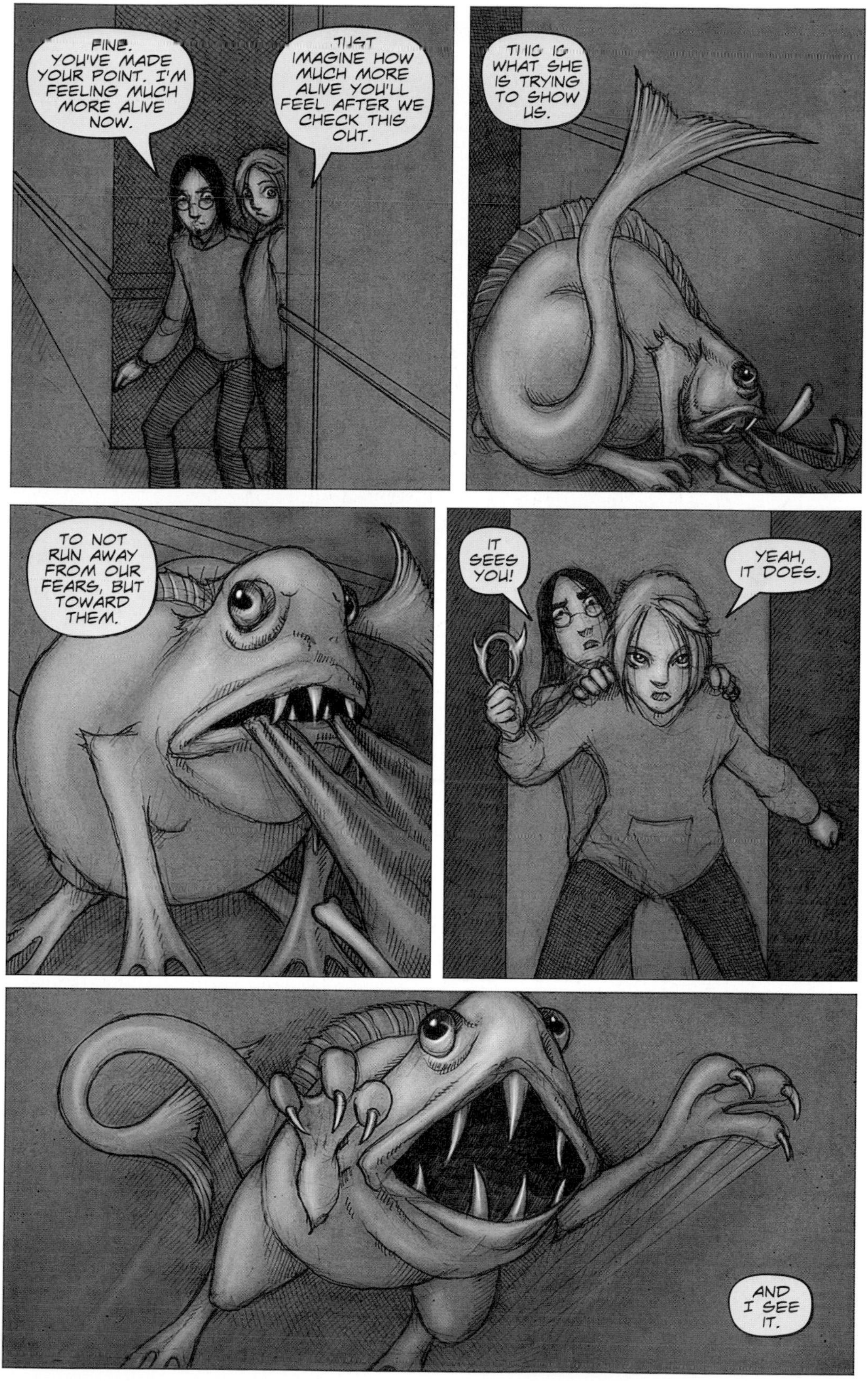
FINE. YOU'VE MADE YOUR POINT. I'M FEELING MUCH MORE ALIVE NOW.
JUST IMAGINE HOW MUCH MORE ALIVE YOU'LL FEEL AFTER WE CHECK THIS OUT.
THIS IS WHAT SHE IS TRYING TO SHOW US.
TO NOT RUN AWAY FROM OUR FEARS, BUT TOWARD THEM.
IT SEES YOU!
YEAH, IT DOES.
AND I SEE IT.

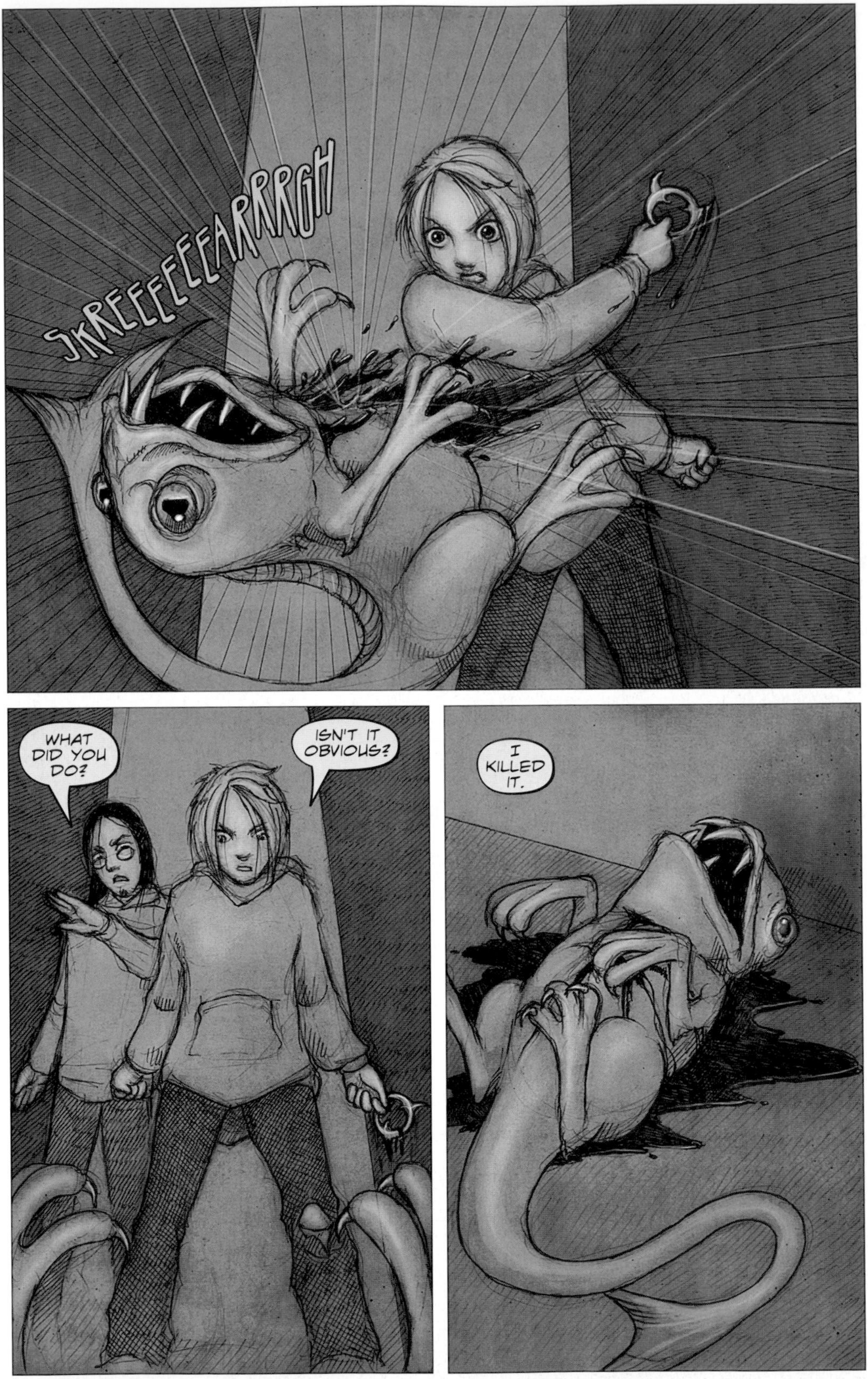
SKREEEEEEARRRRGH
WHAT DID YOU DO?
ISN'T IT OBVIOUS?
I KILLED IT.

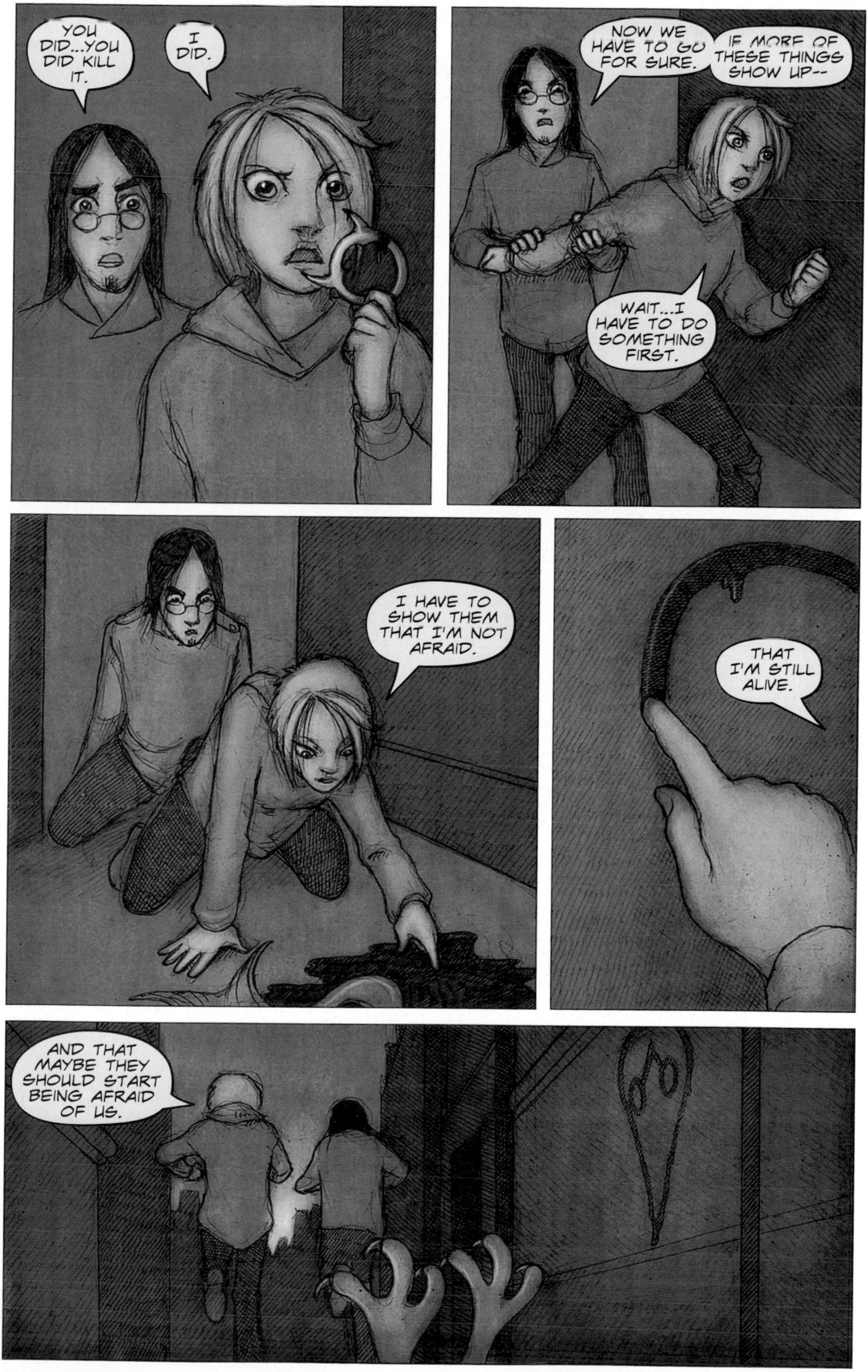
YOU DID...YOU DID KILL IT.
I DID.
NOW WE HAVE TO GO FOR SURE.
IF MORE OF THESE THINGS SHOW UP--
WAIT...I HAVE TO DO SOMETHING FIRST.
I HAVE TO SHOW THEM THAT I'M NOT AFRAID.
THAT I'M STILL ALIVE.
AND THAT MAYBE THEY SHOULD START BEING AFRAID OF US.

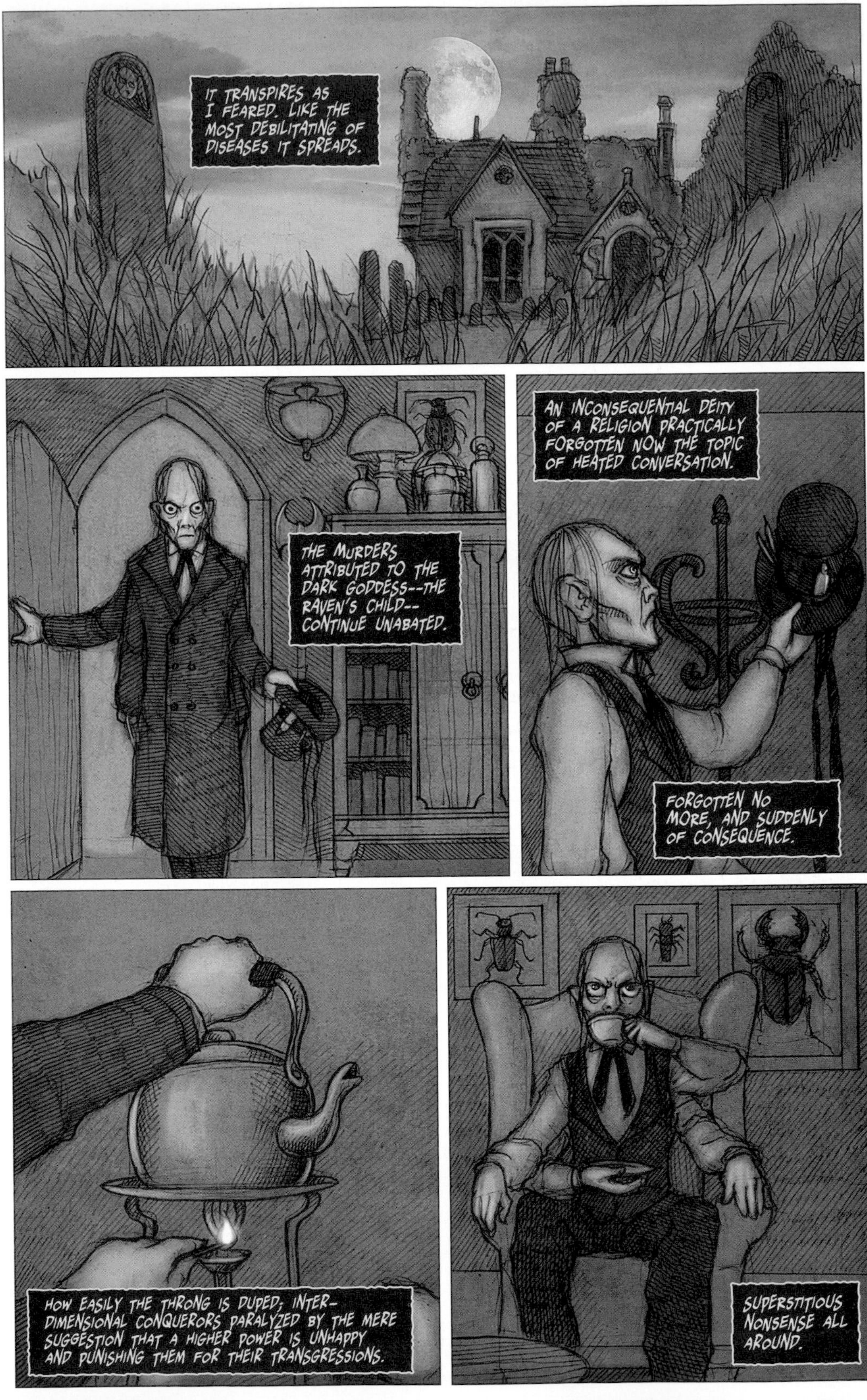
IT TRANSPIRES AS I FEARED. LIKE THE MOST DEBILITATING OF DISEASES IT SPREADS.
THE MURDERS ATTRIBUTED TO THE DARK GODDESS--THE RAVEN'S CHILD--CONTINUE UNABATED.
AN INCONSEQUENTIAL DEITY OF A RELIGION PRACTICALLY FORGOTTEN NOW THE TOPIC OF HEATED CONVERSATION.
FORGOTTEN NO MORE, AND SUDDENLY OF CONSEQUENCE.
HOW EASILY THE THRONG IS DUPED; INTER-DIMENSIONAL CONQUERORS PARALYZED BY THE MERE SUGGESTION THAT A HIGHER POWER IS UNHAPPY AND PUNISHING THEM FOR THEIR TRANSGRESSIONS.
SUPERSTITIOUS NONSENSE ALL AROUND.

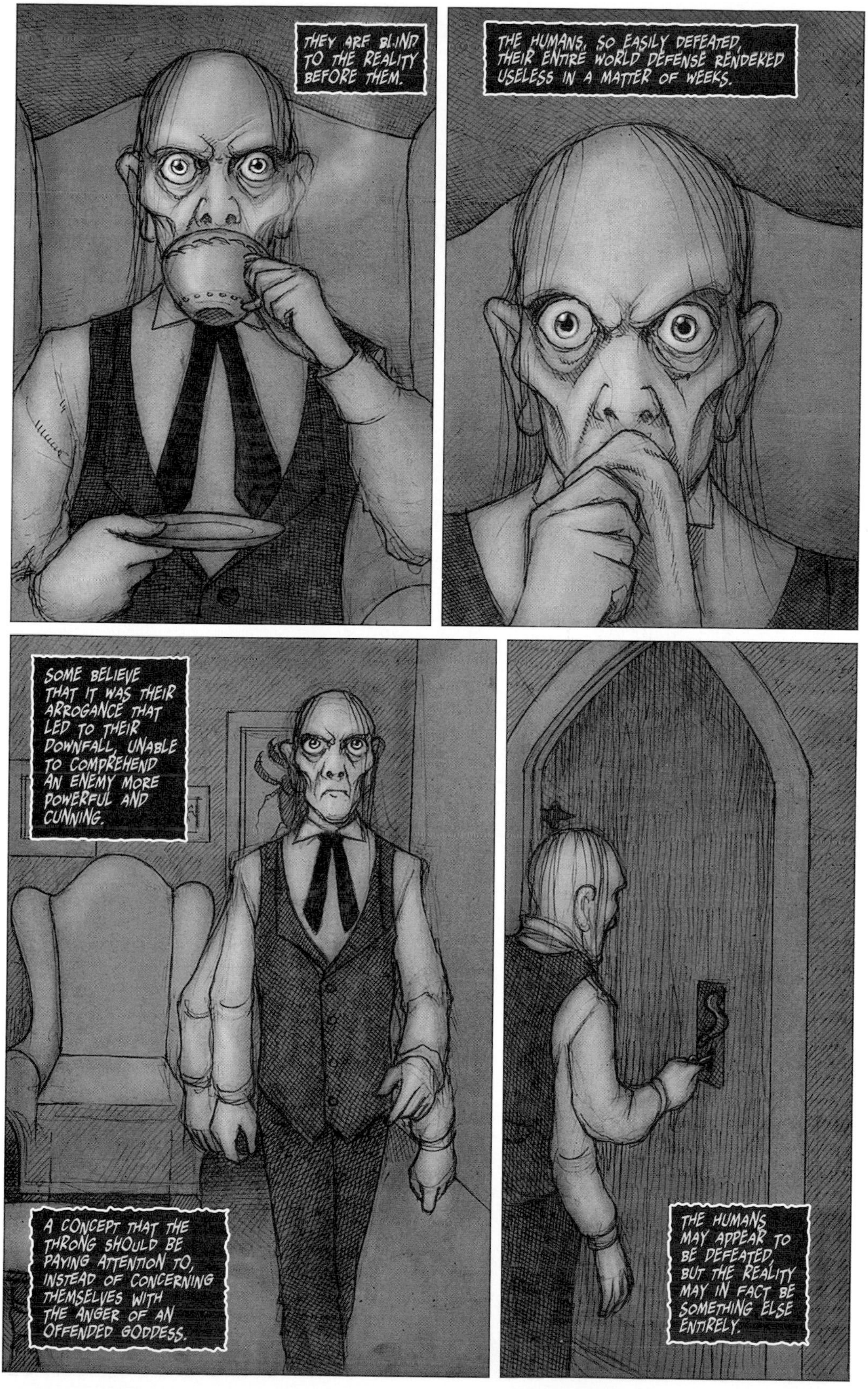
THEY ARE BLIND TO THE REALITY BEFORE THEM.
THE HUMANS, SO EASILY DEFEATED, THEIR ENTIRE WORLD DEFENSE RENDERED USELESS IN A MATTER OF WEEKS.
SOME BELIEVE THAT IT WAS THEIR ARROGANCE THAT LED TO THEIR DOWNFALL, UNABLE TO COMPREHEND AN ENEMY MORE POWERFUL AND CUNNING.
A CONCEPT THAT THE THRONG SHOULD BE PAYING ATTENTION TO, INSTEAD OF CONCERNING THEMSELVES WITH THE ANGER OF AN OFFENDED GODDESS.
THE HUMANS MAY APPEAR TO BE DEFEATED, BUT THE REALITY MAY IN FACT BE SOMETHING ELSE ENTIRELY.

THEY ARE FAR MORE DEVIOUS THAN THEY ARE GIVEN CREDIT FOR.

BUT THIS IS AN OPINION NOT SHARED BY MOST. HUMANITY BEING NOTHING MORE TO THEM THAN A MINOR ANNOYANCE...PESTS...

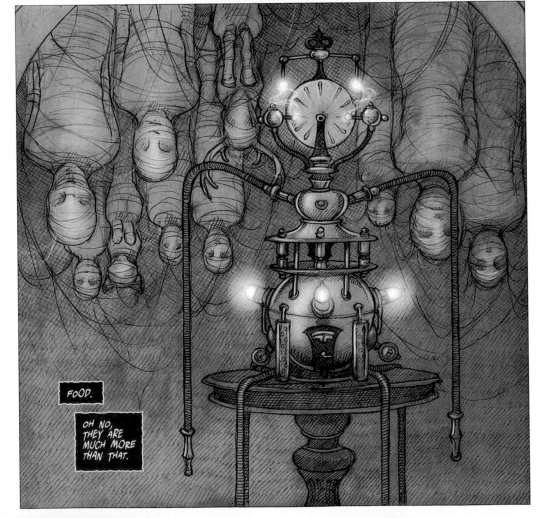

FOOD.

OH NO, THEY ARE MUCH MORE THAN THAT.

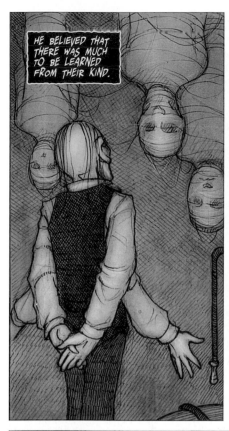

HE BELIEVED THAT THERE WAS MUCH TO BE LEARNED FROM THEIR KIND.

ONE JUST NEEDED TO HAVE THE PROPER AMOUNT OF PATIENCE...

...AND TO ASK THE RIGHT QUESTIONS.

IS THIS IT? OH GOD...ARE YOU GOING TO...? PLEASE...PLEASE... I'LL TELL YOU ANY-THING YOU NEED TO KNOW... PLEASE!

IN OUR PREVIOUS DISCUSSIONS I TOLD YOU ABOUT THE GODDESS.

YES, THE RAVEN'S CHILD...AN ANGRY DEITY...ONE WHO IT IS FORETOLD WILL COME TO PUNISH YOU ALL IF DISPLEASED.

YES, EXACTLY. OF COURSE WE KNOW THIS IS FOOLISHNESS... THE LEGEND'S NOTHING BUT STORIES TO SWAY THE VARIOUS THRONG RACES TO BEHAVE.

BUT SOMEONE HAS LEARNED OF THESE LEGENDS, AND NOW ATTEMPTS TO USE MY KIND'S RABID SUPERSTITIONS AGAINST US.

A HUMAN SOMEONE, I DO BELIEVE.

A HUMAN SOMEONE WHO HAS ACTUALLY MANAGED TO INSTILL A CREEPING FEAR INTO MY PEOPLE.

FEAR IS A DEADLY WEAPON...A MEANS TO OBTAINING POWER OVER YOUR OPPONENT.

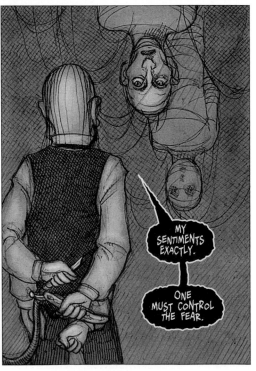

MY SENTIMENTS EXACTLY.

ONE MUST CONTROL THE FEAR.

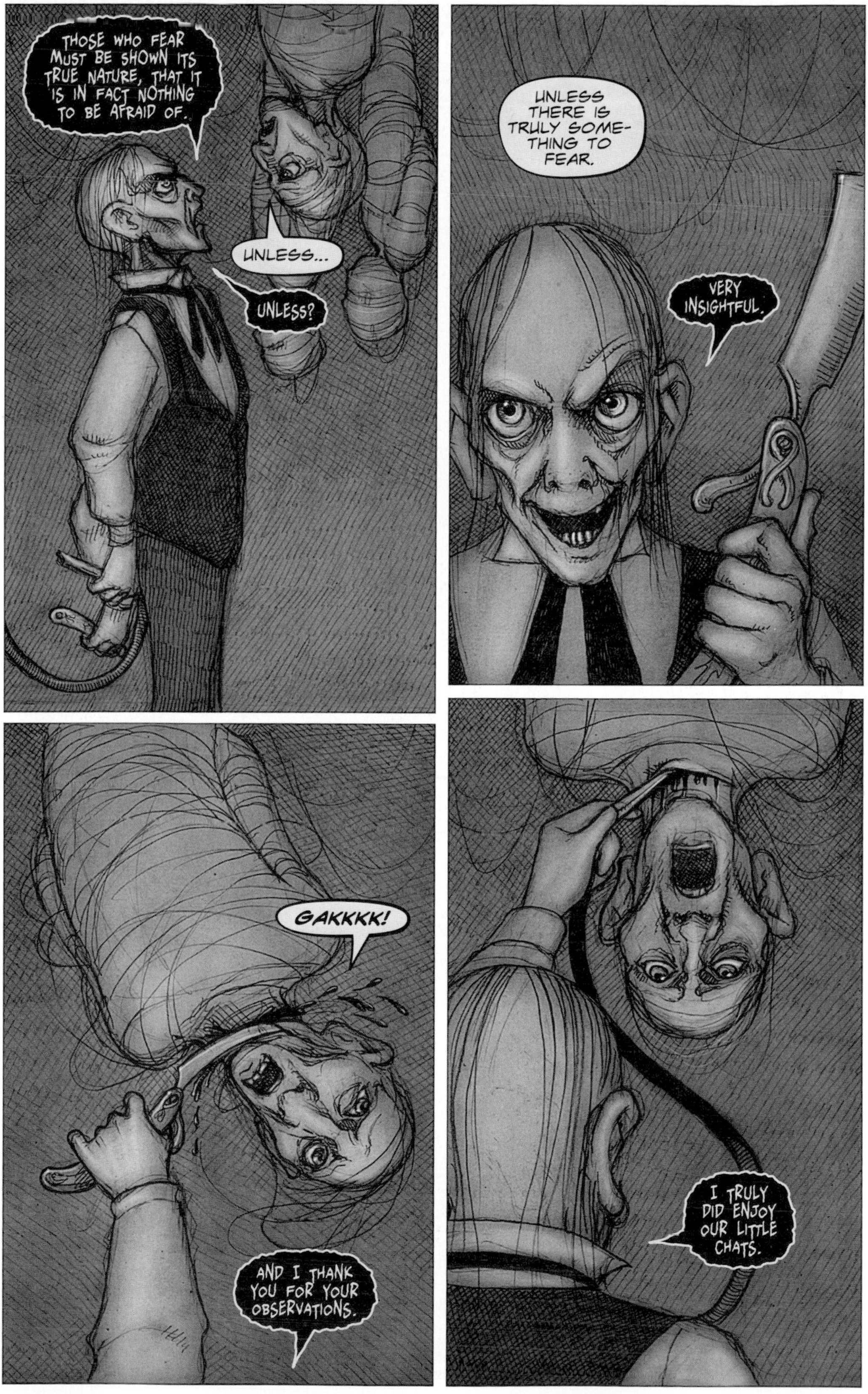
THOSE WHO FEAR MUST BE SHOWN ITS TRUE NATURE, THAT IT IS IN FACT NOTHING TO BE AFRAID OF.
UNLESS...
UNLESS?
UNLESS THERE IS TRULY SOME-THING TO FEAR.
VERY INSIGHTFUL.
GAKKKK!
AND I THANK YOU FOR YOUR OBSERVATIONS.
I TRULY DID ENJOY OUR LITTLE CHATS.

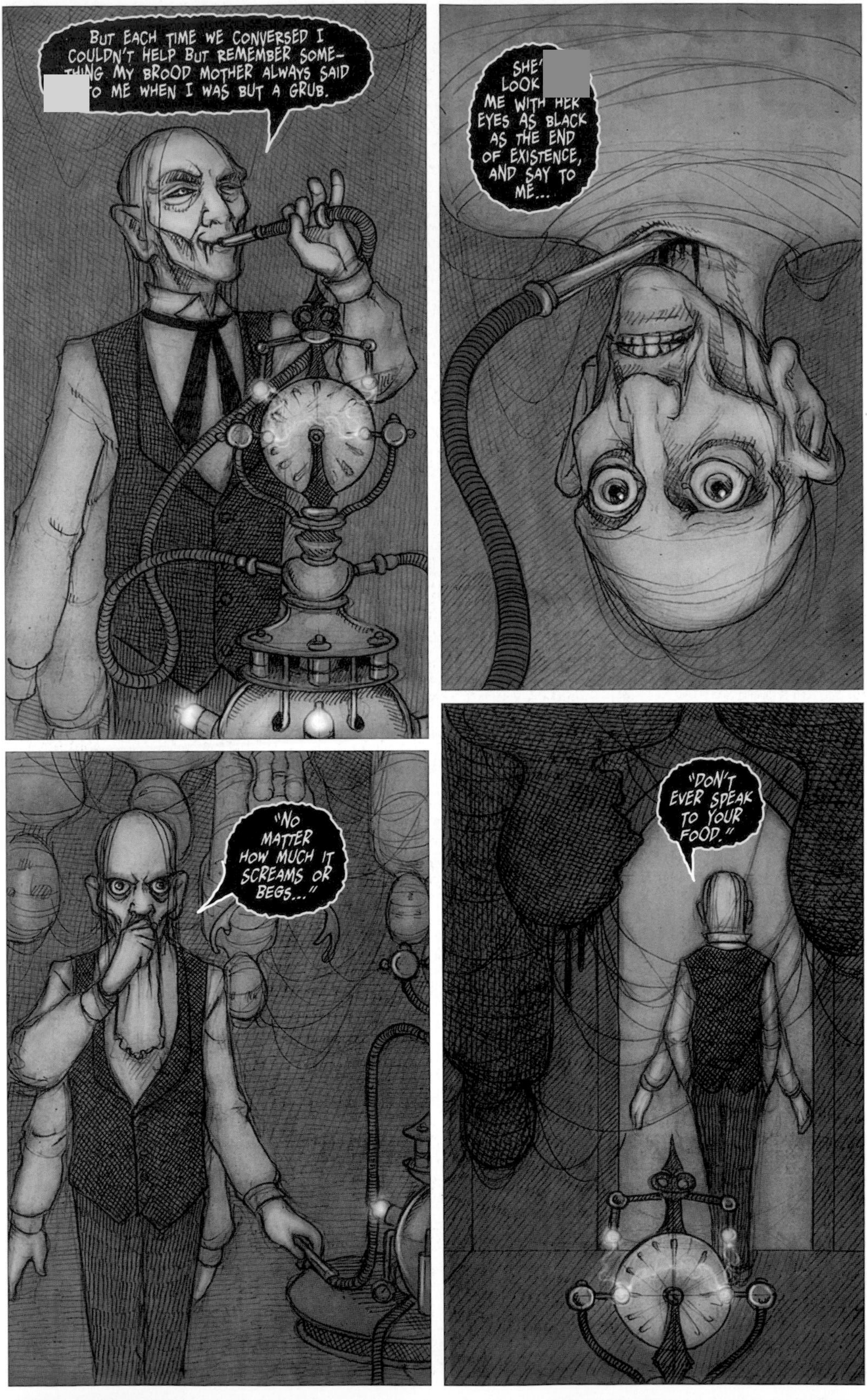
BUT EACH TIME WE CONVERSED I COULDN'T HELP BUT REMEMBER SOME-THING MY BROOD MOTHER ALWAYS SAID O ME WHEN I WAS BUT A GRUB.
SHE' LOOK ME WITH HER EYES AS BLACK AS THE END OF EXISTENCE, AND SAY TO ME...
"NO MATTER HOW MUCH IT SCREAMS OR BEGS..."
"DON'T EVER SPEAK TO YOUR FOOD."

WHAT IS LIFE WITHOUT CHALLENGE?

INTERMINABLE PERIODS OF TIME BETWEEN CONFLICTS, UNTIL A NEW TRIAL ARISES.

SINCE CONQUERING THIS WORLD THE DISSENTION HAS BEEN MINOR, EASILY CRUSHED BENEATH THE WEIGHT OF THOSE I COMMAND.

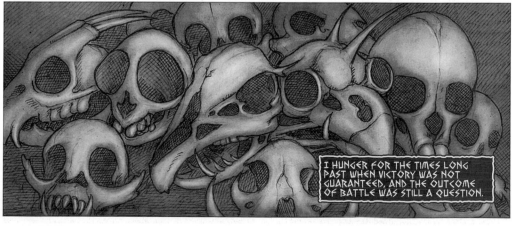

I HUNGER FOR THE TIMES LONG PAST WHEN VICTORY WAS NOT GUARANTEED, AND THE OUTCOME OF BATTLE WAS STILL A QUESTION.

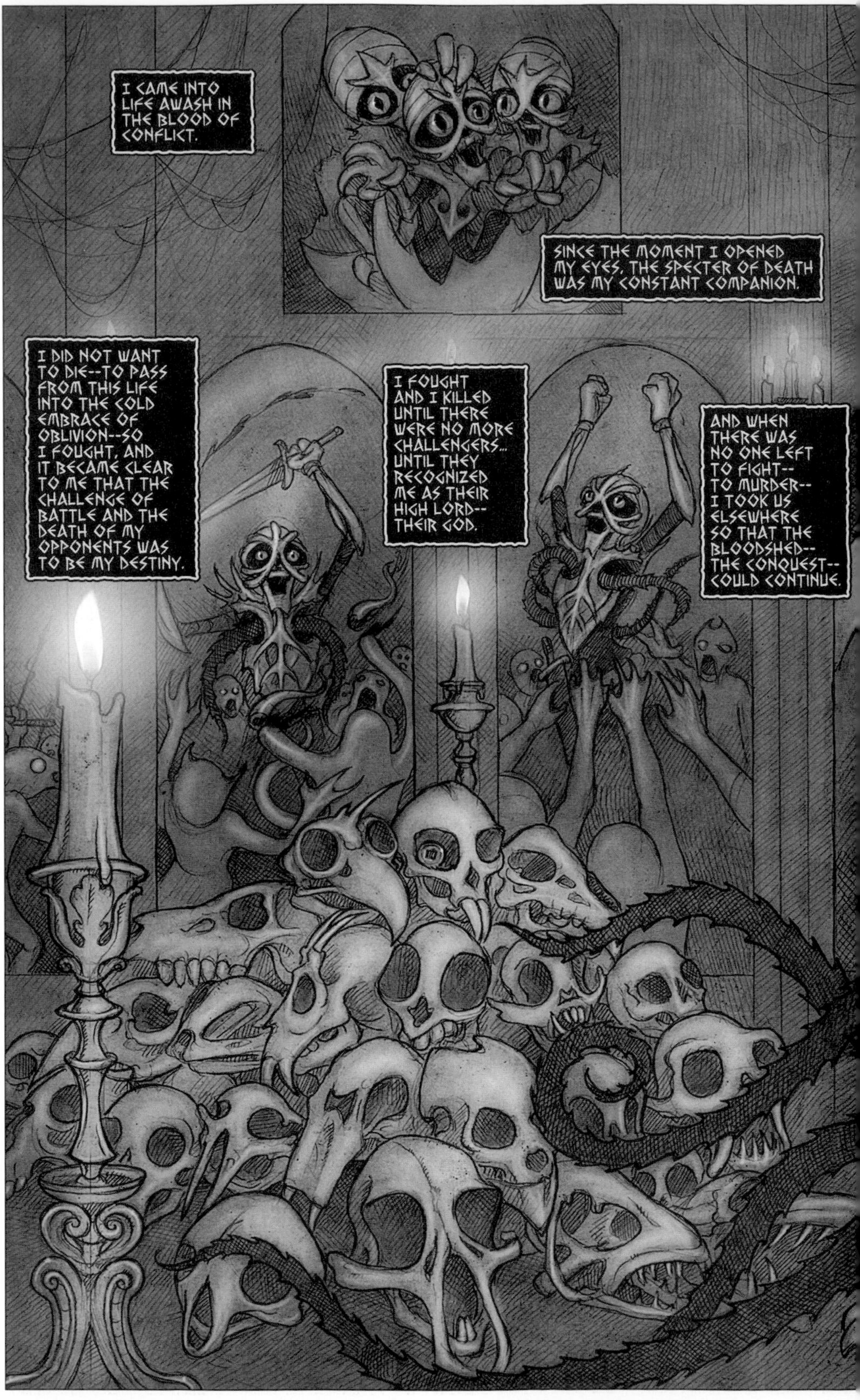
I CAME INTO LIFE AWASH IN THE BLOOD OF CONFLICT.
SINCE THE MOMENT I OPENED MY EYES, THE SPECTER OF DEATH WAS MY CONSTANT COMPANION.
I DID NOT WANT TO DIE--TO PASS FROM THIS LIFE INTO THE COLD EMBRACE OF OBLIVION--SO I FOUGHT, AND IT BECAME CLEAR TO ME THAT THE CHALLENGE OF BATTLE AND THE DEATH OF MY OPPONENTS WAS TO BE MY DESTINY.
I FOUGHT AND I KILLED UNTIL THERE WERE NO MORE CHALLENGERS... UNTIL THEY RECOGNIZED ME AS THEIR HIGH LORD--THEIR GOD.
AND WHEN THERE WAS NO ONE LEFT TO FIGHT--TO MURDER--I TOOK US ELSEWHERE SO THAT THE BLOODSHED--THE CONQUEST--COULD CONTINUE.

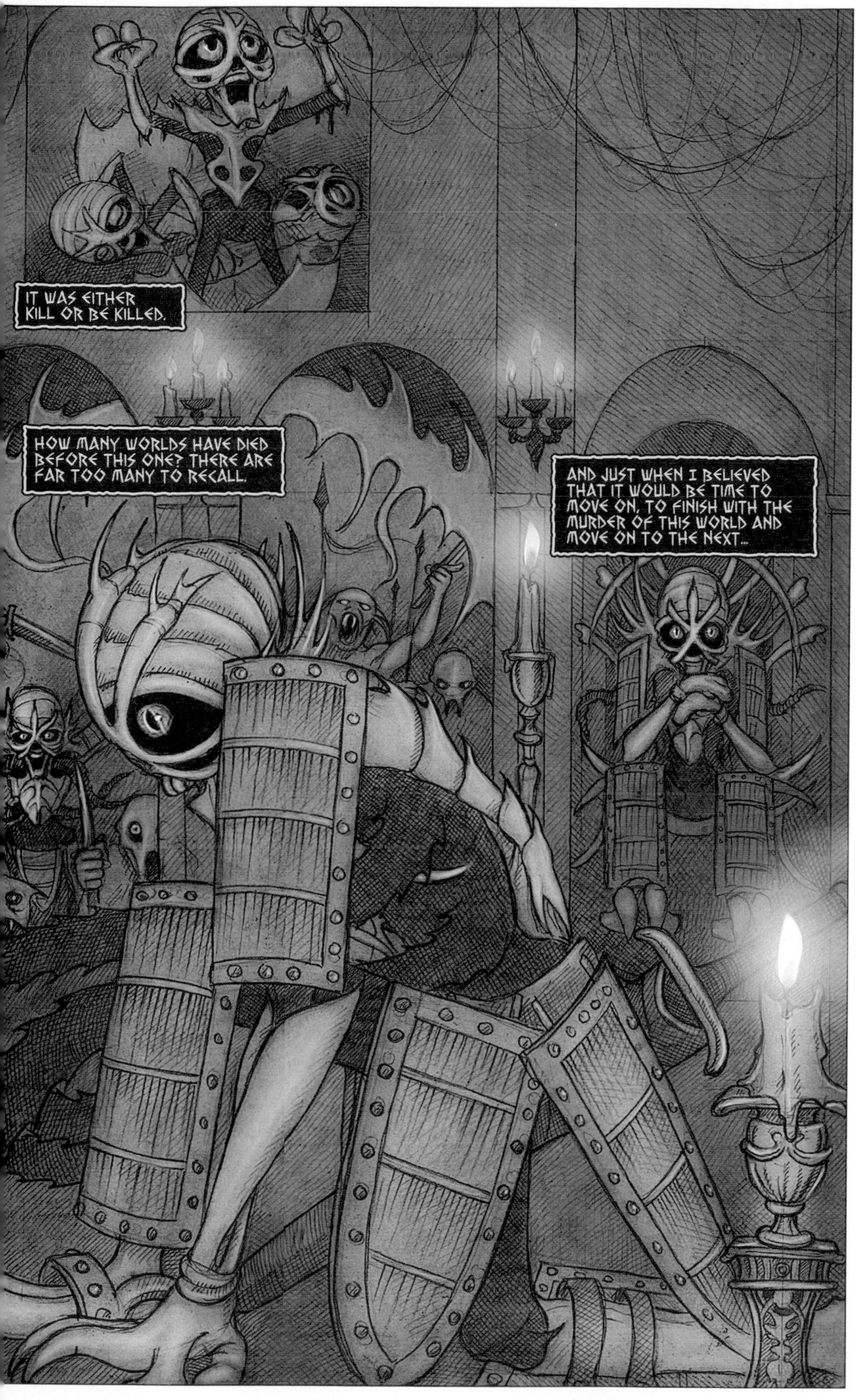
IT WAS EITHER
KILL OR BE KILLED.
HOW MANY WORLDS HAVE DIED
BEFORE THIS ONE? THERE ARE
FAR TOO MANY TO RECALL.
AND JUST WHEN I BELIEVED
THAT IT WOULD BE TIME TO
MOVE ON, TO FINISH WITH THE
MURDER OF THIS WORLD AND
MOVE ON TO THE NEXT...

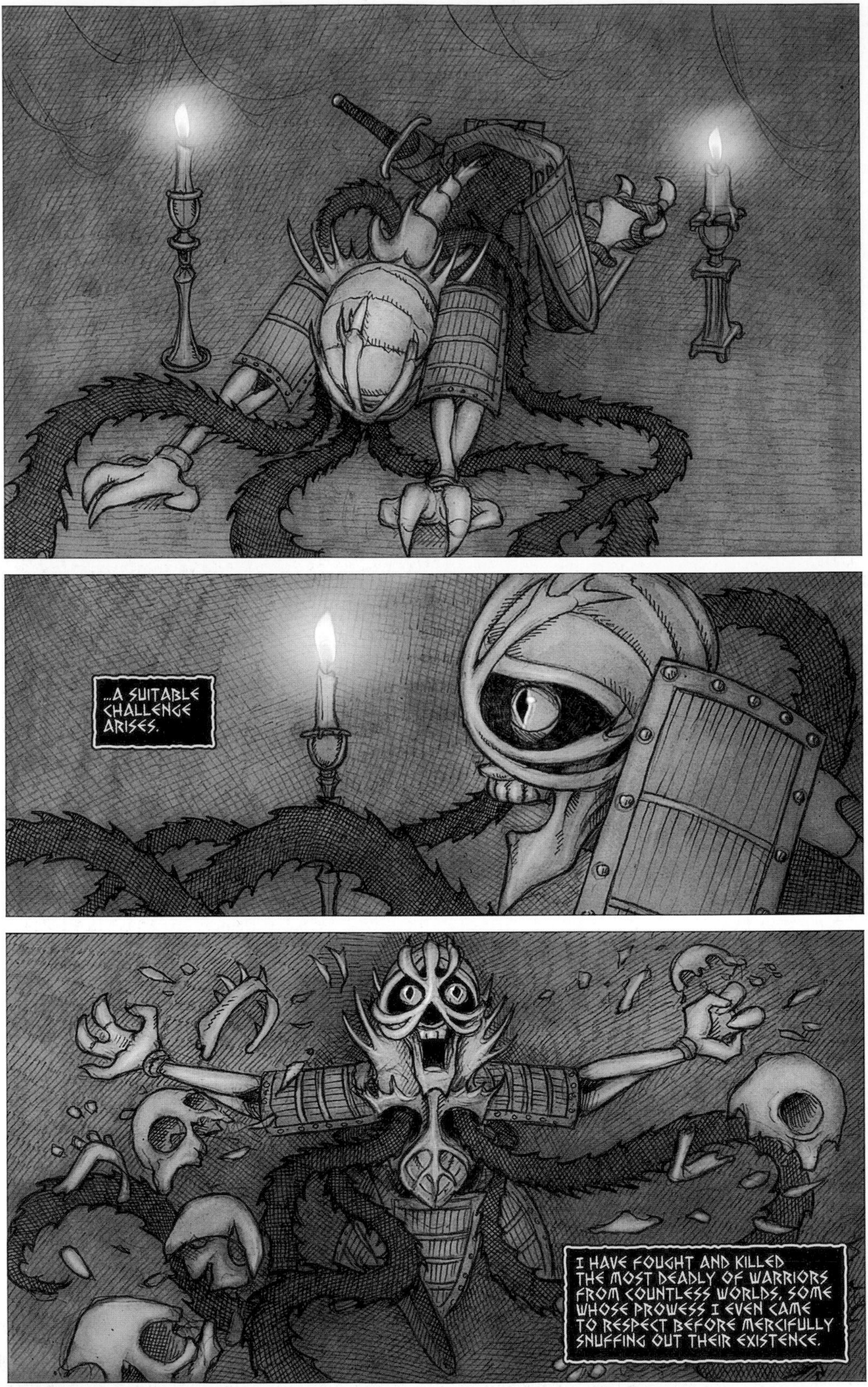
...A SUITABLE CHALLENGE ARISES.
I HAVE FOUGHT AND KILLED THE MOST DEADLY OF WARRIORS FROM COUNTLESS WORLDS, SOME WHOSE PROWESS I EVEN CAME TO RESPECT BEFORE MERCIFULLY SNUFFING OUT THEIR EXISTENCE.

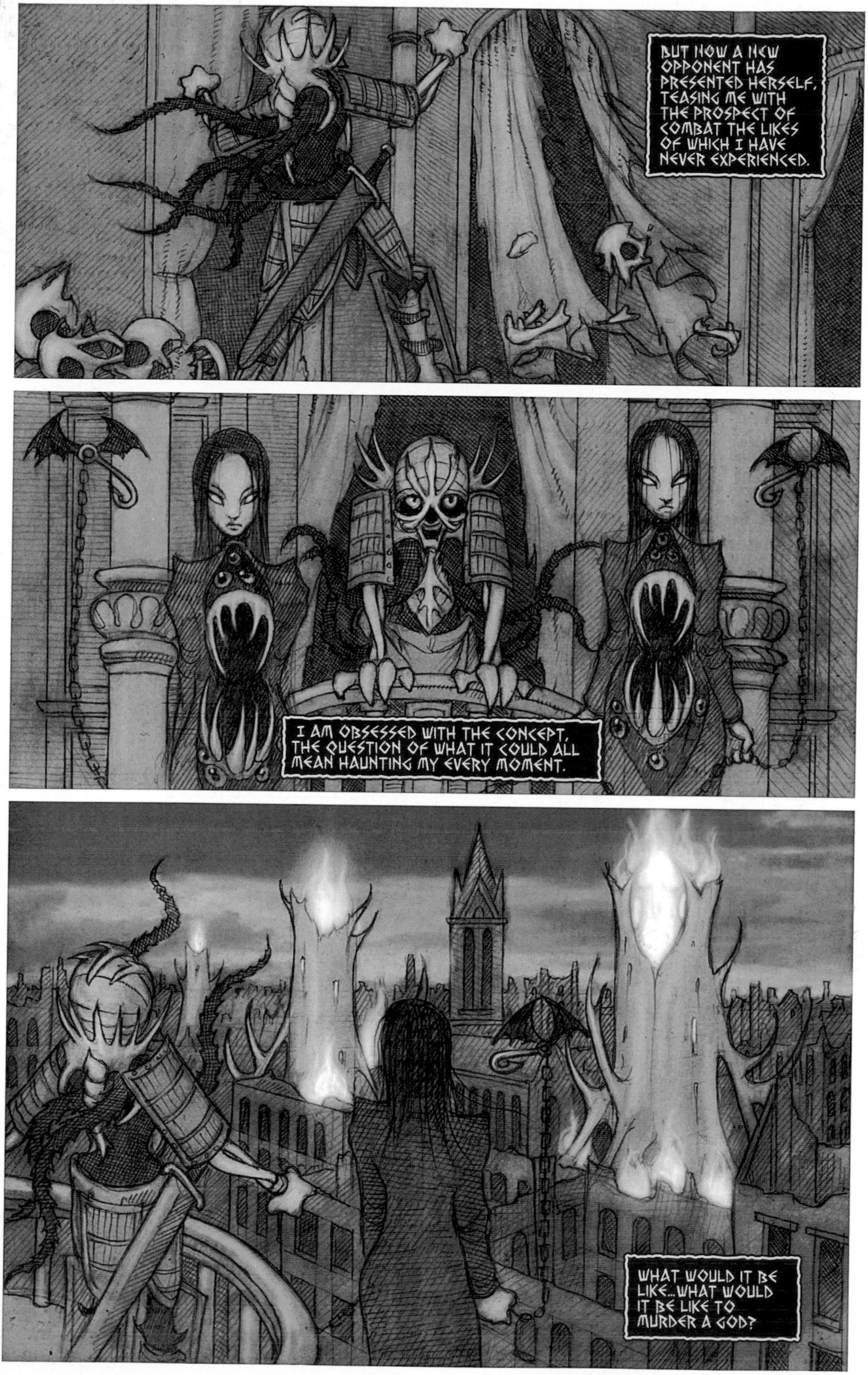

BUT NOW A NEW OPPONENT HAS PRESENTED HERSELF, TEASING ME WITH THE PROSPECT OF COMBAT THE LIKES OF WHICH I HAVE NEVER EXPERIENCED.
I AM OBSESSED WITH THE CONCEPT, THE QUESTION OF WHAT IT COULD ALL MEAN HAUNTING MY EVERY MOMENT.
WHAT WOULD IT BE LIKE...WHAT WOULD IT BE LIKE TO MURDER A GOD?

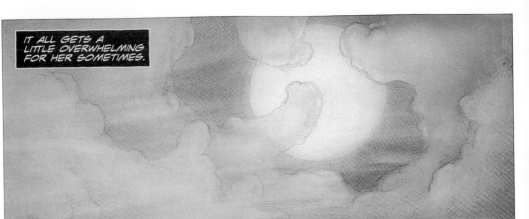

IT ALL GETS A LITTLE OVERWHELMING FOR HER SOMETIMES.

DOWN ON THE STREETS IT'S ALL SO CLOSE-UP AND IN YOUR FACE IT'S EASY TO LOSE SIGHT.

UP HERE THOUGH, UP HERE SHE CAN THINK.

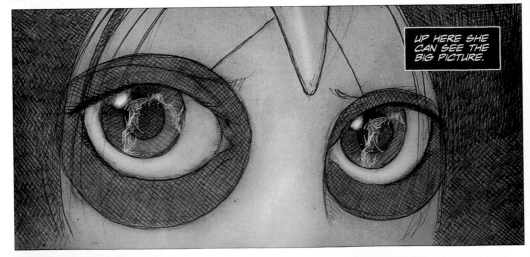

UP HERE SHE CAN SEE THE BIG PICTURE.

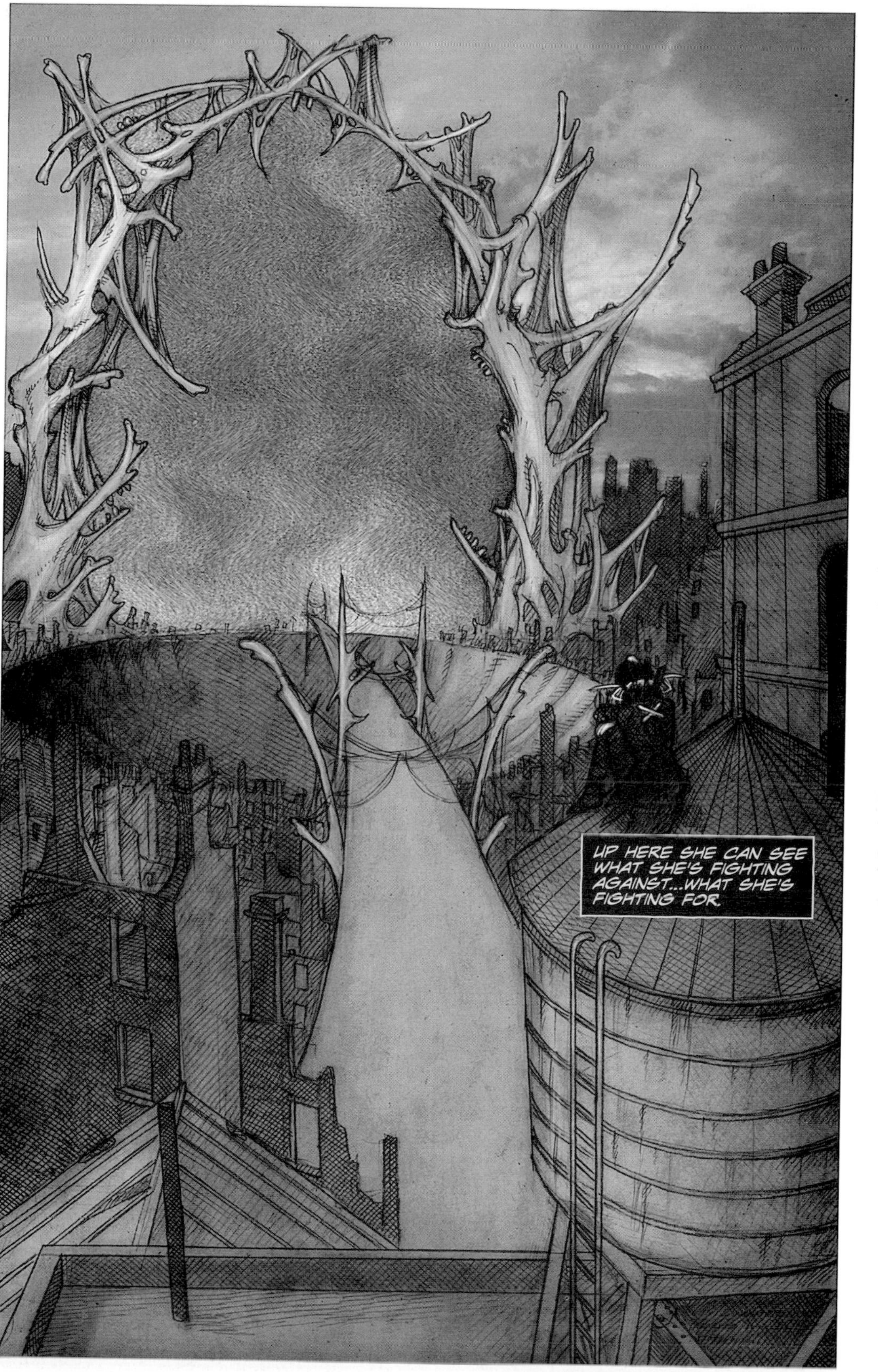
UP HERE SHE CAN SEE WHAT SHE'S FIGHTING AGAINST...WHAT SHE'S FIGHTING FOR.

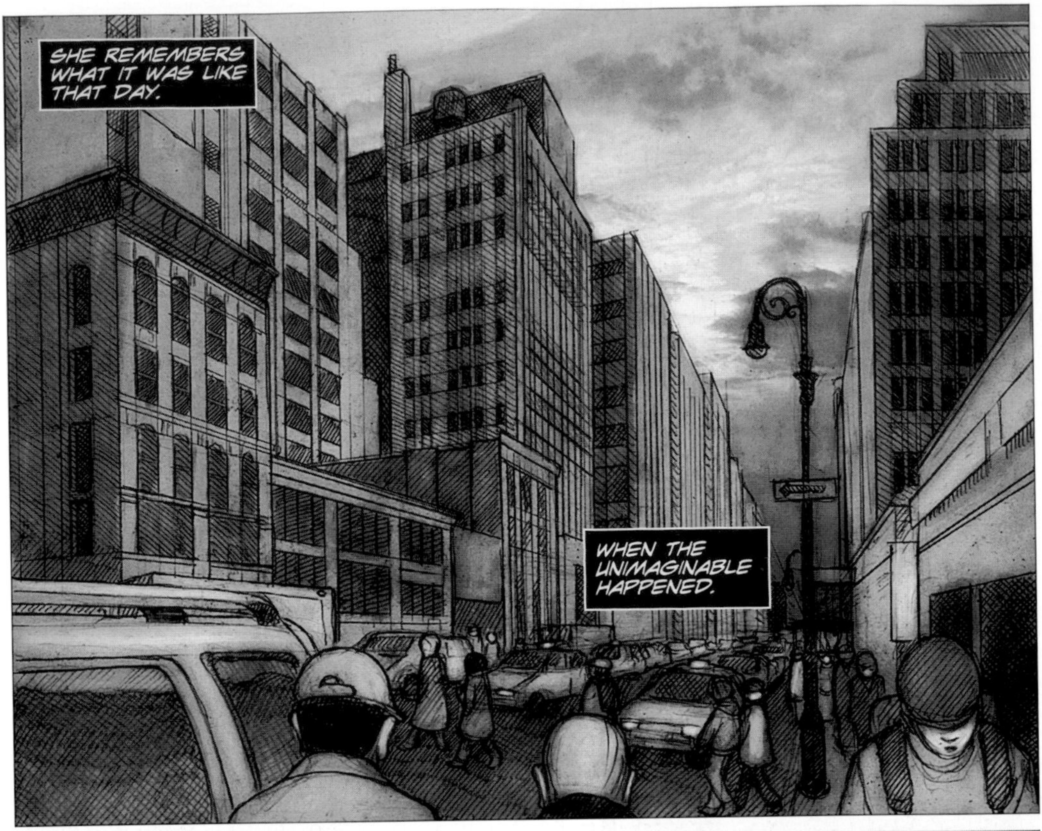
SHE REMEMBERS WHAT IT WAS LIKE THAT DAY.
WHEN THE UNIMAGINABLE HAPPENED.

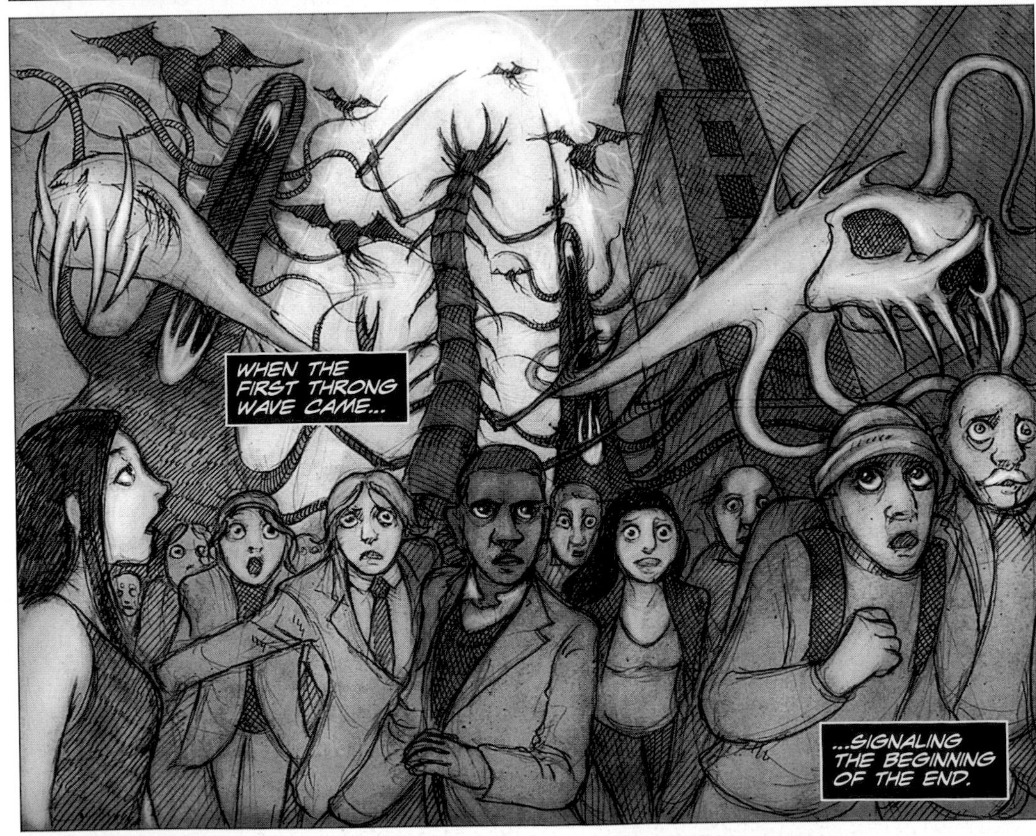
WHEN THE FIRST THRONG WAVE CAME...
...SIGNALING THE BEGINNING OF THE END.

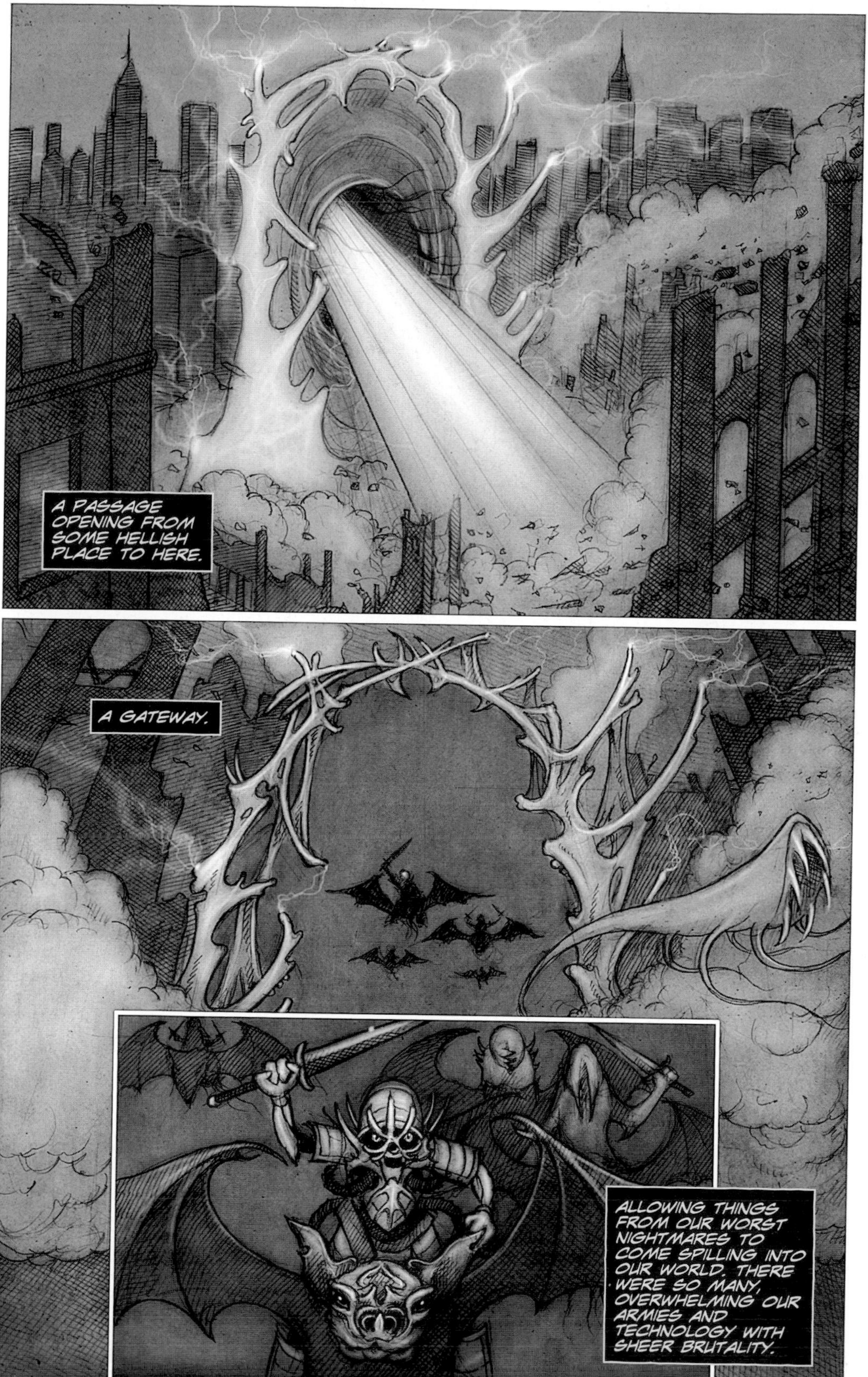

A PASSAGE OPENING FROM SOME HELLISH PLACE TO HERE.
A GATEWAY.
ALLOWING THINGS FROM OUR WORST NIGHTMARES TO COME SPILLING INTO OUR WORLD. THERE WERE SO MANY, OVERWHELMING OUR ARMIES AND TECHNOLOGY WITH SHEER BRUTALITY.

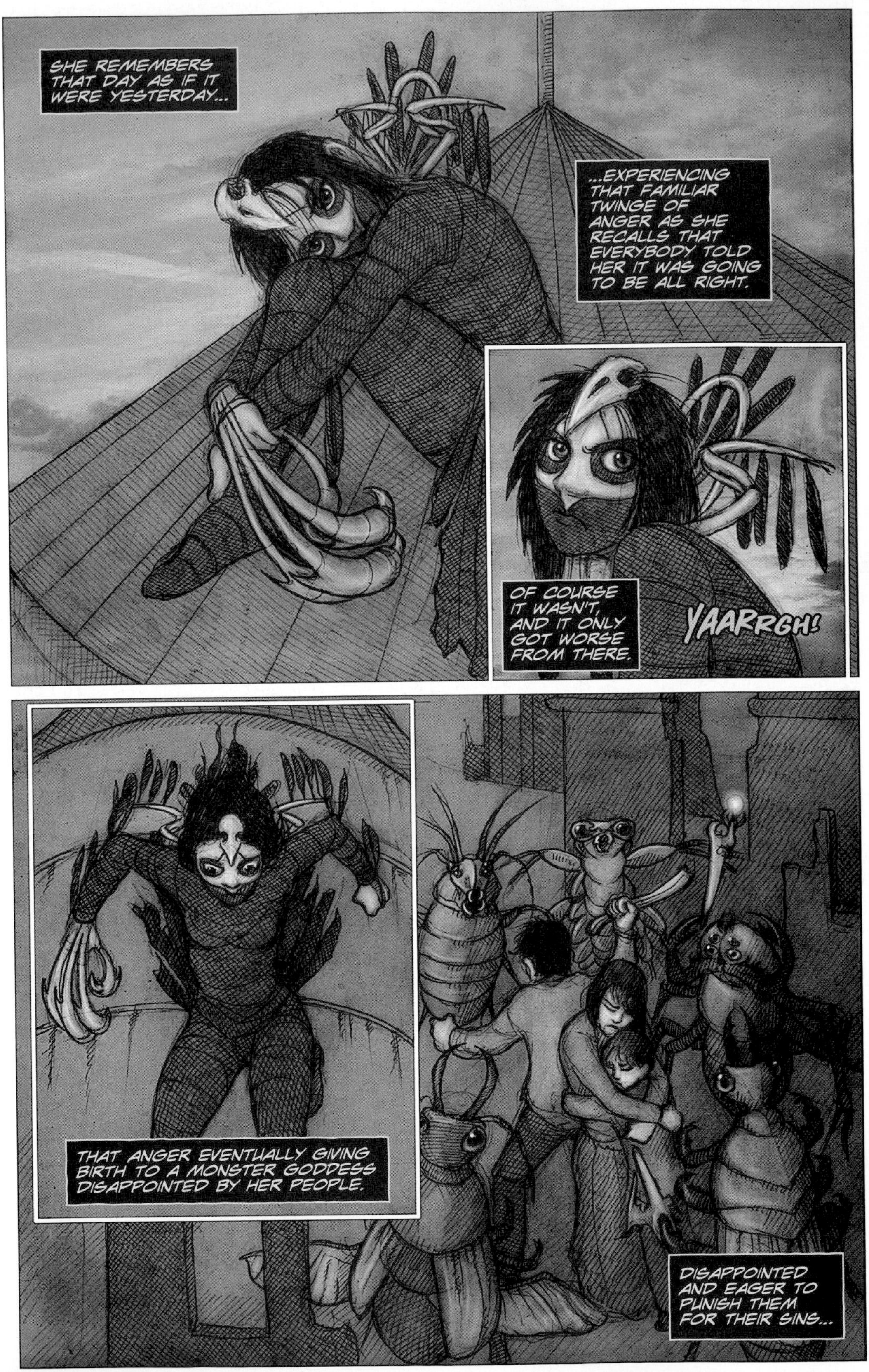
SHE REMEMBERS THAT DAY AS IF IT WERE YESTERDAY...
...EXPERIENCING THAT FAMILIAR TWINGE OF ANGER AS SHE RECALLS THAT EVERYBODY TOLD HER IT WAS GOING TO BE ALL RIGHT.
OF COURSE IT WASN'T, AND IT ONLY GOT WORSE FROM THERE.
YAARRGH!
THAT ANGER EVENTUALLY GIVING BIRTH TO A MONSTER GODDESS DISAPPOINTED BY HER PEOPLE.
DISAPPOINTED AND EAGER TO PUNISH THEM FOR THEIR SINS...

BUT ALSO TO INSPIRE HUMANITY...

GAAAAK!

...TO FIGHT BACK, AND RECLAIM WHAT HAD BEEN STOLEN FROM THEM.

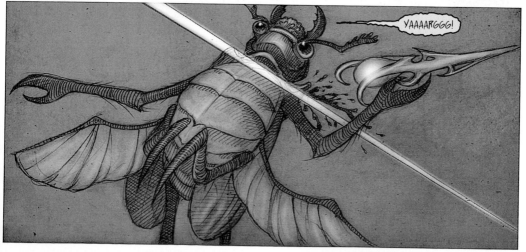

YAAAARGGG!

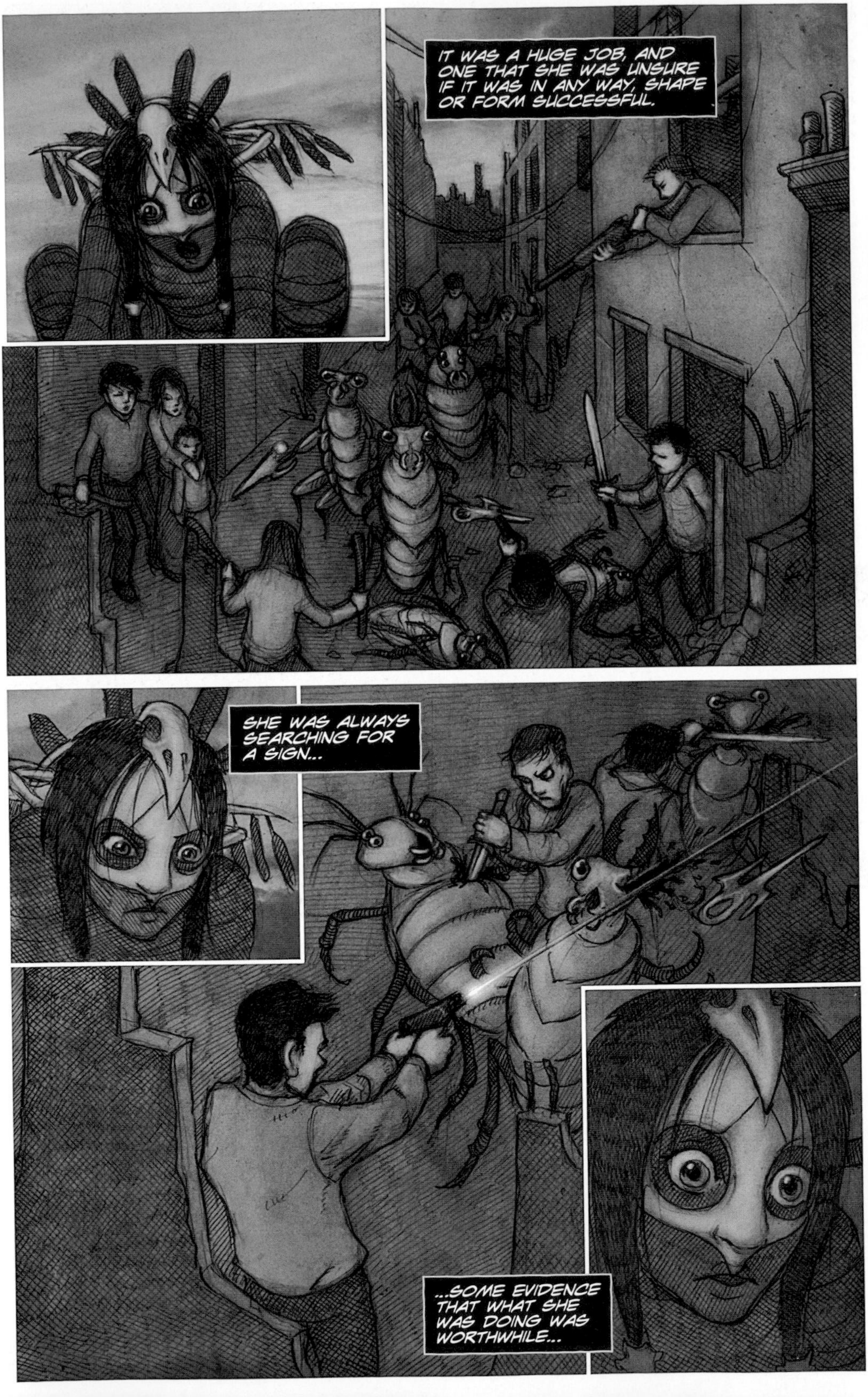
IT WAS A HUGE JOB, AND ONE THAT SHE WAS UNSURE IF IT WAS IN ANY WAY, SHAPE OR FORM SUCCESSFUL.
SHE WAS ALWAYS SEARCHING FOR A SIGN...
...SOME EVIDENCE THAT WHAT SHE WAS DOING WAS WORTHWHILE...

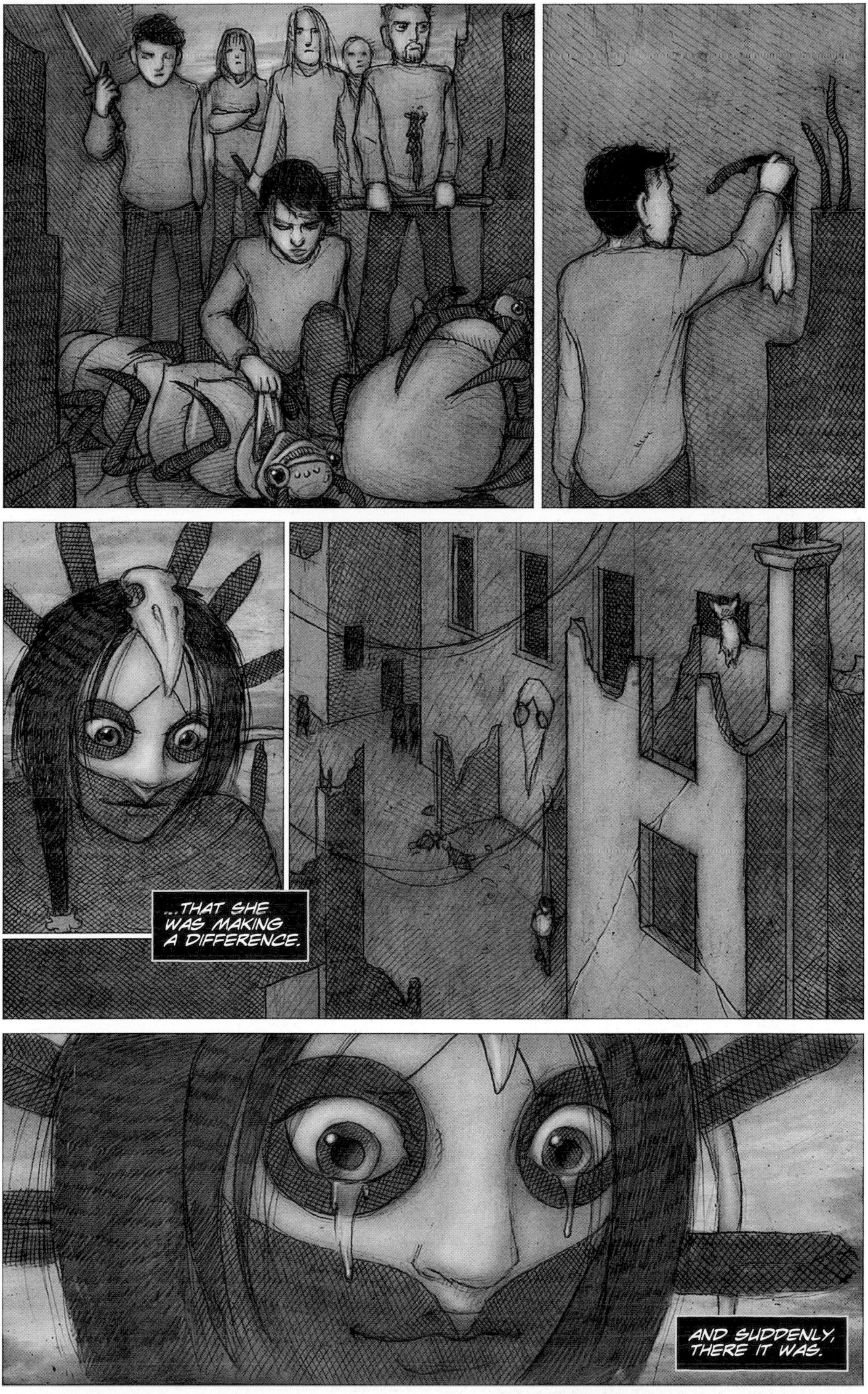
...THAT SHE WAS MAKING A DIFFERENCE.
AND SUDDENLY, THERE IT WAS.

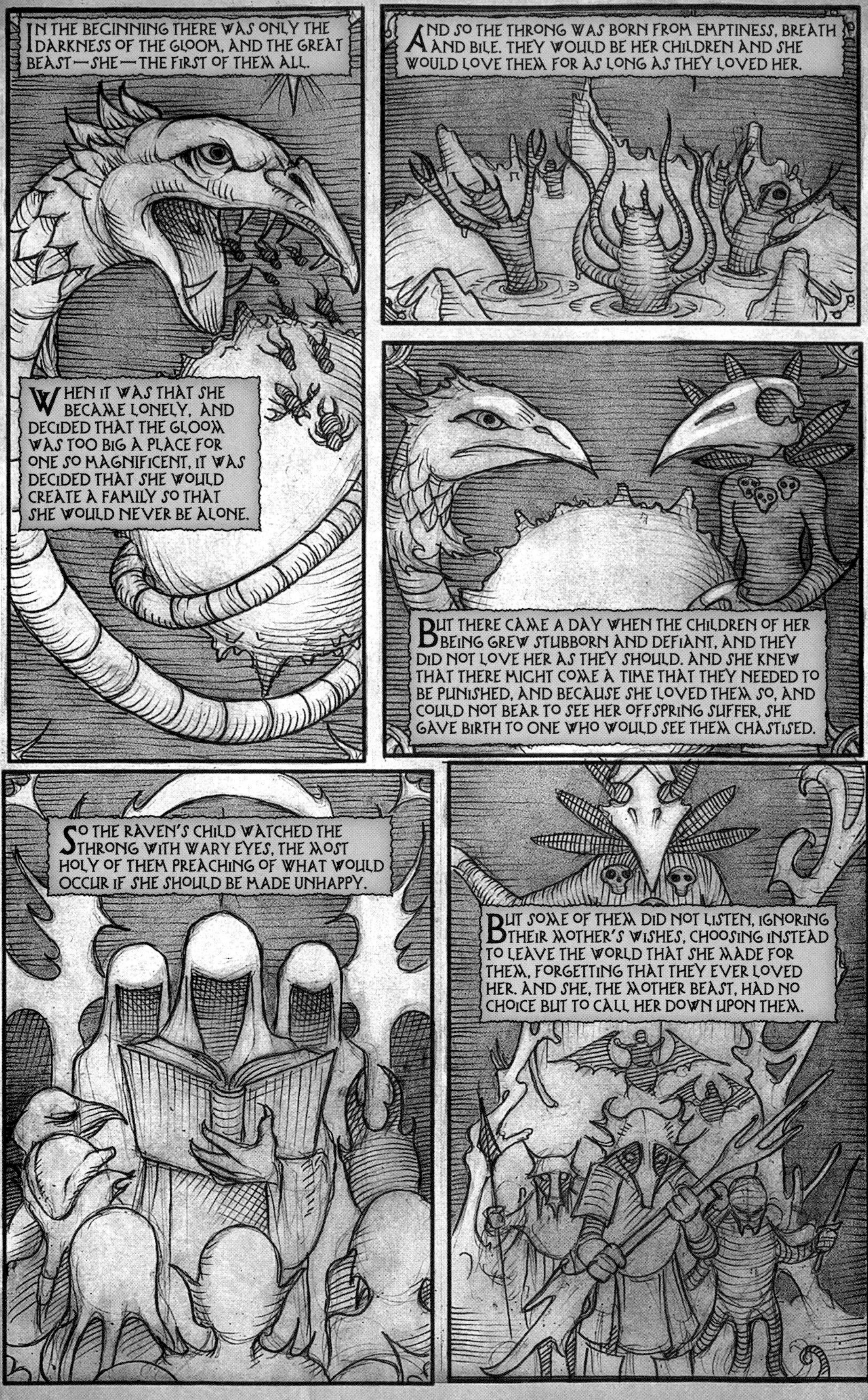
In the beginning there was only the darkness of the Gloom, and the great beast—she—the first of them all.
When it was that she became lonely, and decided that the Gloom was too big a place for one so magnificent, it was decided that she would create a family so that she would never be alone.
And so the throng was born from emptiness, breath and bile. They would be her children and she would love them for as long as they loved her.
But there came a day when the children of her being grew stubborn and defiant, and they did not love her as they should. And she knew that there might come a time that they needed to be punished, and because she loved them so, and could not bear to see her offspring suffer, she gave birth to one who would see them chastised.
So the Raven's Child watched the throng with wary eyes, the most holy of them preaching of what would occur if she should be made unhappy.
But some of them did not listen, ignoring their mother's wishes, choosing instead to leave the world that she made for them, forgetting that they ever loved her. And she, the Mother Beast, had no choice but to call her down upon them.

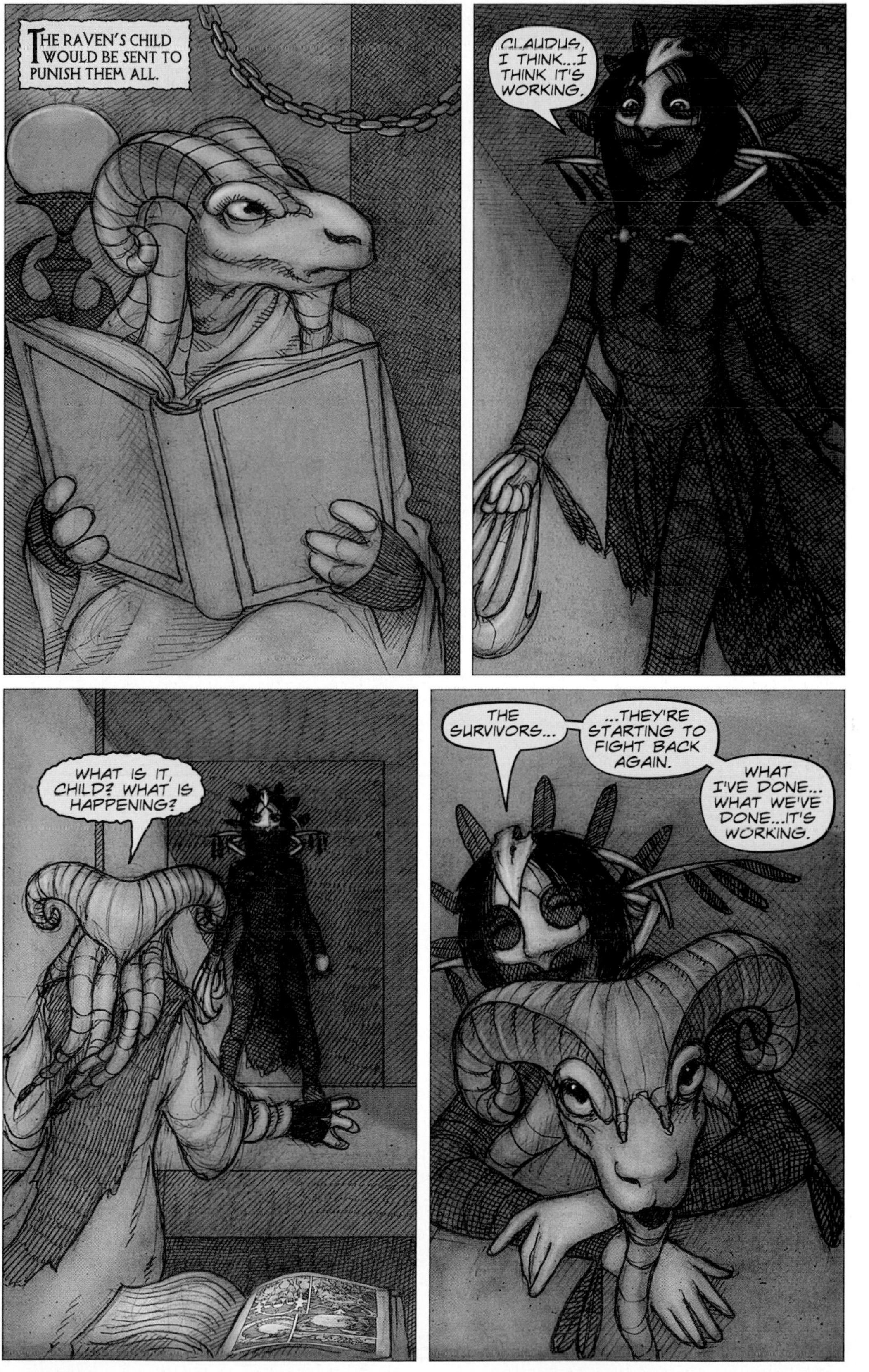
THE RAVEN'S CHILD WOULD BE SENT TO PUNISH THEM ALL.
CLAUDUS, I THINK...I THINK IT'S WORKING.
WHAT IS IT, CHILD? WHAT IS HAPPENING?
THE SURVIVORS...
...THEY'RE STARTING TO FIGHT BACK AGAIN.
WHAT I'VE DONE... WHAT WE'VE DONE...IT'S WORKING.

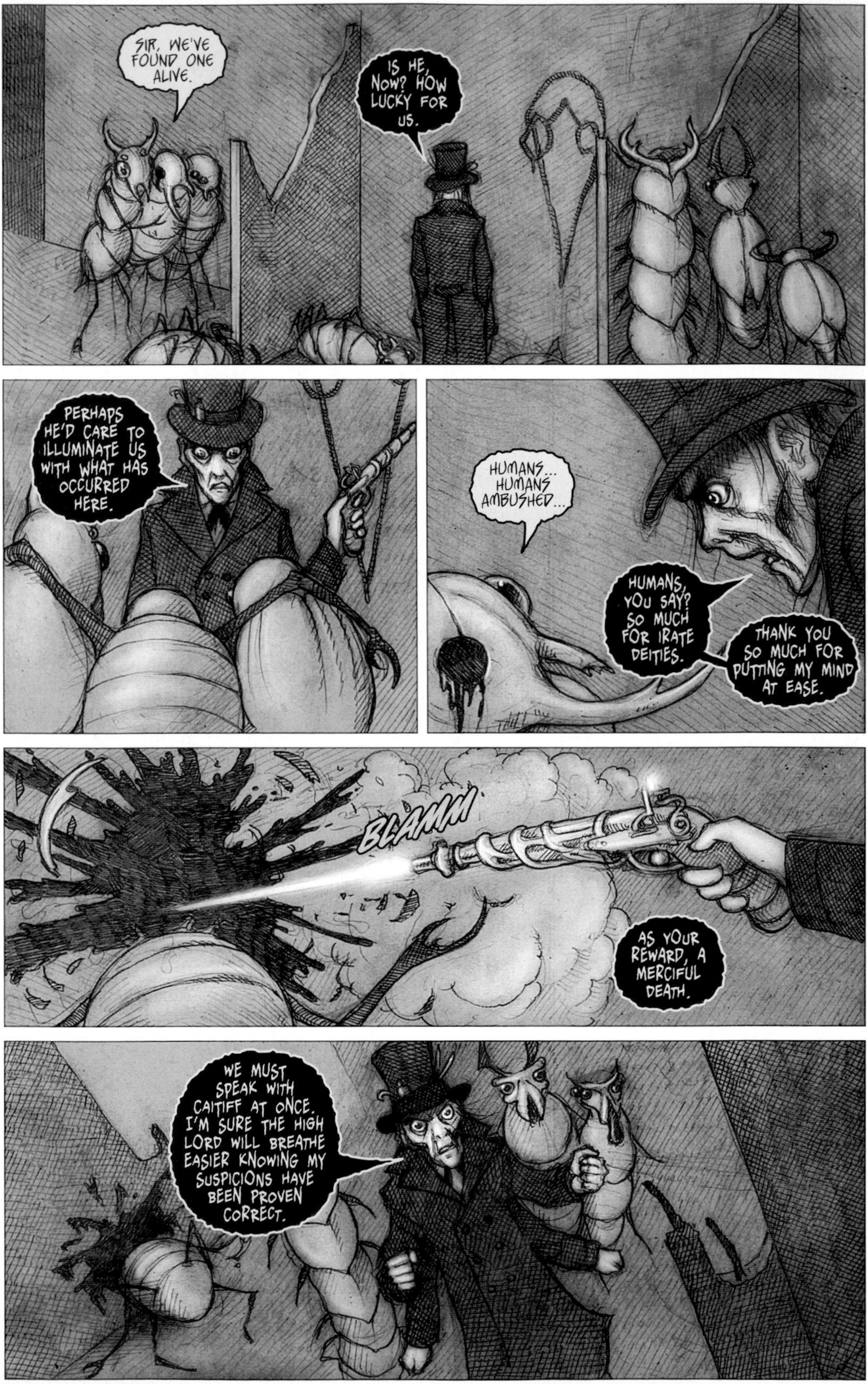
SIR, WE'VE FOUND ONE ALIVE.
IS HE, NOW? HOW LUCKY FOR US.
PERHAPS HE'D CARE TO ILLUMINATE US WITH WHAT HAS OCCURRED HERE.
HUMANS... HUMANS AMBUSHED...
HUMANS, YOU SAY? SO MUCH FOR IRATE DEITIES.
THANK YOU SO MUCH FOR PUTTING MY MIND AT EASE.
BLAMM
AS YOUR REWARD, A MERCIFUL DEATH.
WE MUST SPEAK WITH CAITIFF AT ONCE. I'M SURE THE HIGH LORD WILL BREATHE EASIER KNOWING MY SUSPICIONS HAVE BEEN PROVEN CORRECT.

And when the mother beast has had too much, the raven's child will descend upon them.

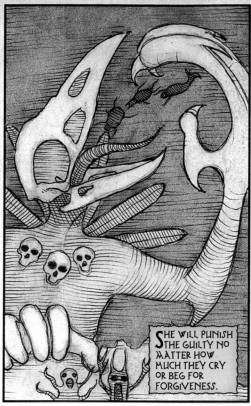

She will punish the guilty no matter how much they cry or beg for forgiveness.

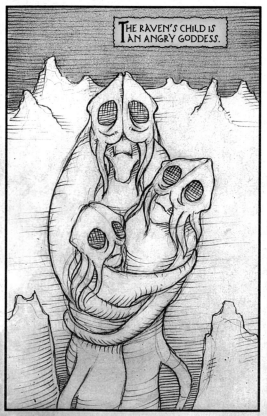

The raven's child is an angry goddess.

See that she is not angry at you.

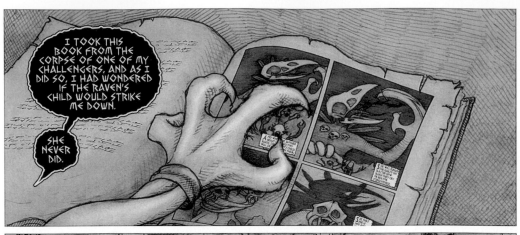

I TOOK THIS BOOK FROM THE CORPSE OF ONE OF MY CHALLENGERS, AND AS I DID SO, I HAD WONDERED IF THE RAVEN'S CHILD WOULD STRIKE ME DOWN.

SHE NEVER DID.

THAT'S BECAUSE SHE DOESN'T EXIST, AND WAS IN FACT A CREATION OF RELIGIOUS ZEALOTS ATTEMPTING TO AMASS POWER...

...AND HAS NOW BECOME SOME SORT OF SYMBOL OF ANARCHY FOR A DYING HUMANITY.

I'M FAR ANGRIER THAN I BELIEVED I'D BE... DISAPPOINTED, REALLY. I WAS RATHER LOOKING FORWARD TO BATTLING A GODDESS.

THEN LET ME DISTRACT YOU WITH SOMETHING THAT WILL HOPEFULLY CRUSH ANY HUMAN PLANS FOR FURTHER REVOLT.

WE NEED TO DRAW THE IMPOSTER OUT...TO EXTRACT HER FROM THE SHADOWS. THE HUMANS INSPIRED BY HER ACTIONS WILL BE THE LURE.

AN EXCELLENT PLAN, MAGISTRATE, AND WITH IT I WILL HAVE THE PLEASURE OF SHOWING THE BITCH THAT IT ISN'T WISE TO DISAPPOINT A THRONG HIGH LORD.

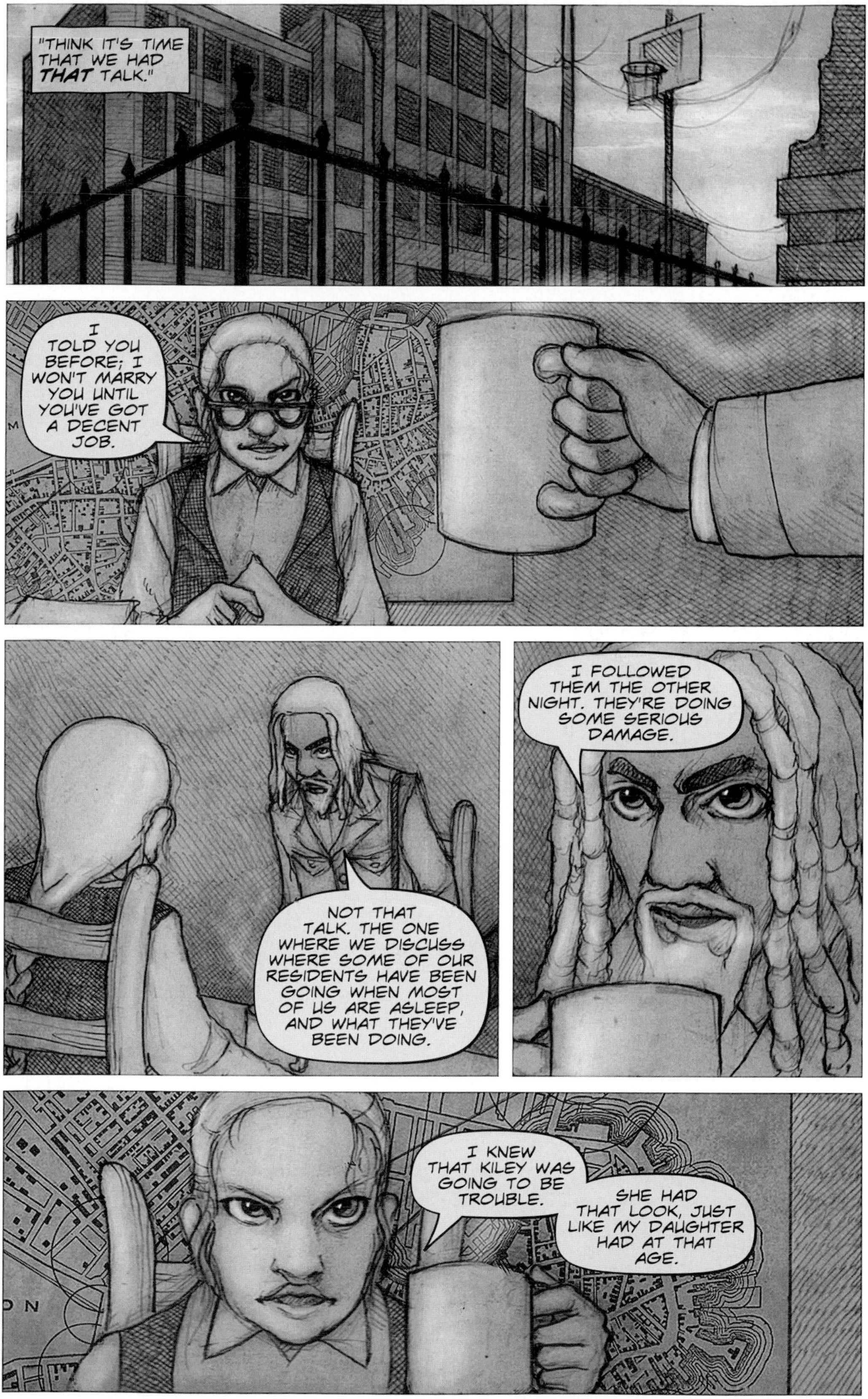
"THINK IT'S TIME THAT WE HAD **THAT** TALK."
I TOLD YOU BEFORE; I WON'T MARRY YOU UNTIL YOU'VE GOT A DECENT JOB.
NOT THAT TALK. THE ONE WHERE WE DISCUSS WHERE SOME OF OUR RESIDENTS HAVE BEEN GOING WHEN MOST OF US ARE ASLEEP, AND WHAT THEY'VE BEEN DOING.
I FOLLOWED THEM THE OTHER NIGHT. THEY'RE DOING SOME SERIOUS DAMAGE.
I KNEW THAT KILEY WAS GOING TO BE TROUBLE.
SHE HAD THAT LOOK, JUST LIKE MY DAUGHTER HAD AT THAT AGE.

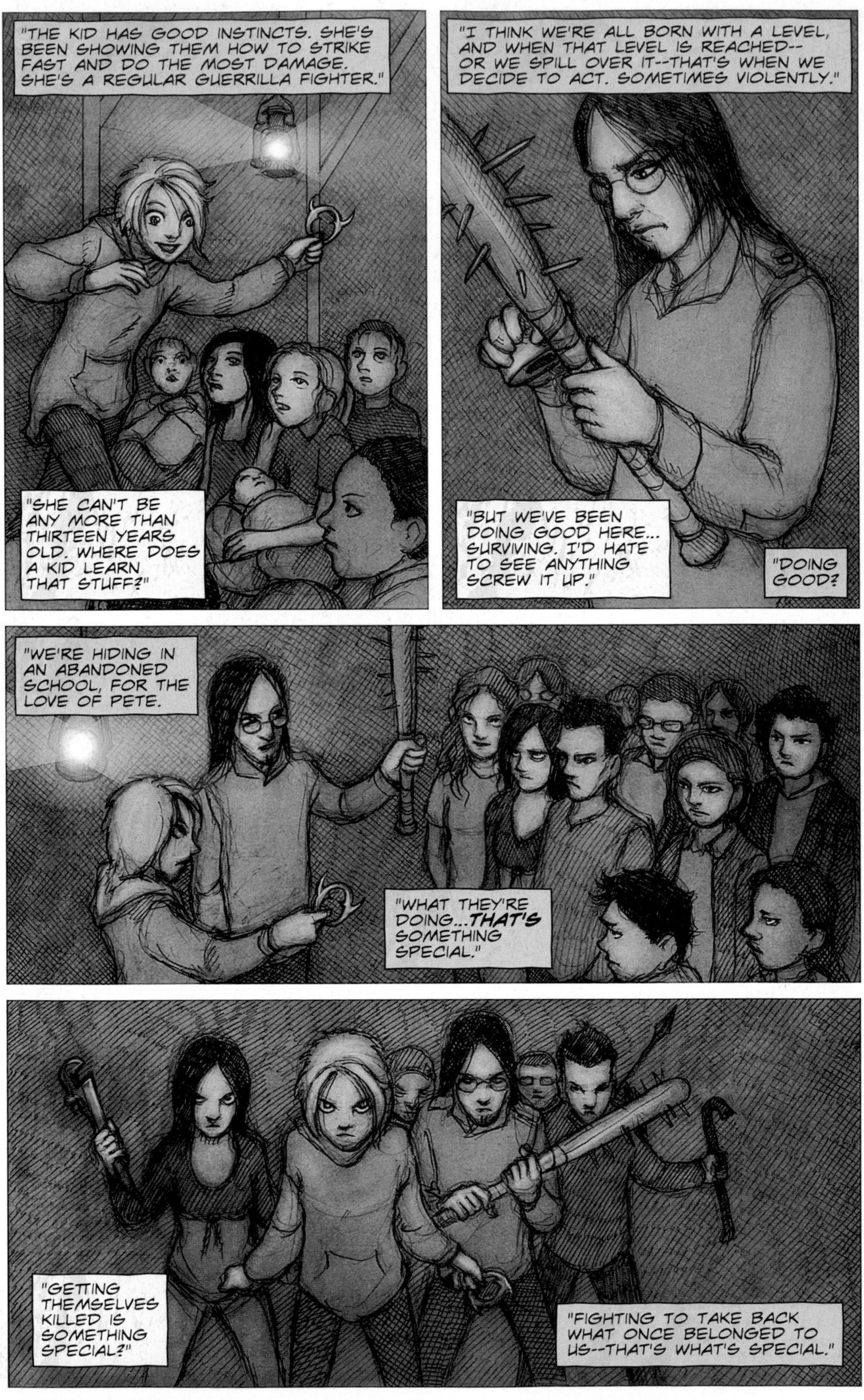
"THE KID HAS GOOD INSTINCTS. SHE'S BEEN SHOWING THEM HOW TO STRIKE FAST AND DO THE MOST DAMAGE. SHE'S A REGULAR GUERRILLA FIGHTER."
"SHE CAN'T BE ANY MORE THAN THIRTEEN YEARS OLD. WHERE DOES A KID LEARN THAT STUFF?"
"I THINK WE'RE ALL BORN WITH A LEVEL, AND WHEN THAT LEVEL IS REACHED-- OR WE SPILL OVER IT--THAT'S WHEN WE DECIDE TO ACT. SOMETIMES VIOLENTLY."
"BUT WE'VE BEEN DOING GOOD HERE... SURVIVING. I'D HATE TO SEE ANYTHING SCREW IT UP."
"DOING GOOD?
"WE'RE HIDING IN AN ABANDONED SCHOOL, FOR THE LOVE OF PETE.
"WHAT THEY'RE DOING...THAT'S SOMETHING SPECIAL."
"GETTING THEMSELVES KILLED IS SOMETHING SPECIAL?"
"FIGHTING TO TAKE BACK WHAT ONCE BELONGED TO US--THAT'S WHAT'S SPECIAL."

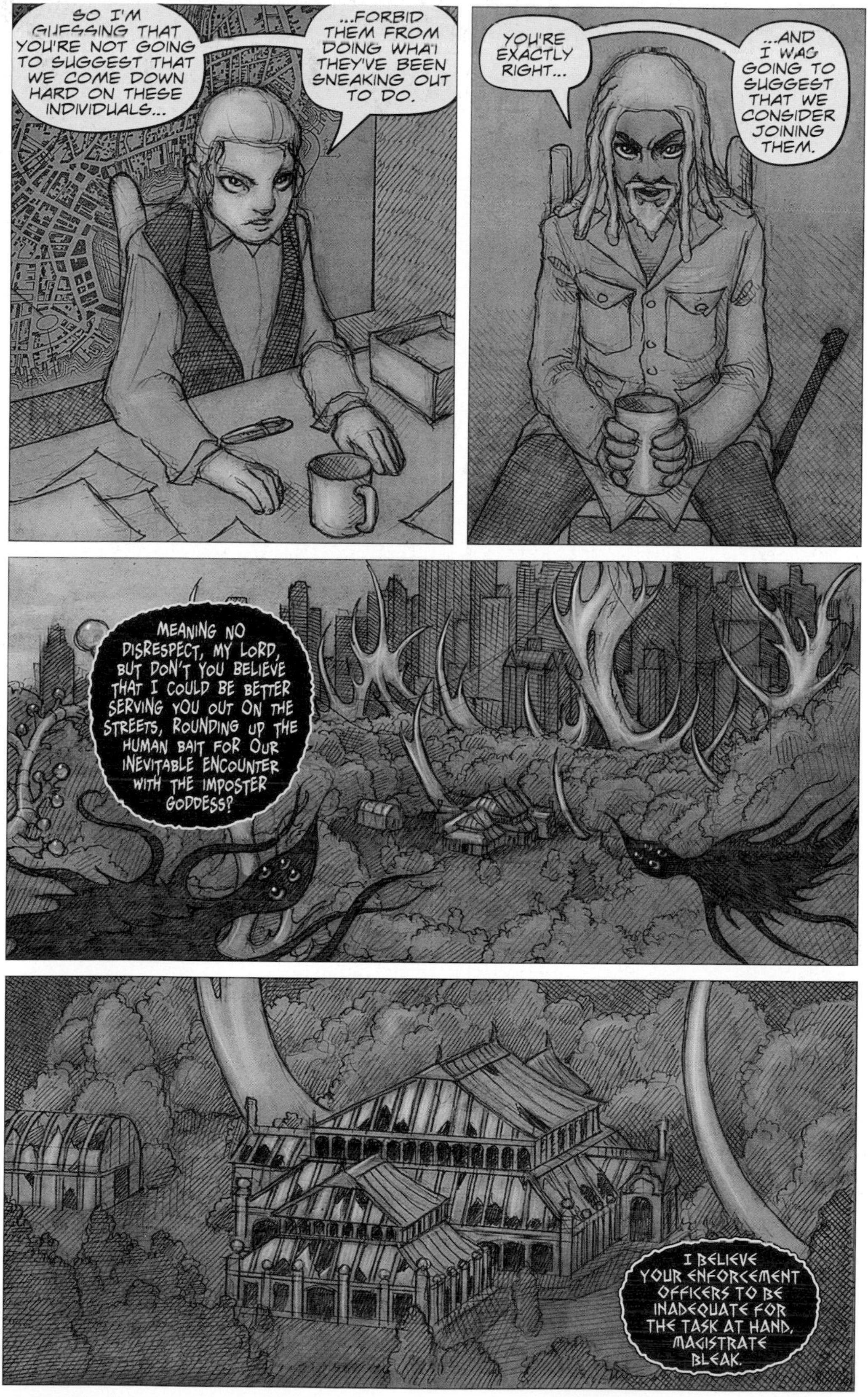
SO I'M GUESSING THAT YOU'RE NOT GOING TO SUGGEST THAT WE COME DOWN HARD ON THESE INDIVIDUALS...
...FORBID THEM FROM DOING WHAT THEY'VE BEEN SNEAKING OUT TO DO.
YOU'RE EXACTLY RIGHT...
...AND I WAS GOING TO SUGGEST THAT WE CONSIDER JOINING THEM.
MEANING NO DISRESPECT, MY LORD, BUT DON'T YOU BELIEVE THAT I COULD BE BETTER SERVING YOU OUT ON THE STREETS, ROUNDING UP THE HUMAN BAIT FOR OUR INEVITABLE ENCOUNTER WITH THE IMPOSTER GODDESS?
I BELIEVE YOUR ENFORCEMENT OFFICERS TO BE INADEQUATE FOR THE TASK AT HAND, MAGISTRATE BLEAK.

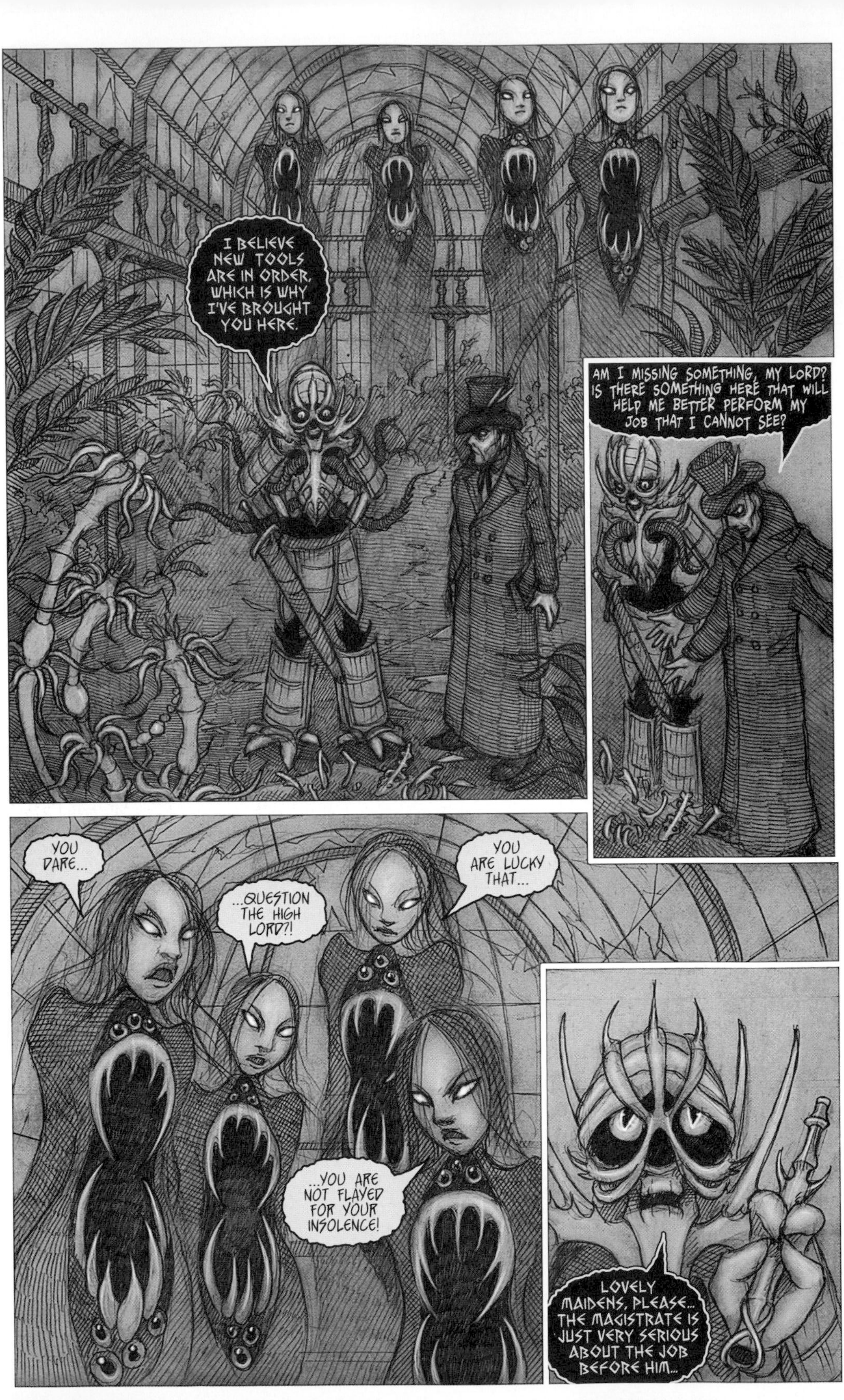
I BELIEVE NEW TOOLS ARE IN ORDER, WHICH IS WHY I'VE BROUGHT YOU HERE.
AM I MISSING SOMETHING, MY LORD? IS THERE SOMETHING HERE THAT WILL HELP ME BETTER PERFORM MY JOB THAT I CANNOT SEE?
YOU DARE...
...QUESTION THE HIGH LORD?!
YOU ARE LUCKY THAT...
...YOU ARE NOT FLAYED FOR YOUR INSOLENCE!
LOVELY MAIDENS, PLEASE... THE MAGISTRATE IS JUST VERY SERIOUS ABOUT THE JOB BEFORE HIM...

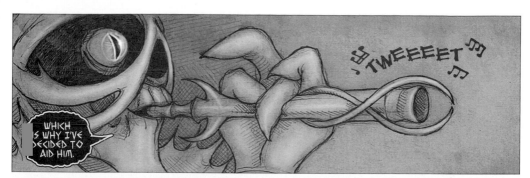

WHICH IS WHY I'VE DECIDED TO AID HIM.

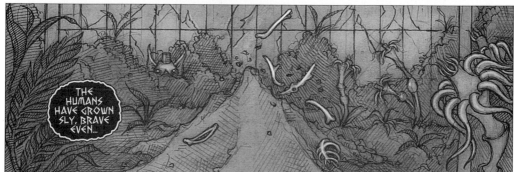

THE HUMANS HAVE GROWN SLY, BRAVE EVEN...

...A CHALLENGE FOR THE OFFICERS UNDER HIS COMMAND.

A SPECIAL KIND OF ENFORCER WILL BE NEEDED TO FULFILL THE JOB PROPERLY.

OH MY... WHAT ARE THEY?

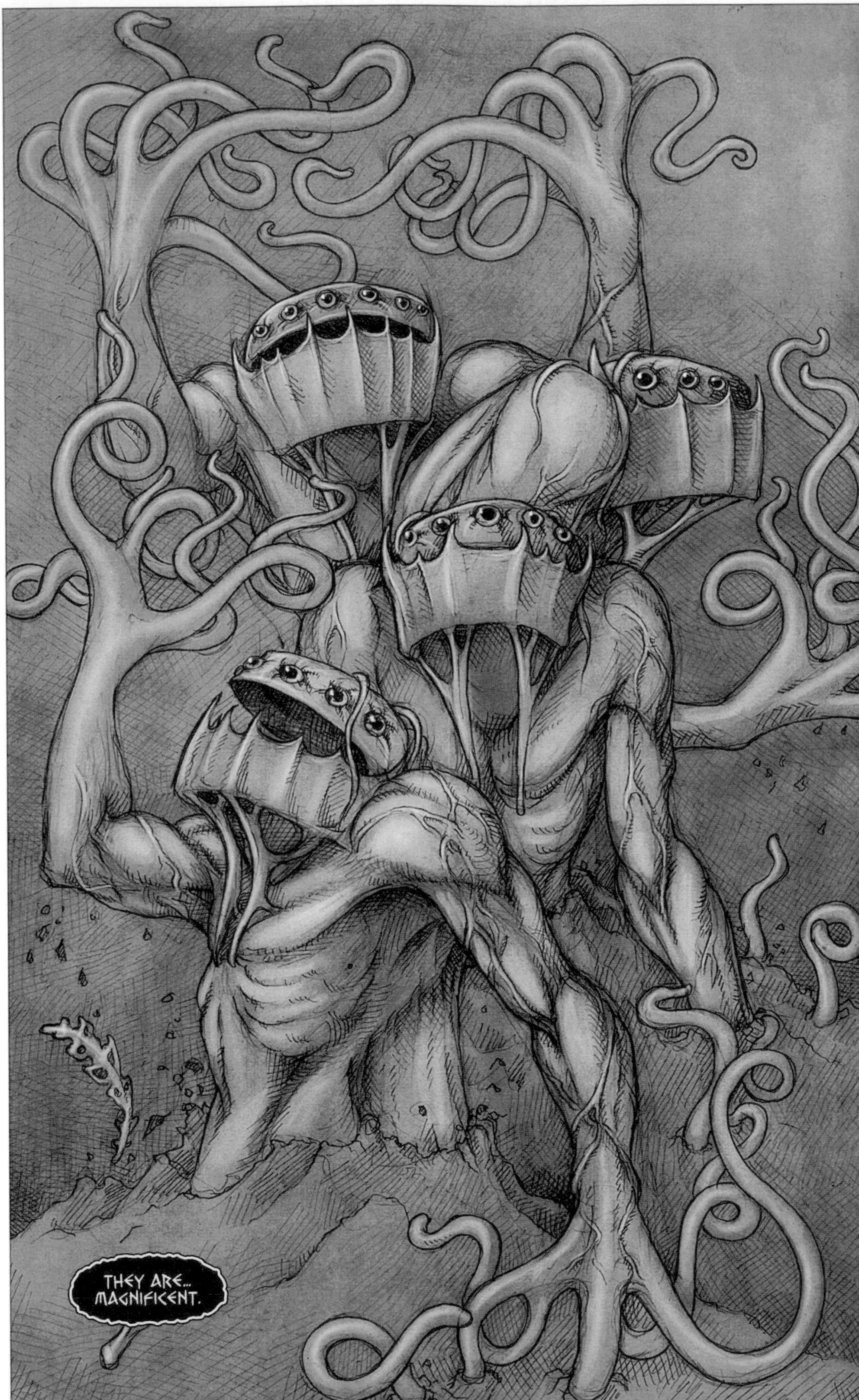
THEY ARE... MAGNIFICENT.

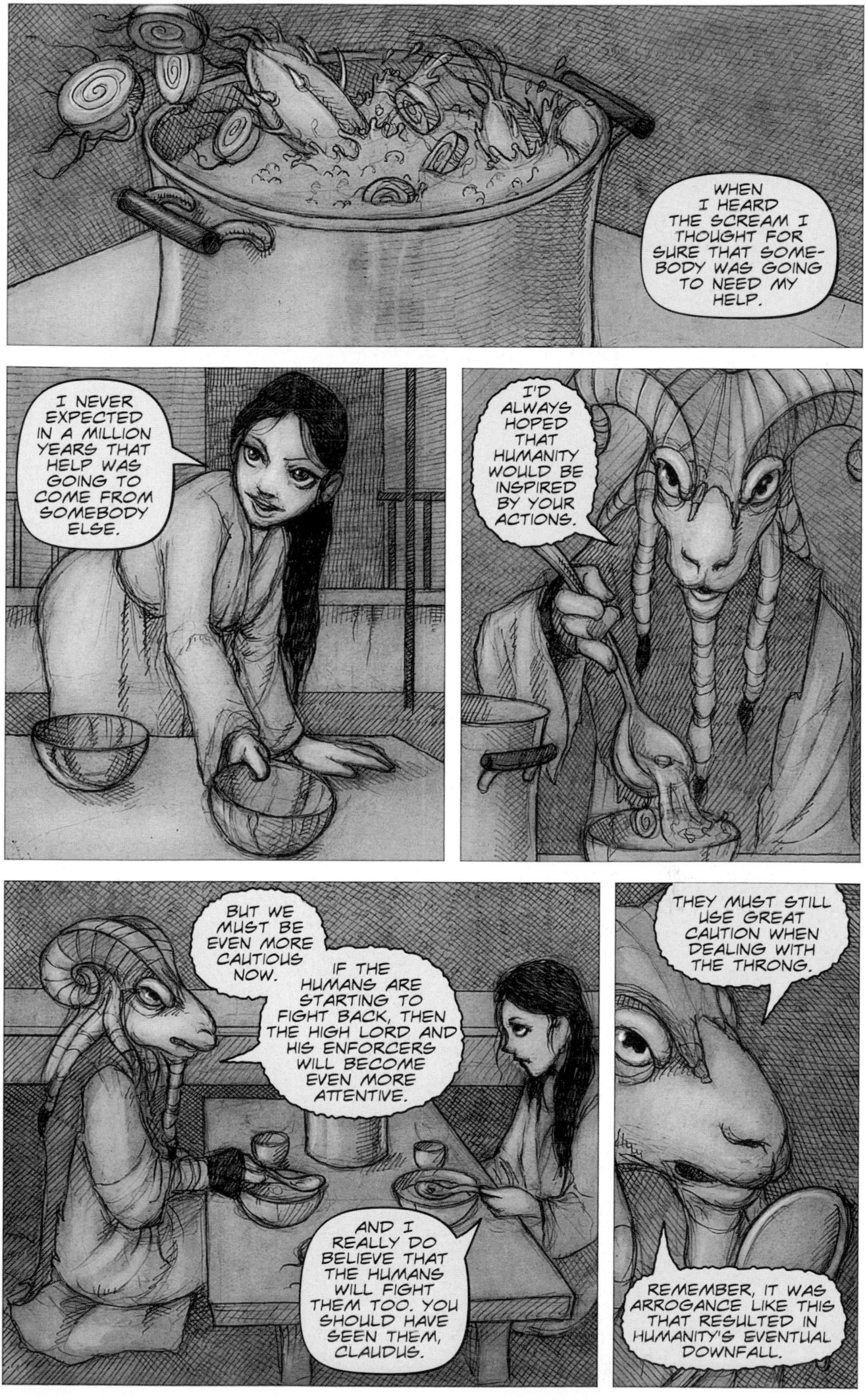
WHEN I HEARD THE SCREAM I THOUGHT FOR SURE THAT SOME-BODY WAS GOING TO NEED MY HELP.
I NEVER EXPECTED IN A MILLION YEARS THAT HELP WAS GOING TO COME FROM SOMEBODY ELSE.
I'D ALWAYS HOPED THAT HUMANITY WOULD BE INSPIRED BY YOUR ACTIONS.
BUT WE MUST BE EVEN MORE CAUTIOUS NOW.
IF THE HUMANS ARE STARTING TO FIGHT BACK, THEN THE HIGH LORD AND HIS ENFORCERS WILL BECOME EVEN MORE ATTENTIVE.
AND I REALLY DO BELIEVE THAT THE HUMANS WILL FIGHT THEM TOO. YOU SHOULD HAVE SEEN THEM, CLAUDUS.
THEY MUST STILL USE GREAT CAUTION WHEN DEALING WITH THE THRONG.
REMEMBER, IT WAS ARROGANCE LIKE THIS THAT RESULTED IN HUMANITY'S EVENTUAL DOWNFALL.

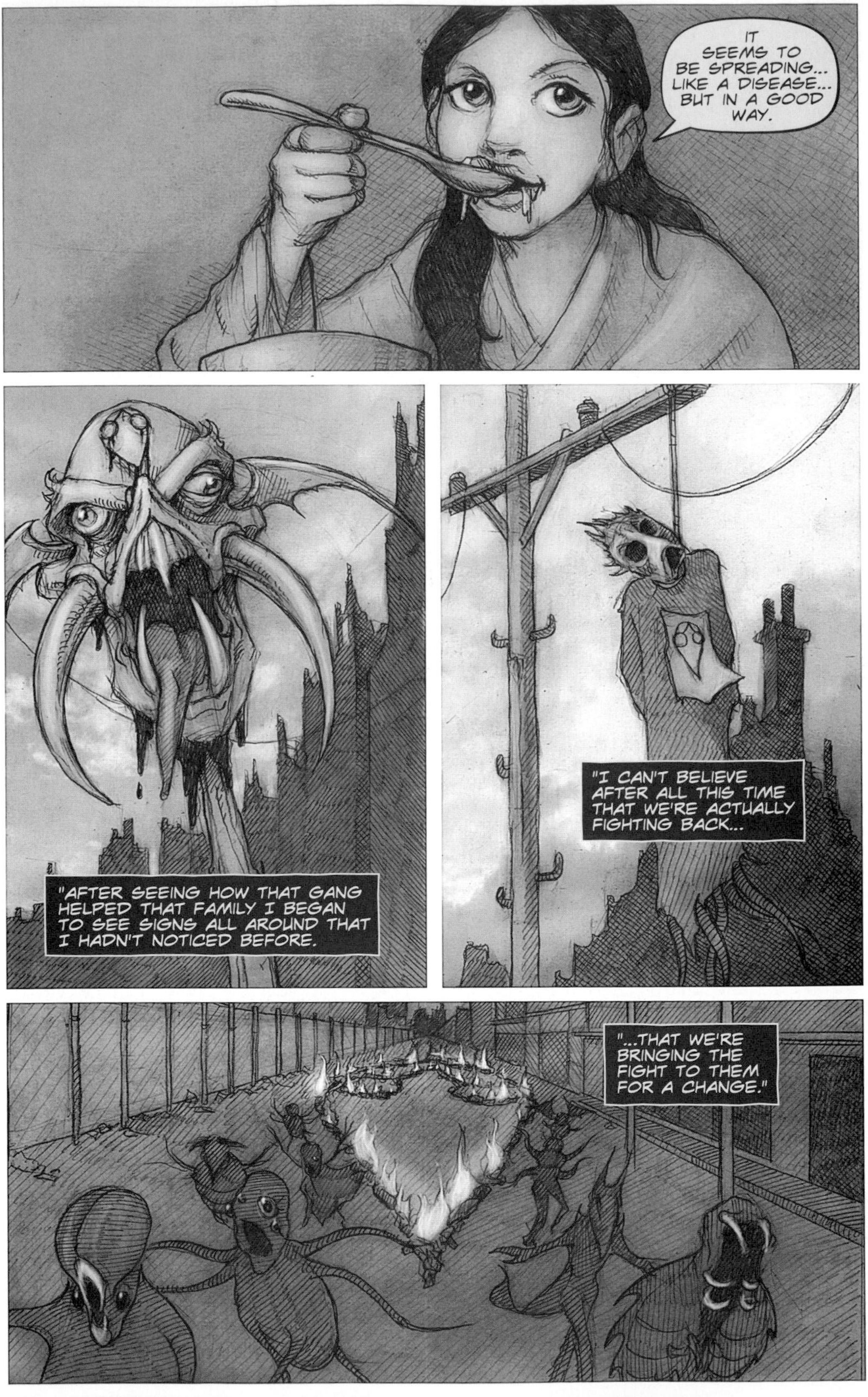
IT SEEMS TO BE SPREADING... LIKE A DISEASE... BUT IN A GOOD WAY.
"AFTER SEEING HOW THAT GANG HELPED THAT FAMILY I BEGAN TO SEE SIGNS ALL AROUND THAT I HADN'T NOTICED BEFORE.
"I CAN'T BELIEVE AFTER ALL THIS TIME THAT WE'RE ACTUALLY FIGHTING BACK...
"...THAT WE'RE BRINGING THE FIGHT TO THEM FOR A CHANGE."

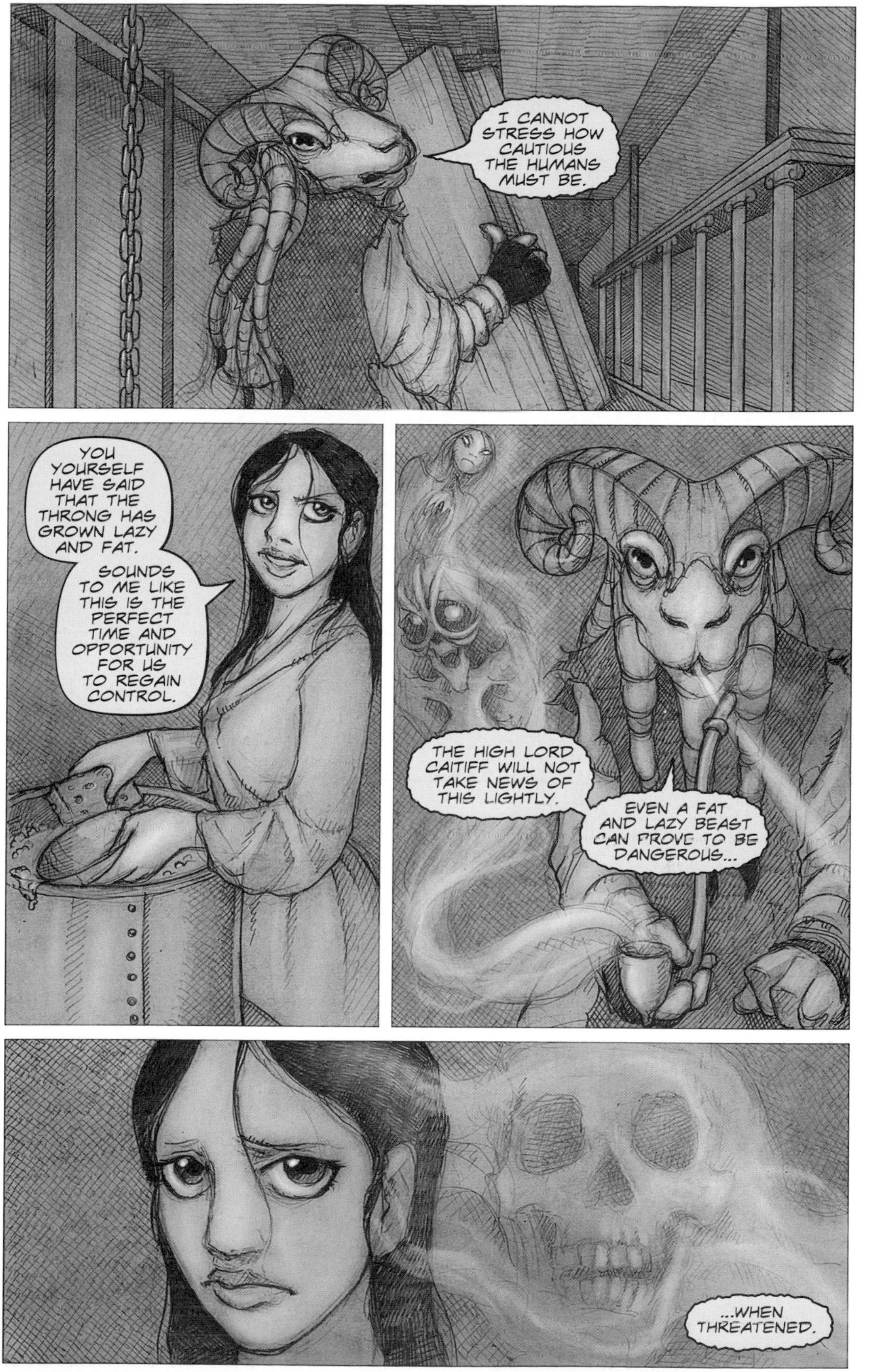
I CANNOT STRESS HOW CAUTIOUS THE HUMANS MUST BE.
YOU YOURSELF HAVE SAID THAT THE THRONG HAS GROWN LAZY AND FAT.
SOUNDS TO ME LIKE THIS IS THE PERFECT TIME AND OPPORTUNITY FOR US TO REGAIN CONTROL.
THE HIGH LORD CAITIFF WILL NOT TAKE NEWS OF THIS LIGHTLY.
EVEN A FAT AND LAZY BEAST CAN PROVE TO BE DANGEROUS...
...WHEN THREATENED.

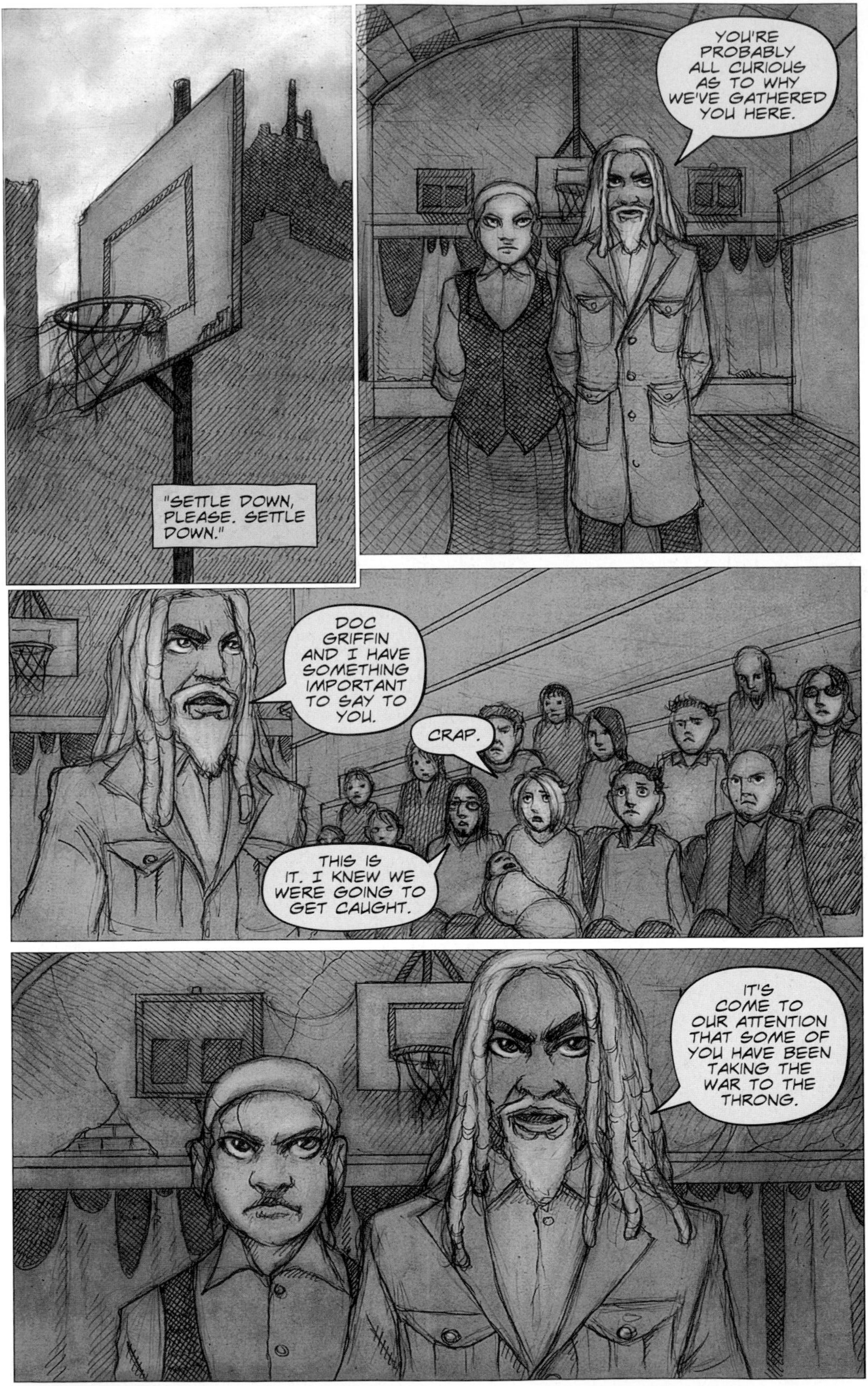
"SETTLE DOWN, PLEASE. SETTLE DOWN."
YOU'RE PROBABLY ALL CURIOUS AS TO WHY WE'VE GATHERED YOU HERE.
DOC GRIFFIN AND I HAVE SOMETHING IMPORTANT TO SAY TO YOU.
CRAP.
THIS IS IT. I KNEW WE WERE GOING TO GET CAUGHT.
IT'S COME TO OUR ATTENTION THAT SOME OF YOU HAVE BEEN TAKING THE WAR TO THE THRONG.

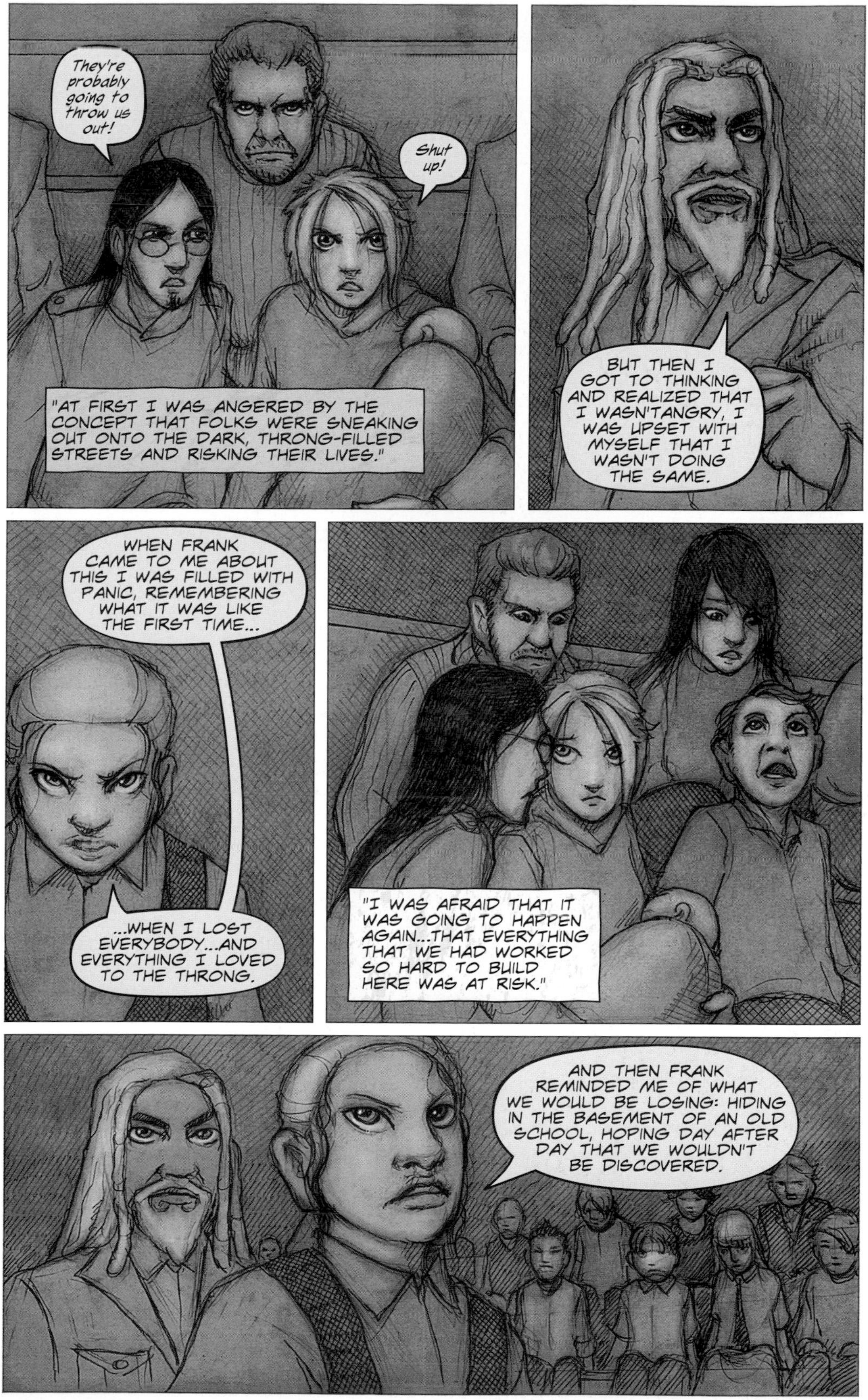
They're probably going to throw us out!
Shut up!
"AT FIRST I WAS ANGERED BY THE CONCEPT THAT FOLKS WERE SNEAKING OUT ONTO THE DARK, THRONG-FILLED STREETS AND RISKING THEIR LIVES."
BUT THEN I GOT TO THINKING AND REALIZED THAT I WASN'TANGRY, I WAS UPSET WITH MYSELF THAT I WASN'T DOING THE SAME.
WHEN FRANK CAME TO ME ABOUT THIS I WAS FILLED WITH PANIC, REMEMBERING WHAT IT WAS LIKE THE FIRST TIME...
...WHEN I LOST EVERYBODY...AND EVERYTHING I LOVED TO THE THRONG.
"I WAS AFRAID THAT IT WAS GOING TO HAPPEN AGAIN...THAT EVERYTHING THAT WE HAD WORKED SO HARD TO BUILD HERE WAS AT RISK."
AND THEN FRANK REMINDED ME OF WHAT WE WOULD BE LOSING: HIDING IN THE BASEMENT OF AN OLD SCHOOL, HOPING DAY AFTER DAY THAT WE WOULDN'T BE DISCOVERED.

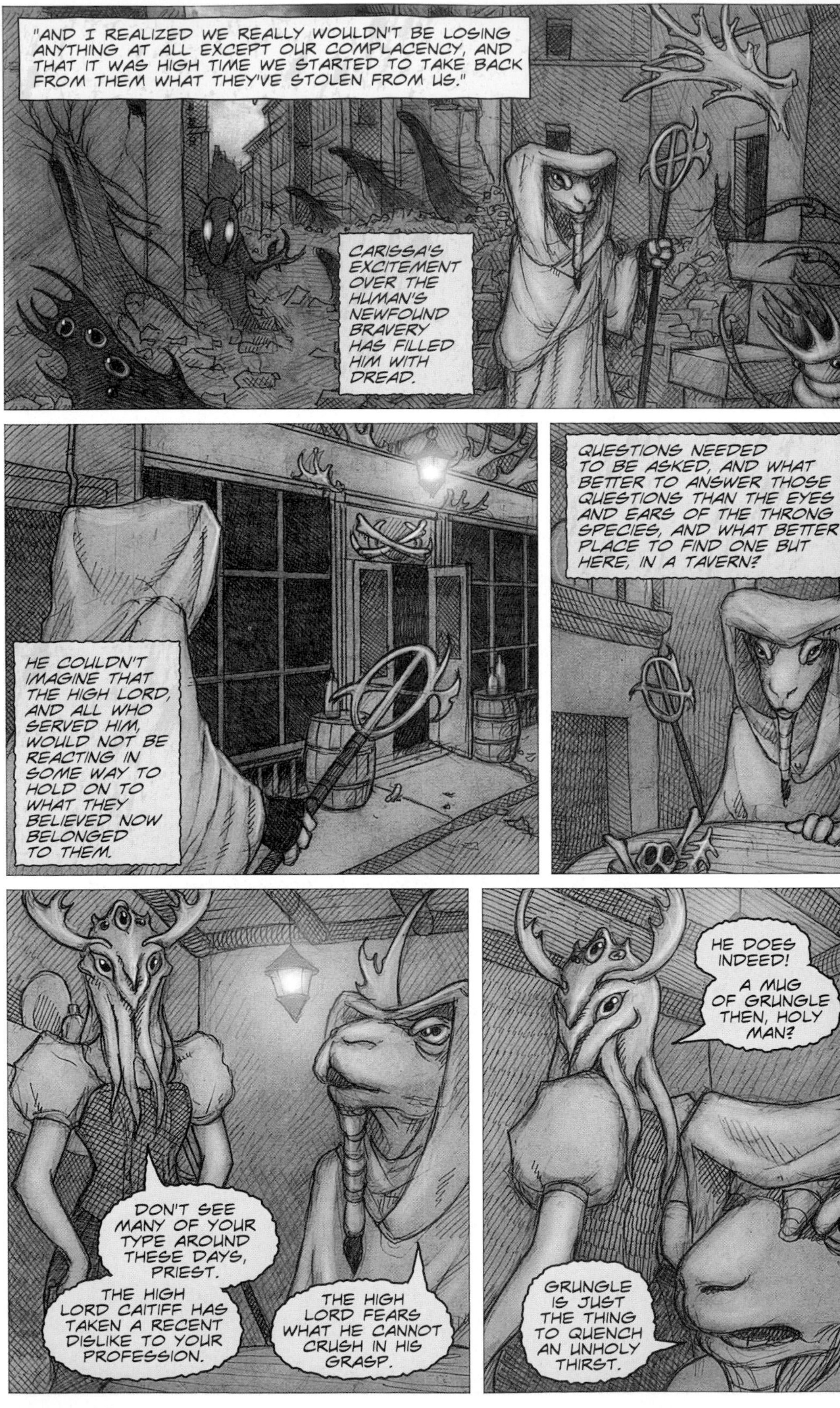
"AND I REALIZED WE REALLY WOULDN'T BE LOSING ANYTHING AT ALL EXCEPT OUR COMPLACENCY, AND THAT IT WAS HIGH TIME WE STARTED TO TAKE BACK FROM THEM WHAT THEY'VE STOLEN FROM US."
CARISSA'S EXCITEMENT OVER THE HUMAN'S NEWFOUND BRAVERY HAS FILLED HIM WITH DREAD.
HE COULDN'T IMAGINE THAT THE HIGH LORD, AND ALL WHO SERVED HIM, WOULD NOT BE REACTING IN SOME WAY TO HOLD ON TO WHAT THEY BELIEVED NOW BELONGED TO THEM.
QUESTIONS NEEDED TO BE ASKED, AND WHAT BETTER TO ANSWER THOSE QUESTIONS THAN THE EYES AND EARS OF THE THRONG SPECIES, AND WHAT BETTER PLACE TO FIND ONE BUT HERE, IN A TAVERN?
DON'T SEE MANY OF YOUR TYPE AROUND THESE DAYS, PRIEST.
THE HIGH LORD CAITIFF HAS TAKEN A RECENT DISLIKE TO YOUR PROFESSION.
THE HIGH LORD FEARS WHAT HE CANNOT CRUSH IN HIS GRASP.
HE DOES INDEED!
A MUG OF GRUNGLE THEN, HOLY MAN?
GRUNGLE IS JUST THE THING TO QUENCH AN UNHOLY THIRST.

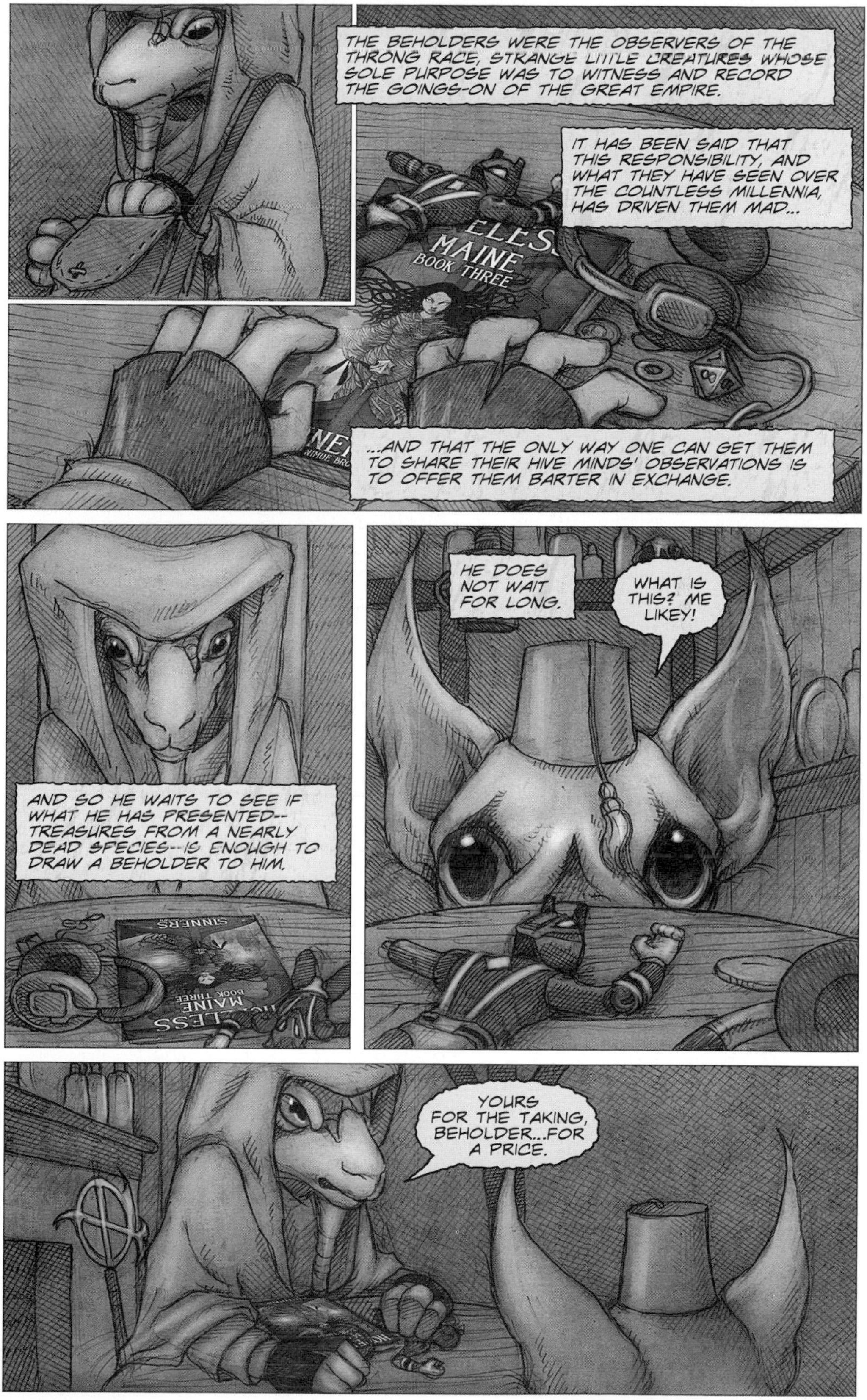
THE BEHOLDERS WERE THE OBSERVERS OF THE THRONG RACE, STRANGE LITTLE CREATURES WHOSE SOLE PURPOSE WAS TO WITNESS AND RECORD THE GOINGS-ON OF THE GREAT EMPIRE.
IT HAS BEEN SAID THAT THIS RESPONSIBILITY, AND WHAT THEY HAVE SEEN OVER THE COUNTLESS MILLENNIA, HAS DRIVEN THEM MAD...
MAINE
BOOK THREE
...AND THAT THE ONLY WAY ONE CAN GET THEM TO SHARE THEIR HIVE MINDS' OBSERVATIONS IS TO OFFER THEM BARTER IN EXCHANGE.
AND SO HE WAITS TO SEE IF WHAT HE HAS PRESENTED--TREASURES FROM A NEARLY DEAD SPECIES--IS ENOUGH TO DRAW A BEHOLDER TO HIM.
SINNERS
HE DOES NOT WAIT FOR LONG.
WHAT IS THIS? ME LIKEY!
YOURS FOR THE TAKING, BEHOLDER...FOR A PRICE.

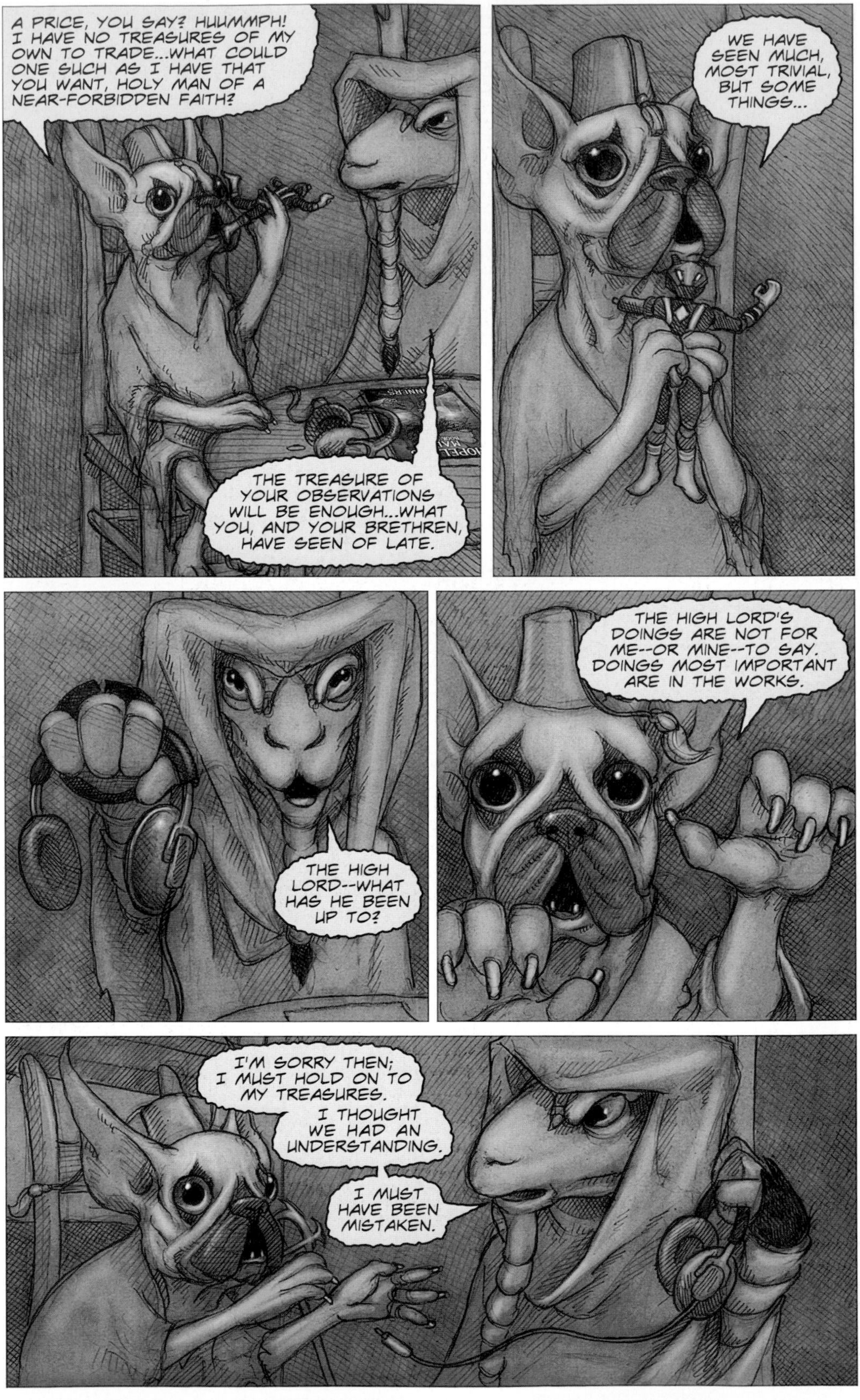
A PRICE, YOU SAY? HUUMMPH! I HAVE NO TREASURES OF MY OWN TO TRADE...WHAT COULD ONE SUCH AS I HAVE THAT YOU WANT, HOLY MAN OF A NEAR-FORBIDDEN FAITH?
THE TREASURE OF YOUR OBSERVATIONS WILL BE ENOUGH...WHAT YOU, AND YOUR BRETHREN, HAVE SEEN OF LATE.
WE HAVE SEEN MUCH, MOST TRIVIAL, BUT SOME THINGS...
THE HIGH LORD--WHAT HAS HE BEEN UP TO?
THE HIGH LORD'S DOINGS ARE NOT FOR ME--OR MINE--TO SAY. DOINGS MOST IMPORTANT ARE IN THE WORKS.
I'M SORRY THEN; I MUST HOLD ON TO MY TREASURES.
I THOUGHT WE HAD AN UNDERSTANDING.
I MUST HAVE BEEN MISTAKEN.

A TASTE OF WHAT HAS BEEN SEEN, THEN.

THE IMPOSTER GODDESS HAS GONE TOO FAR.

LORD CAITIFF HAS HAD ENOUGH OF HER ANTICS...

...AND THE HUMANS MUST BE MADE TO SUFFER.

ONE BY ONE THEY WILL BE PLUCKED FROM THEIR HIDEY-HOLES...

...AND THE FALSE GODDESS WILL LEARN WHAT IT IS LIKE TO ANGER A HIGH LORD.

OH YES.

YOU'VE EARNED YOUR TREASURES, BEHOLDER. HOARD THEM WELL. THERE ARE PLACES I MUST GO.

LOTS OF THINGS TO SEE SOON.

BIG CHANGES ARE COMING I BELIEVE.

MAYBE I'LL BE SEEING YOU AGAIN?

HE NEEDS TO GET BACK, TO WARN CARISSA THAT HIS SUSPICIONS WERE CORRECT. THEY'RE GOING TO NEED TO BE VERY CAREFUL AS THEY CONTINUE WITH THEIR MISSION.

WHERE'S THE PRIEST?

GONE. THINGS TO DO I THINK. IMPORTANT THINGS.

HOPELESS MAINE
BOOK THREE

SINNER

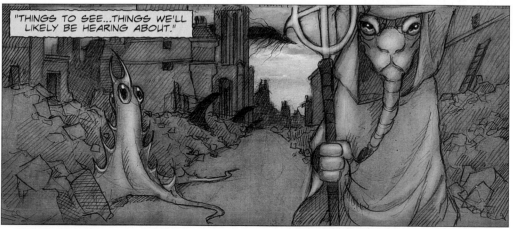

"THINGS TO SEE...THINGS WE'LL LIKELY BE HEARING ABOUT."

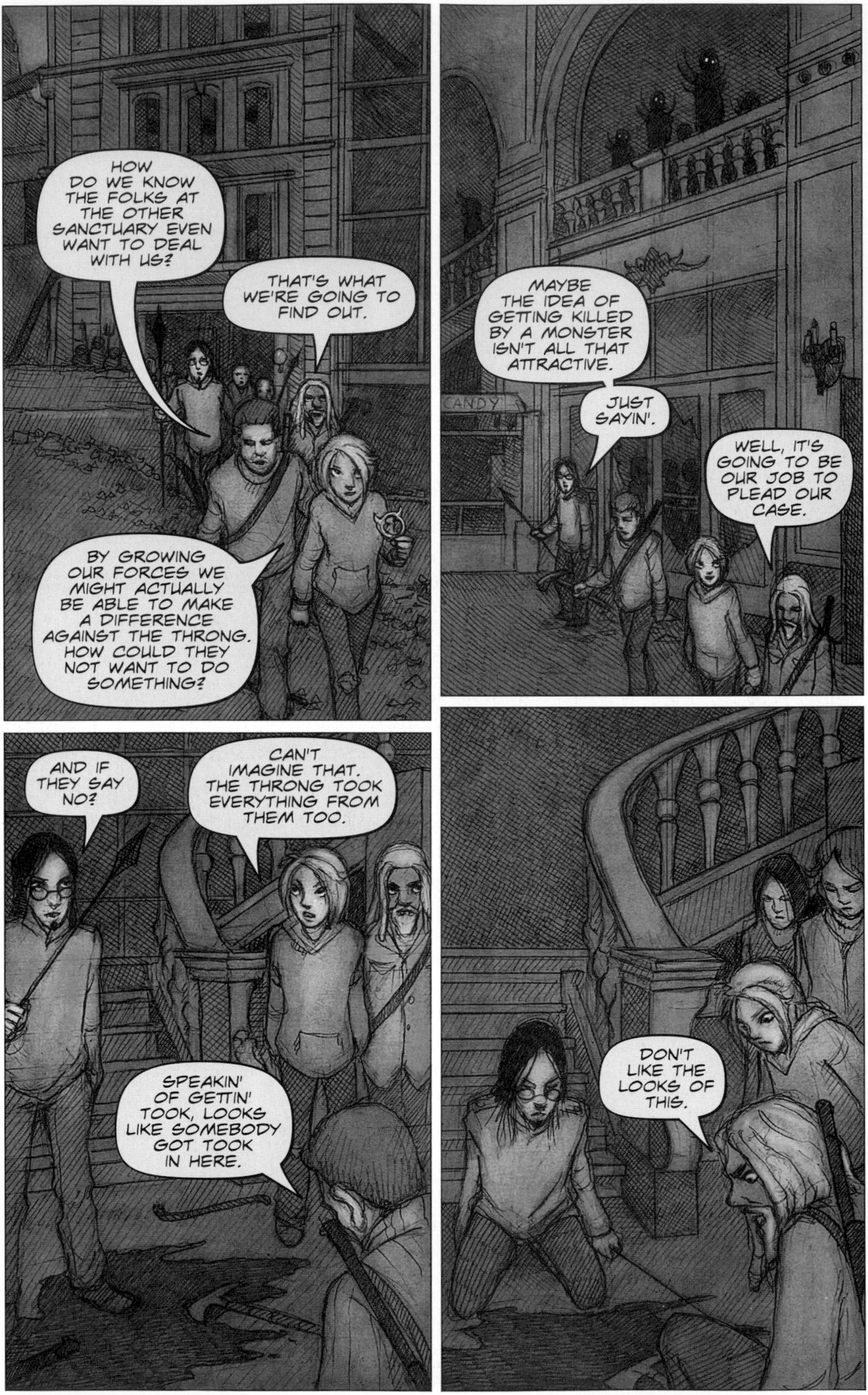
HOW DO WE KNOW THE FOLKS AT THE OTHER SANCTUARY EVEN WANT TO DEAL WITH US?
THAT'S WHAT WE'RE GOING TO FIND OUT.
BY GROWING OUR FORCES WE MIGHT ACTUALLY BE ABLE TO MAKE A DIFFERENCE AGAINST THE THRONG. HOW COULD THEY NOT WANT TO DO SOMETHING?
MAYBE THE IDEA OF GETTING KILLED BY A MONSTER ISN'T ALL THAT ATTRACTIVE.
JUST SAYIN'.
CANDY
WELL, IT'S GOING TO BE OUR JOB TO PLEAD OUR CASE.
AND IF THEY SAY NO?
CAN'T IMAGINE THAT. THE THRONG TOOK EVERYTHING FROM THEM TOO.
SPEAKIN' OF GETTIN' TOOK, LOOKS LIKE SOMEBODY GOT TOOK IN HERE.
DON'T LIKE THE LOOKS OF THIS.

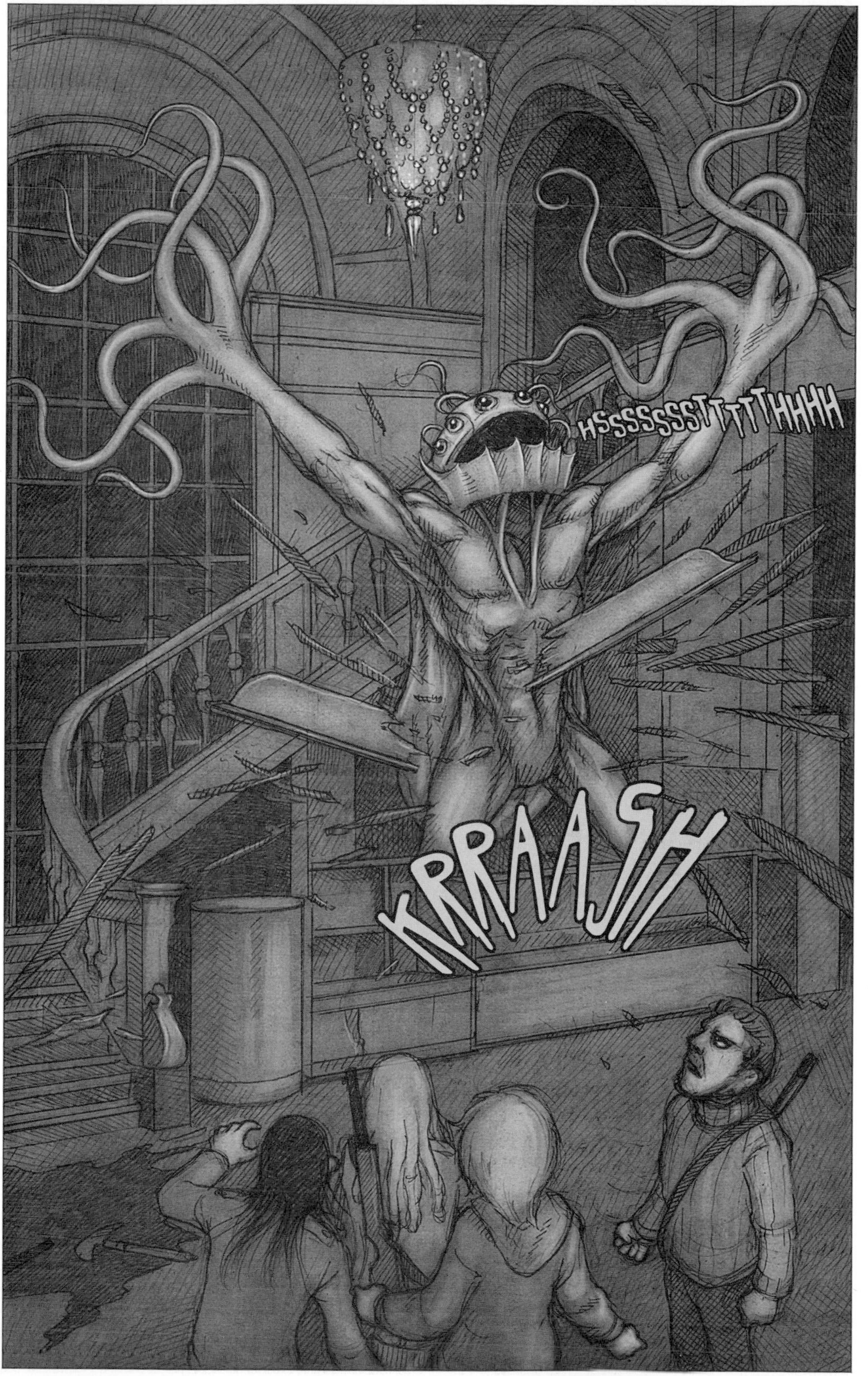
HSSSSSSSTTTTTHHHH
KRRAASH

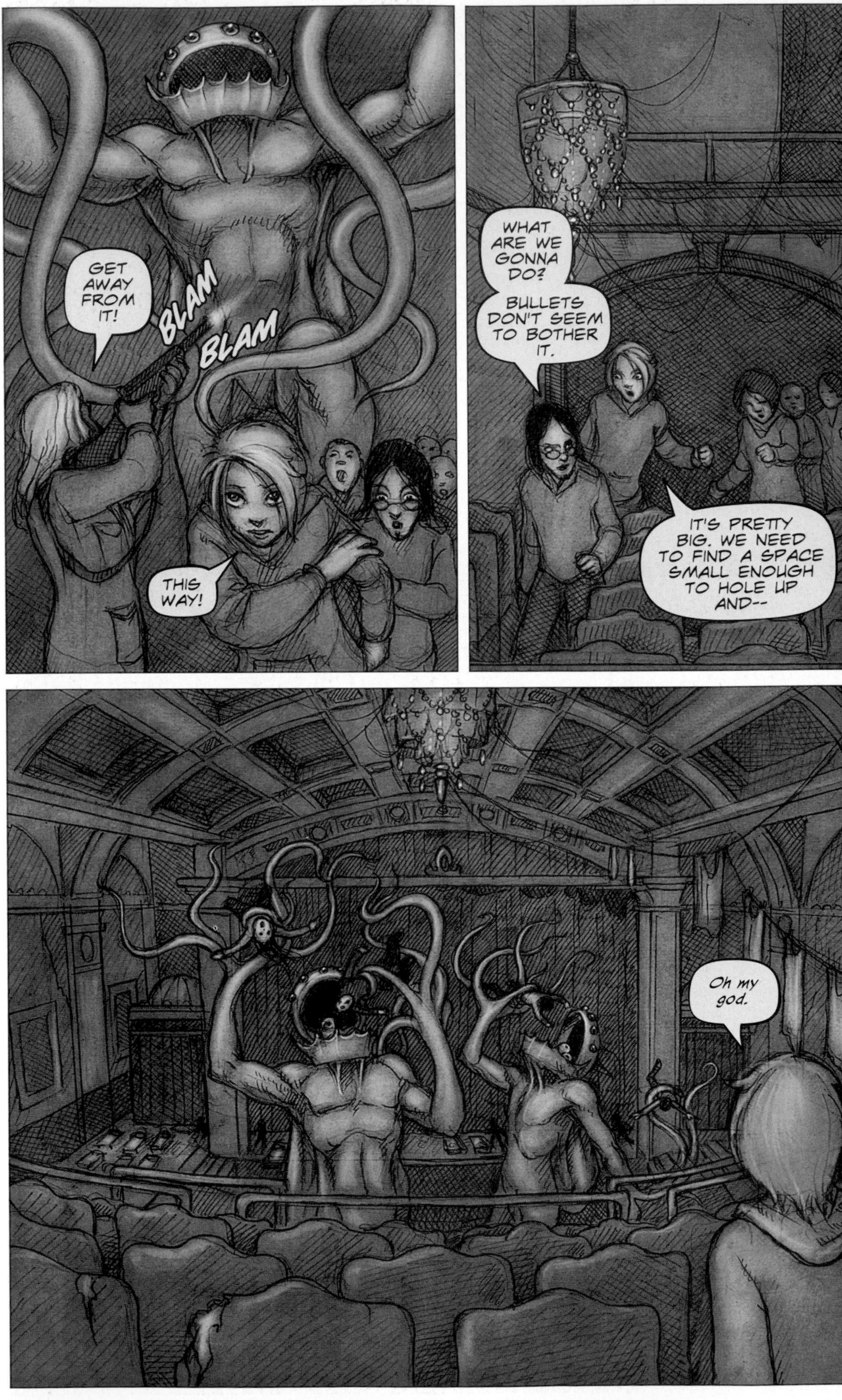
GET AWAY FROM IT!
BLAM
BLAM
THIS WAY!
WHAT ARE WE GONNA DO?
BULLETS DON'T SEEM TO BOTHER IT.
IT'S PRETTY BIG. WE NEED TO FIND A SPACE SMALL ENOUGH TO HOLE UP AND--
Oh my god.

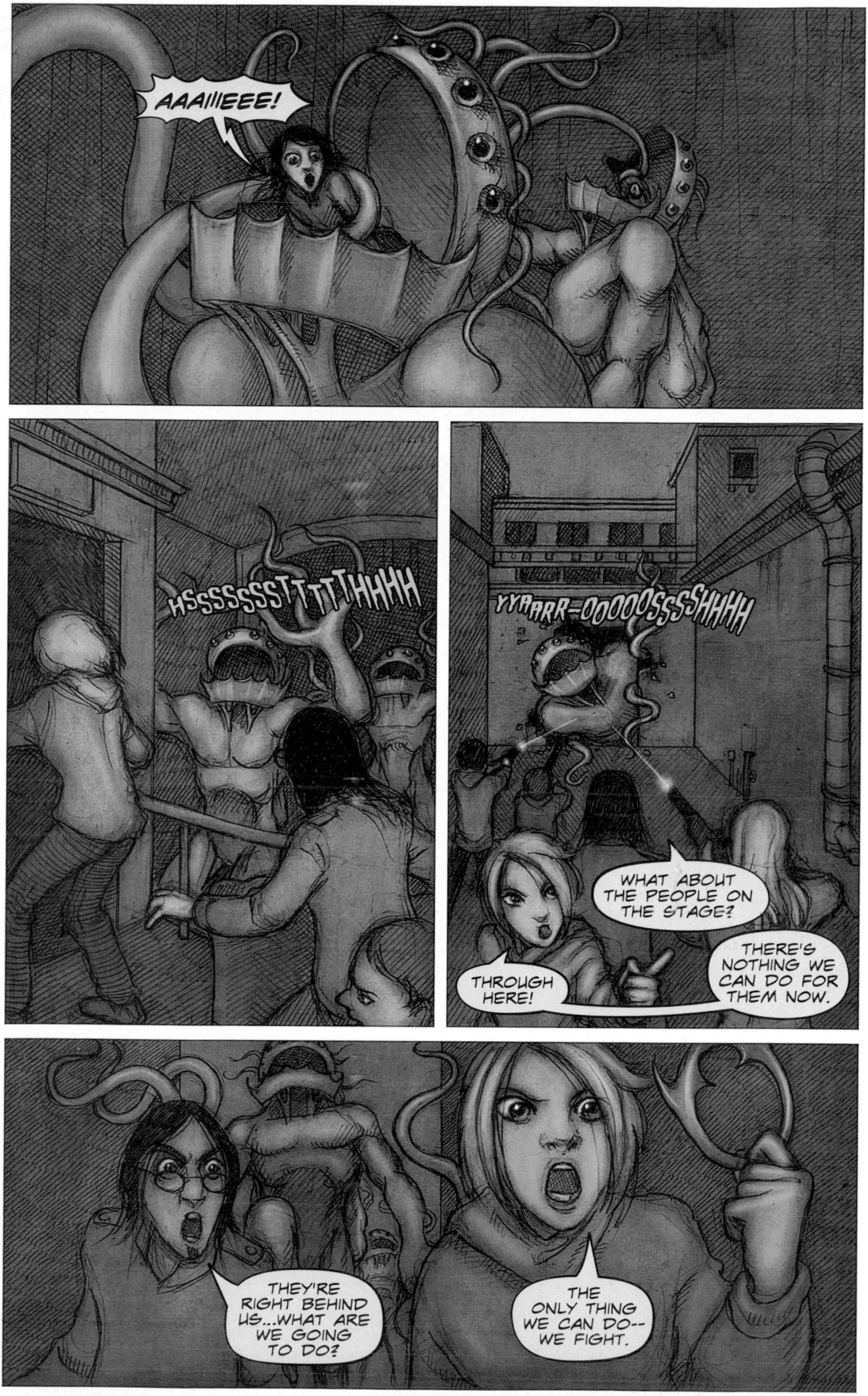
AAAIIIEEE!
HSSSSSSSTTTTTHHHH
YYRARR-OOOOOSSSSHHHH
THROUGH HERE!
WHAT ABOUT THE PEOPLE ON THE STAGE?
THERE'S NOTHING WE CAN DO FOR THEM NOW.
THEY'RE RIGHT BEHIND US...WHAT ARE WE GOING TO DO?
THE ONLY THING WE CAN DO-- WE FIGHT.

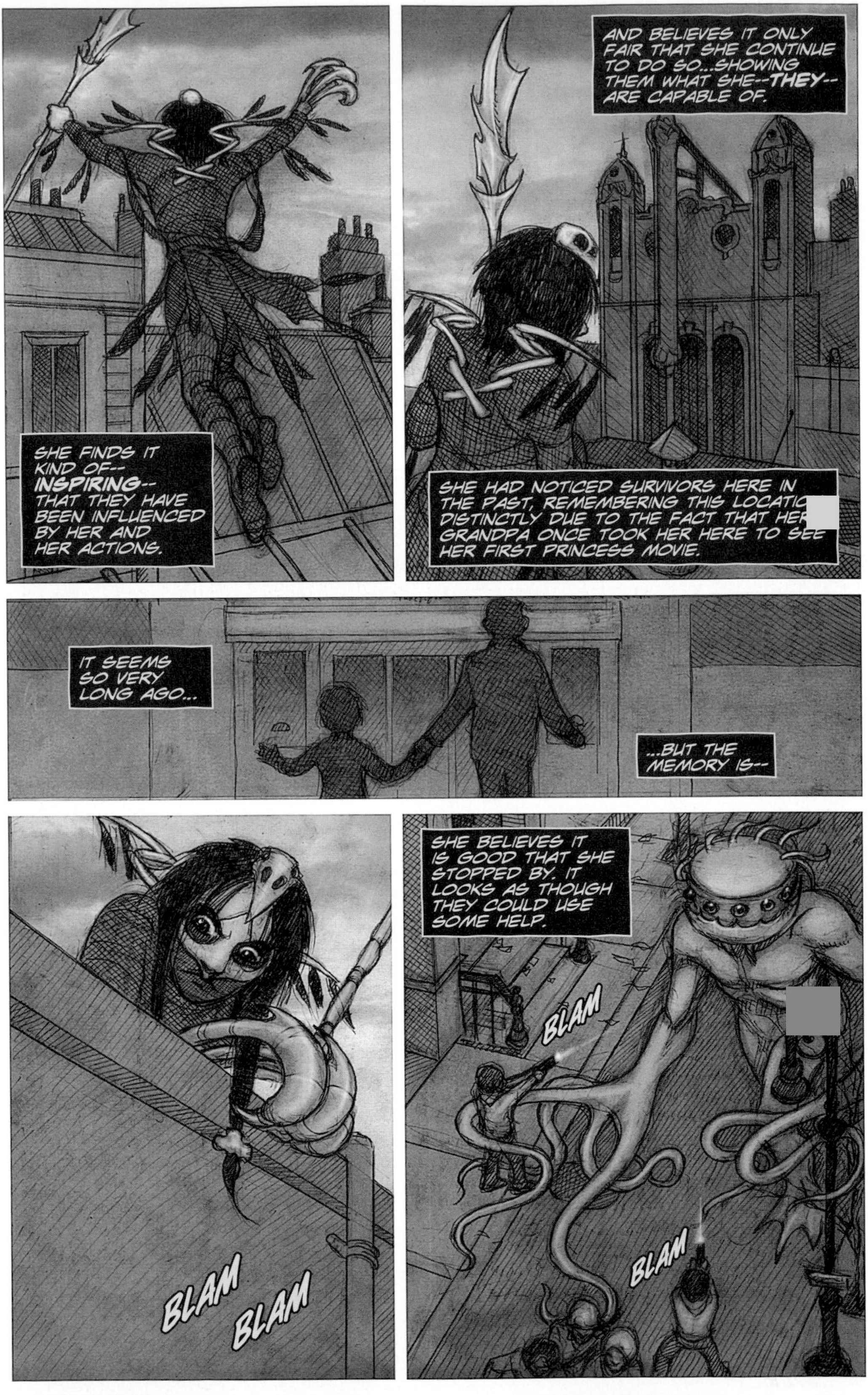
SHE FINDS IT KIND OF-- **INSPIRING**-- THAT THEY HAVE BEEN INFLUENCED BY HER AND HER ACTIONS.
AND BELIEVES IT ONLY FAIR THAT SHE CONTINUE TO DO SO...SHOWING THEM WHAT SHE--**THEY**-- ARE CAPABLE OF.
SHE HAD NOTICED SURVIVORS HERE IN THE PAST, REMEMBERING THIS LOCATIO DISTINCTLY DUE TO THE FACT THAT HER GRANDPA ONCE TOOK HER HERE TO SEE HER FIRST PRINCESS MOVIE.
IT SEEMS SO VERY LONG AGO...
...BUT THE MEMORY IS--
BLAM
BLAM
SHE BELIEVES IT IS GOOD THAT SHE STOPPED BY. IT LOOKS AS THOUGH THEY COULD USE SOME HELP.
BLAM
BLAM

SHOW THEM WE'RE NOT AFRAID!

IT AMAZES HER HOW FAST IT CAN ALL GO WRONG.

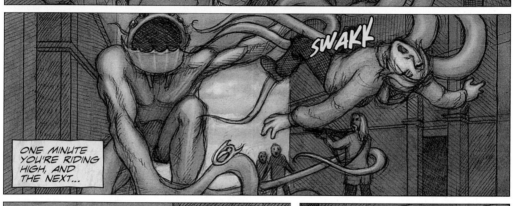

SWAKK

ONE MINUTE YOU'RE RIDING HIGH, AND THE NEXT...

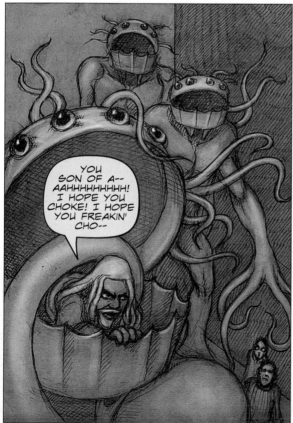

YOU SON OF A-- AAHHHHHHHHH! I HOPE YOU CHOKE! I HOPE YOU FREAKIN' CHO--

SHE THINKS ABOUT PRAYING, BUT DOUBTS THAT ANYBODY WOULD BE LISTENING. SHE'S CONVINCED THAT HUMANITY IS IN THIS ALONE.

BUT THEN SHE HEARS THE SOUND.

AT FIRST SHE THINKS IT'S ONE OF HER FRIENDS SCREAMING, BUT QUICKLY REALIZES THAT IT'S NOT A SCREAM OF FEAR.

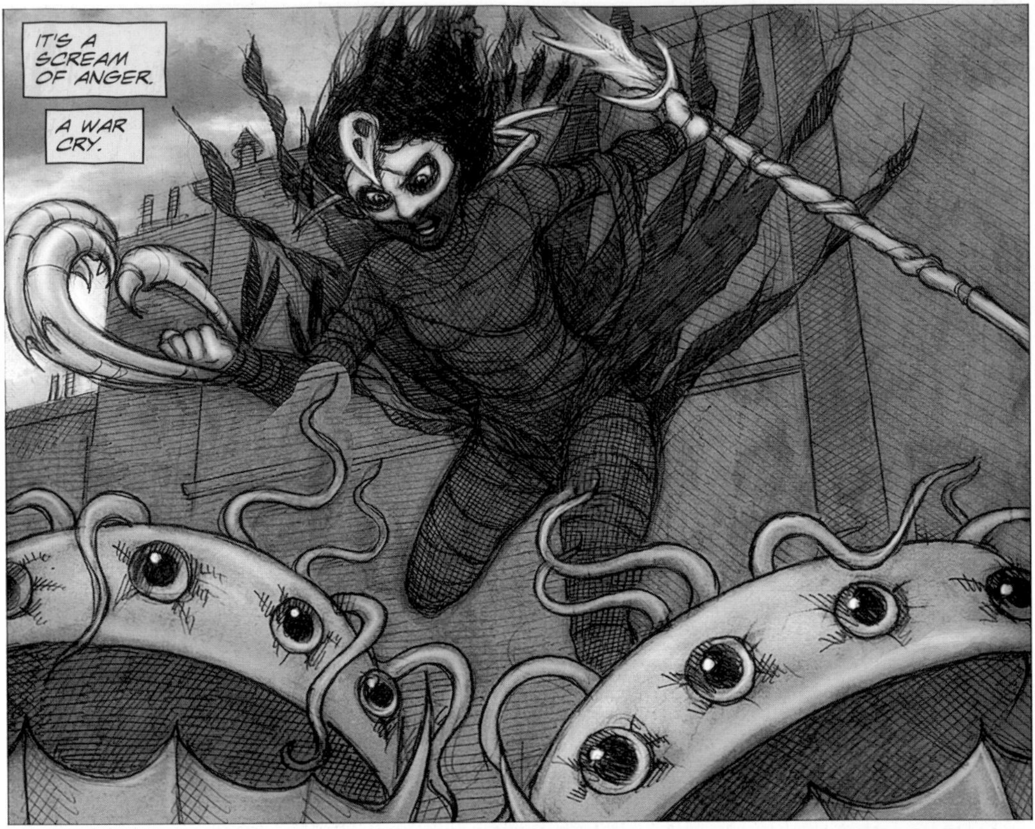
IT'S A SCREAM OF ANGER.
A WAR CRY.

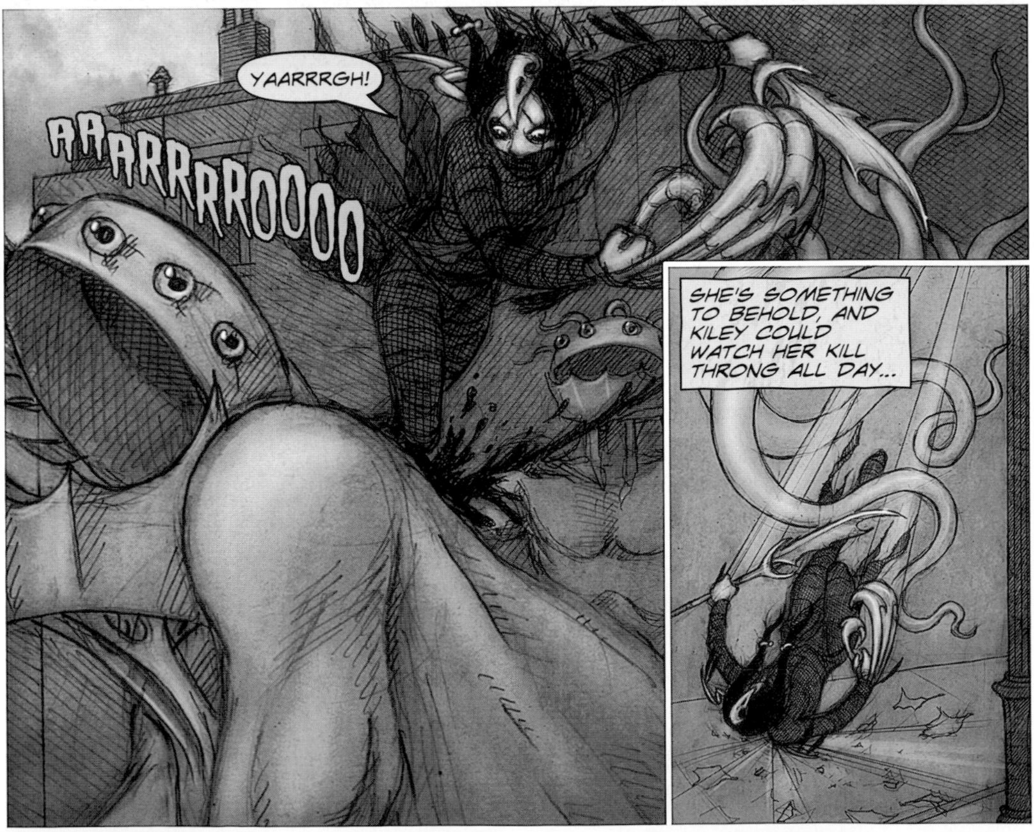
YAARRRGH!
AAARRRRROOOO
SHE'S SOMETHING TO BEHOLD, AND KILEY COULD WATCH HER KILL THRONG ALL DAY...

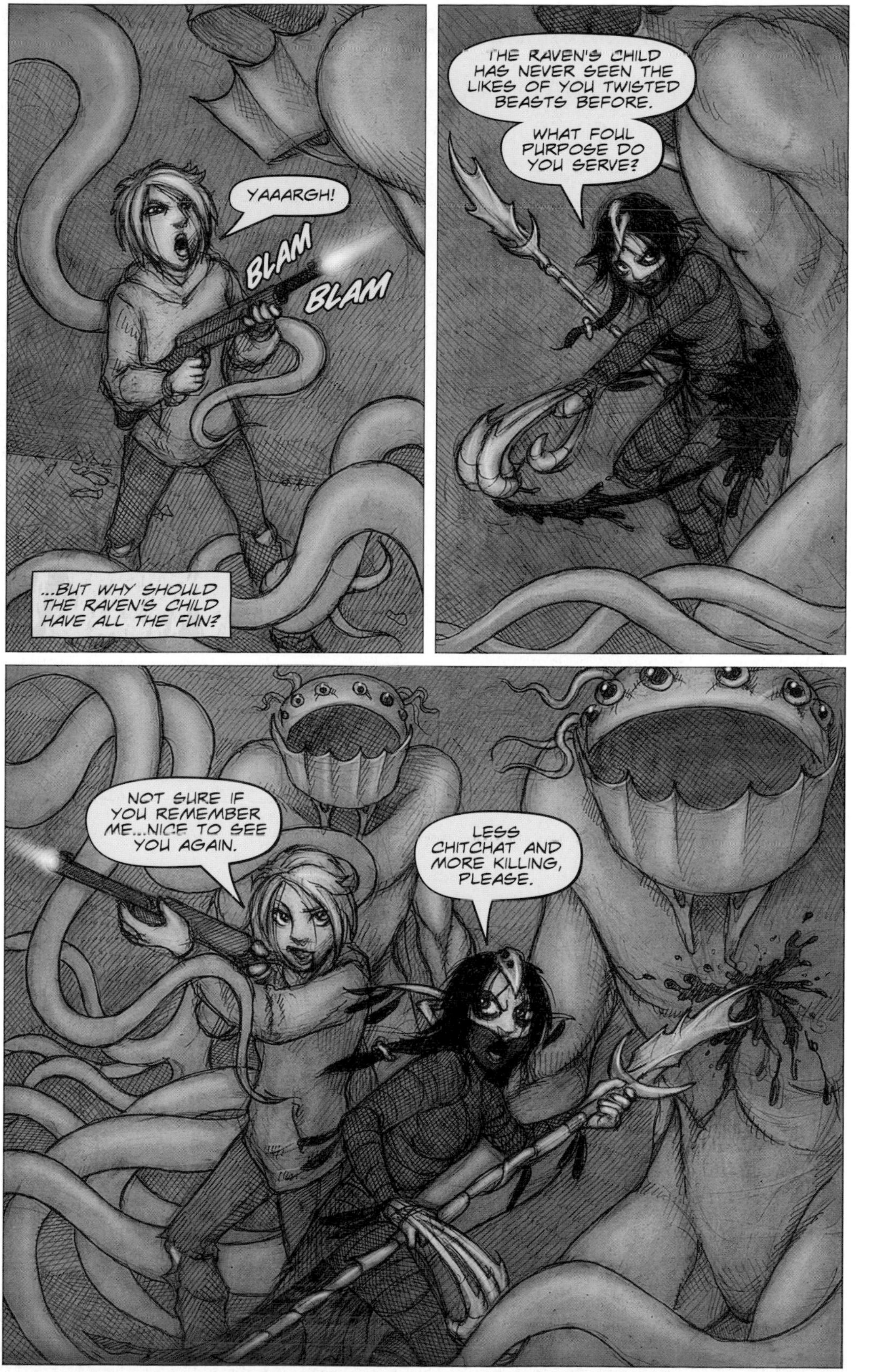
YAAARGH!
BLAM
BLAM
...BUT WHY SHOULD THE RAVEN'S CHILD HAVE ALL THE FUN?
THE RAVEN'S CHILD HAS NEVER SEEN THE LIKES OF YOU TWISTED BEASTS BEFORE.
WHAT FOUL PURPOSE DO YOU SERVE?
NOT SURE IF YOU REMEMBER ME...NICE TO SEE YOU AGAIN.
LESS CHITCHAT AND MORE KILLING, PLEASE.

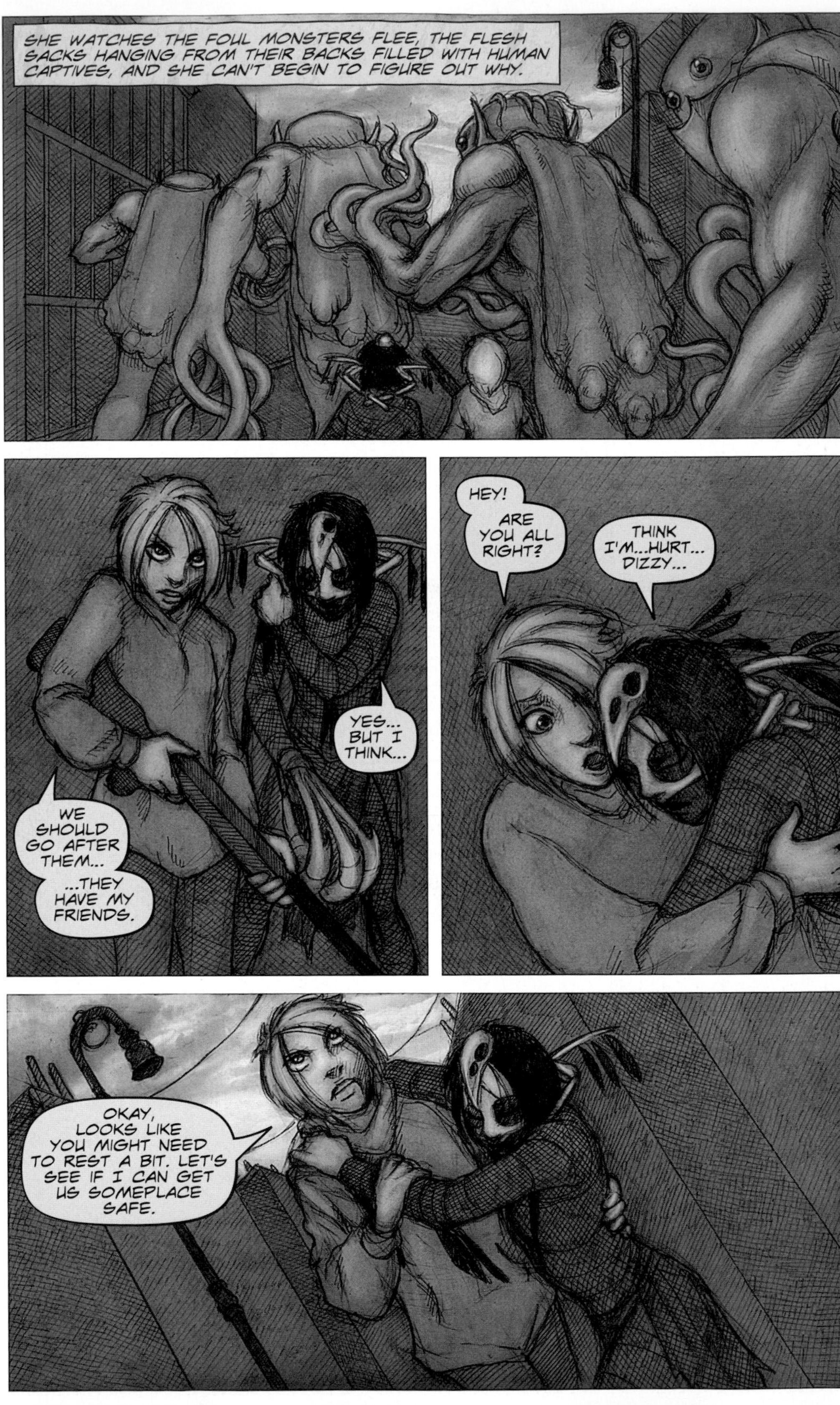
SHE WATCHES THE FOUL MONSTERS FLEE, THE FLESH SACKS HANGING FROM THEIR BACKS FILLED WITH HUMAN CAPTIVES, AND SHE CAN'T BEGIN TO FIGURE OUT WHY.
WE SHOULD GO AFTER THEM...
...THEY HAVE MY FRIENDS.
YES... BUT I THINK...
HEY! ARE YOU ALL RIGHT?
THINK I'M...HURT... DIZZY...
OKAY, LOOKS LIKE YOU MIGHT NEED TO REST A BIT. LET'S SEE IF I CAN GET US SOMEPLACE SAFE.

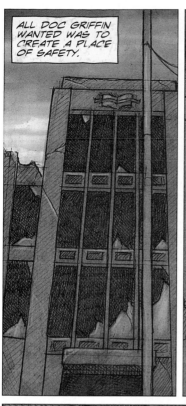

ALL DOC GRIFFIN WANTED WAS TO CREATE A PLACE OF SAFETY.

A PLACE WHERE THOSE DISENFRANCHISED BY THE THRONG INVASION MIGHT FIND SHELTER.

A SANCTUARY FROM THE HORRORS OF THE WORLD OUTSIDE.

A PLACE TO KEEP THE TERROR AT BAY.

SHE SHOULD HAVE KNOWN IT WOULDN'T LAST.

GET THE KIDS TO SAFETY... I'LL TRY TO HOLD THEM OFF!

BLAM BLAM

BLAM

BLAM

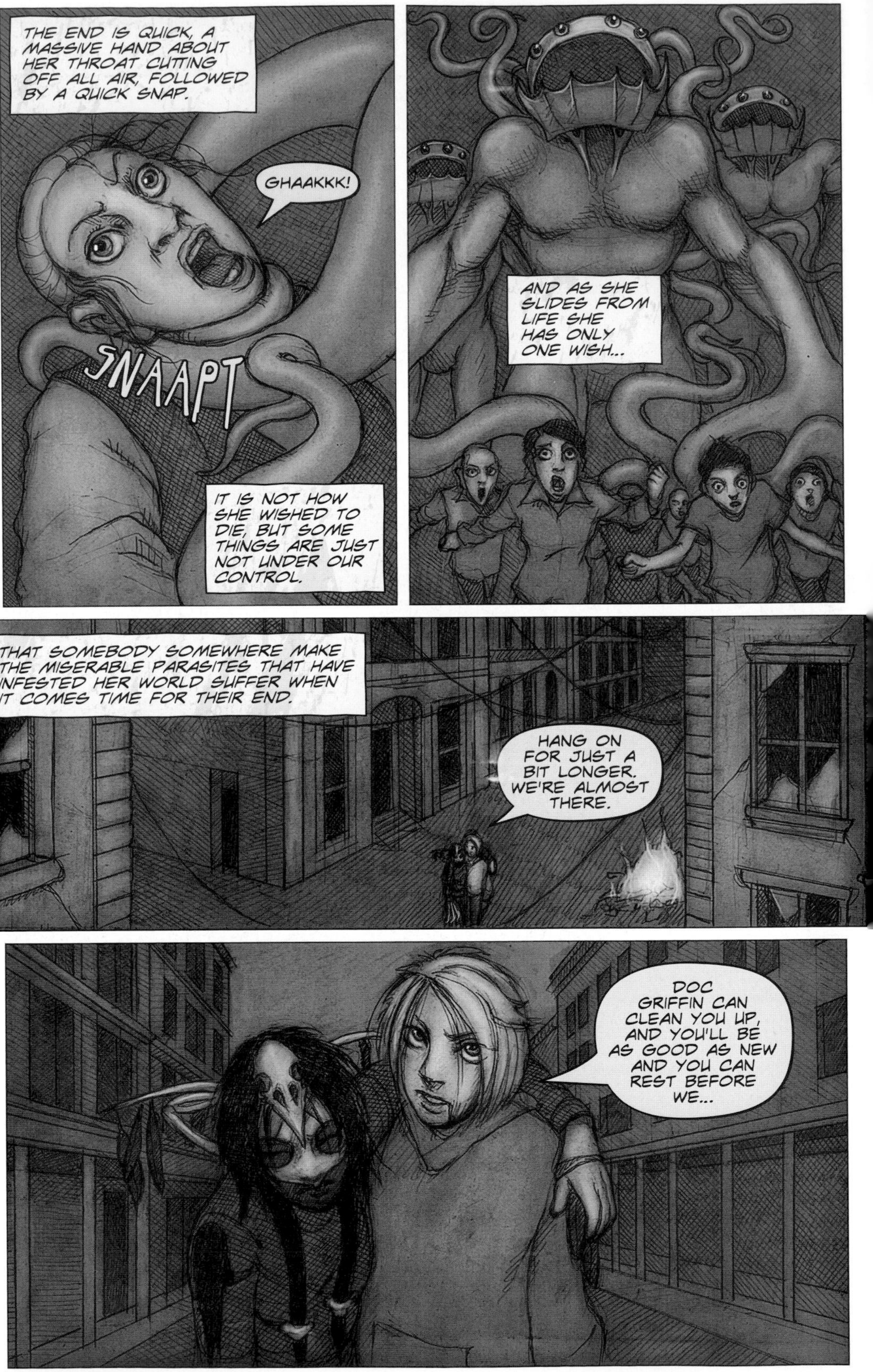
THE END IS QUICK, A MASSIVE HAND ABOUT HER THROAT CUTTING OFF ALL AIR, FOLLOWED BY A QUICK SNAP.
GHAAKKK!
SNAAPT
IT IS NOT HOW SHE WISHED TO DIE, BUT SOME THINGS ARE JUST NOT UNDER OUR CONTROL.
AND AS SHE SLIDES FROM LIFE SHE HAS ONLY ONE WISH...
THAT SOMEBODY SOMEWHERE MAKE THE MISERABLE PARASITES THAT HAVE INFESTED HER WORLD SUFFER WHEN IT COMES TIME FOR THEIR END.
HANG ON FOR JUST A BIT LONGER. WE'RE ALMOST THERE.
DOC GRIFFIN CAN CLEAN YOU UP, AND YOU'LL BE AS GOOD AS NEW AND YOU CAN REST BEFORE WE...

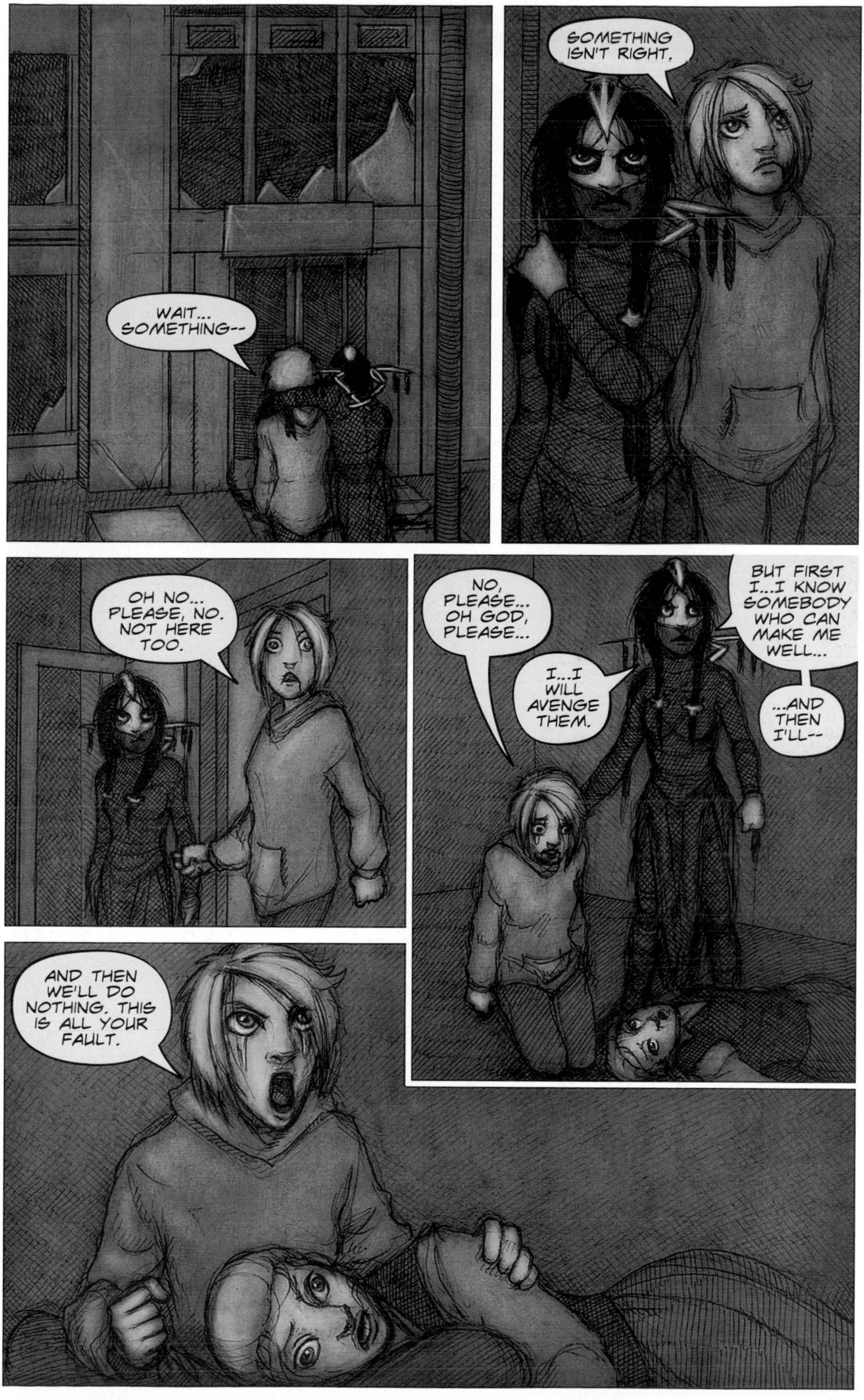
WAIT... SOMETHING--
SOMETHING ISN'T RIGHT.
OH NO... PLEASE, NO. NOT HERE TOO.
NO, PLEASE... OH GOD, PLEASE...
I...I WILL AVENGE THEM.
BUT FIRST I...I KNOW SOMEBODY WHO CAN MAKE ME WELL...
...AND THEN I'LL--
AND THEN WE'LL DO NOTHING. THIS IS ALL YOUR FAULT.

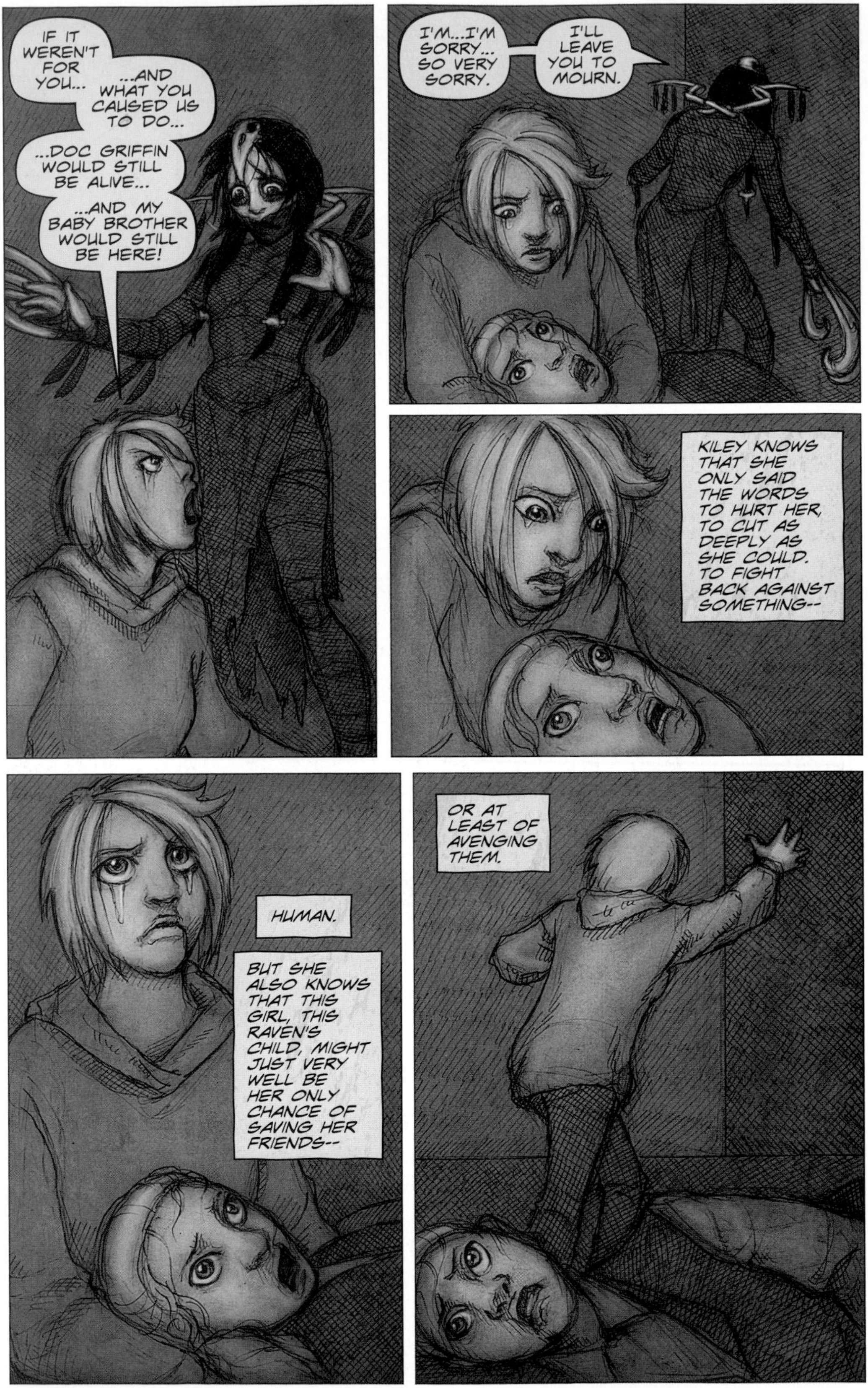
IF IT WEREN'T FOR YOU...
...AND WHAT YOU CAUSED US TO DO...
...DOC GRIFFIN WOULD STILL BE ALIVE...
...AND MY BABY BROTHER WOULD STILL BE HERE!
I'M...I'M SORRY... SO VERY SORRY.
I'LL LEAVE YOU TO MOURN.
KILEY KNOWS THAT SHE ONLY SAID THE WORDS TO HURT HER, TO CUT AS DEEPLY AS SHE COULD. TO FIGHT BACK AGAINST SOMETHING--
HUMAN.
BUT SHE ALSO KNOWS THAT THIS GIRL, THIS RAVEN'S CHILD, MIGHT JUST VERY WELL BE HER ONLY CHANCE OF SAVING HER FRIENDS--
OR AT LEAST OF AVENGING THEM.

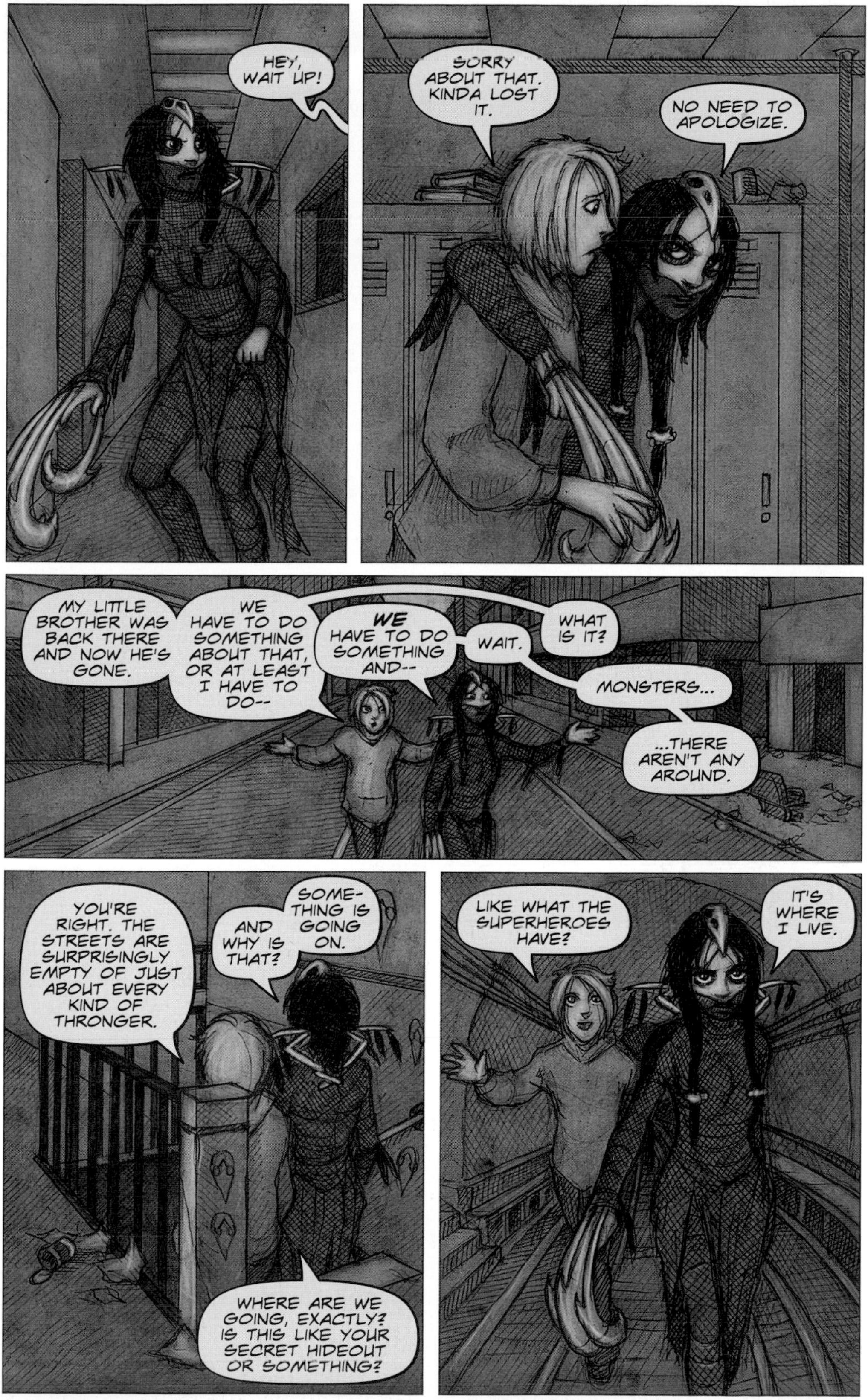
HEY, WAIT UP!
SORRY ABOUT THAT. KINDA LOST IT.
NO NEED TO APOLOGIZE.
MY LITTLE BROTHER WAS BACK THERE AND NOW HE'S GONE.
WE HAVE TO DO SOMETHING ABOUT THAT, OR AT LEAST I HAVE TO DO--
WE HAVE TO DO SOMETHING AND--
WAIT.
WHAT IS IT?
MONSTERS...
...THERE AREN'T ANY AROUND.
YOU'RE RIGHT. THE STREETS ARE SURPRISINGLY EMPTY OF JUST ABOUT EVERY KIND OF THRONGER.
AND WHY IS THAT?
SOMETHING IS GOING ON.
WHERE ARE WE GOING, EXACTLY? IS THIS LIKE YOUR SECRET HIDEOUT OR SOMETHING?
LIKE WHAT THE SUPERHEROES HAVE?
IT'S WHERE I LIVE.

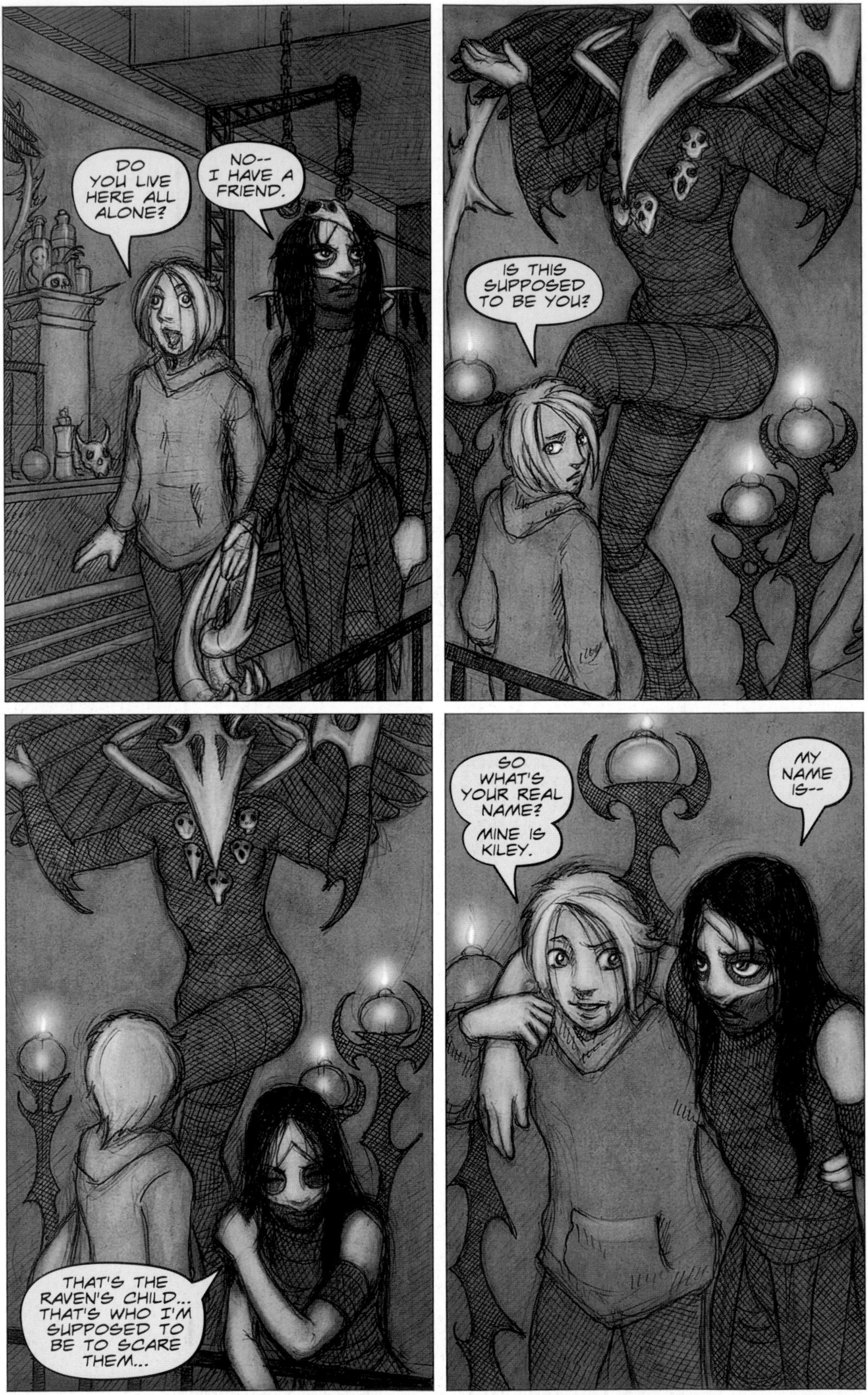
DO YOU LIVE HERE ALL ALONE?
NO-- I HAVE A FRIEND.
IS THIS SUPPOSED TO BE YOU?
THAT'S THE RAVEN'S CHILD... THAT'S WHO I'M SUPPOSED TO BE TO SCARE THEM...
SO WHAT'S YOUR REAL NAME? MINE IS KILEY.
MY NAME IS--

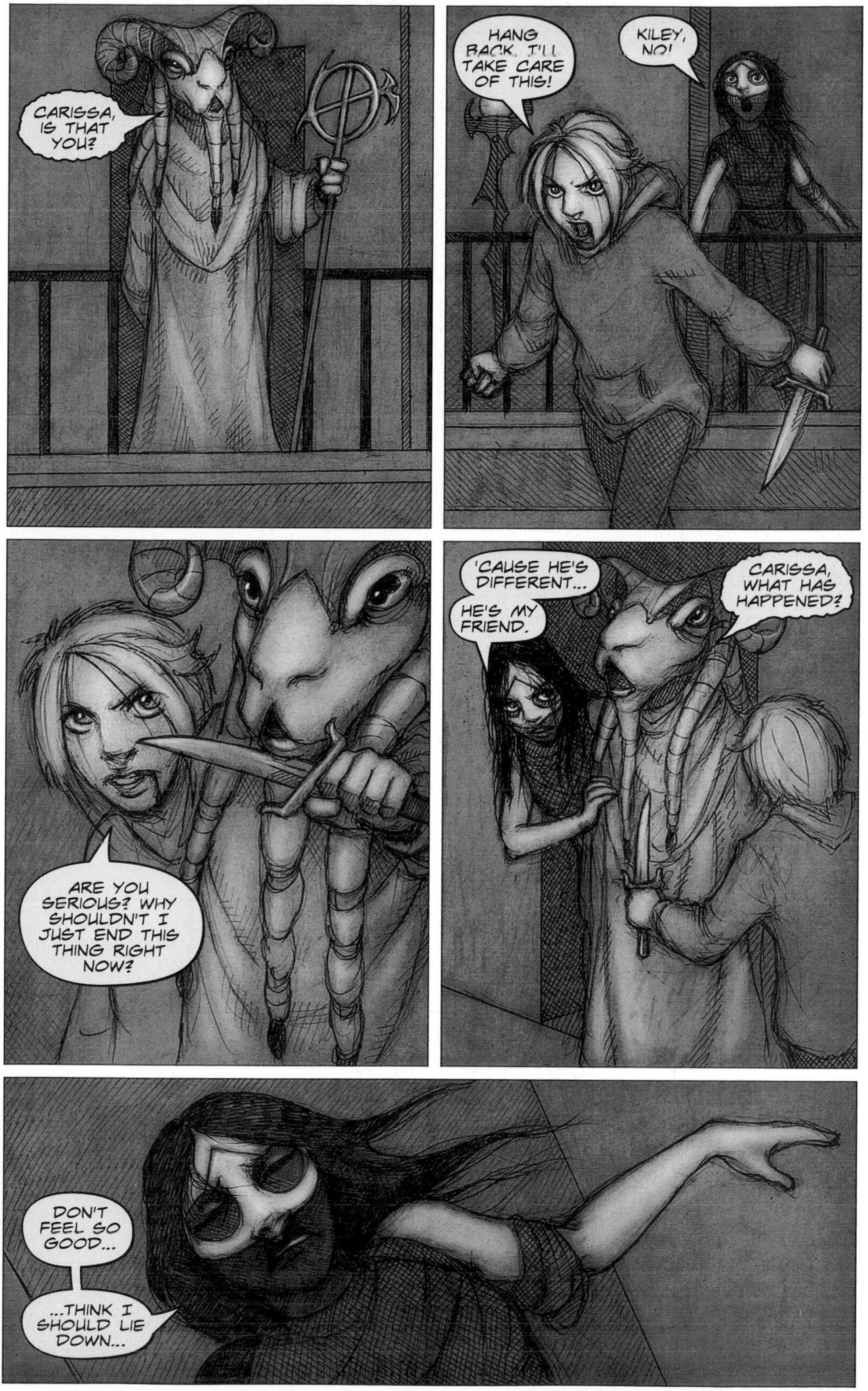
CARISSA, IS THAT YOU?
HANG BACK. I'LL TAKE CARE OF THIS!
KILEY, NO!
ARE YOU SERIOUS? WHY SHOULDN'T I JUST END THIS THING RIGHT NOW?
'CAUSE HE'S DIFFERENT...
HE'S MY FRIEND.
CARISSA, WHAT HAS HAPPENED?
DON'T FEEL SO GOOD...
...THINK I SHOULD LIE DOWN...

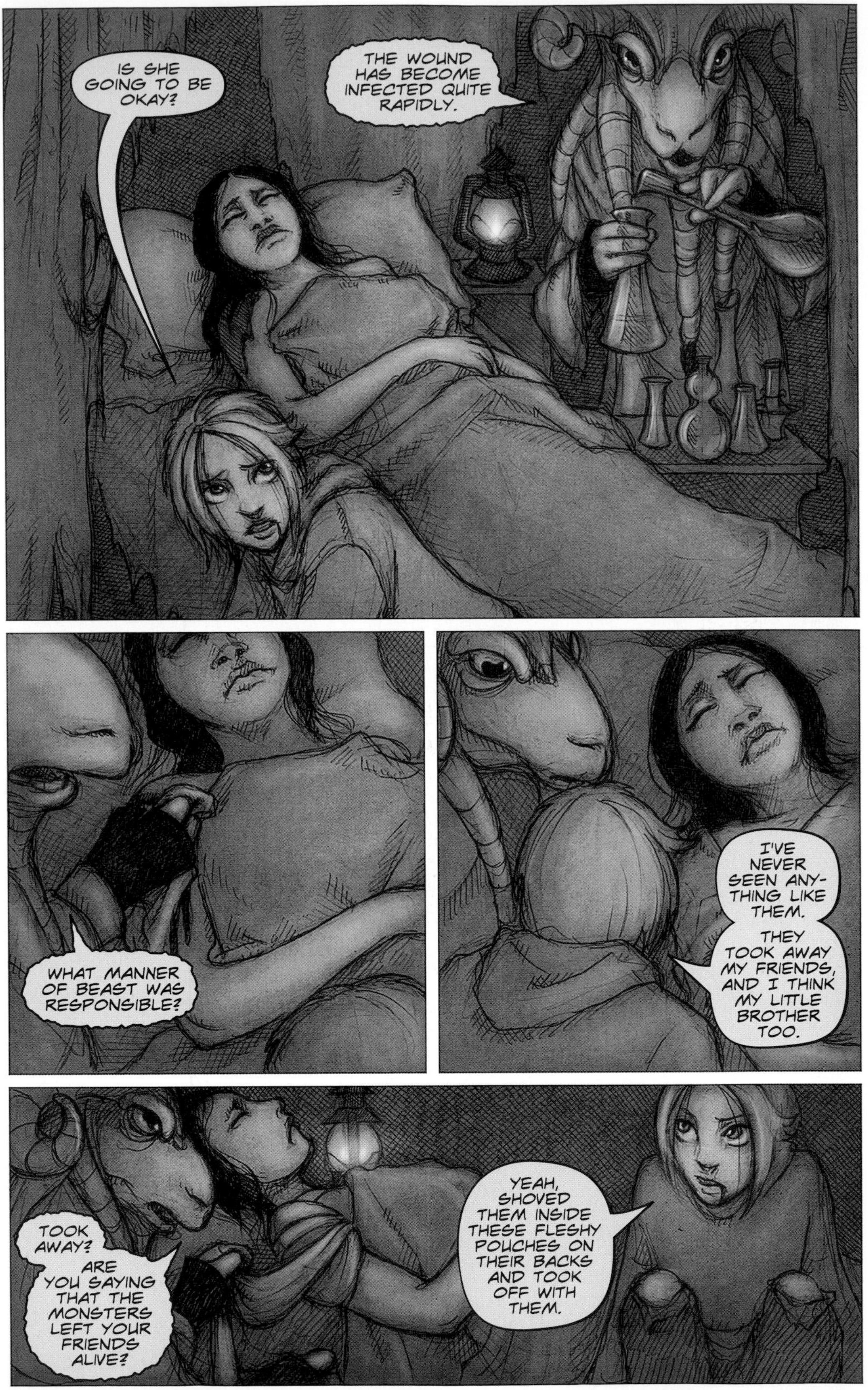
IS SHE GOING TO BE OKAY?
THE WOUND HAS BECOME INFECTED QUITE RAPIDLY.
WHAT MANNER OF BEAST WAS RESPONSIBLE?
I'VE NEVER SEEN ANY-THING LIKE THEM.
THEY TOOK AWAY MY FRIENDS, AND I THINK MY LITTLE BROTHER TOO.
TOOK AWAY? ARE YOU SAYING THAT THE MONSTERS LEFT YOUR FRIENDS ALIVE?
YEAH, SHOVED THEM INSIDE THESE FLESHY POUCHES ON THEIR BACKS AND TOOK OFF WITH THEM.

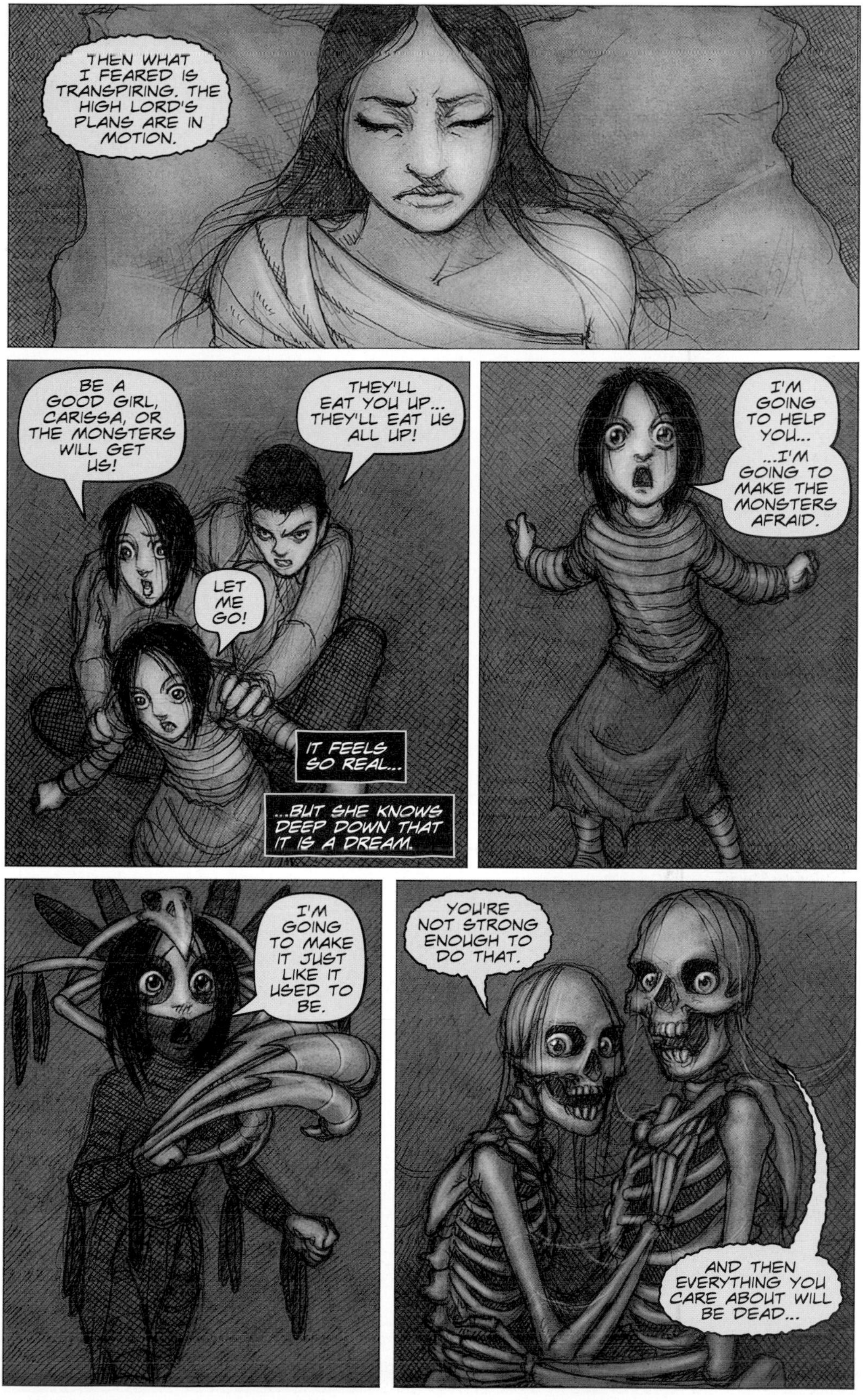
THEN WHAT I FEARED IS TRANSPIRING. THE HIGH LORD'S PLANS ARE IN MOTION.
BE A GOOD GIRL, CARISSA, OR THE MONSTERS WILL GET US!
THEY'LL EAT YOU UP... THEY'LL EAT US ALL UP!
LET ME GO!
IT FEELS SO REAL...
...BUT SHE KNOWS DEEP DOWN THAT IT IS A DREAM.
I'M GOING TO HELP YOU... ...I'M GOING TO MAKE THE MONSTERS AFRAID.
I'M GOING TO MAKE IT JUST LIKE IT USED TO BE.
YOU'RE NOT STRONG ENOUGH TO DO THAT.
AND THEN EVERYTHING YOU CARE ABOUT WILL BE DEAD...

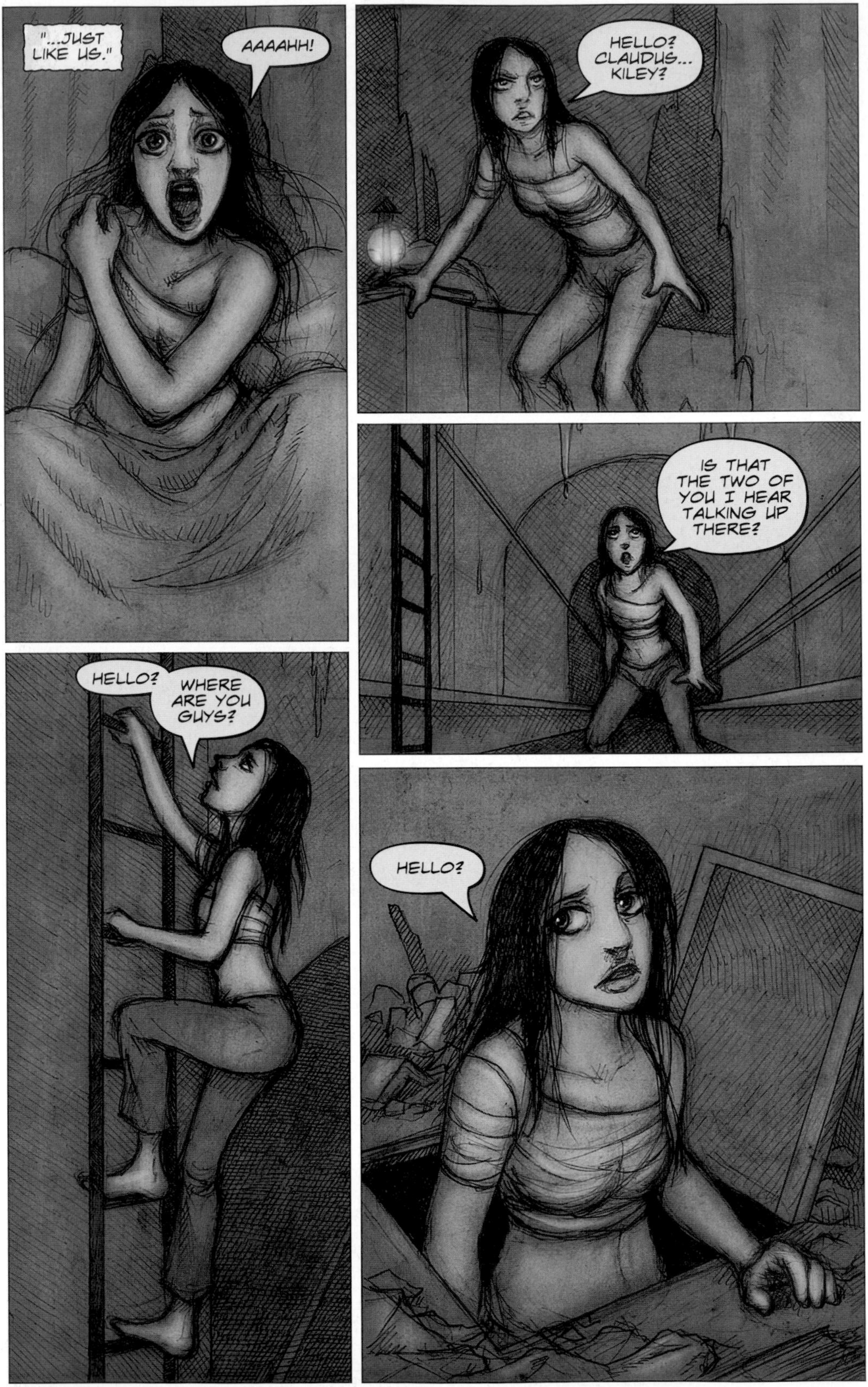
"...JUST LIKE US."
AAAAHH!
HELLO? CLAUDUS... KILEY?
IS THAT THE TWO OF YOU I HEAR TALKING UP THERE?
HELLO?
WHERE ARE YOU GUYS?
HELLO?

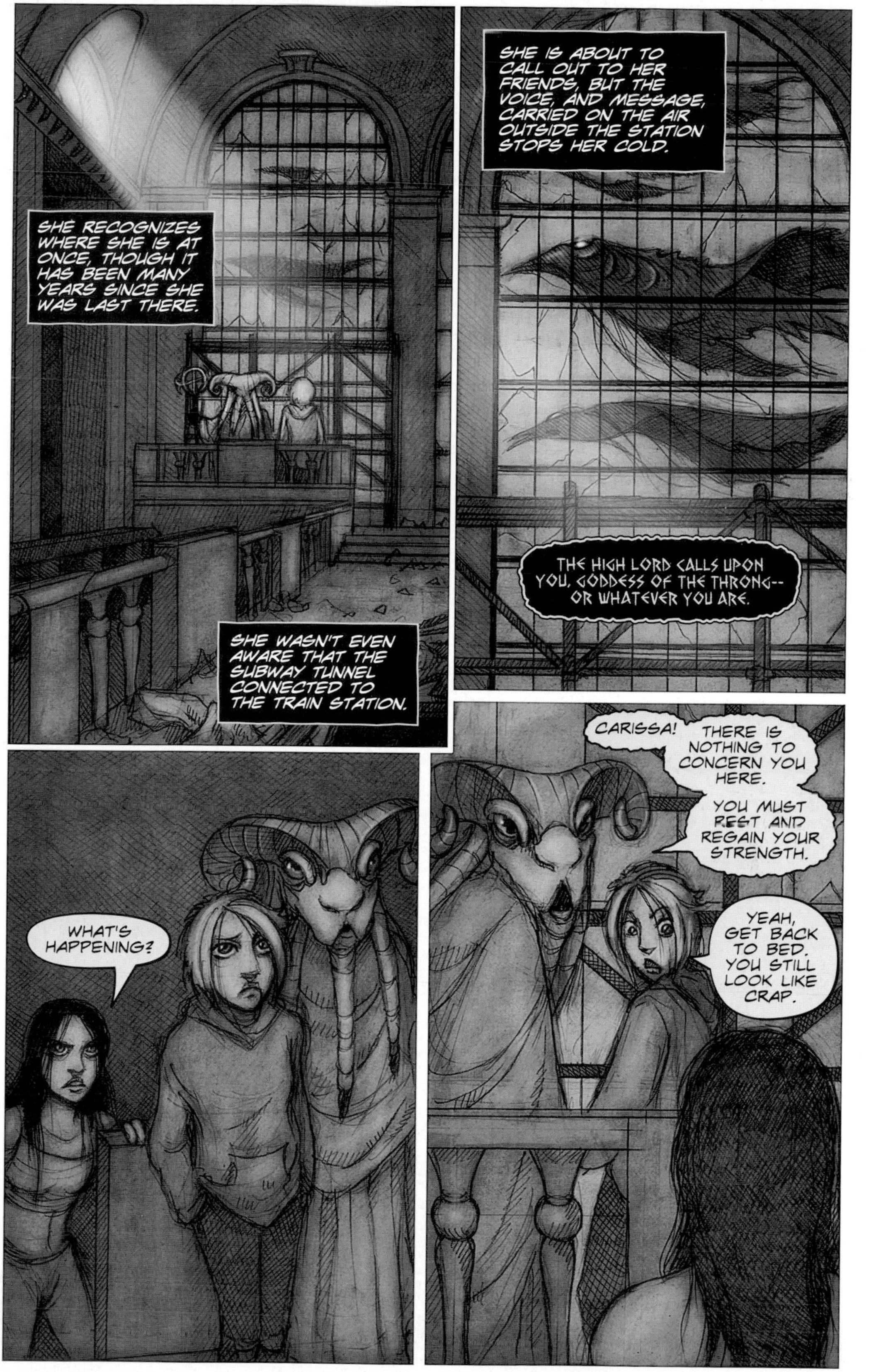
SHE RECOGNIZES WHERE SHE IS AT ONCE, THOUGH IT HAS BEEN MANY YEARS SINCE SHE WAS LAST THERE.
SHE WASN'T EVEN AWARE THAT THE SUBWAY TUNNEL CONNECTED TO THE TRAIN STATION.
SHE IS ABOUT TO CALL OUT TO HER FRIENDS, BUT THE VOICE, AND MESSAGE, CARRIED ON THE AIR OUTSIDE THE STATION STOPS HER COLD.
THE HIGH LORD CALLS UPON YOU, GODDESS OF THE THRONG-- OR WHATEVER YOU ARE.
WHAT'S HAPPENING?
CARISSA!
THERE IS NOTHING TO CONCERN YOU HERE.
YOU MUST REST AND REGAIN YOUR STRENGTH.
YEAH, GET BACK TO BED. YOU STILL LOOK LIKE CRAP.

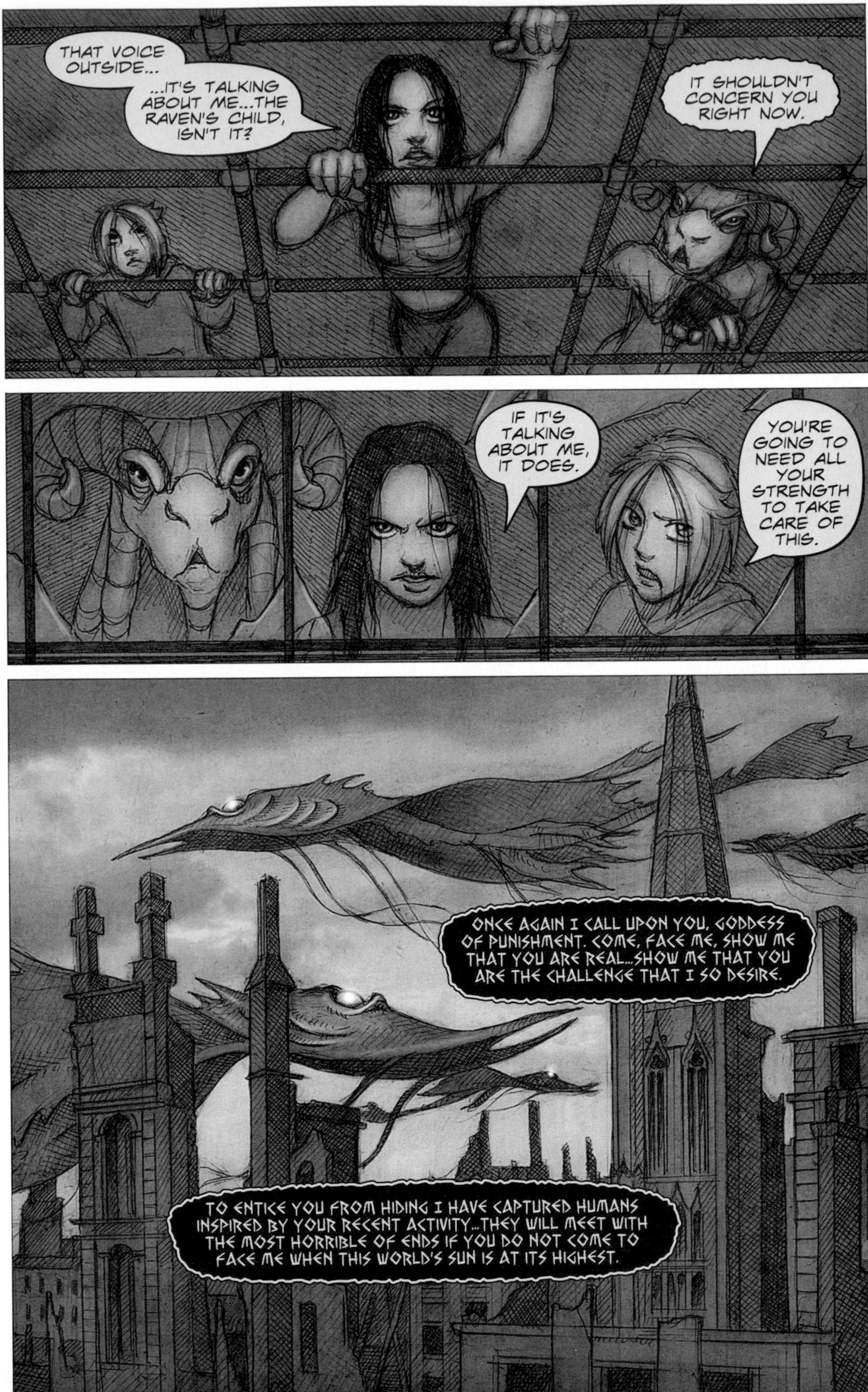
THAT VOICE OUTSIDE...
...IT'S TALKING ABOUT ME...THE RAVEN'S CHILD, ISN'T IT?
IT SHOULDN'T CONCERN YOU RIGHT NOW.
IF IT'S TALKING ABOUT ME, IT DOES.
YOU'RE GOING TO NEED ALL YOUR STRENGTH TO TAKE CARE OF THIS.
ONCE AGAIN I CALL UPON YOU, GODDESS OF PUNISHMENT. COME, FACE ME, SHOW ME THAT YOU ARE REAL...SHOW ME THAT YOU ARE THE CHALLENGE THAT I SO DESIRE.
TO ENTICE YOU FROM HIDING I HAVE CAPTURED HUMANS INSPIRED BY YOUR RECENT ACTIVITY...THEY WILL MEET WITH THE MOST HORRIBLE OF ENDS IF YOU DO NOT COME TO FACE ME WHEN THIS WORLD'S SUN IS AT ITS HIGHEST.

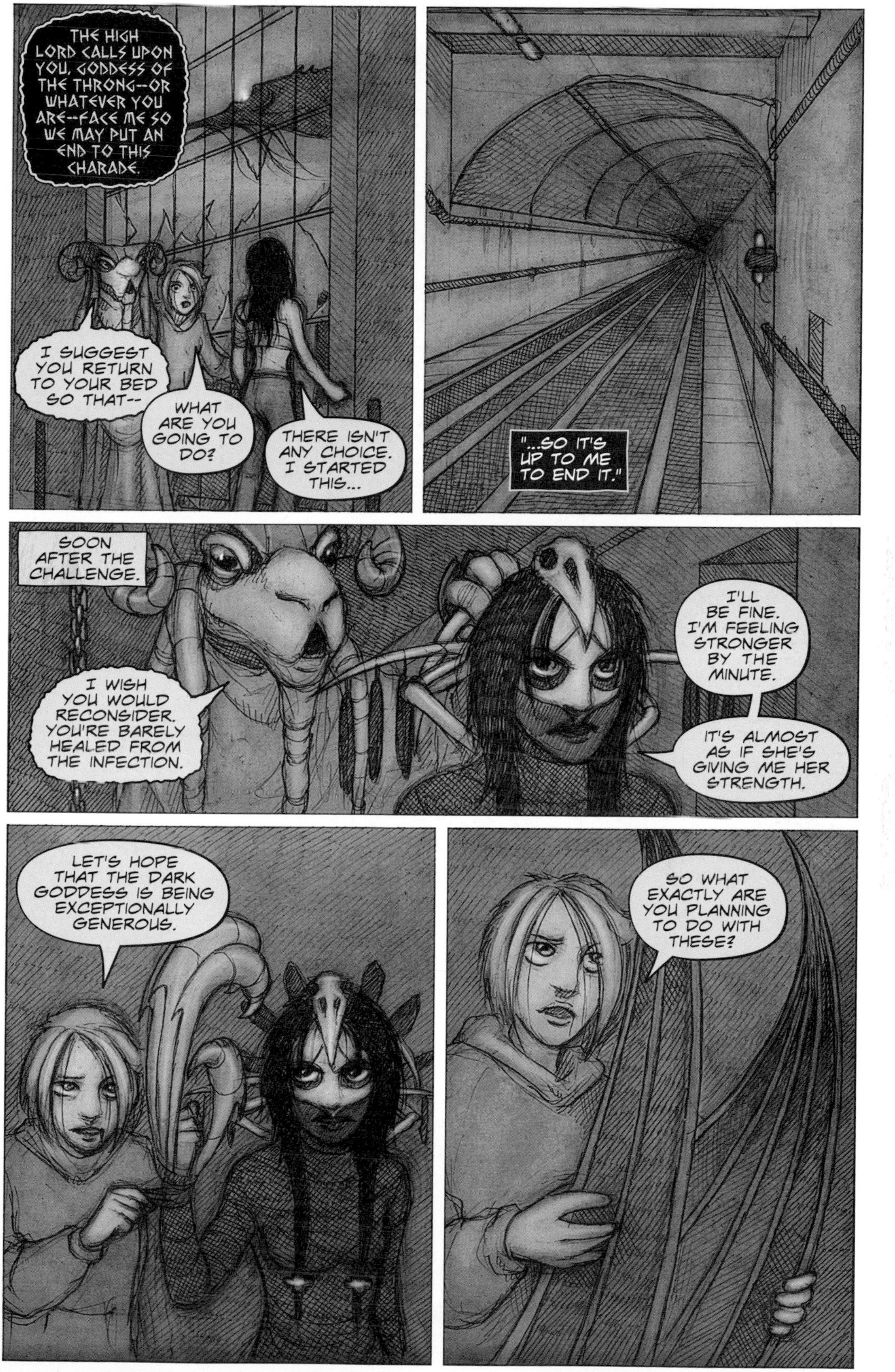
THE HIGH LORD CALLS UPON YOU, GODDESS OF THE THRONG--OR WHATEVER YOU ARE--FACE ME SO WE MAY PUT AN END TO THIS CHARADE.
I SUGGEST YOU RETURN TO YOUR BED SO THAT--
WHAT ARE YOU GOING TO DO?
THERE ISN'T ANY CHOICE. I STARTED THIS...
"...SO IT'S UP TO ME TO END IT."
SOON AFTER THE CHALLENGE.
I WISH YOU WOULD RECONSIDER. YOU'RE BARELY HEALED FROM THE INFECTION.
I'LL BE FINE. I'M FEELING STRONGER BY THE MINUTE.
IT'S ALMOST AS IF SHE'S GIVING ME HER STRENGTH.
LET'S HOPE THAT THE DARK GODDESS IS BEING EXCEPTIONALLY GENEROUS.
SO WHAT EXACTLY ARE YOU PLANNING TO DO WITH THESE?

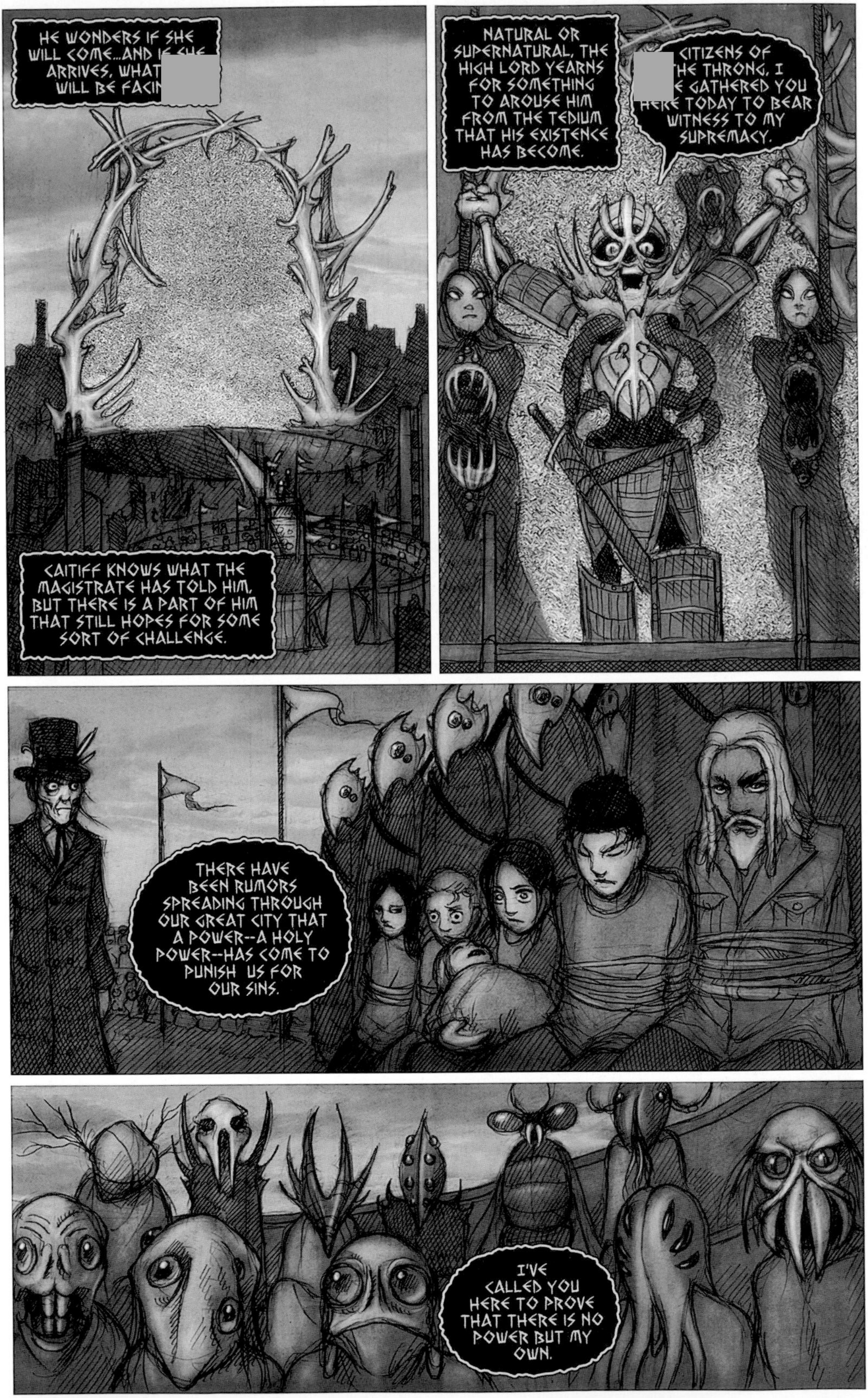

HE WONDERS IF SHE WILL COME...AND IF SHE ARRIVES, WHAT [redacted] WILL BE FACIN[redacted]
CAITIFF KNOWS WHAT THE MAGISTRATE HAS TOLD HIM, BUT THERE IS A PART OF HIM THAT STILL HOPES FOR SOME SORT OF CHALLENGE.
NATURAL OR SUPERNATURAL, THE HIGH LORD YEARNS FOR SOMETHING TO AROUSE HIM FROM THE TEDIUM THAT HIS EXISTENCE HAS BECOME.
CITIZENS OF [redacted]THE THRONG, I [redacted]E GATHERED YOU HERE TODAY TO BEAR WITNESS TO MY SUPREMACY.
THERE HAVE BEEN RUMORS SPREADING THROUGH OUR GREAT CITY THAT A POWER--A HOLY POWER--HAS COME TO PUNISH US FOR OUR SINS.
I'VE CALLED YOU HERE TO PROVE THAT THERE IS NO POWER BUT MY OWN.

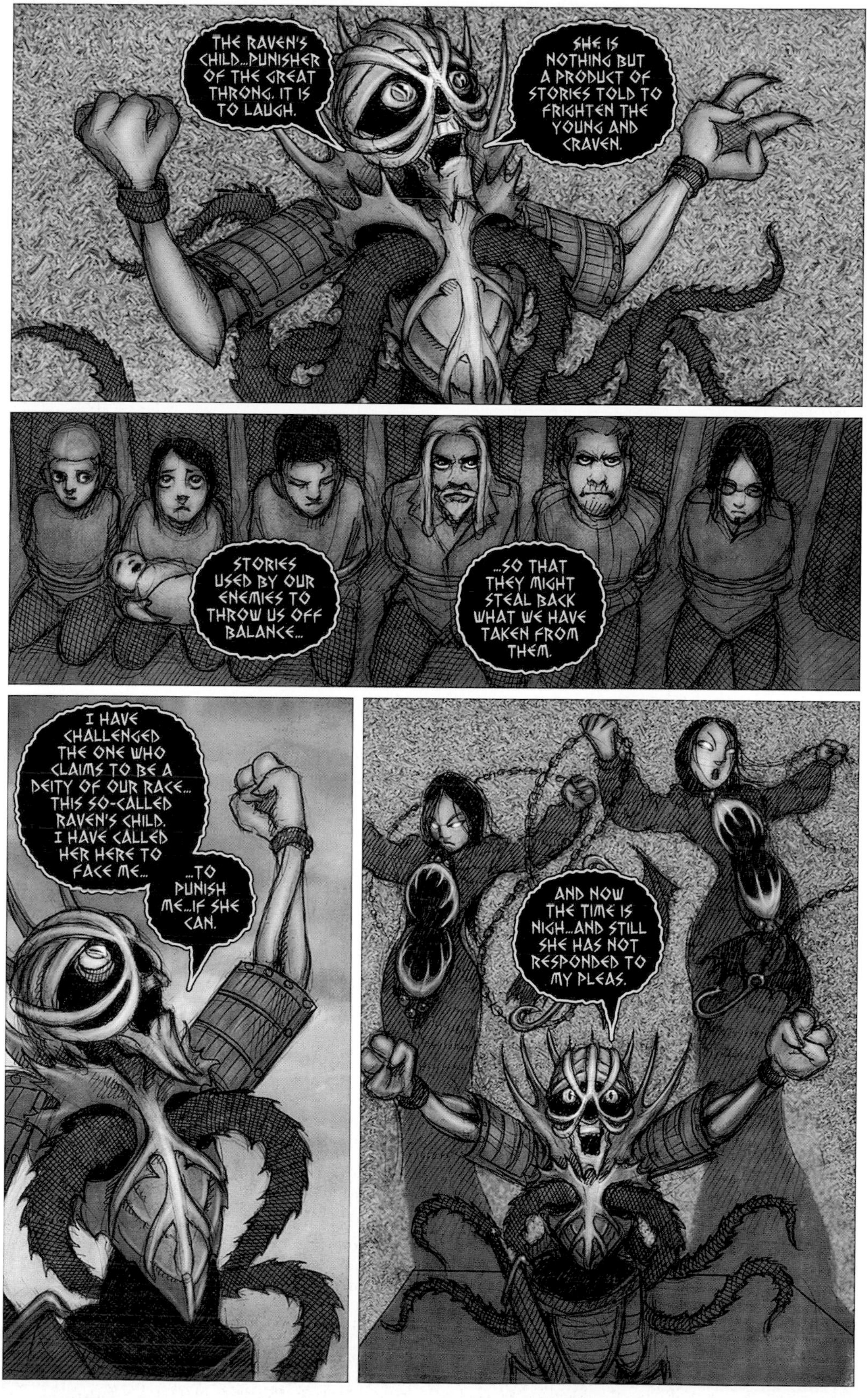
THE RAVEN'S CHILD...PUNISHER OF THE GREAT THRONG. IT IS TO LAUGH.
SHE IS NOTHING BUT A PRODUCT OF STORIES TOLD TO FRIGHTEN THE YOUNG AND CRAVEN.
STORIES USED BY OUR ENEMIES TO THROW US OFF BALANCE...
...SO THAT THEY MIGHT STEAL BACK WHAT WE HAVE TAKEN FROM THEM.
I HAVE CHALLENGED THE ONE WHO CLAIMS TO BE A DEITY OF OUR RACE... THIS SO-CALLED RAVEN'S CHILD. I HAVE CALLED HER HERE TO FACE ME...
...TO PUNISH ME...IF SHE CAN.
AND NOW THE TIME IS NIGH...AND STILL SHE HAS NOT RESPONDED TO MY PLEAS.

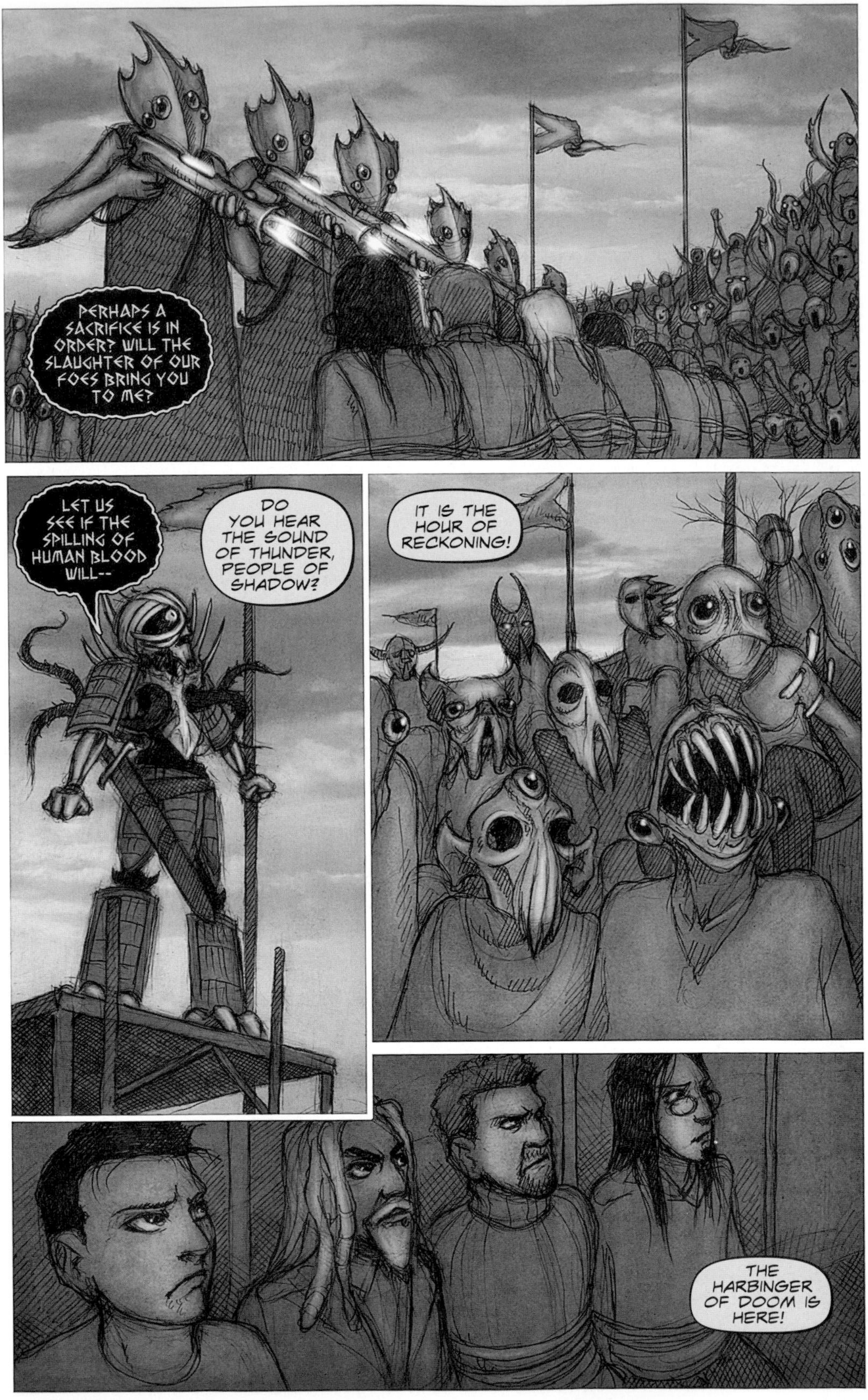
PERHAPS A SACRIFICE IS IN ORDER? WILL THE SLAUGHTER OF OUR FOES BRING YOU TO ME?
LET US SEE IF THE SPILLING OF HUMAN BLOOD WILL--
DO YOU HEAR THE SOUND OF THUNDER, PEOPLE OF SHADOW?
IT IS THE HOUR OF RECKONING!
THE HARBINGER OF DOOM IS HERE!

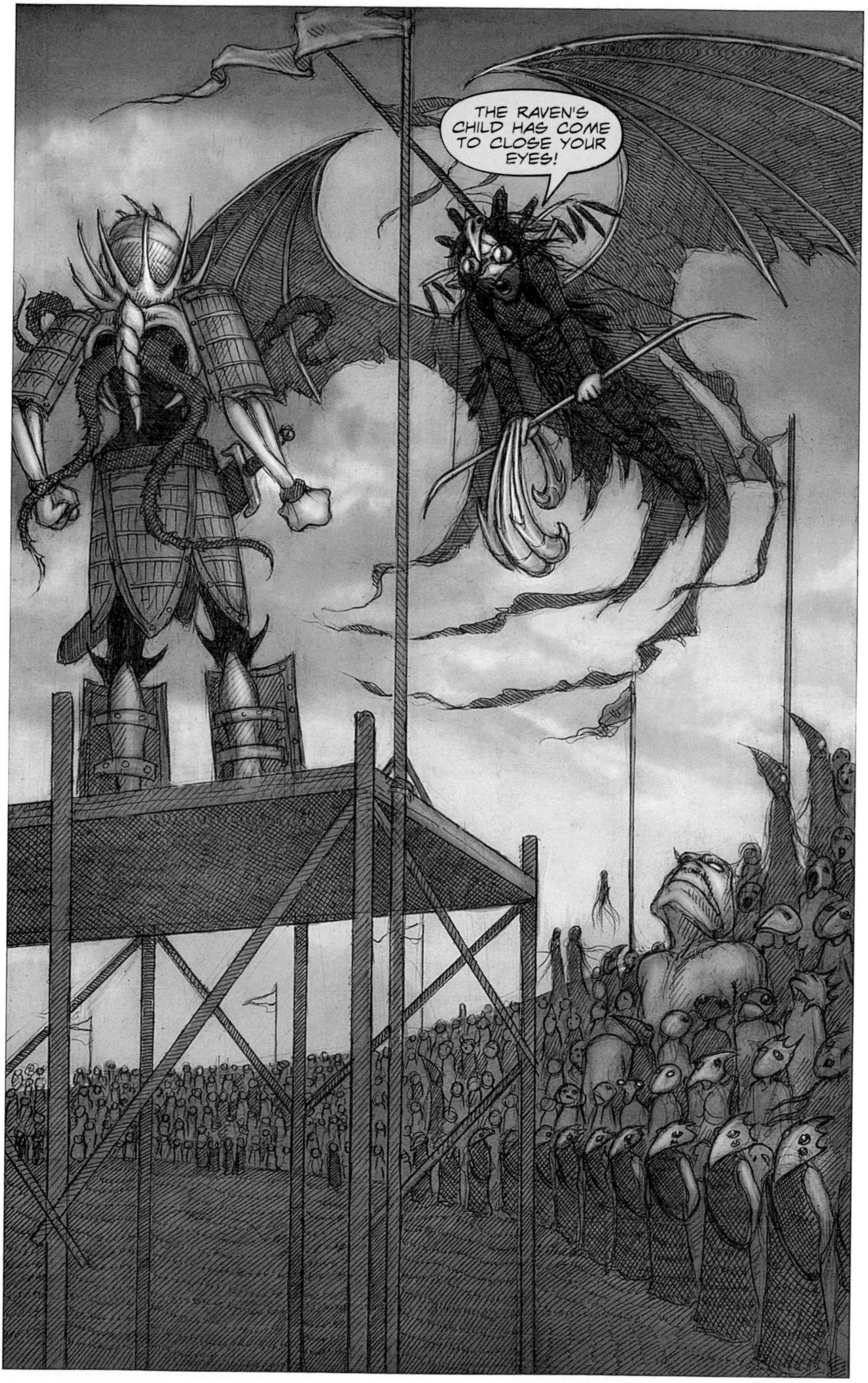
THE RAVEN'S CHILD HAS COME TO CLOSE YOUR EYES!

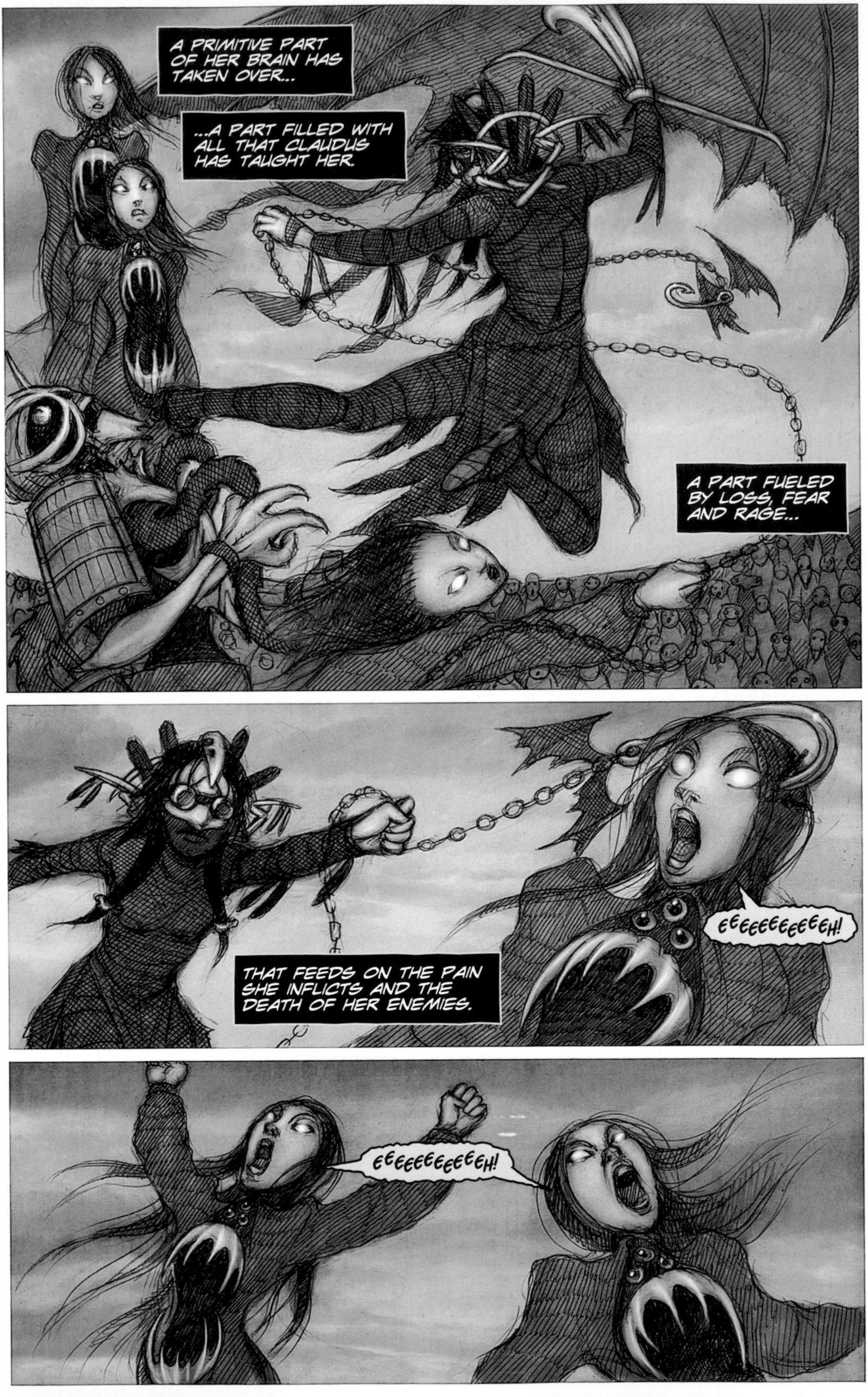
A PRIMITIVE PART OF HER BRAIN HAS TAKEN OVER...
...A PART FILLED WITH ALL THAT CLAUDUS HAS TAUGHT HER.
A PART FUELED BY LOSS, FEAR AND RAGE...
THAT FEEDS ON THE PAIN SHE INFLICTS AND THE DEATH OF HER ENEMIES.
EEEEEEEEEEEH!
EEEEEEEEEEEH!

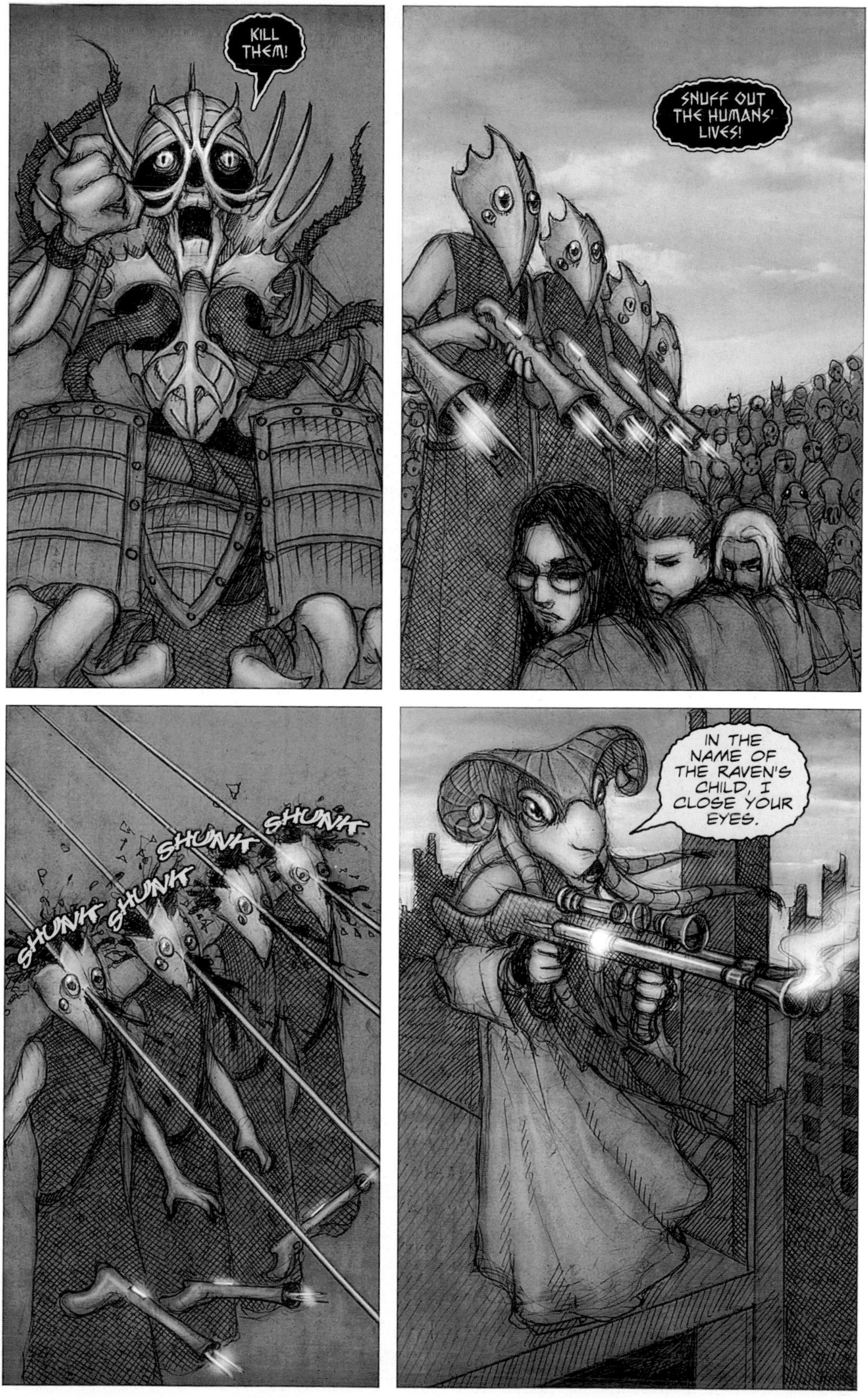
KILL THEM!
SNUFF OUT THE HUMANS' LIVES!
SHUNK SHUNK SHUNK SHUNK
IN THE NAME OF THE RAVEN'S CHILD, I CLOSE YOUR EYES.

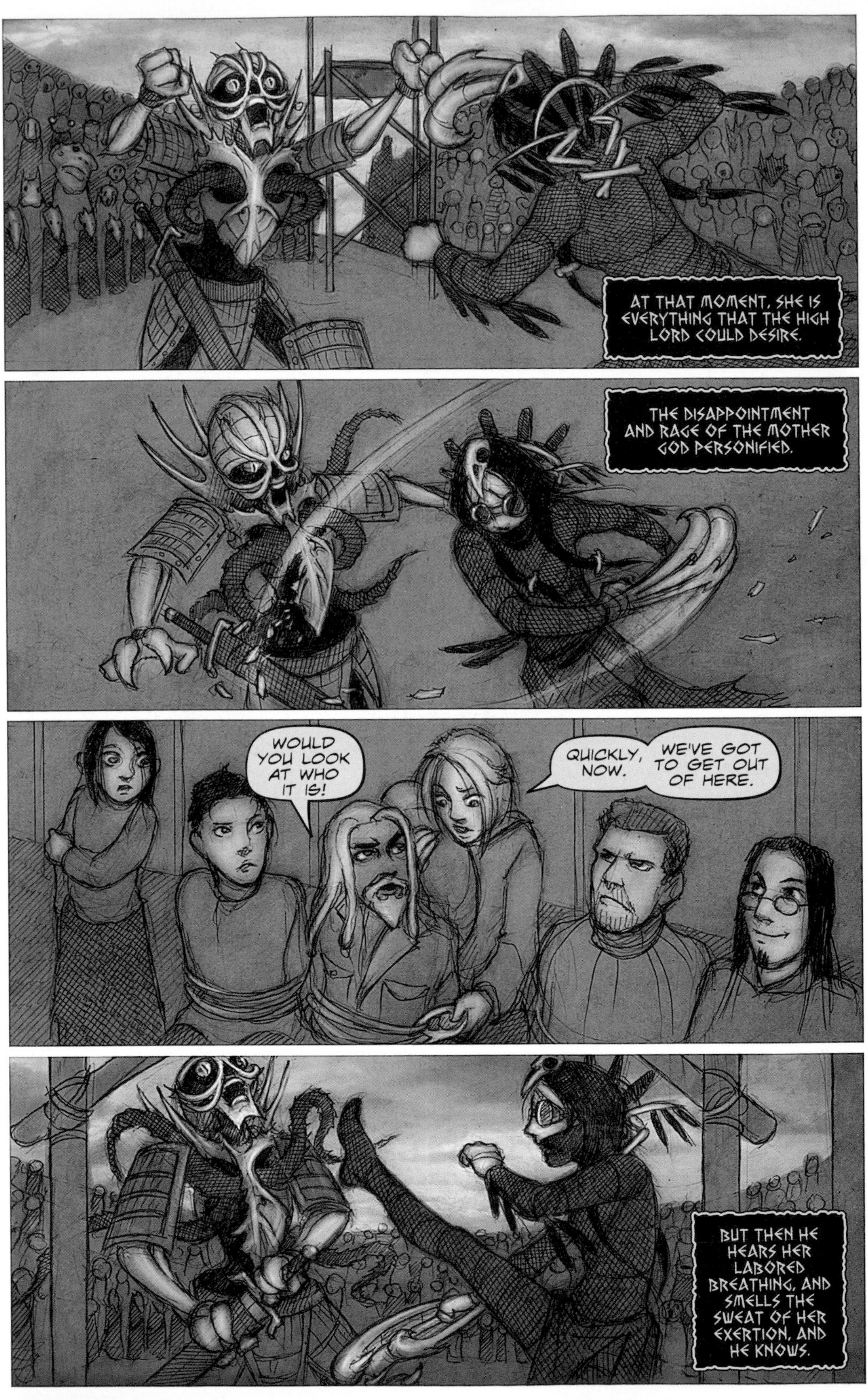
AT THAT MOMENT, SHE IS EVERYTHING THAT THE HIGH LORD COULD DESIRE.
THE DISAPPOINTMENT AND RAGE OF THE MOTHER GOD PERSONIFIED.
WOULD YOU LOOK AT WHO IT IS!
QUICKLY, NOW.
WE'VE GOT TO GET OUT OF HERE.
BUT THEN HE HEARS HER LABORED BREATHING, AND SMELLS THE SWEAT OF HER EXERTION, AND HE KNOWS.

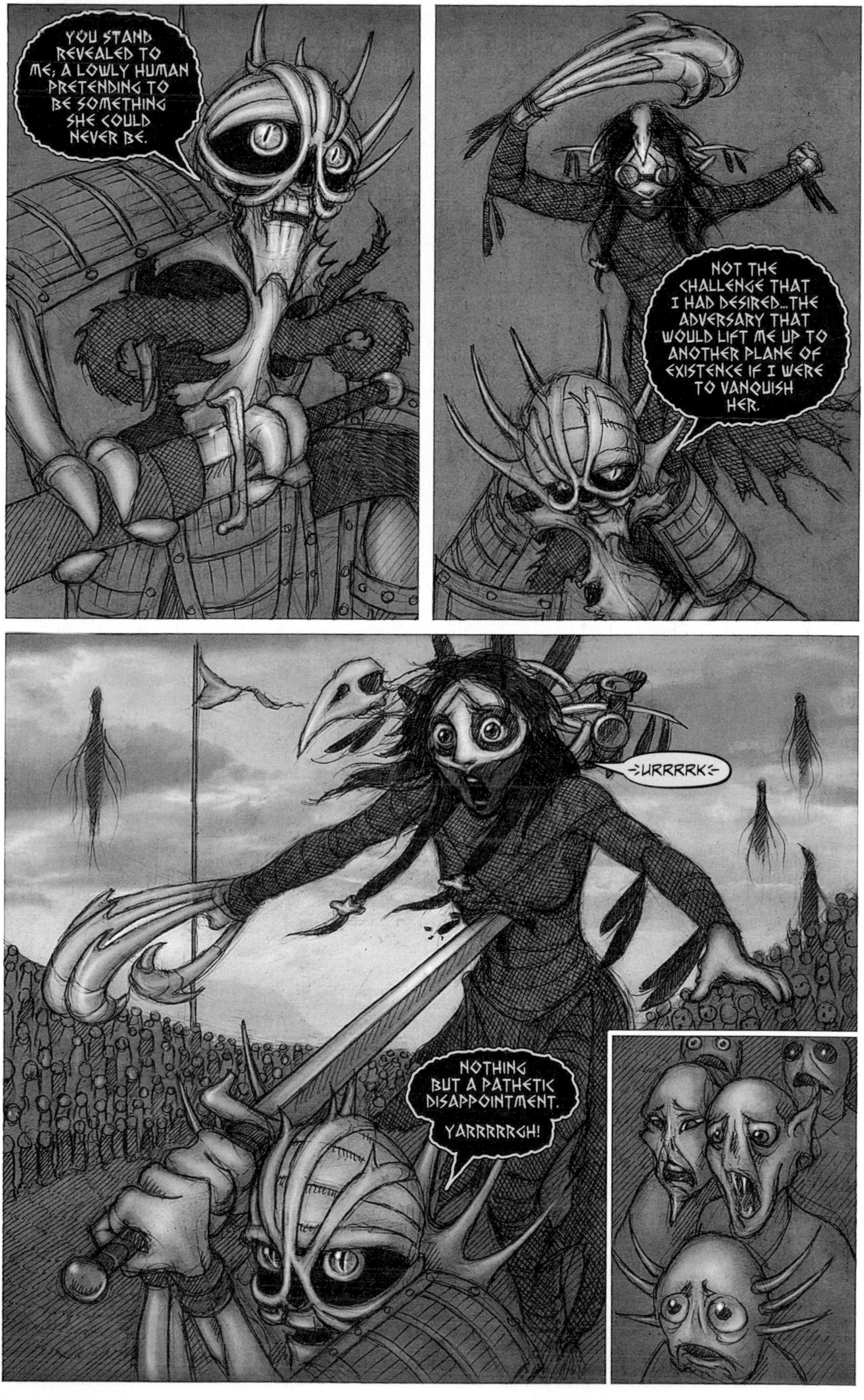
YOU STAND REVEALED TO ME; A LOWLY HUMAN PRETENDING TO BE SOMETHING SHE COULD NEVER BE.
NOT THE CHALLENGE THAT I HAD DESIRED...THE ADVERSARY THAT WOULD LIFT ME UP TO ANOTHER PLANE OF EXISTENCE IF I WERE TO VANQUISH HER.
URRRRK
NOTHING BUT A PATHETIC DISAPPOINTMENT.
YARRRRRGH!

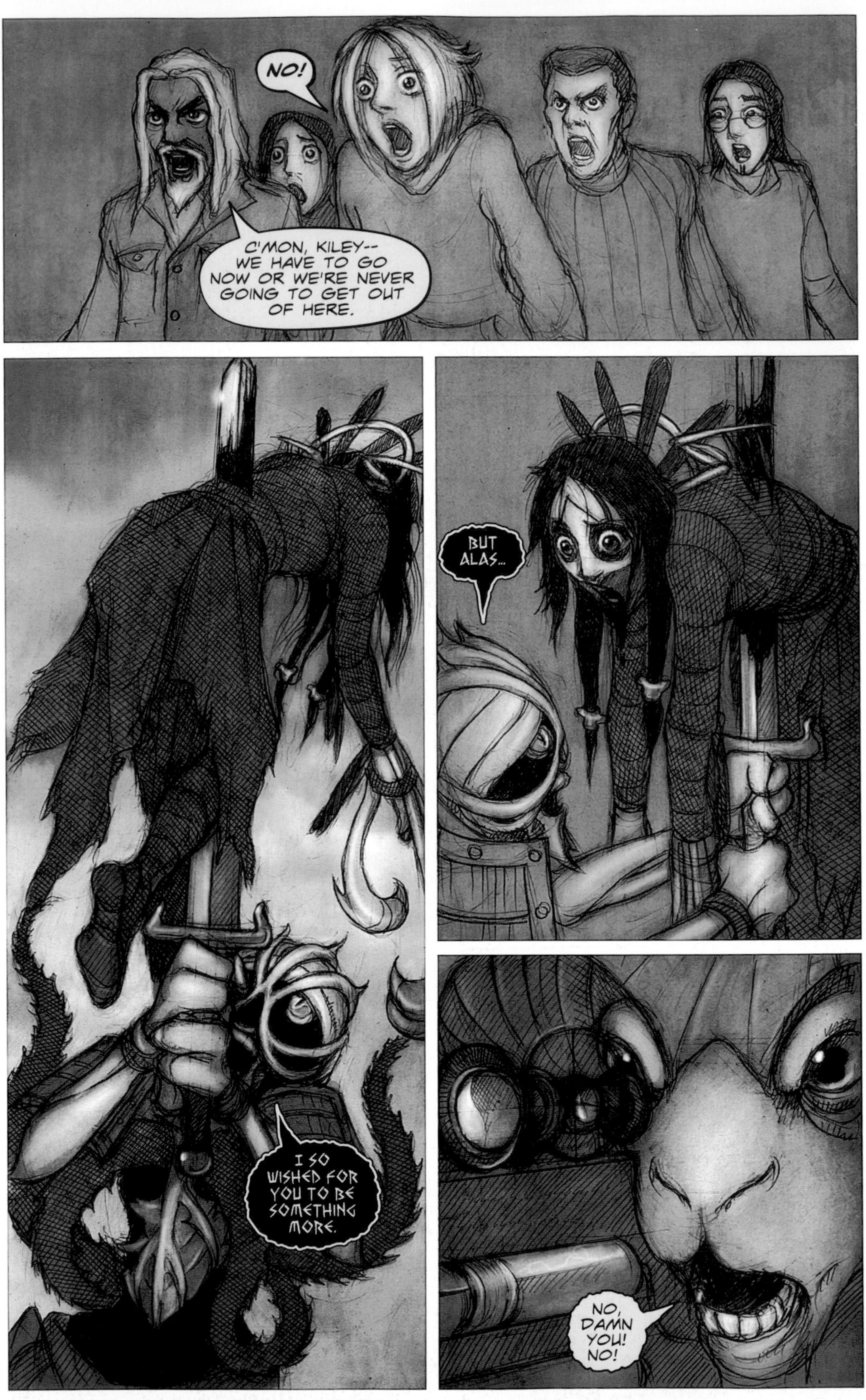
NO!
C'MON, KILEY-- WE HAVE TO GO NOW OR WE'RE NEVER GOING TO GET OUT OF HERE.
I SO WISHED FOR YOU TO BE SOMETHING MORE.
BUT ALAS...
NO, DAMN YOU! NO!

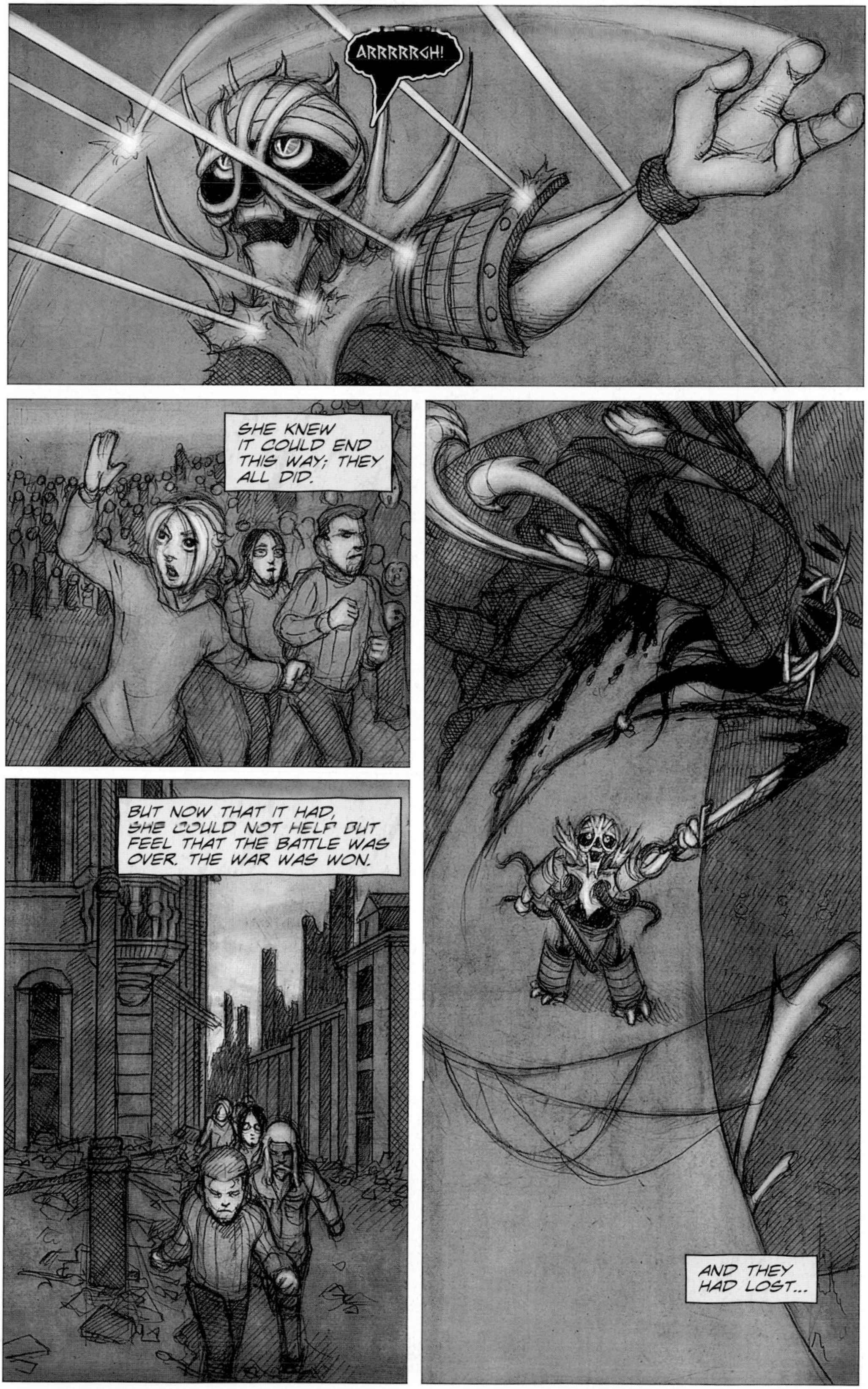
ARRRRRGH!
SHE KNEW IT COULD END THIS WAY; THEY ALL DID.
BUT NOW THAT IT HAD, SHE COULD NOT HELP BUT FEEL THAT THE BATTLE WAS OVER. THE WAR WAS WON.
AND THEY HAD LOST...

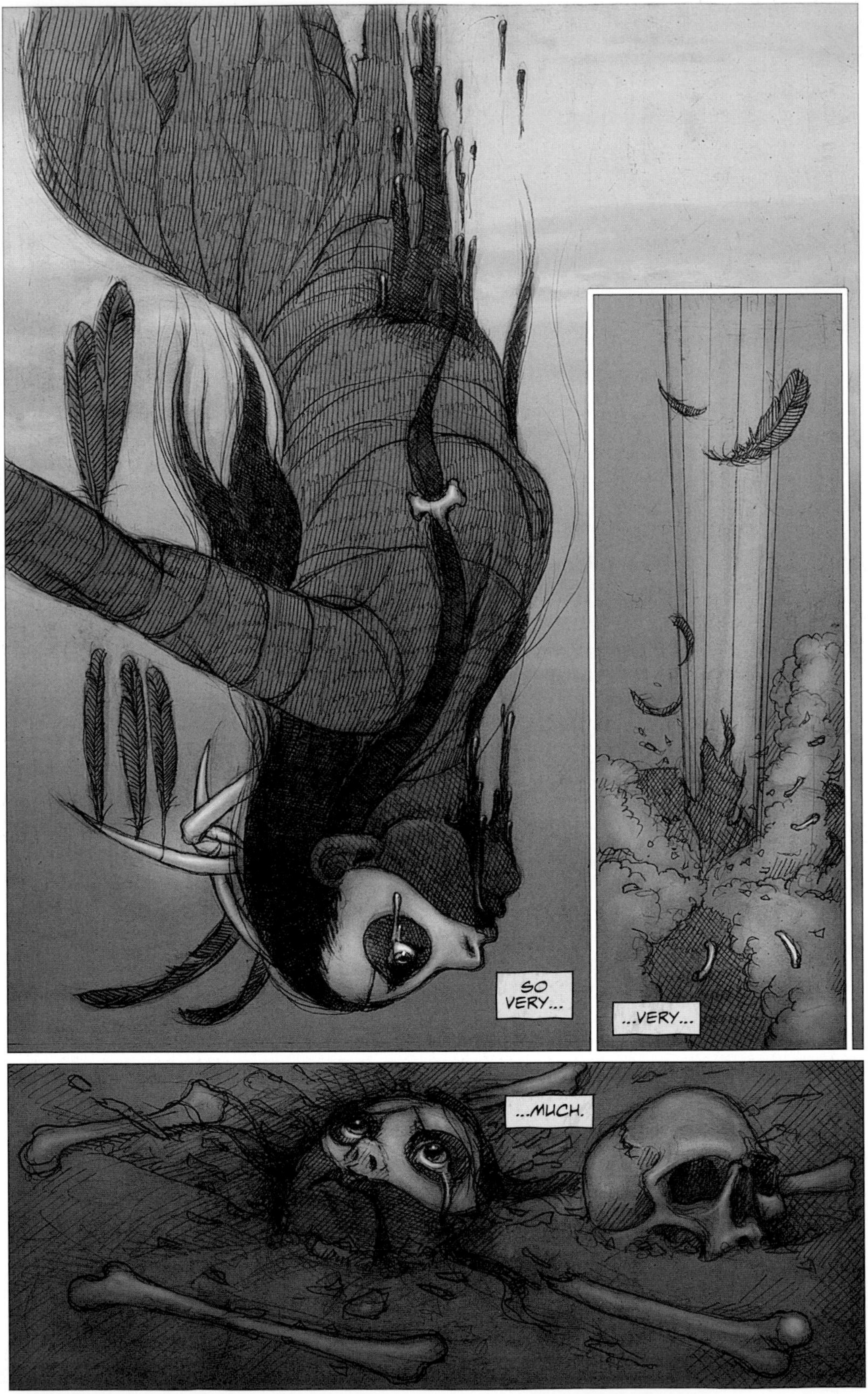
SO VERY...
...VERY...
...MUCH.

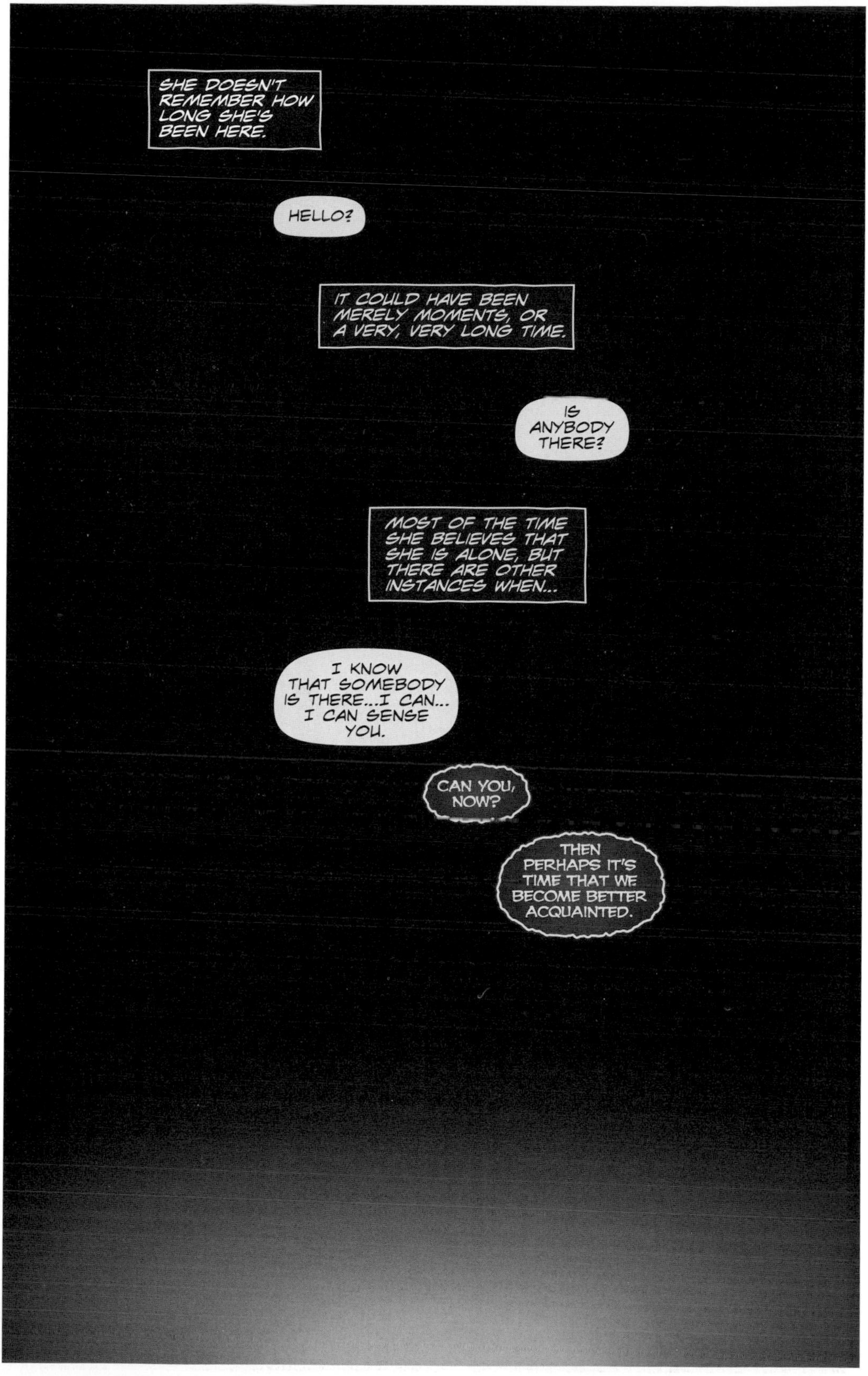
SHE DOESN'T REMEMBER HOW LONG SHE'S BEEN HERE.
HELLO?
IT COULD HAVE BEEN MERELY MOMENTS, OR A VERY, VERY LONG TIME.
IS ANYBODY THERE?
MOST OF THE TIME SHE BELIEVES THAT SHE IS ALONE, BUT THERE ARE OTHER INSTANCES WHEN...
I KNOW THAT SOMEBODY IS THERE...I CAN... I CAN SENSE YOU.
CAN YOU, NOW?
THEN PERHAPS IT'S TIME THAT WE BECOME BETTER ACQUAINTED.

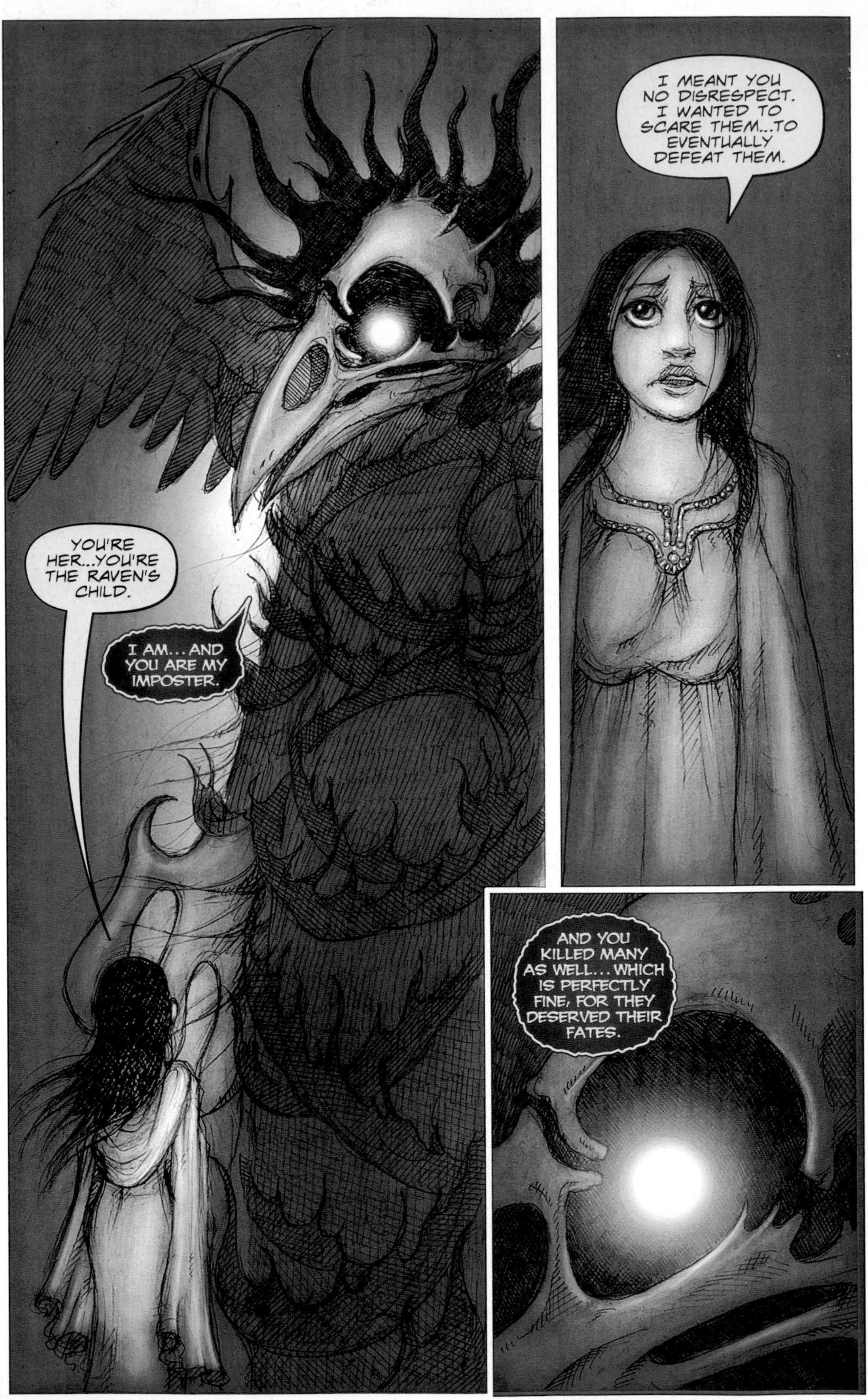
YOU'RE HER...YOU'RE THE RAVEN'S CHILD.
I AM... AND YOU ARE MY IMPOSTER.
I MEANT YOU NO DISRESPECT. I WANTED TO SCARE THEM...TO EVENTUALLY DEFEAT THEM.
AND YOU KILLED MANY AS WELL... WHICH IS PERFECTLY FINE, FOR THEY DESERVED THEIR FATES.

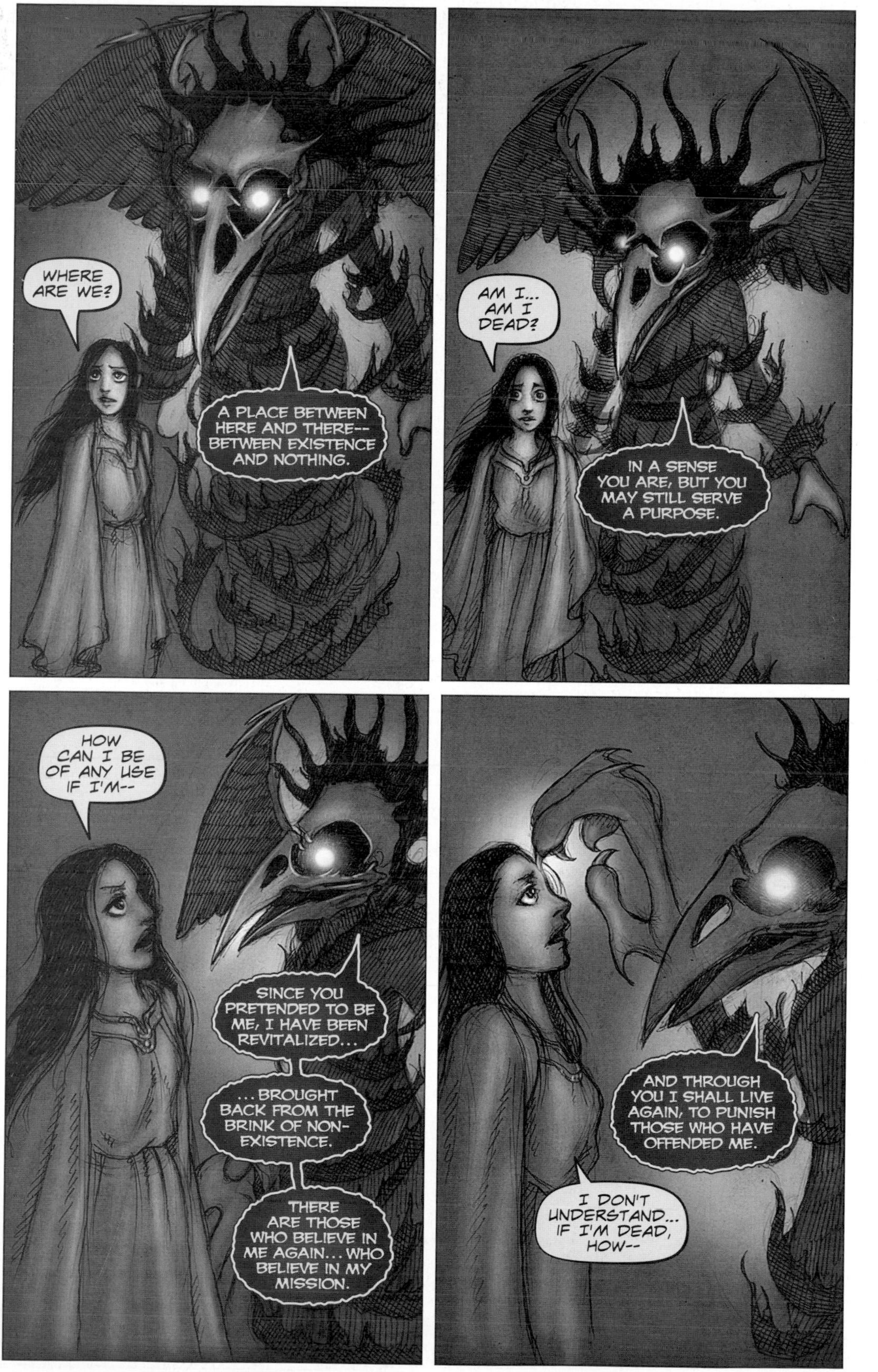
WHERE ARE WE?
A PLACE BETWEEN HERE AND THERE-- BETWEEN EXISTENCE AND NOTHING.
AM I... AM I DEAD?
IN A SENSE YOU ARE, BUT YOU MAY STILL SERVE A PURPOSE.
HOW CAN I BE OF ANY USE IF I'M--
SINCE YOU PRETENDED TO BE ME, I HAVE BEEN REVITALIZED...
...BROUGHT BACK FROM THE BRINK OF NON-EXISTENCE.
THERE ARE THOSE WHO BELIEVE IN ME AGAIN... WHO BELIEVE IN MY MISSION.
AND THROUGH YOU I SHALL LIVE AGAIN, TO PUNISH THOSE WHO HAVE OFFENDED ME.
I DON'T UNDERSTAND... IF I'M DEAD, HOW--

"GRANT ME PERMISSION TO USE YOUR FORM, AS YOU ONCE USED MINE.

"I WILL WORK THROUGH YOU TO SEE BOTH OUR MISSIONS REALIZED."

YOU WANT ME TO GIVE YOU...GIVE YOU MY BODY?

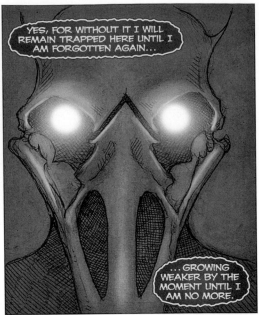

YES, FOR WITHOUT IT I WILL REMAIN TRAPPED HERE UNTIL I AM FORGOTTEN AGAIN...

...GROWING WEAKER BY THE MOMENT UNTIL I AM NO MORE.

"WILL YOU DO THIS, CARISSA? WILL YOU BE MY HOST SO THAT I CAN PUNISH THE GUILTY?"

"FOR ALL THAT HAS BEEN TAKEN FROM ME...

"...MY MOTHER AND FATHER... MY FRIENDS...

"...MY CITY... MY WORLD..."

"...YES."

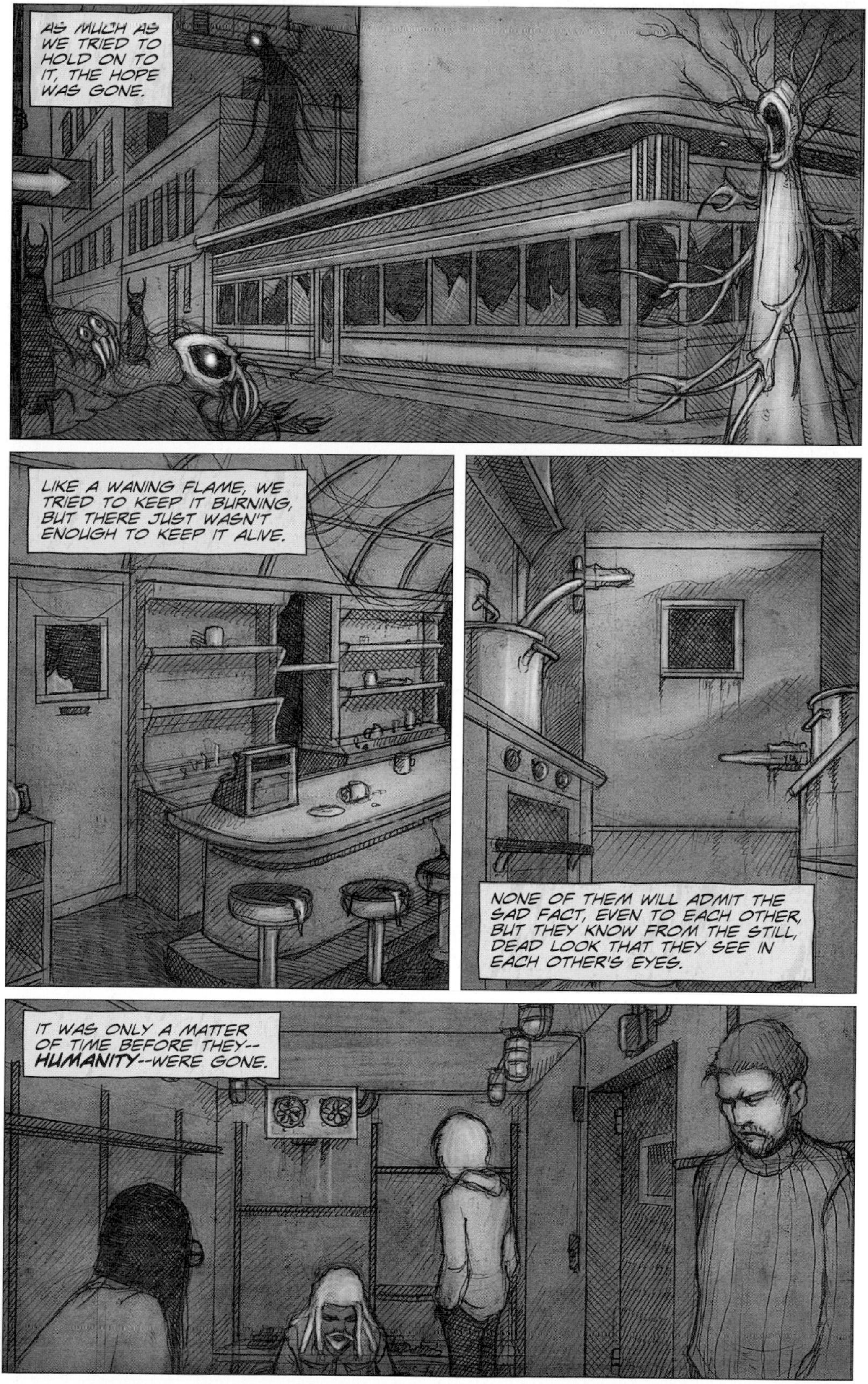
AS MUCH AS WE TRIED TO HOLD ON TO IT, THE HOPE WAS GONE.
LIKE A WANING FLAME, WE TRIED TO KEEP IT BURNING, BUT THERE JUST WASN'T ENOUGH TO KEEP IT ALIVE.
NONE OF THEM WILL ADMIT THE SAD FACT, EVEN TO EACH OTHER, BUT THEY KNOW FROM THE STILL, DEAD LOOK THAT THEY SEE IN EACH OTHER'S EYES.
IT WAS ONLY A MATTER OF TIME BEFORE THEY-- HUMANITY--WERE GONE.

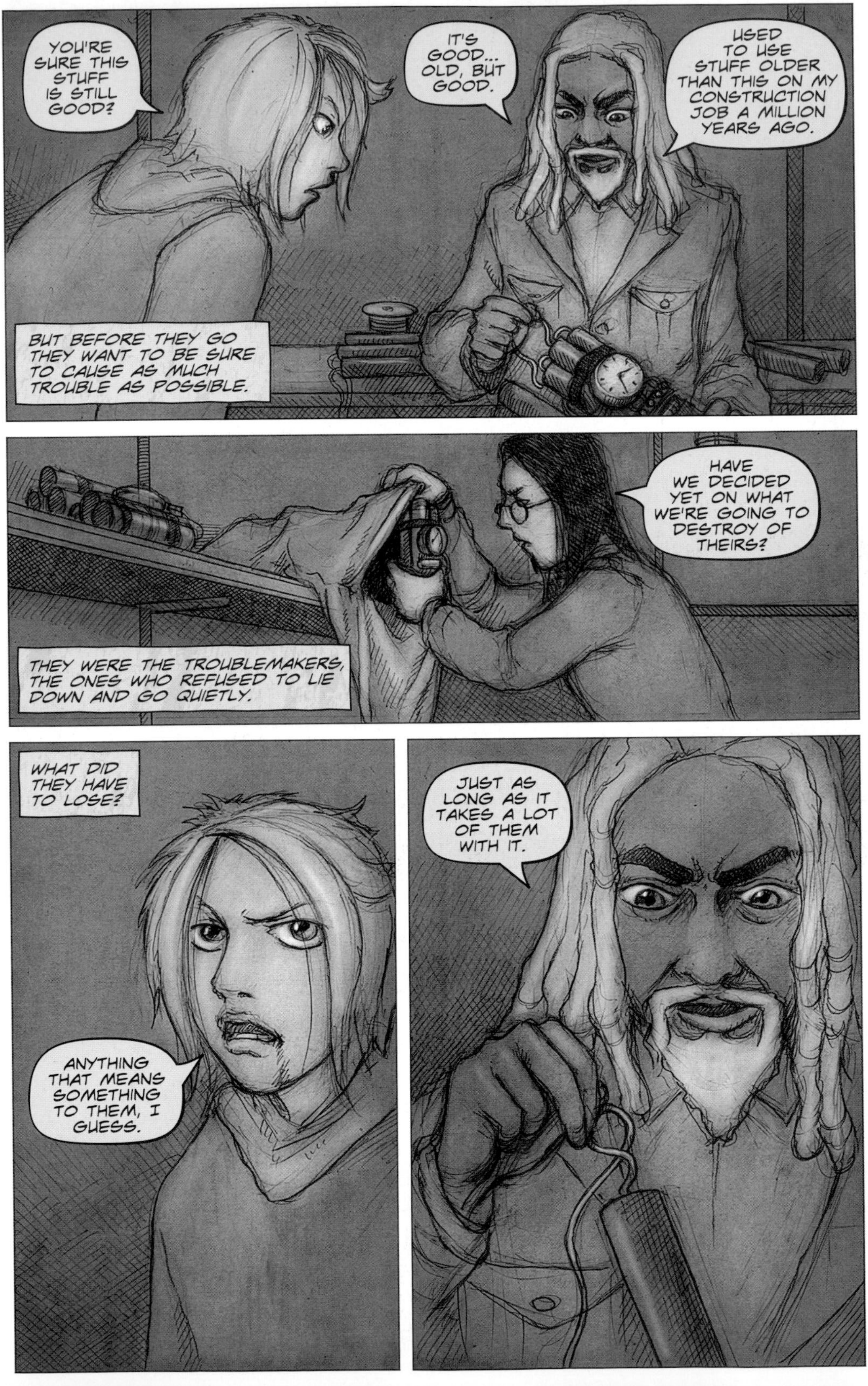
YOU'RE SURE THIS STUFF IS STILL GOOD?
IT'S GOOD... OLD, BUT GOOD.
USED TO USE STUFF OLDER THAN THIS ON MY CONSTRUCTION JOB A MILLION YEARS AGO.
BUT BEFORE THEY GO THEY WANT TO BE SURE TO CAUSE AS MUCH TROUBLE AS POSSIBLE.
HAVE WE DECIDED YET ON WHAT WE'RE GOING TO DESTROY OF THEIRS?
THEY WERE THE TROUBLEMAKERS, THE ONES WHO REFUSED TO LIE DOWN AND GO QUIETLY.
WHAT DID THEY HAVE TO LOSE?
ANYTHING THAT MEANS SOMETHING TO THEM, I GUESS.
JUST AS LONG AS IT TAKES A LOT OF THEM WITH IT.

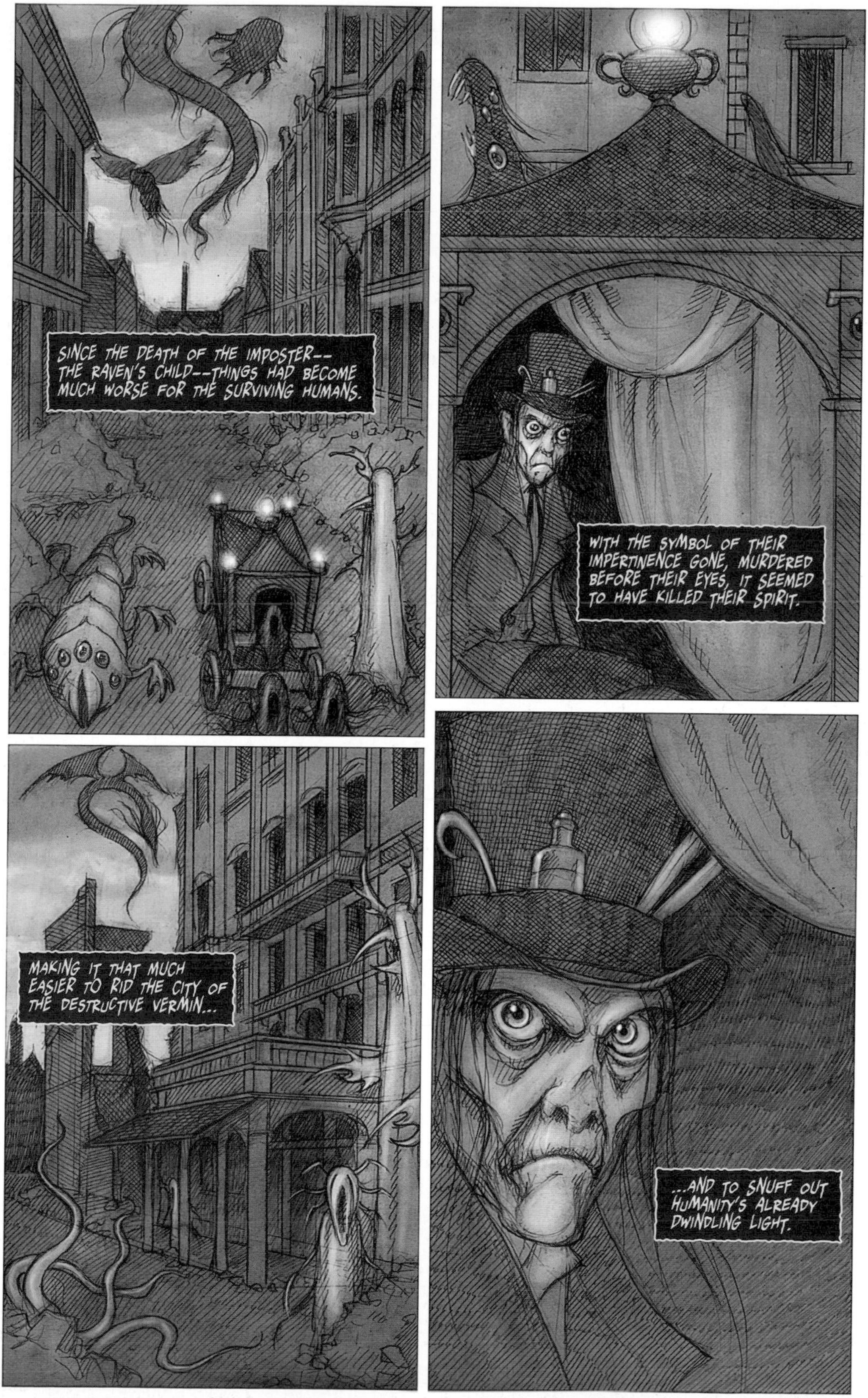
SINCE THE DEATH OF THE IMPOSTER--
THE RAVEN'S CHILD--THINGS HAD BECOME
MUCH WORSE FOR THE SURVIVING HUMANS.
WITH THE SYMBOL OF THEIR
IMPERTINENCE GONE, MURDERED
BEFORE THEIR EYES, IT SEEMED
TO HAVE KILLED THEIR SPIRIT.
MAKING IT THAT MUCH
EASIER TO RID THE CITY OF
THE DESTRUCTIVE VERMIN...
...AND TO SNUFF OUT
HUMANITY'S ALREADY
DWINDLING LIGHT.

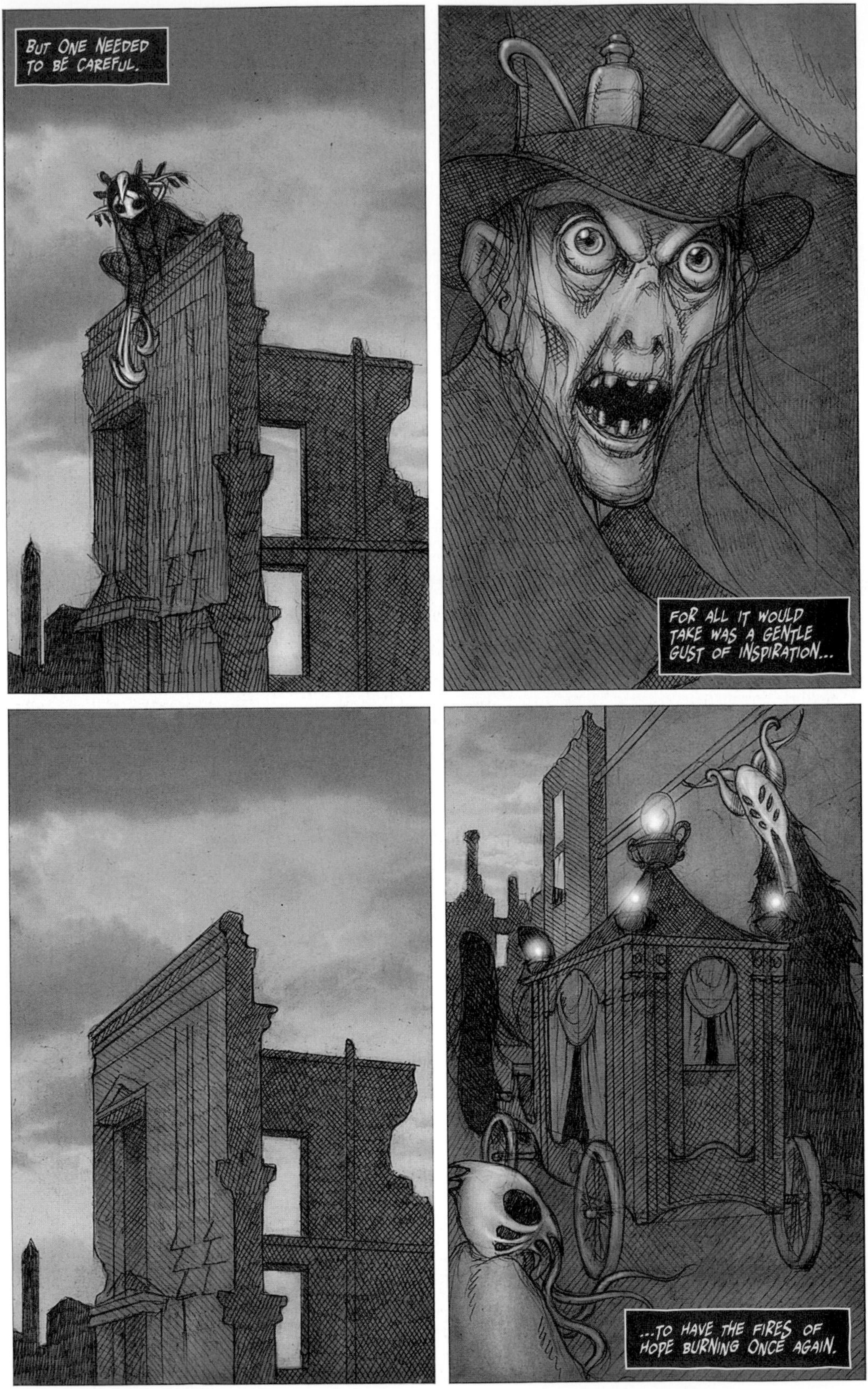
BUT ONE NEEDED TO BE CAREFUL.
FOR ALL IT WOULD TAKE WAS A GENTLE GUST OF INSPIRATION...
...TO HAVE THE FIRES OF HOPE BURNING ONCE AGAIN.

I HAVE EVERYTHING THAT I COULD HOPE FOR.

MY FORCES AROUND THE WORLD TELL ME THAT HUMANITY WILL SOON BE BUT A DISTANT MEMORY, DRIVEN TO EXTINCTION.

ANOTHER WORLD BELONGS TO ME--BELONGS TO THE THRONG.

DO YOU HEAR THEM, MY DARK LORD?

THE CRIES OF HOPELESSNESS FROM THE HUMAN VERMIN AS THEY MEET THEIR FATES?

IT IS LIKE SWEET, SWEET MUSIC TO OUR EARS.

THEN WHY DO I FEEL SO-- EMPTY? WHY CAN I NOT STOP THINKING OF HER?

IT DROWNS OUT THE HORRIBLE SILENCE OF OUR MISSING SISTER.

THE LOWLY HUMAN PRETENDING TO BE A GODDESS.

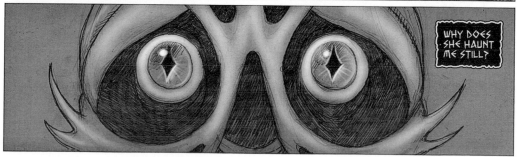

WHY DOES SHE HAUNT ME STILL?

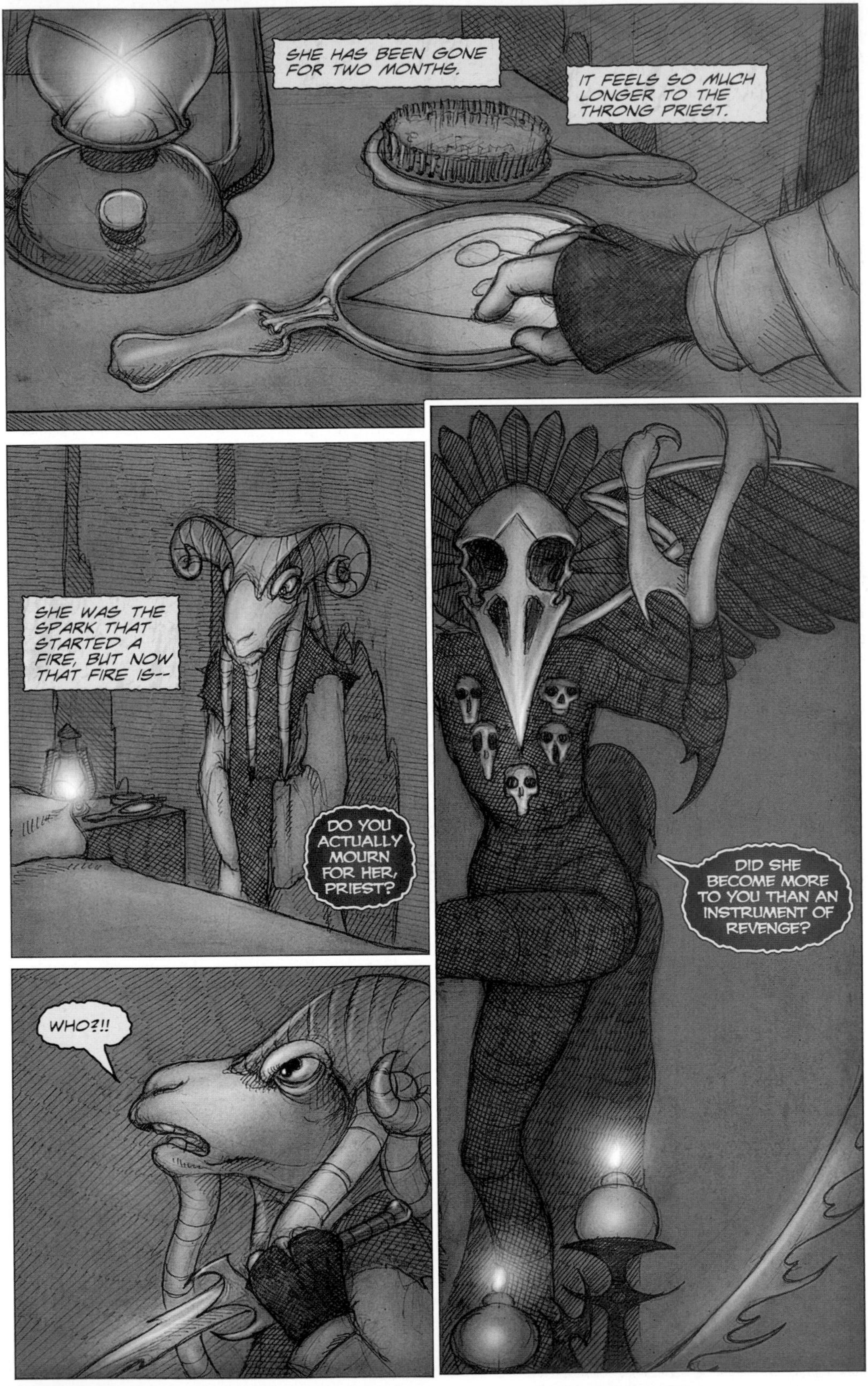
SHE HAS BEEN GONE FOR TWO MONTHS.
IT FEELS SO MUCH LONGER TO THE THRONG PRIEST.
SHE WAS THE SPARK THAT STARTED A FIRE, BUT NOW THAT FIRE IS--
DO YOU ACTUALLY MOURN FOR HER, PRIEST?
DID SHE BECOME MORE TO YOU THAN AN INSTRUMENT OF REVENGE?
WHO?!!

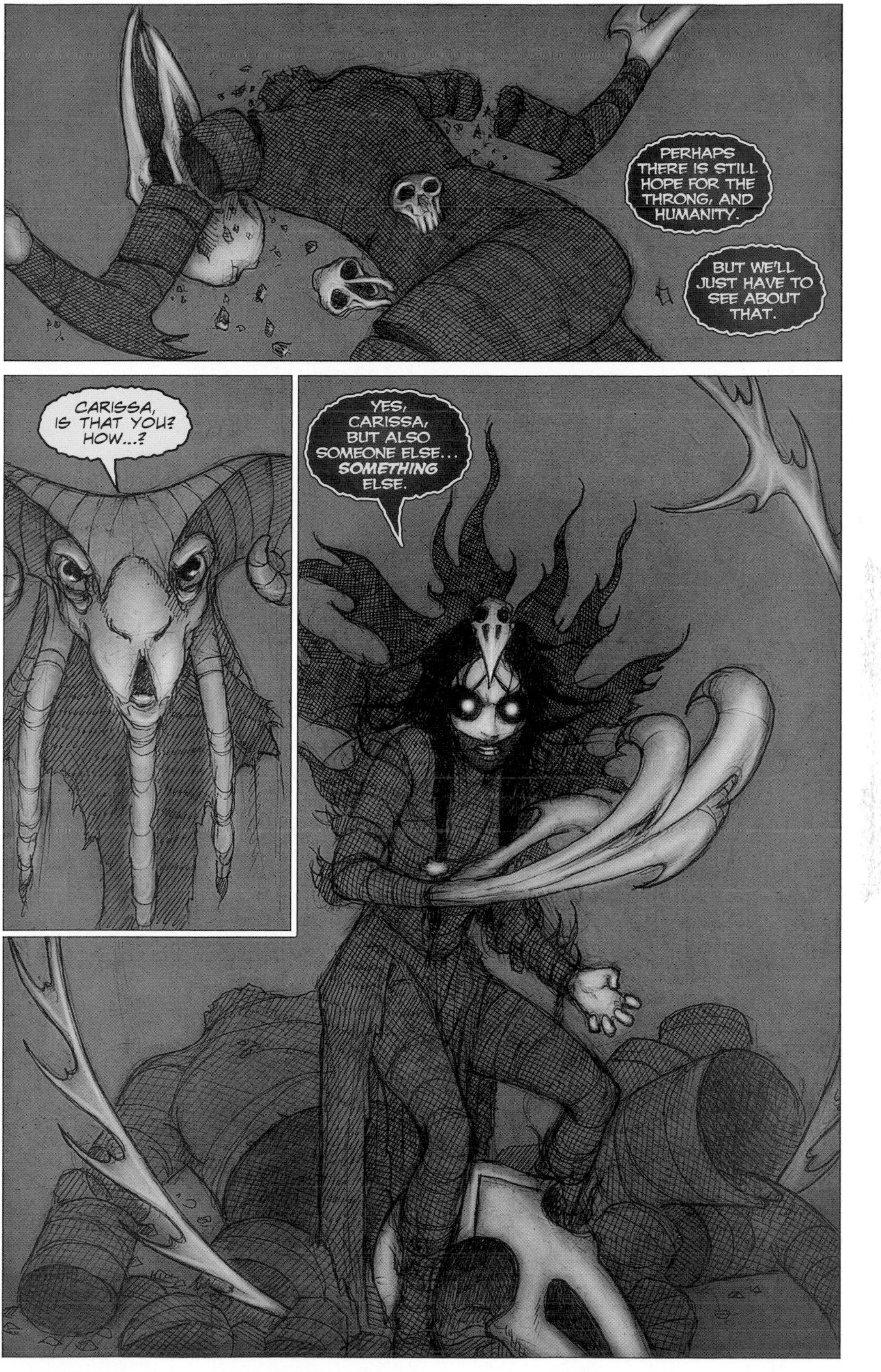
PERHAPS THERE IS STILL HOPE FOR THE THRONG, AND HUMANITY.
BUT WE'LL JUST HAVE TO SEE ABOUT THAT.
CARISSA, IS THAT YOU? HOW...?
YES, CARISSA, BUT ALSO SOMEONE ELSE... *SOMETHING* ELSE.

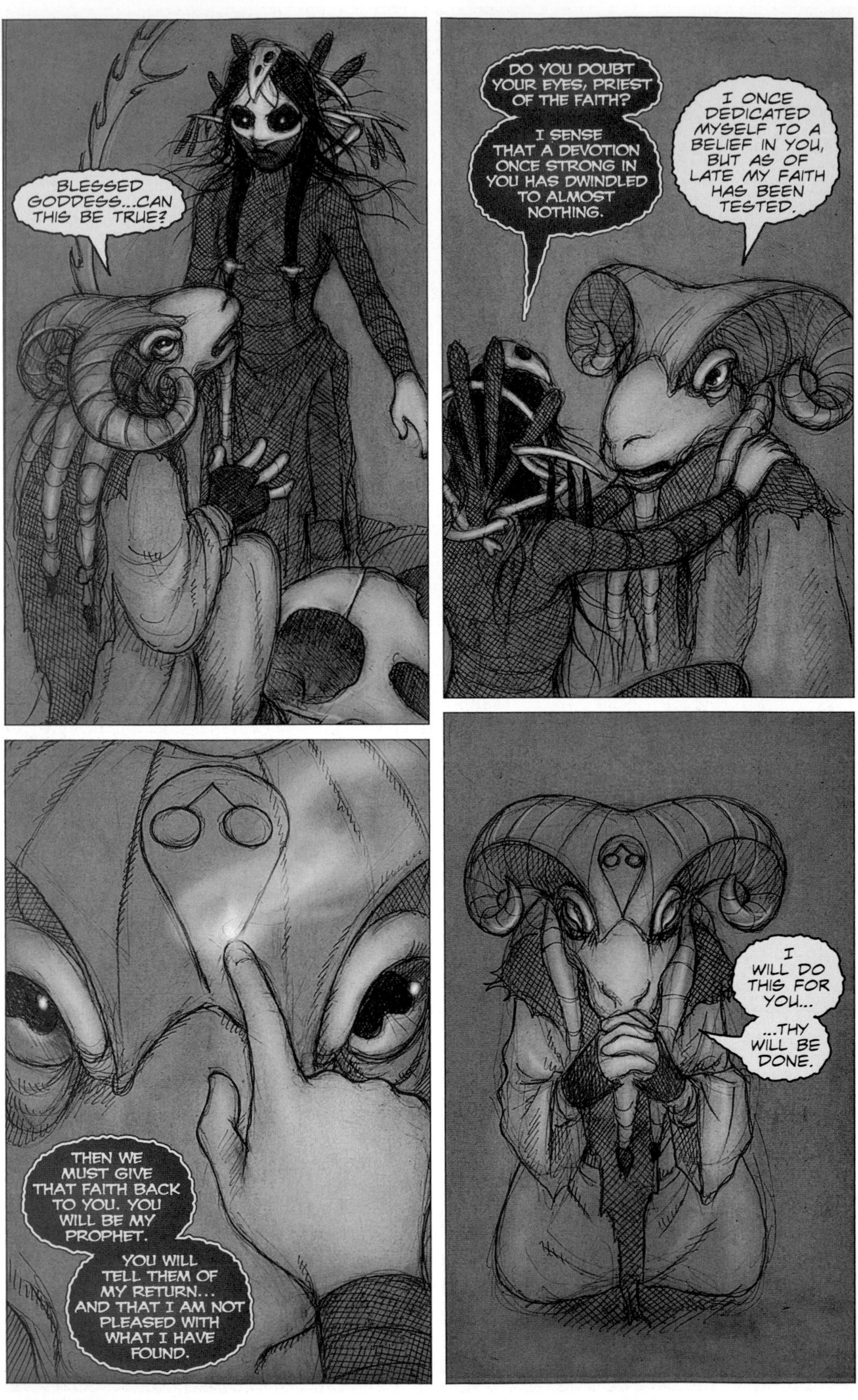
BLESSED GODDESS...CAN THIS BE TRUE?
DO YOU DOUBT YOUR EYES, PRIEST OF THE FAITH?
I SENSE THAT A DEVOTION ONCE STRONG IN YOU HAS DWINDLED TO ALMOST NOTHING.
I ONCE DEDICATED MYSELF TO A BELIEF IN YOU, BUT AS OF LATE MY FAITH HAS BEEN TESTED.
THEN WE MUST GIVE THAT FAITH BACK TO YOU. YOU WILL BE MY PROPHET.
YOU WILL TELL THEM OF MY RETURN... AND THAT I AM NOT PLEASED WITH WHAT I HAVE FOUND.
I WILL DO THIS FOR YOU...
...THY WILL BE DONE.

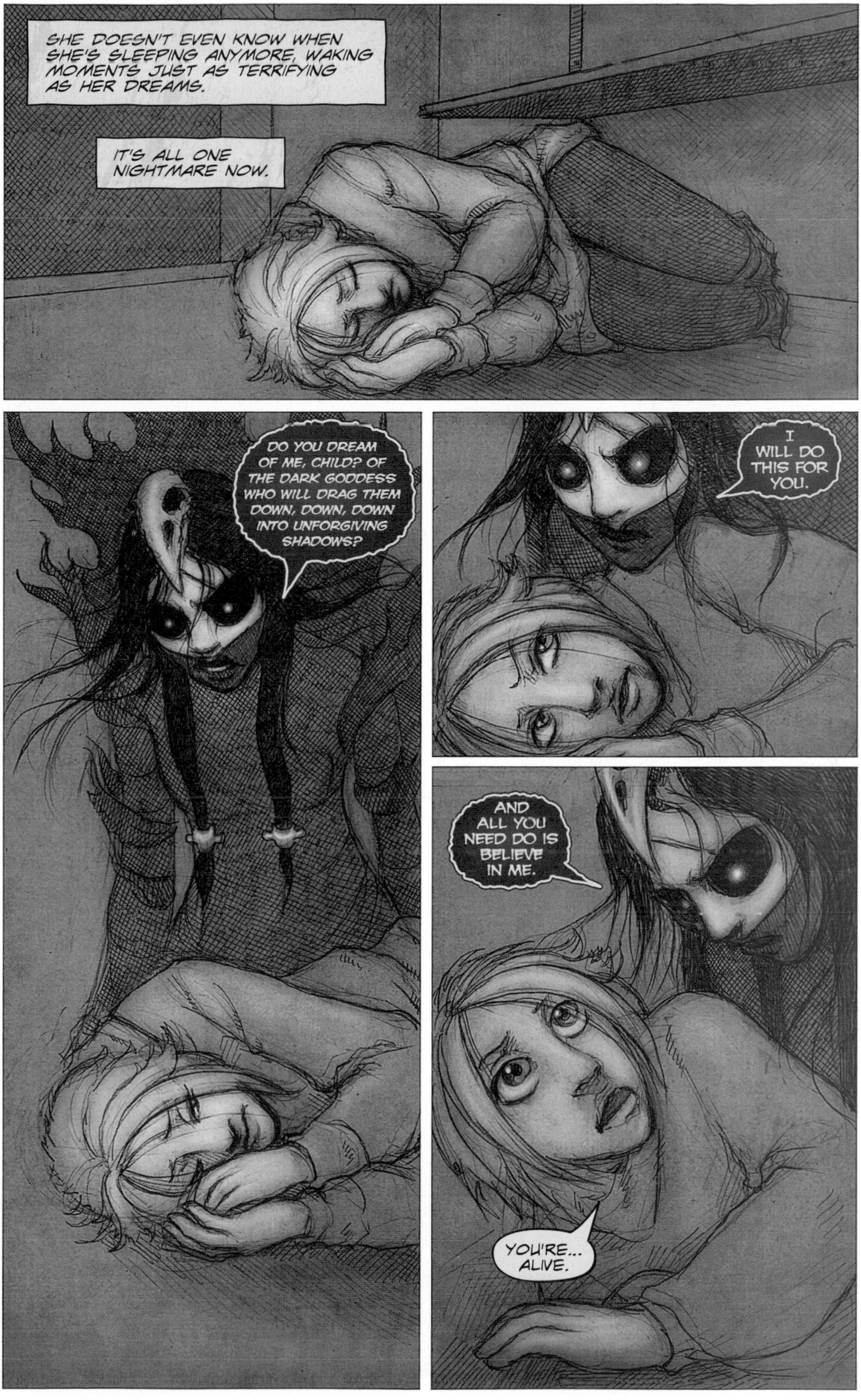
SHE DOESN'T EVEN KNOW WHEN SHE'S SLEEPING ANYMORE, WAKING MOMENTS JUST AS TERRIFYING AS HER DREAMS.
IT'S ALL ONE NIGHTMARE NOW.
DO YOU DREAM OF ME, CHILD? OF THE DARK GODDESS WHO WILL DRAG THEM DOWN, DOWN, DOWN INTO UNFORGIVING SHADOWS?
I WILL DO THIS FOR YOU.
AND ALL YOU NEED DO IS BELIEVE IN ME.
YOU'RE... ALIVE.

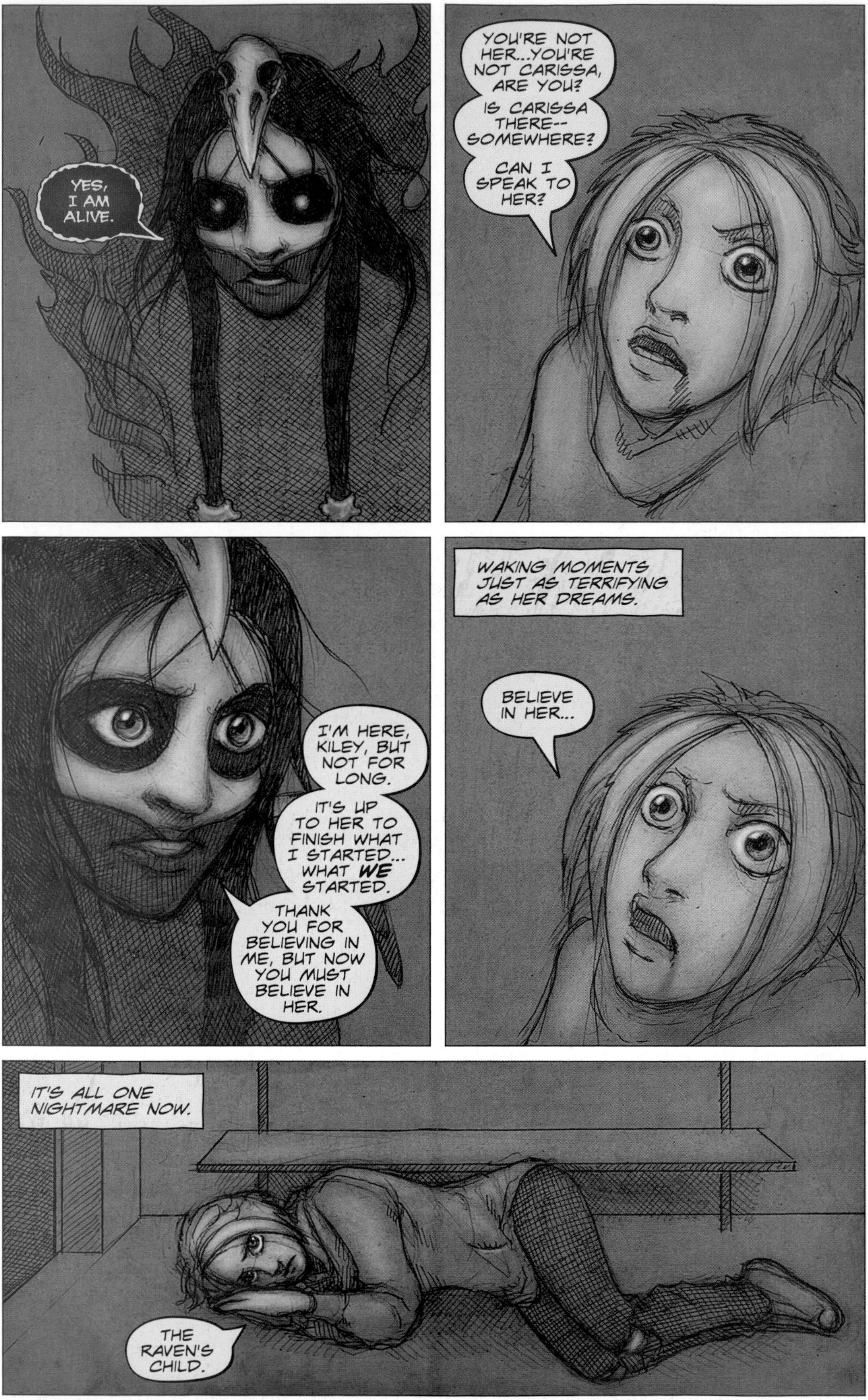
YES, I AM ALIVE.
YOU'RE NOT HER...YOU'RE NOT CARISSA, ARE YOU?
IS CARISSA THERE-- SOMEWHERE?
CAN I SPEAK TO HER?
I'M HERE, KILEY, BUT NOT FOR LONG.
IT'S UP TO HER TO FINISH WHAT I STARTED... WHAT WE STARTED.
THANK YOU FOR BELIEVING IN ME, BUT NOW YOU MUST BELIEVE IN HER.
WAKING MOMENTS JUST AS TERRIFYING AS HER DREAMS.
BELIEVE IN HER...
IT'S ALL ONE NIGHTMARE NOW.
THE RAVEN'S CHILD.

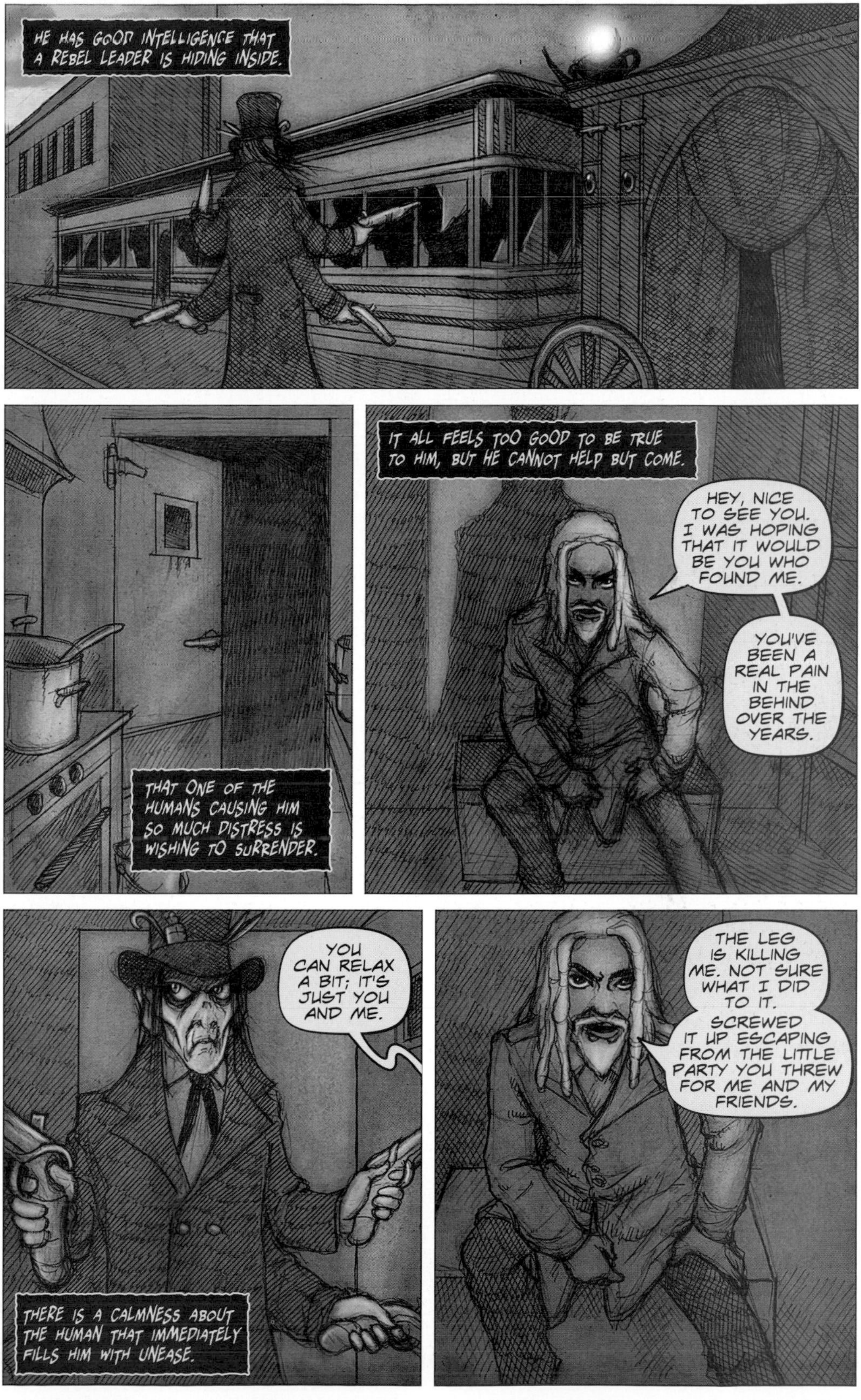
HE HAS GOOD INTELLIGENCE THAT A REBEL LEADER IS HIDING INSIDE.
THAT ONE OF THE HUMANS CAUSING HIM SO MUCH DISTRESS IS WISHING TO SURRENDER.
IT ALL FEELS TOO GOOD TO BE TRUE TO HIM, BUT HE CANNOT HELP BUT COME.
HEY, NICE TO SEE YOU. I WAS HOPING THAT IT WOULD BE YOU WHO FOUND ME.
YOU'VE BEEN A REAL PAIN IN THE BEHIND OVER THE YEARS.
YOU CAN RELAX A BIT; IT'S JUST YOU AND ME.
THERE IS A CALMNESS ABOUT THE HUMAN THAT IMMEDIATELY FILLS HIM WITH UNEASE.
THE LEG IS KILLING ME. NOT SURE WHAT I DID TO IT.
SCREWED IT UP ESCAPING FROM THE LITTLE PARTY YOU THREW FOR ME AND MY FRIENDS.

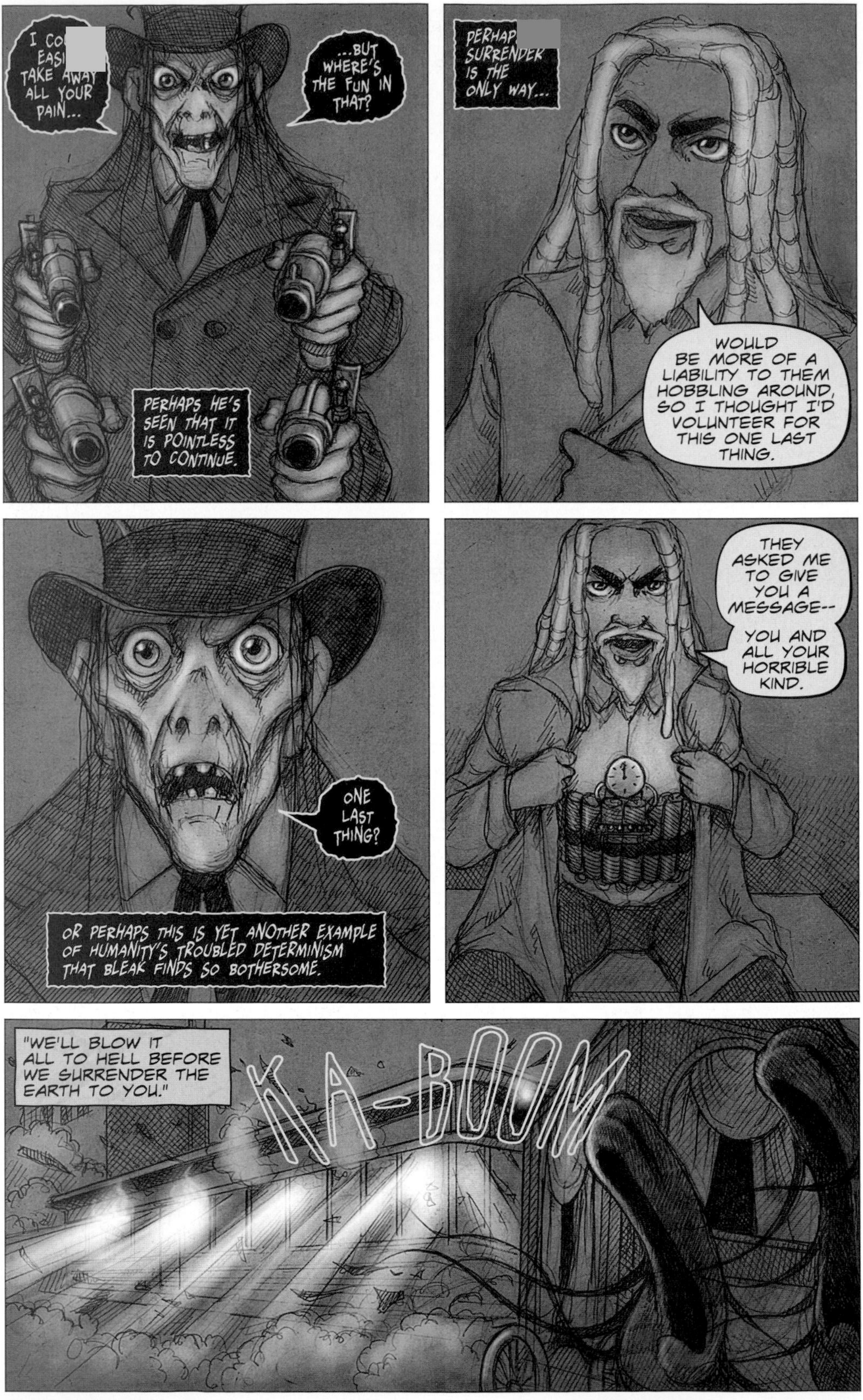
I CO
EASI
TAKE AWAY
ALL YOUR
PAIN...
...BUT WHERE'S THE FUN IN THAT?
PERHAPS HE'S SEEN THAT IT IS POINTLESS TO CONTINUE.
PERHAP
SURRENDER
IS THE
ONLY WAY...
WOULD BE MORE OF A LIABILITY TO THEM HOBBLING AROUND, SO I THOUGHT I'D VOLUNTEER FOR THIS ONE LAST THING.
ONE LAST THING?
OR PERHAPS THIS IS YET ANOTHER EXAMPLE OF HUMANITY'S TROUBLED DETERMINISM THAT BLEAK FINDS SO BOTHERSOME.
THEY ASKED ME TO GIVE YOU A MESSAGE--
YOU AND ALL YOUR HORRIBLE KIND.
"WE'LL BLOW IT ALL TO HELL BEFORE WE SURRENDER THE EARTH TO YOU."
KA-BOOM

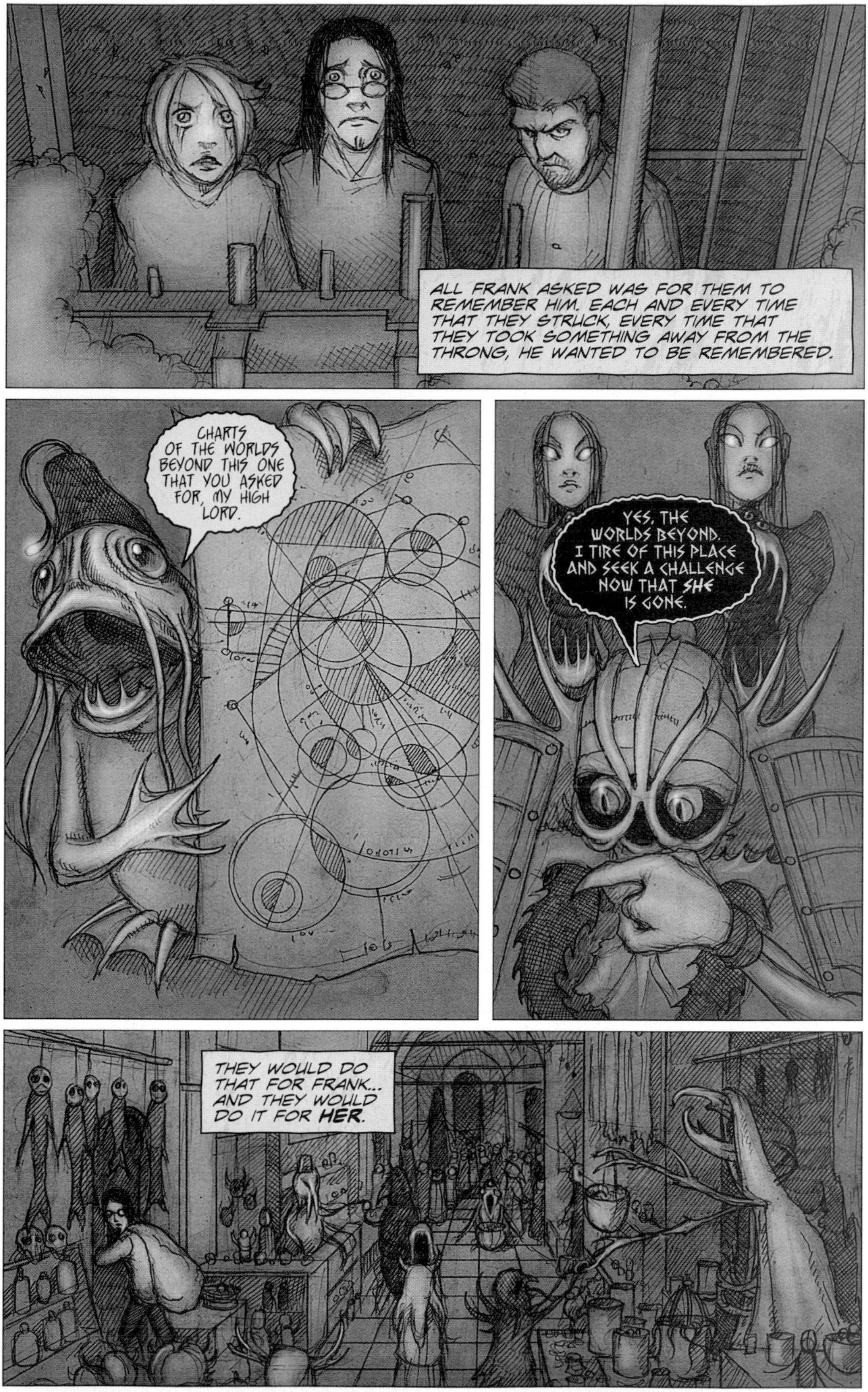
ALL FRANK ASKED WAS FOR THEM TO REMEMBER HIM. EACH AND EVERY TIME THAT THEY STRUCK, EVERY TIME THAT THEY TOOK SOMETHING AWAY FROM THE THRONG, HE WANTED TO BE REMEMBERED.
CHARTS OF THE WORLDS BEYOND THIS ONE THAT YOU ASKED FOR, MY HIGH LORD.
YES, THE WORLDS BEYOND. I TIRE OF THIS PLACE AND SEEK A CHALLENGE NOW THAT SHE IS GONE.
THEY WOULD DO THAT FOR FRANK... AND THEY WOULD DO IT FOR HER.

HIGH LORD CAITIFF--WE MUST SPEAK AT ONCE!

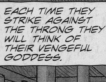

EACH TIME THEY STRIKE AGAINST THE THRONG THEY WILL THINK OF THEIR VENGEFUL GODDESS.

HOW DARE YOU INTERRUPT THE PLANS FOR THE FUTURE OF THE GREAT THRONG EMPIRE!

YOU MUST LISTEN TO ME! IT IS FAR WORSE THAN I--WE-- IMAGINED.

YES, THE IMPOSTER IS DEAD BUT SHE IS STILL VERY MUCH ALIVE!

THE RAVEN'S CHILD IS ALIVE.

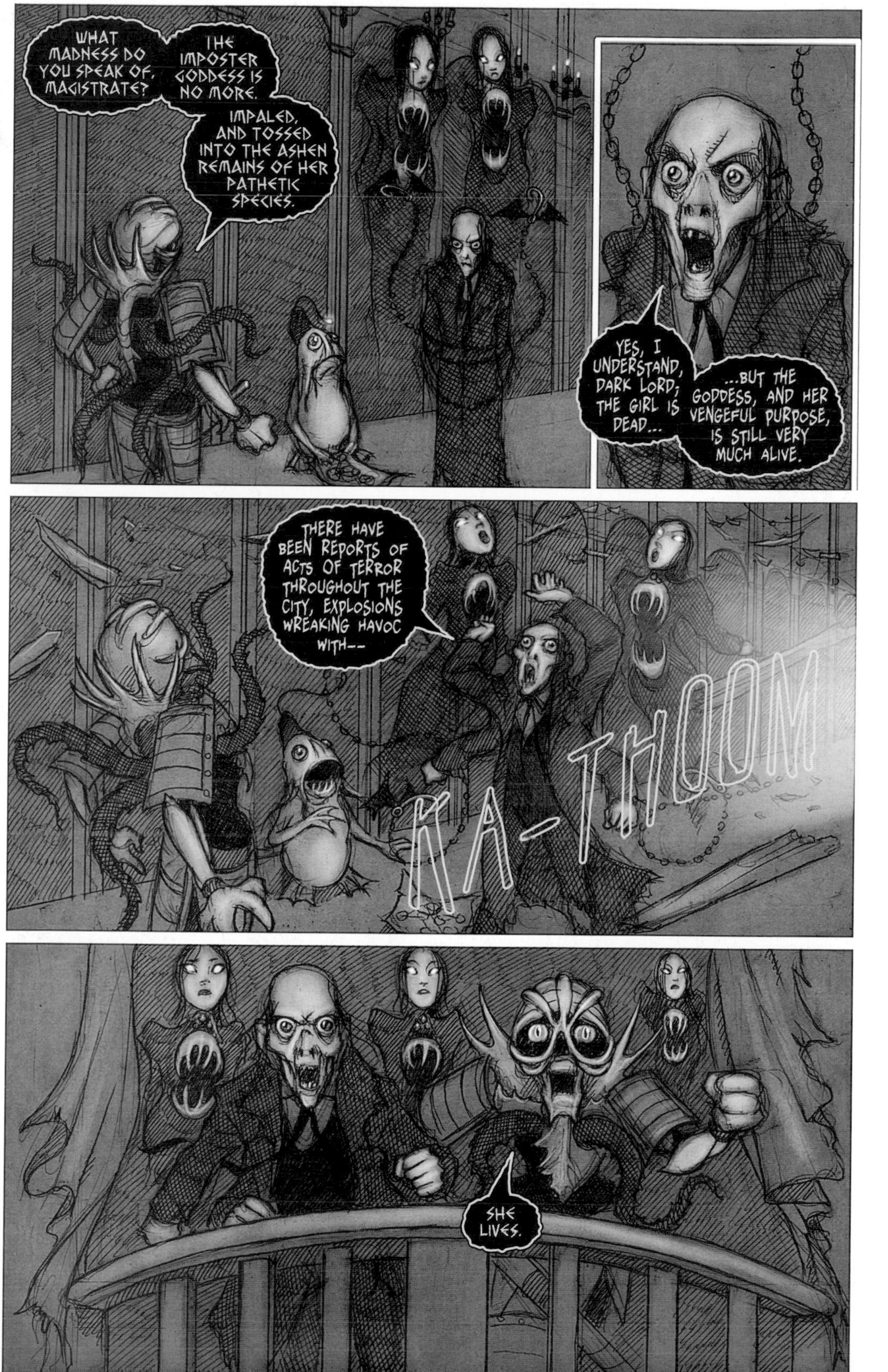
WHAT MADNESS DO YOU SPEAK OF, MAGISTRATE?
THE IMPOSTER GODDESS IS NO MORE.
IMPALED, AND TOSSED INTO THE ASHEN REMAINS OF HER PATHETIC SPECIES.
YES, I UNDERSTAND, DARK LORD; THE GIRL IS DEAD...
...BUT THE GODDESS, AND HER VENGEFUL PURPOSE, IS STILL VERY MUCH ALIVE.
THERE HAVE BEEN REPORTS OF ACTS OF TERROR THROUGHOUT THE CITY, EXPLOSIONS WREAKING HAVOC WITH--
KA-THOOM
SHE LIVES.

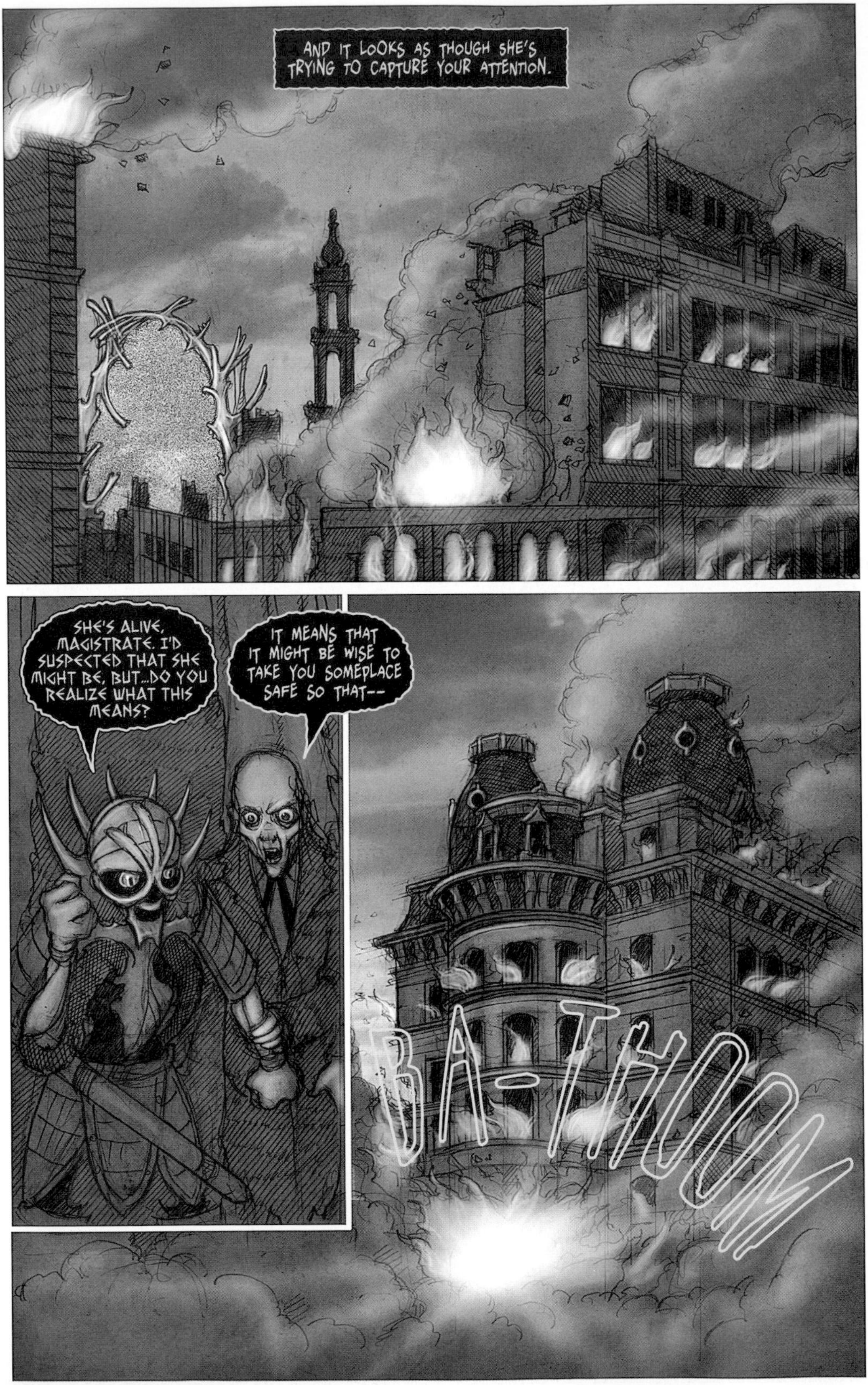
AND IT LOOKS AS THOUGH SHE'S TRYING TO CAPTURE YOUR ATTENTION.
SHE'S ALIVE, MAGISTRATE. I'D SUSPECTED THAT SHE MIGHT BE, BUT...DO YOU REALIZE WHAT THIS MEANS?
IT MEANS THAT IT MIGHT BE WISE TO TAKE YOU SOMEPLACE SAFE SO THAT--
BA-THOOM

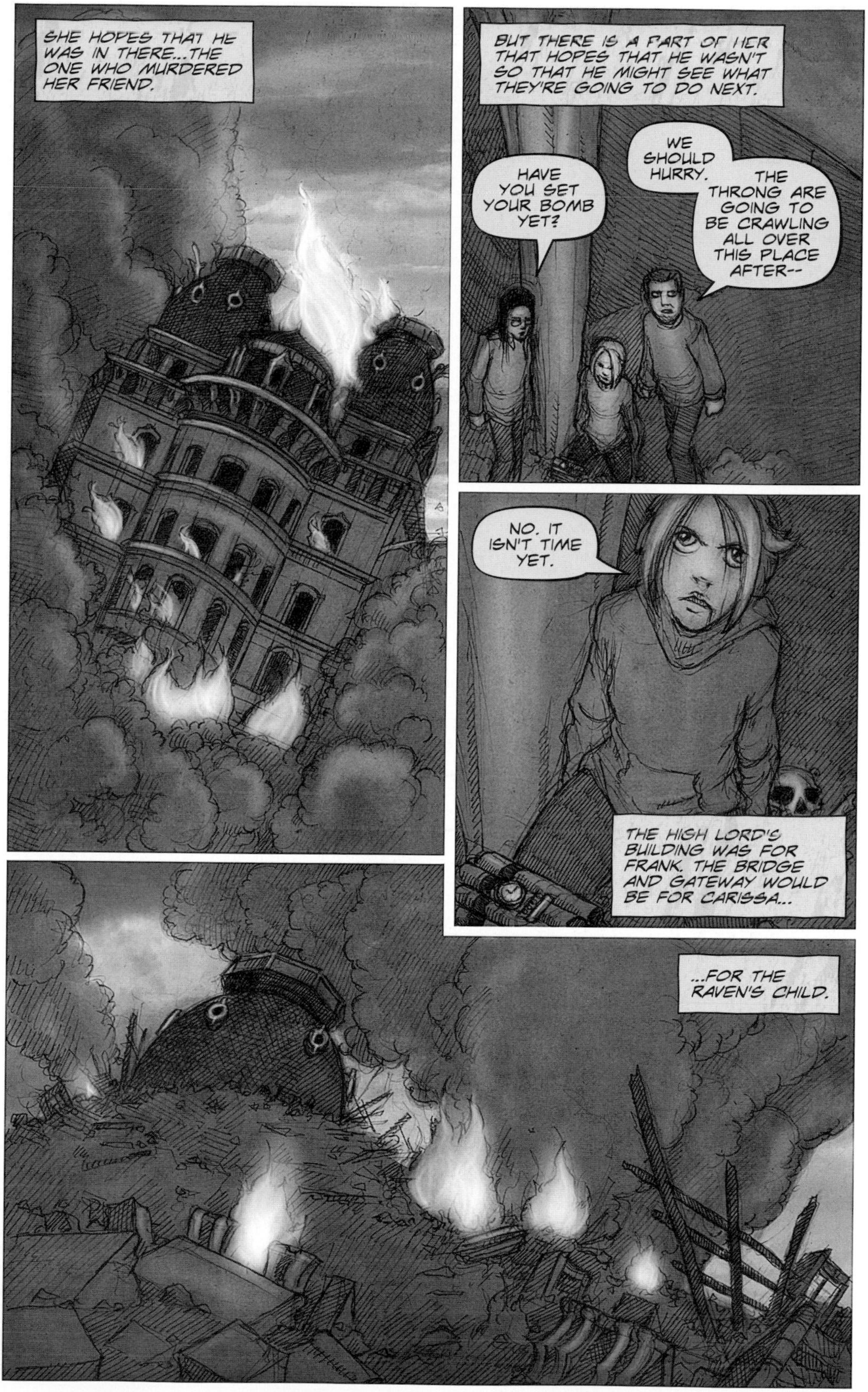
SHE HOPES THAT HE WAS IN THERE...THE ONE WHO MURDERED HER FRIEND.
BUT THERE IS A PART OF HER THAT HOPES THAT HE WASN'T SO THAT HE MIGHT SEE WHAT THEY'RE GOING TO DO NEXT.
HAVE YOU SET YOUR BOMB YET?
WE SHOULD HURRY.
THE THRONG ARE GOING TO BE CRAWLING ALL OVER THIS PLACE AFTER--
NO. IT ISN'T TIME YET.
THE HIGH LORD'S BUILDING WAS FOR FRANK. THE BRIDGE AND GATEWAY WOULD BE FOR CARISSA...
...FOR THE RAVEN'S CHILD.

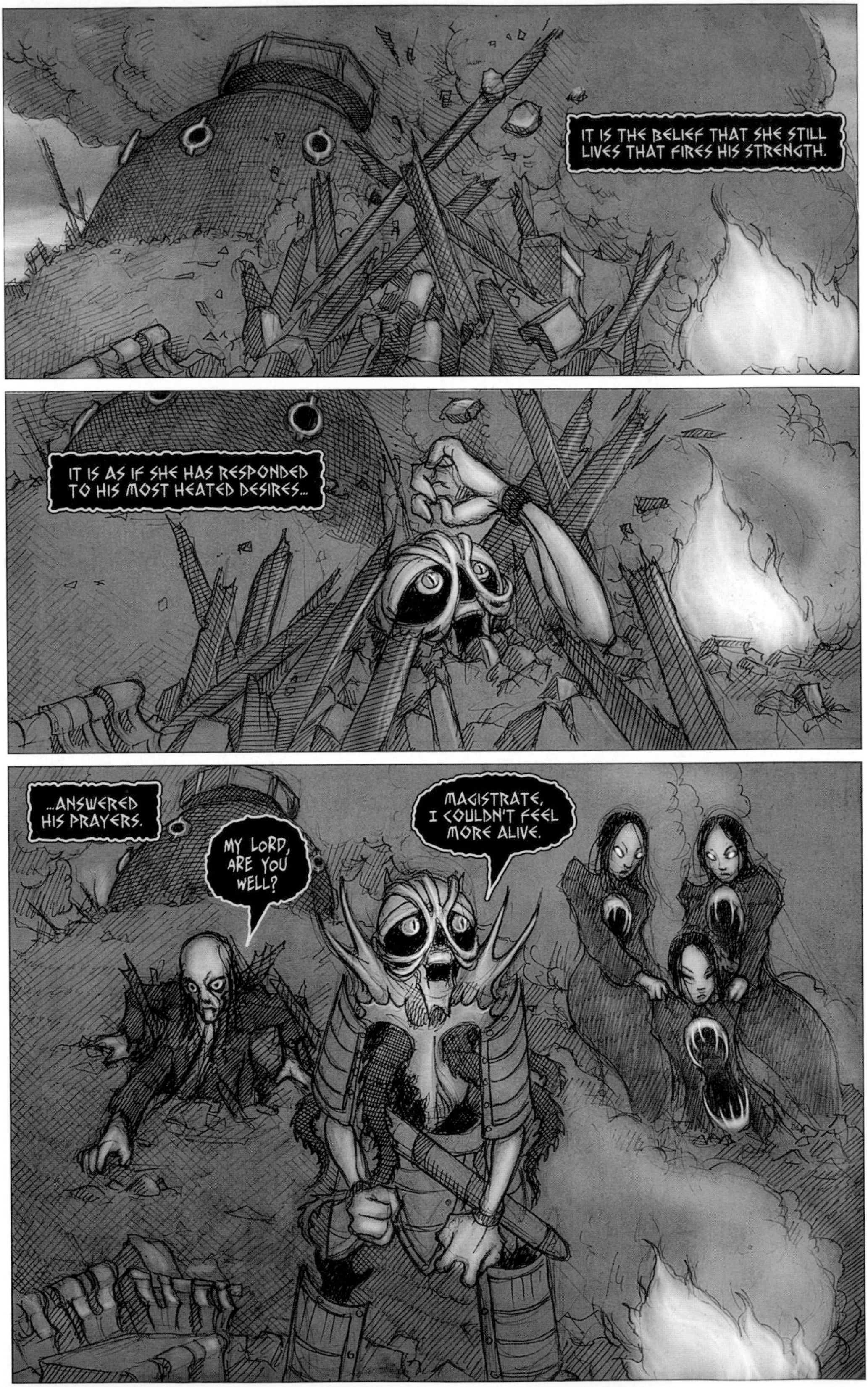
IT IS THE BELIEF THAT SHE STILL LIVES THAT FIRES HIS STRENGTH.
IT IS AS IF SHE HAS RESPONDED TO HIS MOST HEATED DESIRES...
...ANSWERED HIS PRAYERS.
MY LORD, ARE YOU WELL?
MAGISTRATE, I COULDN'T FEEL MORE ALIVE.

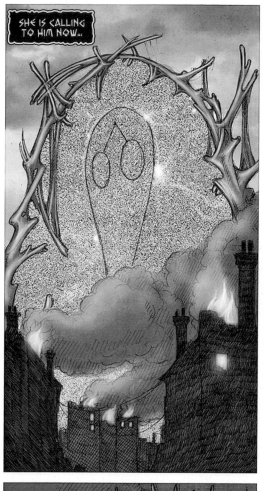

SHE IS CALLING TO HIM NOW...

...AND HE HAS NO CHOICE BUT TO ANSWER.

WE MUST GATHER OUR FORCES AT ONCE AND--

YESSSS...

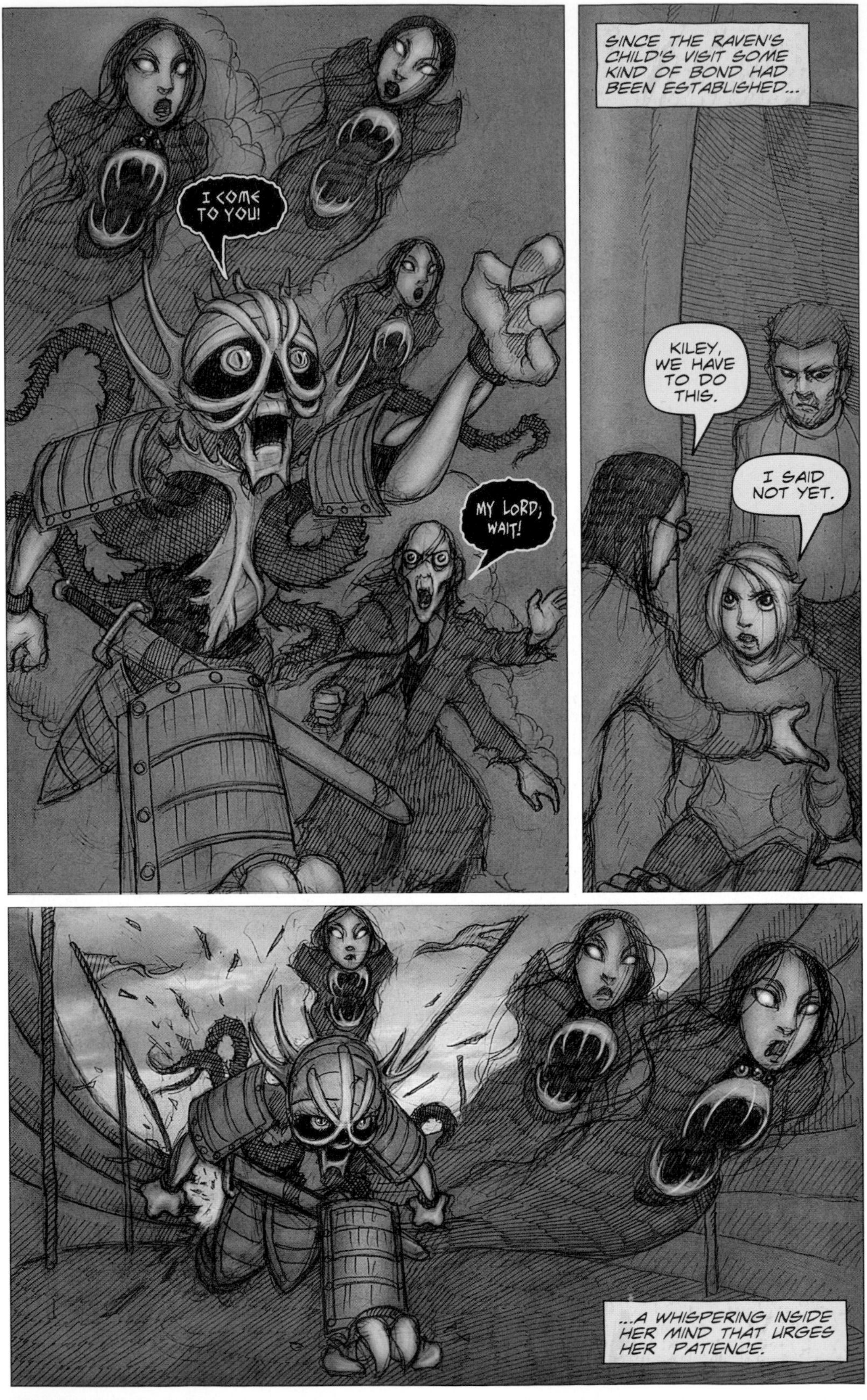
I COME TO YOU!
MY LORD, WAIT!
SINCE THE RAVEN'S CHILD'S VISIT SOME KIND OF BOND HAD BEEN ESTABLISHED...
KILEY, WE HAVE TO DO THIS.
I SAID NOT YET.
...A WHISPERING INSIDE HER MIND THAT URGES HER PATIENCE.

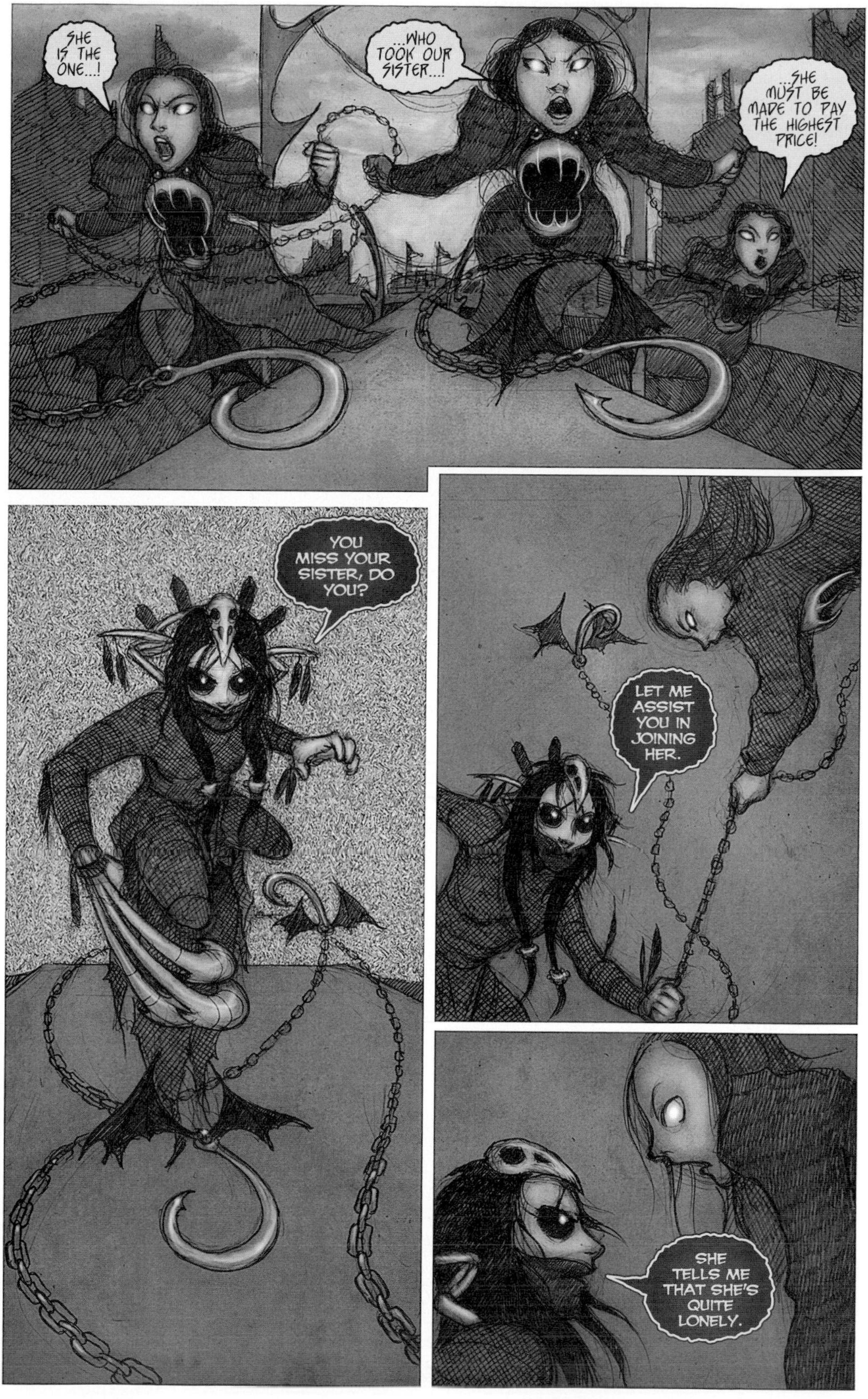
SHE IS THE ONE...!
...WHO TOOK OUR SISTER...!
...SHE MUST BE MADE TO PAY THE HIGHEST PRICE!
YOU MISS YOUR SISTER, DO YOU?
LET ME ASSIST YOU IN JOINING HER.
SHE TELLS ME THAT SHE'S QUITE LONELY.

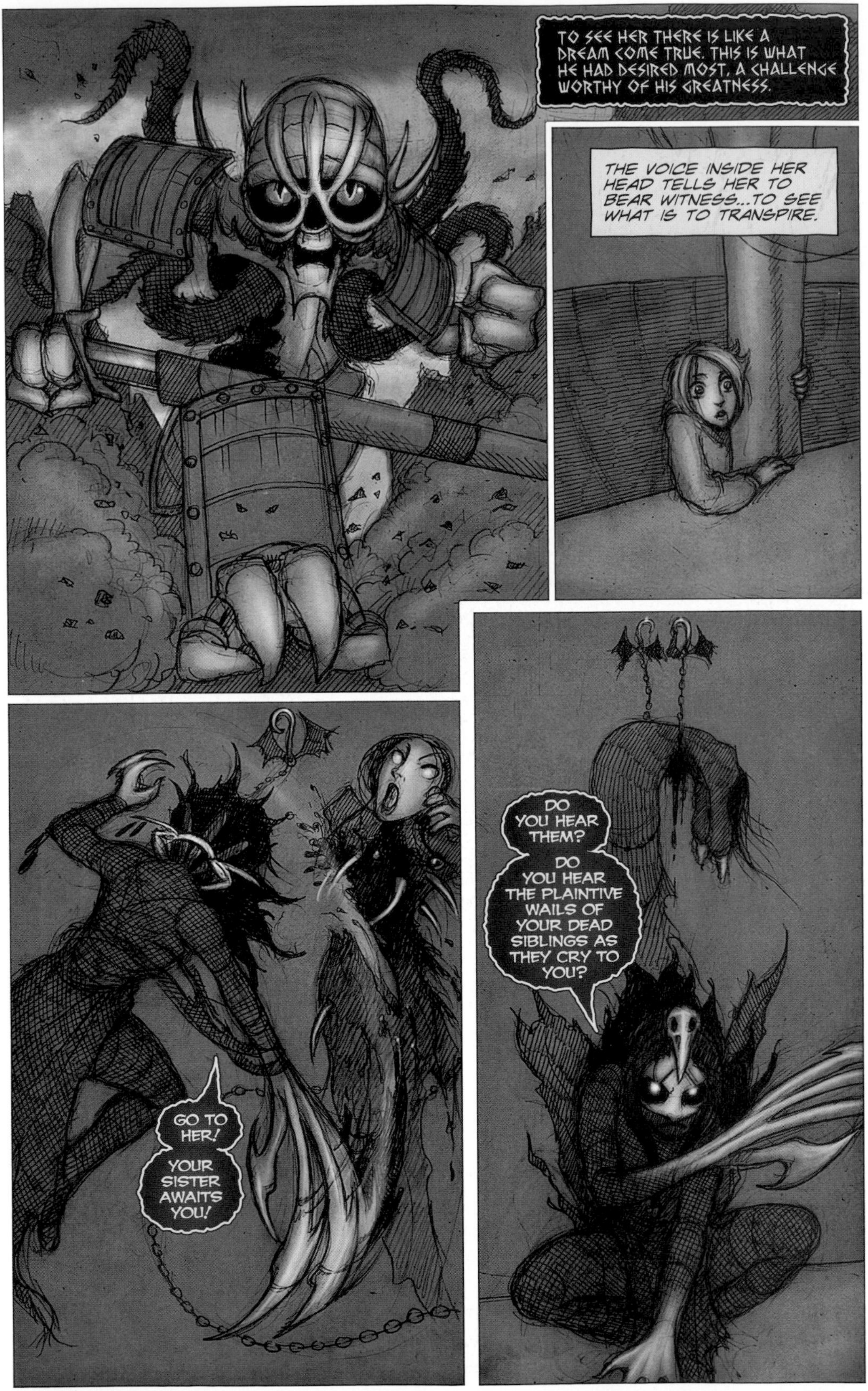
TO SEE HER THERE IS LIKE A DREAM COME TRUE. THIS IS WHAT HE HAD DESIRED MOST, A CHALLENGE WORTHY OF HIS GREATNESS.
THE VOICE INSIDE HER HEAD TELLS HER TO BEAR WITNESS...TO SEE WHAT IS TO TRANSPIRE.
GO TO HER!
YOUR SISTER AWAITS YOU!
DO YOU HEAR THEM?
DO YOU HEAR THE PLAINTIVE WAILS OF YOUR DEAD SIBLINGS AS THEY CRY TO YOU?

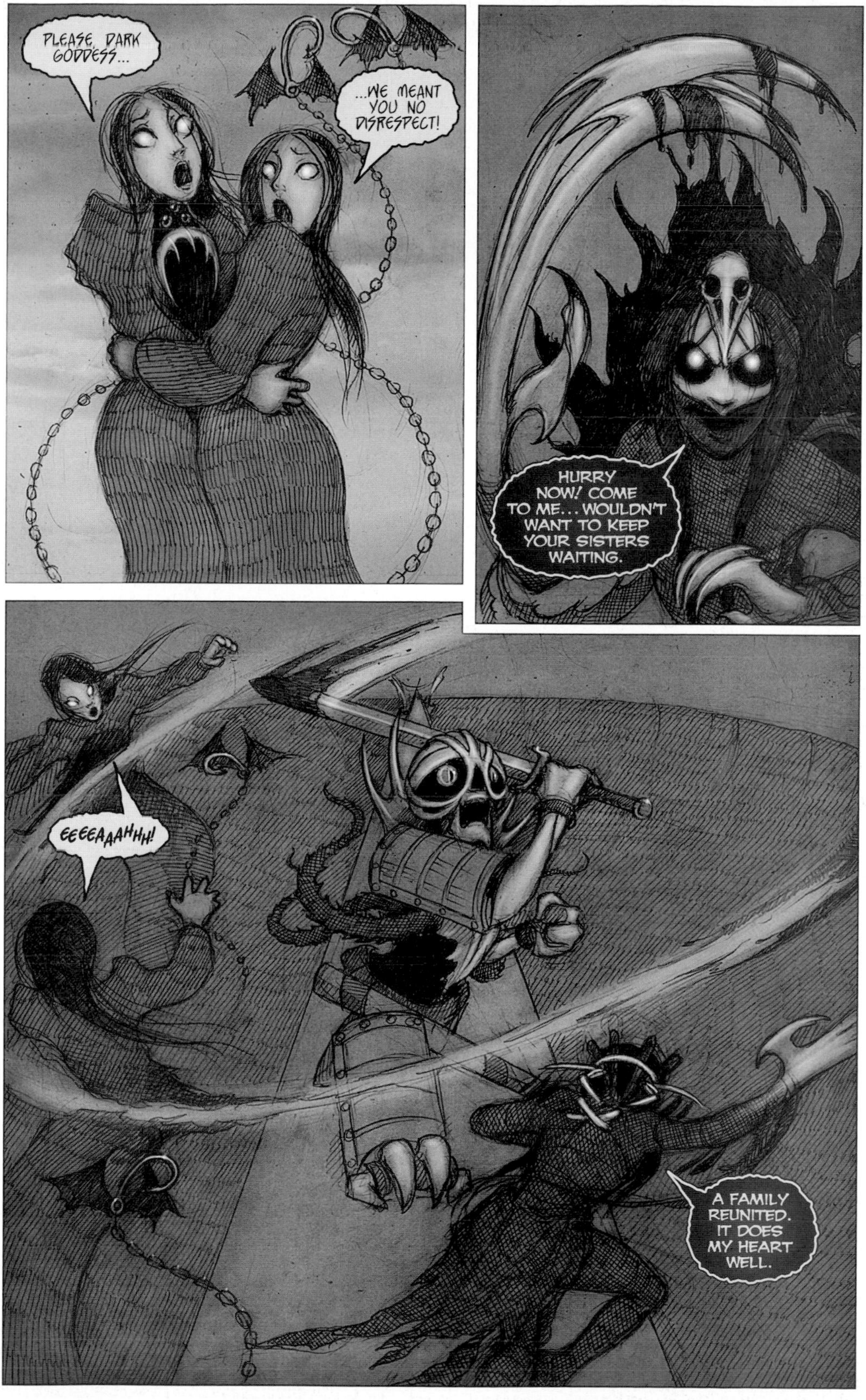
PLEASE, DARK GODDESS...
...WE MEANT YOU NO DISRESPECT!
HURRY NOW! COME TO ME... WOULDN'T WANT TO KEEP YOUR SISTERS WAITING.
EEEEAAAHHH!
A FAMILY REUNITED. IT DOES MY HEART WELL.

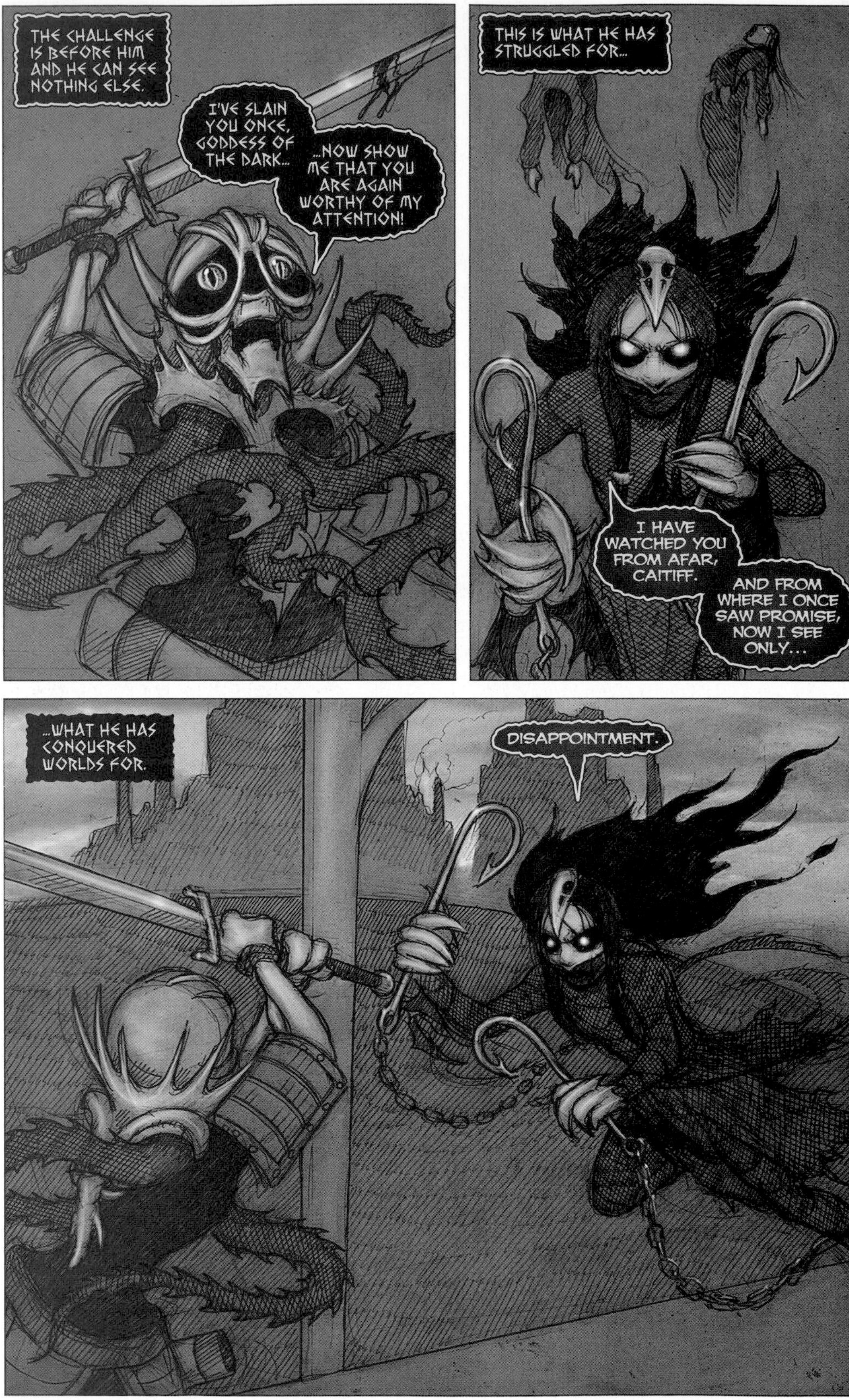
THE CHALLENGE IS BEFORE HIM AND HE CAN SEE NOTHING ELSE.
I'VE SLAIN YOU ONCE, GODDESS OF THE DARK...
...NOW SHOW ME THAT YOU ARE AGAIN WORTHY OF MY ATTENTION!
THIS IS WHAT HE HAS STRUGGLED FOR...
I HAVE WATCHED YOU FROM AFAR, CAITIFF.
AND FROM WHERE I ONCE SAW PROMISE, NOW I SEE ONLY...
...WHAT HE HAS CONQUERED WORLDS FOR.
DISAPPOINTMENT.

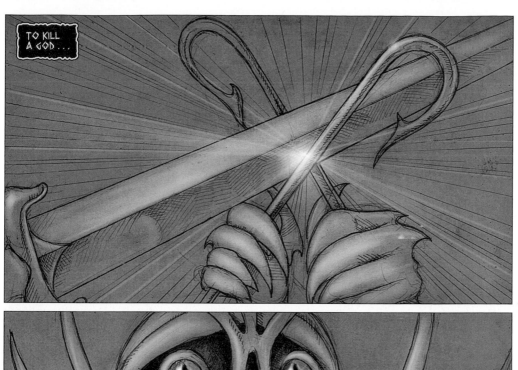

TO KILL A GOD . . .

WILL MAKE HIM ONE HIMSELF.

AND THEN ALL ABOVE, AS WELL AS THOSE BELOW, WILL BOW TO HIM.

COME.

"LET ME TAKE YOU IN MY EMBRACE...

"... AND SHOW YOU OF MY DISPLEASURE.

"LET ME SHOW YOU...

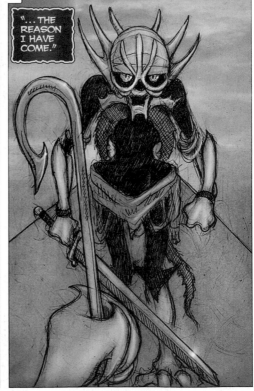

"... THE REASON I HAVE COME."

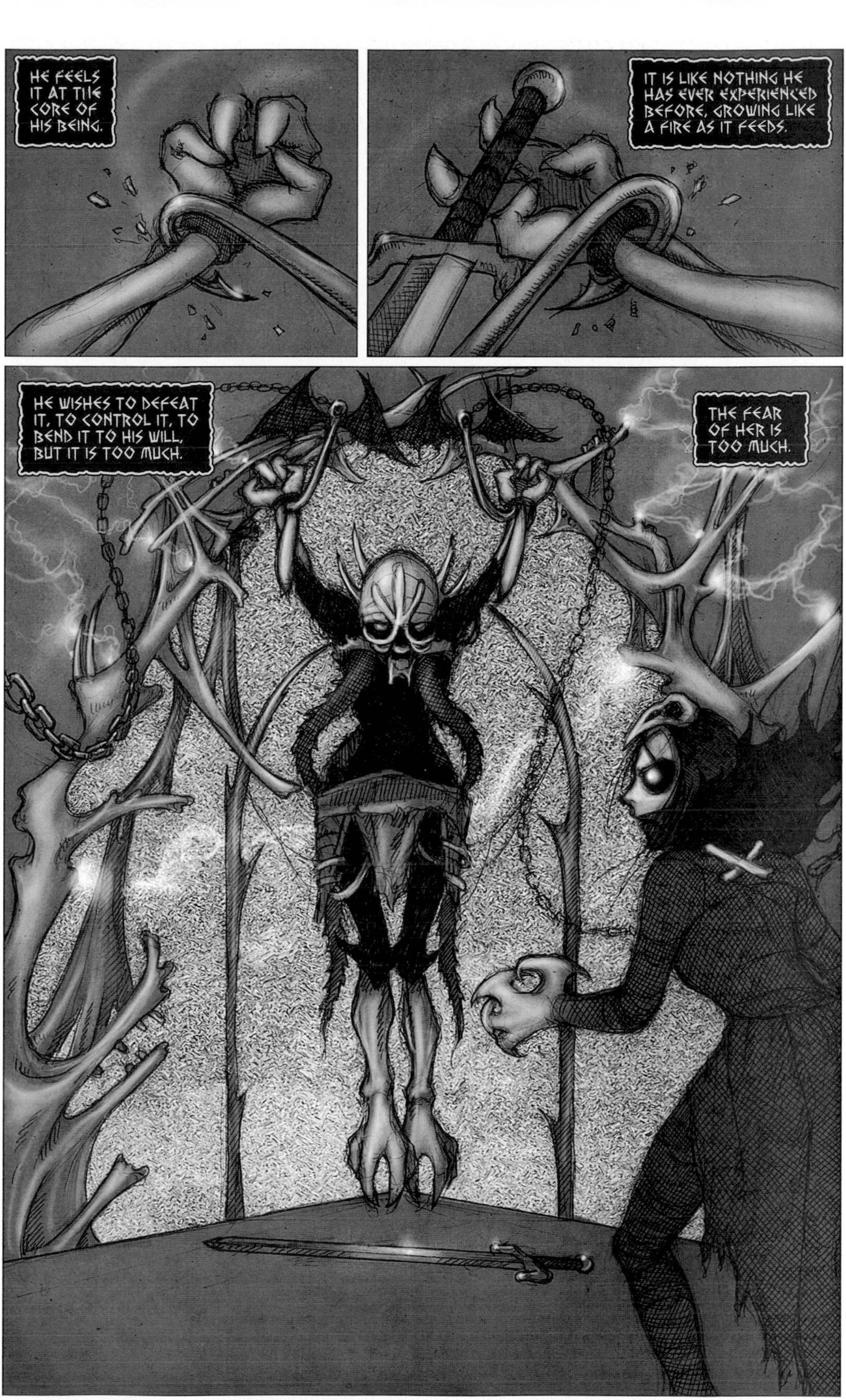
HE FEELS IT AT THE CORE OF HIS BEING.
IT IS LIKE NOTHING HE HAS EVER EXPERIENCED BEFORE, GROWING LIKE A FIRE AS IT FEEDS.
HE WISHES TO DEFEAT IT, TO CONTROL IT, TO BEND IT TO HIS WILL, BUT IT IS TOO MUCH.
THE FEAR OF HER IS TOO MUCH.

ALL BLEAK CAN DO IS STARE AT WHAT IS UNFOLDING BEFORE HIM. HE KNOWS WHAT HE IS LOOKING AT--WHO HE IS LOOKING AT--AND CANNOT BELIEVE HIS EYES.

THE VOICE INSIDE HER HEAD TELLS HER TO WATCH, TO NOT LOOK AWAY.

THAT THIS IS THE BEGINNING OF THE END.

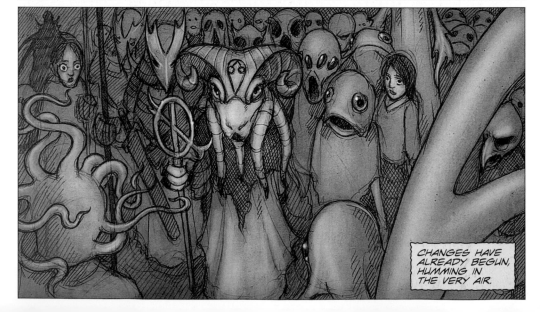

CHANGES HAVE ALREADY BEGUN, HUMMING IN THE VERY AIR.

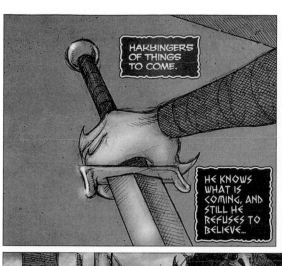

HARBINGERS OF THINGS TO COME.

HE KNOWS WHAT IS COMING, AND STILL HE REFUSES TO BELIEVE...

I AM THE HIGH LORD, AND YOU MUST OBEY ME!

I AM THE CHILD OF RAVENS, SISTER TO THE MOTHER OF SHADOWS, AND I AM HERE TO SHOW YOU THE ERROR OF YOUR WAYS.

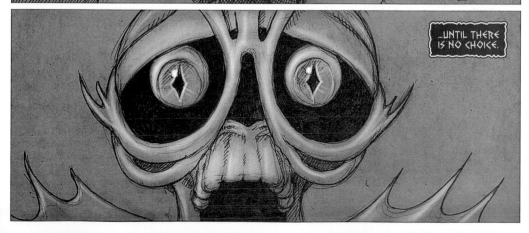

...UNTIL THERE IS NO CHOICE.

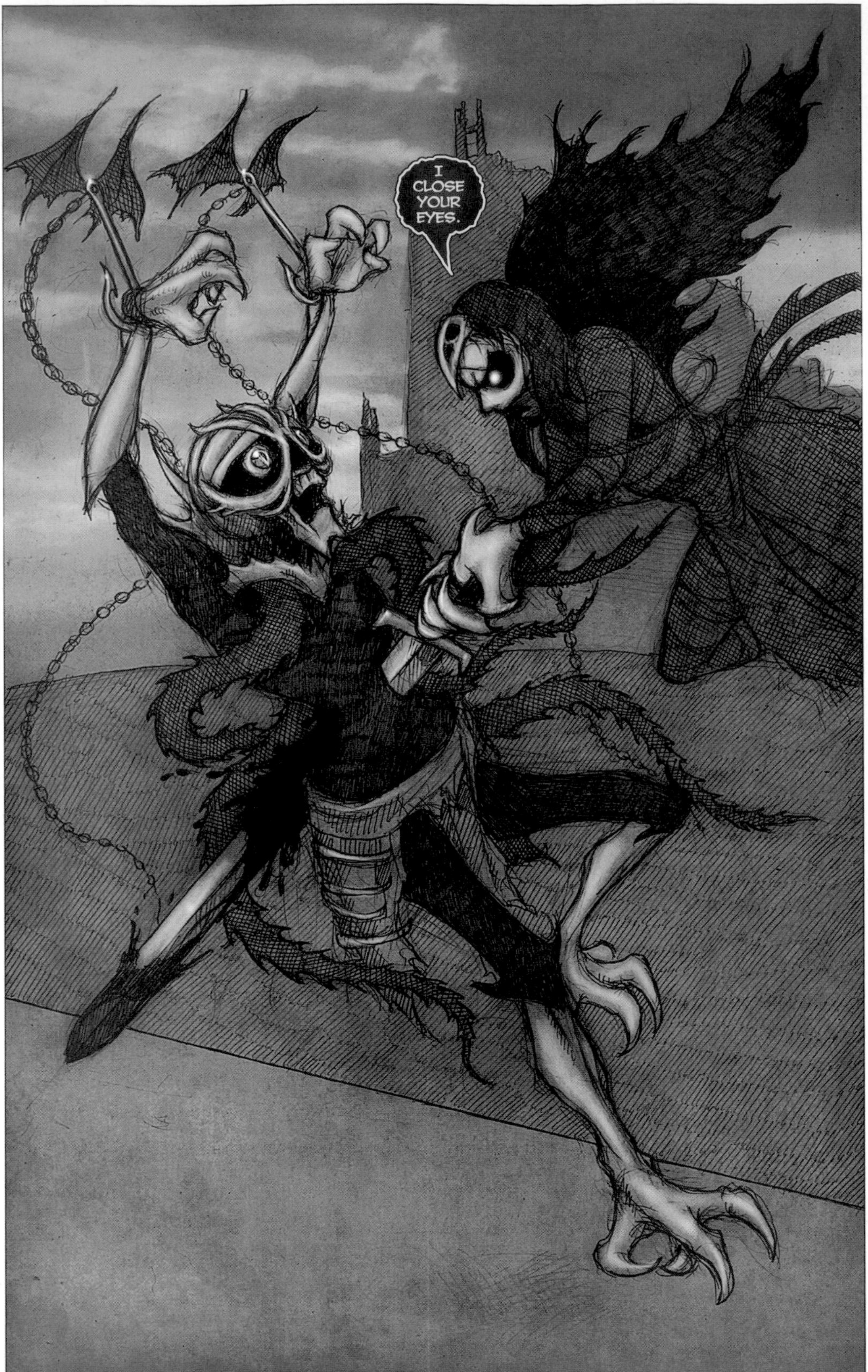
I CLOSE YOUR EYES.

FOR THE FIRST TIME THAT HE CAN RECALL, BLEAK ISN'T SURE HOW TO REACT. HOW DO YOU FIGHT SOMETHING LIKE THAT?

HOW DO YOU FIGHT A GODDESS?

THE BATTLE FOR NOW IS DONE.

THE ANSWER IS YOU DON'T.

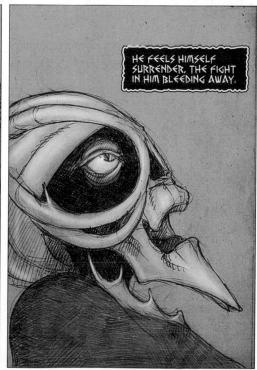

HE FEELS HIMSELF SURRENDER, THE FIGHT IN HIM BLEEDING AWAY.

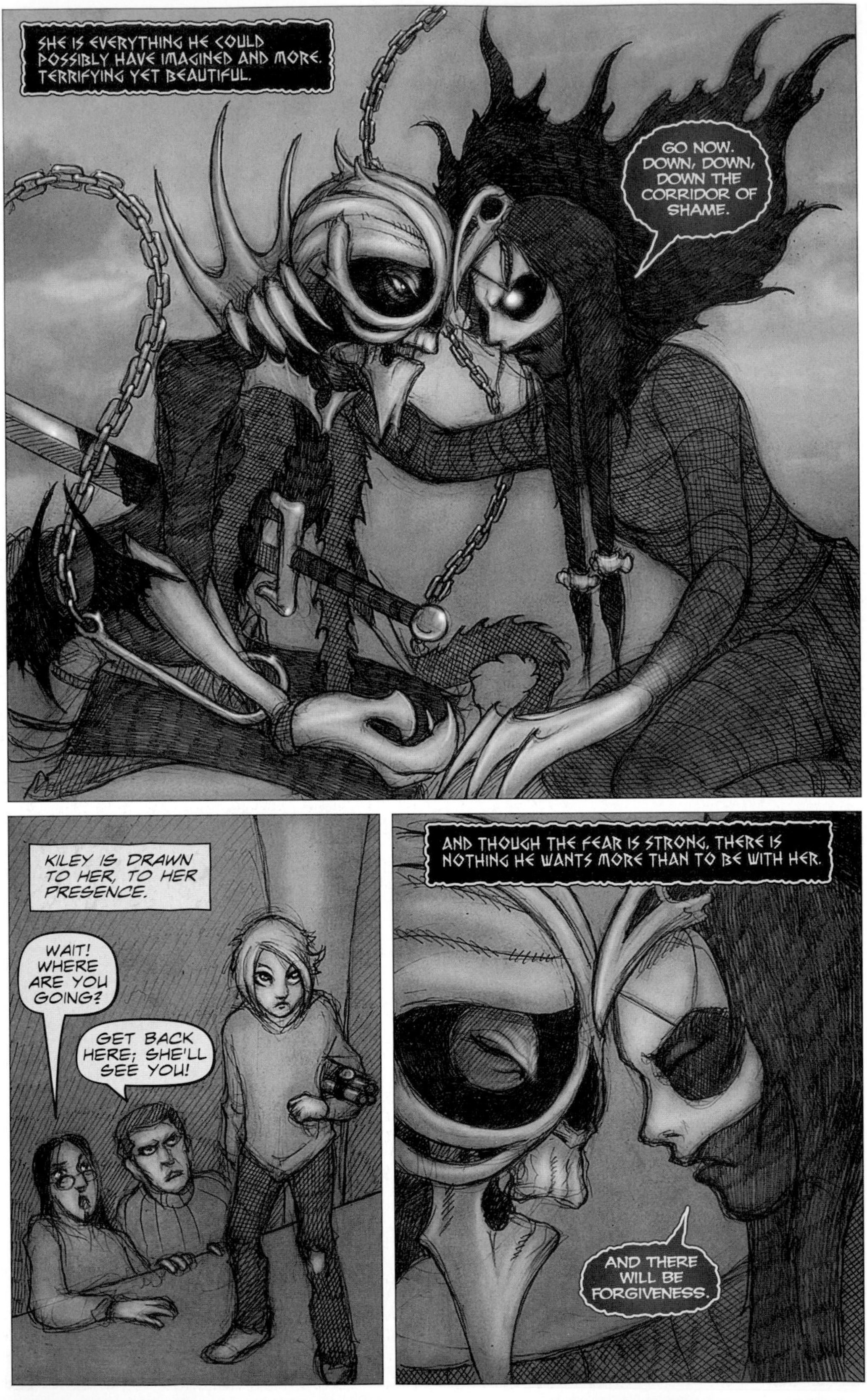
SHE IS EVERYTHING HE COULD POSSIBLY HAVE IMAGINED AND MORE. TERRIFYING YET BEAUTIFUL.
GO NOW. DOWN, DOWN, DOWN THE CORRIDOR OF SHAME.
KILEY IS DRAWN TO HER, TO HER PRESENCE.
WAIT! WHERE ARE YOU GOING?
GET BACK HERE; SHE'LL SEE YOU!
AND THOUGH THE FEAR IS STRONG, THERE IS NOTHING HE WANTS MORE THAN TO BE WITH HER.
AND THERE WILL BE FORGIVENESS.

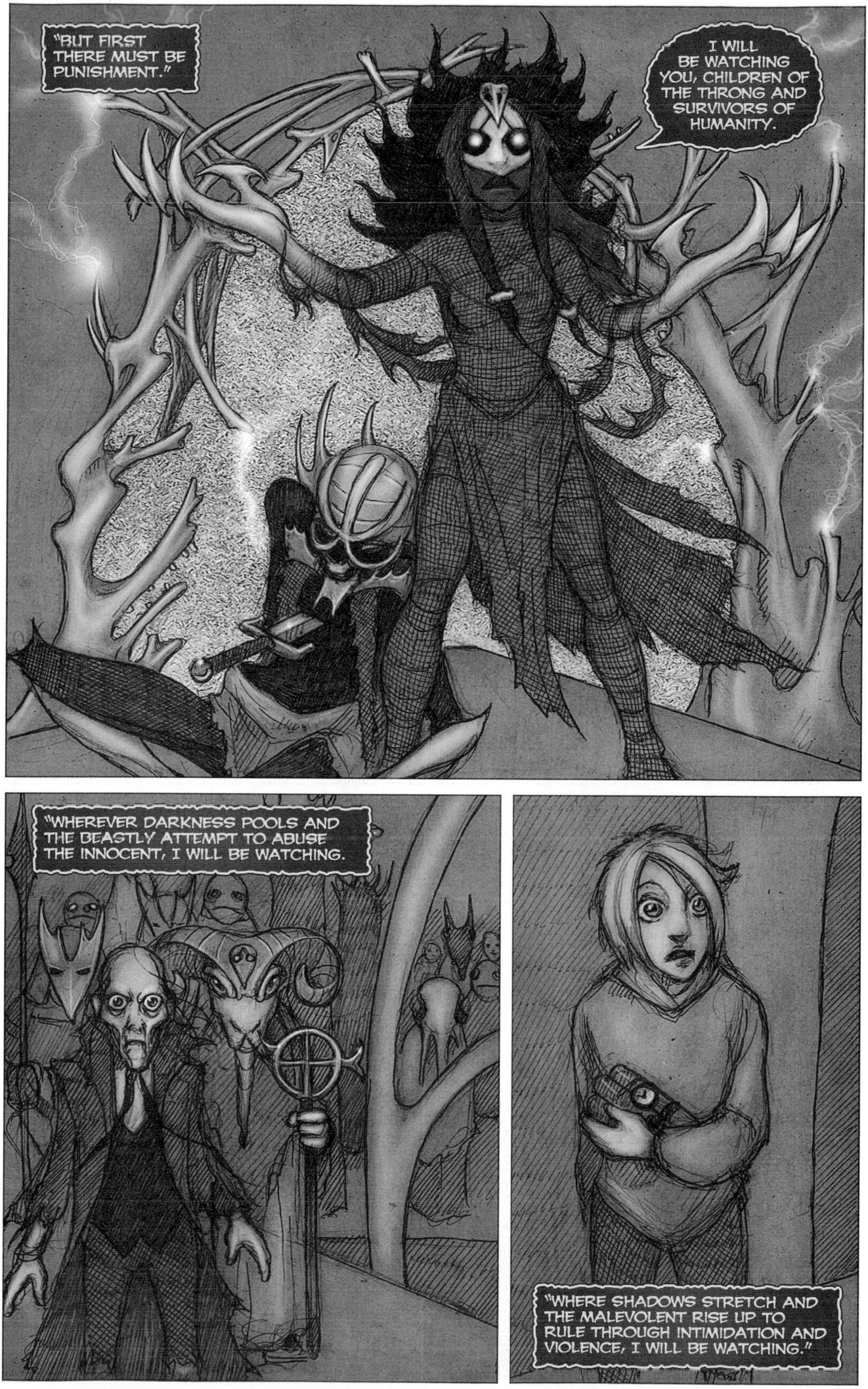
"BUT FIRST THERE MUST BE PUNISHMENT."
I WILL BE WATCHING YOU, CHILDREN OF THE THRONG AND SURVIVORS OF HUMANITY.
"WHEREVER DARKNESS POOLS AND THE BEASTLY ATTEMPT TO ABUSE THE INNOCENT, I WILL BE WATCHING.
"WHERE SHADOWS STRETCH AND THE MALEVOLENT RISE UP TO RULE THROUGH INTIMIDATION AND VIOLENCE, I WILL BE WATCHING."

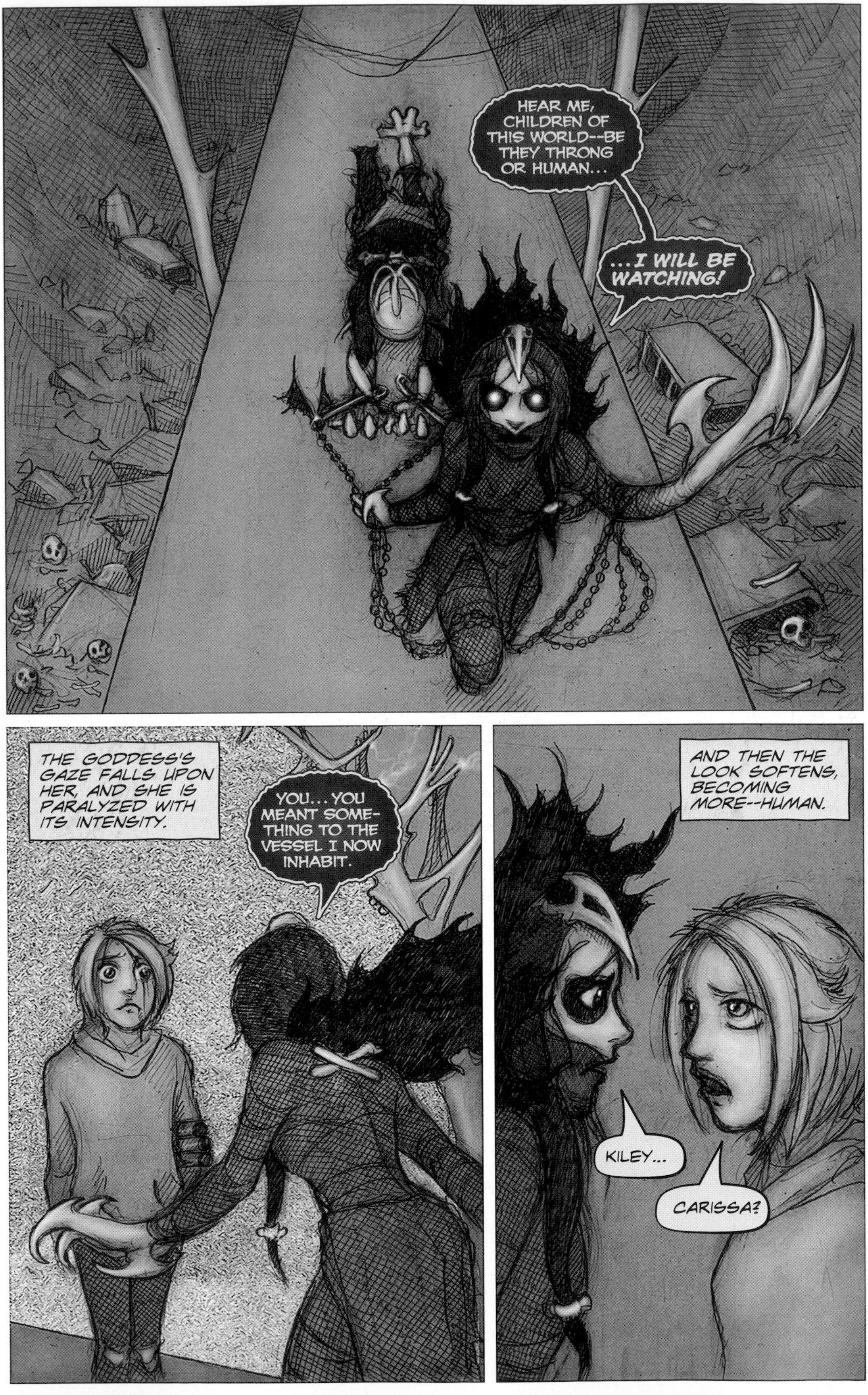
HEAR ME, CHILDREN OF THIS WORLD--BE THEY THRONG OR HUMAN...
...I WILL BE WATCHING!
THE GODDESS'S GAZE FALLS UPON HER, AND SHE IS PARALYZED WITH ITS INTENSITY.
YOU...YOU MEANT SOME-THING TO THE VESSEL I NOW INHABIT.
AND THEN THE LOOK SOFTENS, BECOMING MORE--HUMAN.
KILEY...
CARISSA?

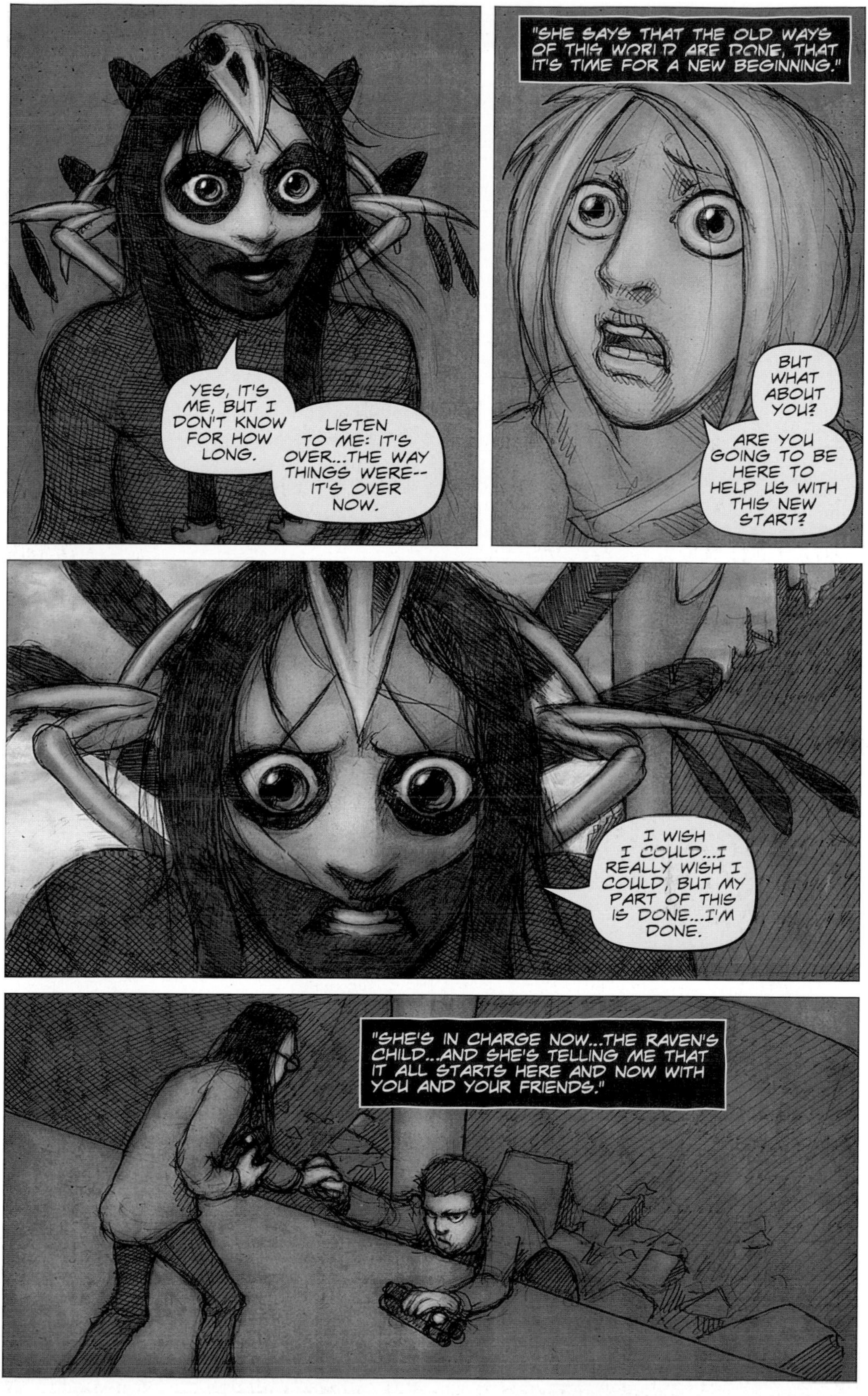
YES, IT'S ME, BUT I DON'T KNOW FOR HOW LONG.
LISTEN TO ME: IT'S OVER...THE WAY THINGS WERE-- IT'S OVER NOW.
"SHE SAYS THAT THE OLD WAYS OF THIS WORLD ARE DONE, THAT IT'S TIME FOR A NEW BEGINNING."
BUT WHAT ABOUT YOU?
ARE YOU GOING TO BE HERE TO HELP US WITH THIS NEW START?
I WISH I COULD...I REALLY WISH I COULD, BUT MY PART OF THIS IS DONE...I'M DONE.
"SHE'S IN CHARGE NOW...THE RAVEN'S CHILD...AND SHE'S TELLING ME THAT IT ALL STARTS HERE AND NOW WITH YOU AND YOUR FRIENDS."

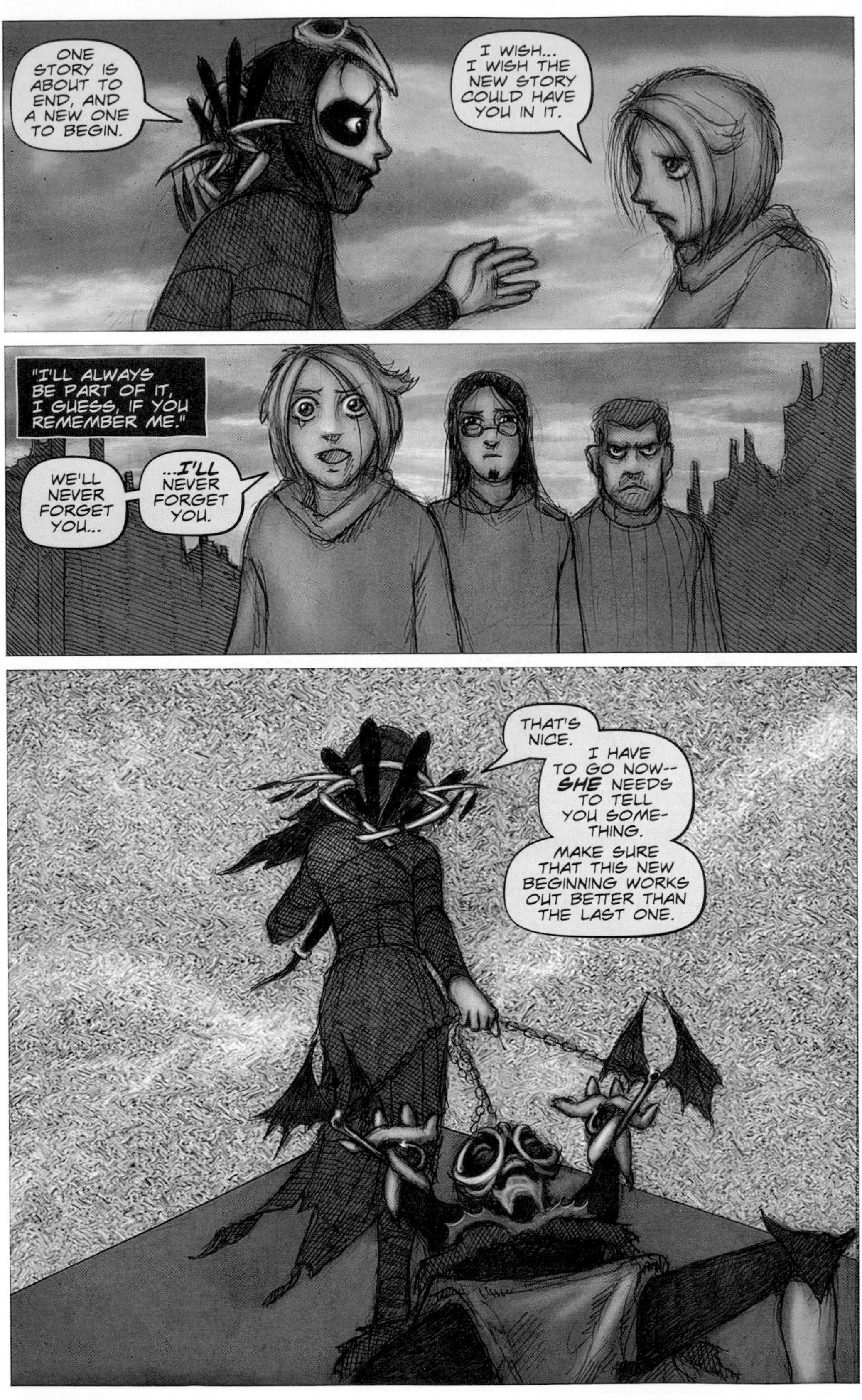
ONE STORY IS ABOUT TO END, AND A NEW ONE TO BEGIN.
I WISH... I WISH THE NEW STORY COULD HAVE YOU IN IT.
"I'LL ALWAYS BE PART OF IT, I GUESS, IF YOU REMEMBER ME."
WE'LL NEVER FORGET YOU...
...I'LL NEVER FORGET YOU.
THAT'S NICE.
I HAVE TO GO NOW-- SHE NEEDS TO TELL YOU SOME-THING.
MAKE SURE THAT THIS NEW BEGINNING WORKS OUT BETTER THAN THE LAST ONE.

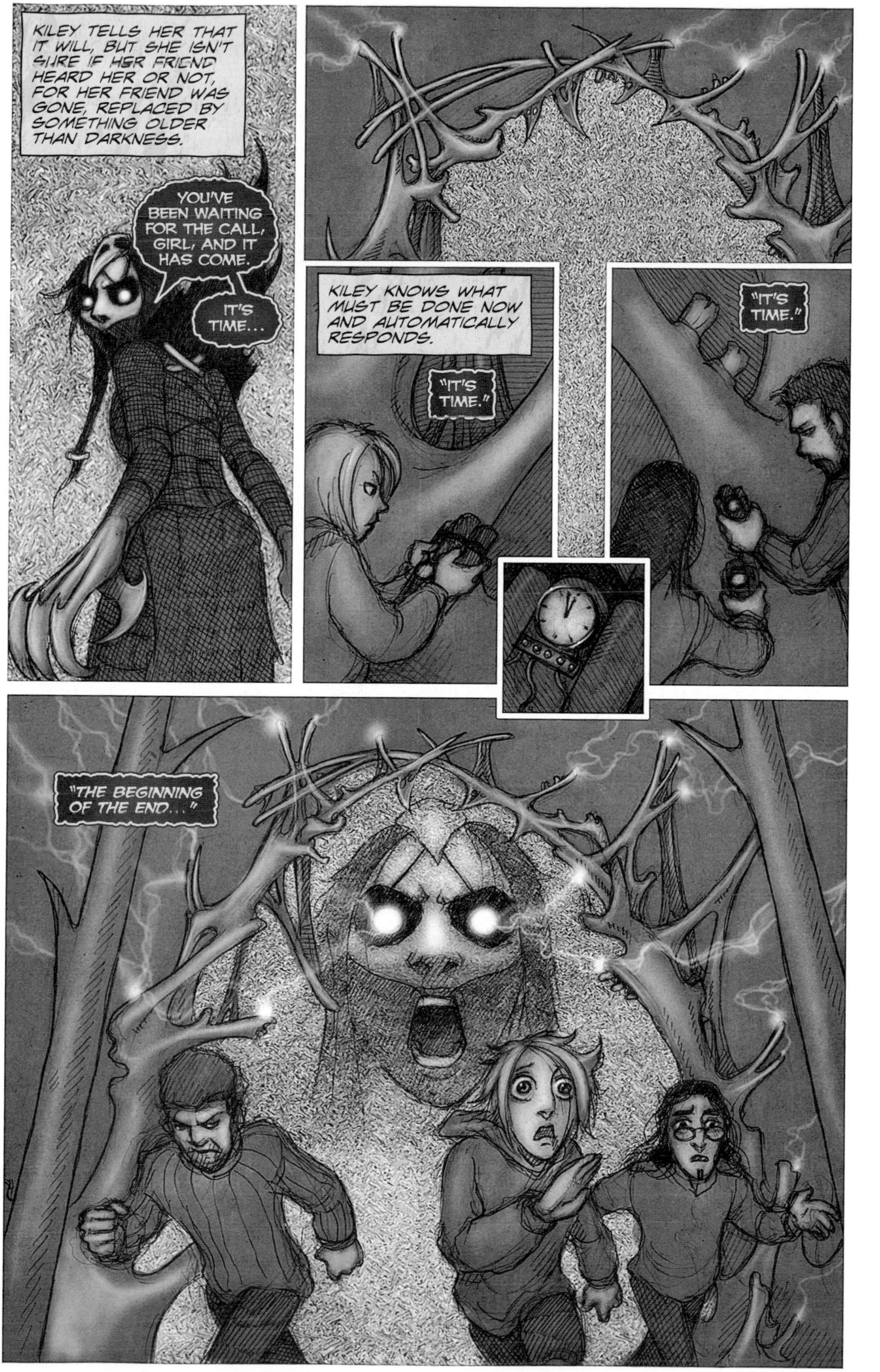
KILEY TELLS HER THAT IT WILL, BUT SHE ISN'T SURE IF HER FRIEND HEARD HER OR NOT, FOR HER FRIEND WAS GONE, REPLACED BY SOMETHING OLDER THAN DARKNESS.
YOU'VE BEEN WAITING FOR THE CALL, GIRL, AND IT HAS COME.
IT'S TIME...
KILEY KNOWS WHAT MUST BE DONE NOW AND AUTOMATICALLY RESPONDS.
"IT'S TIME."
"IT'S TIME."
"THE BEGINNING OF THE END..."

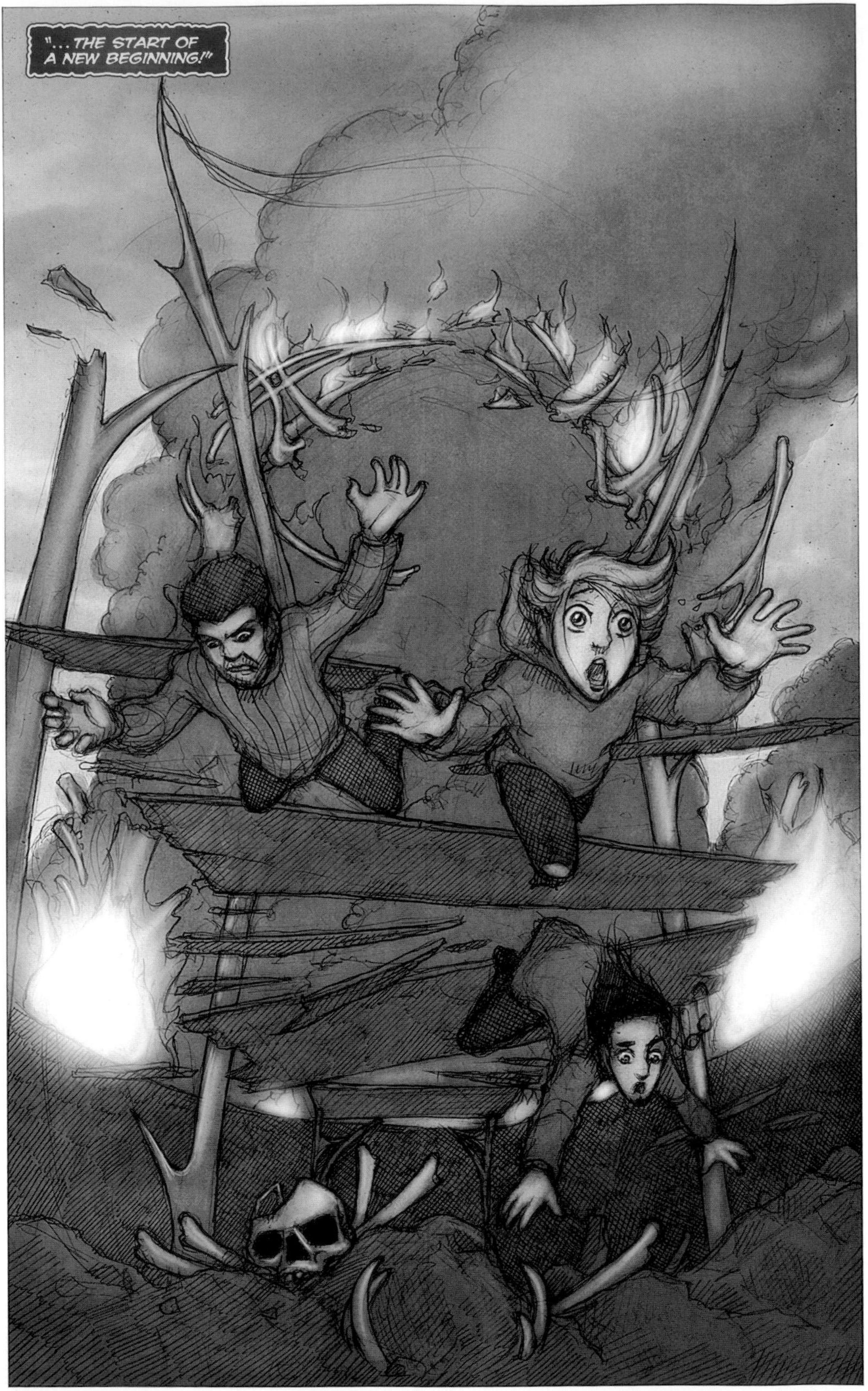
"...THE START OF A NEW BEGINNING!"

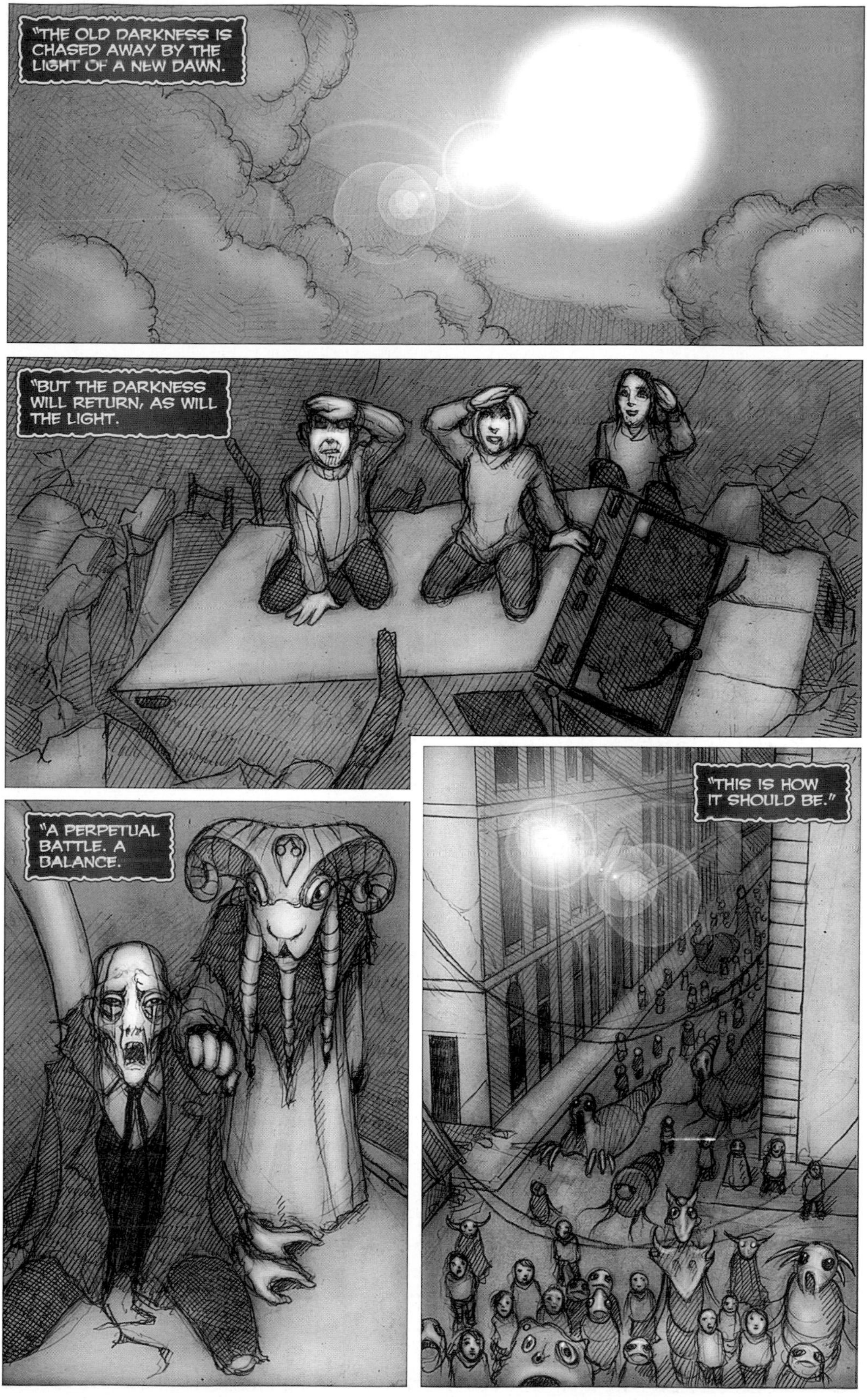
"THE OLD DARKNESS IS CHASED AWAY BY THE LIGHT OF A NEW DAWN.
"BUT THE DARKNESS WILL RETURN, AS WILL THE LIGHT.
"A PERPETUAL BATTLE. A BALANCE.
"THIS IS HOW IT SHOULD BE."

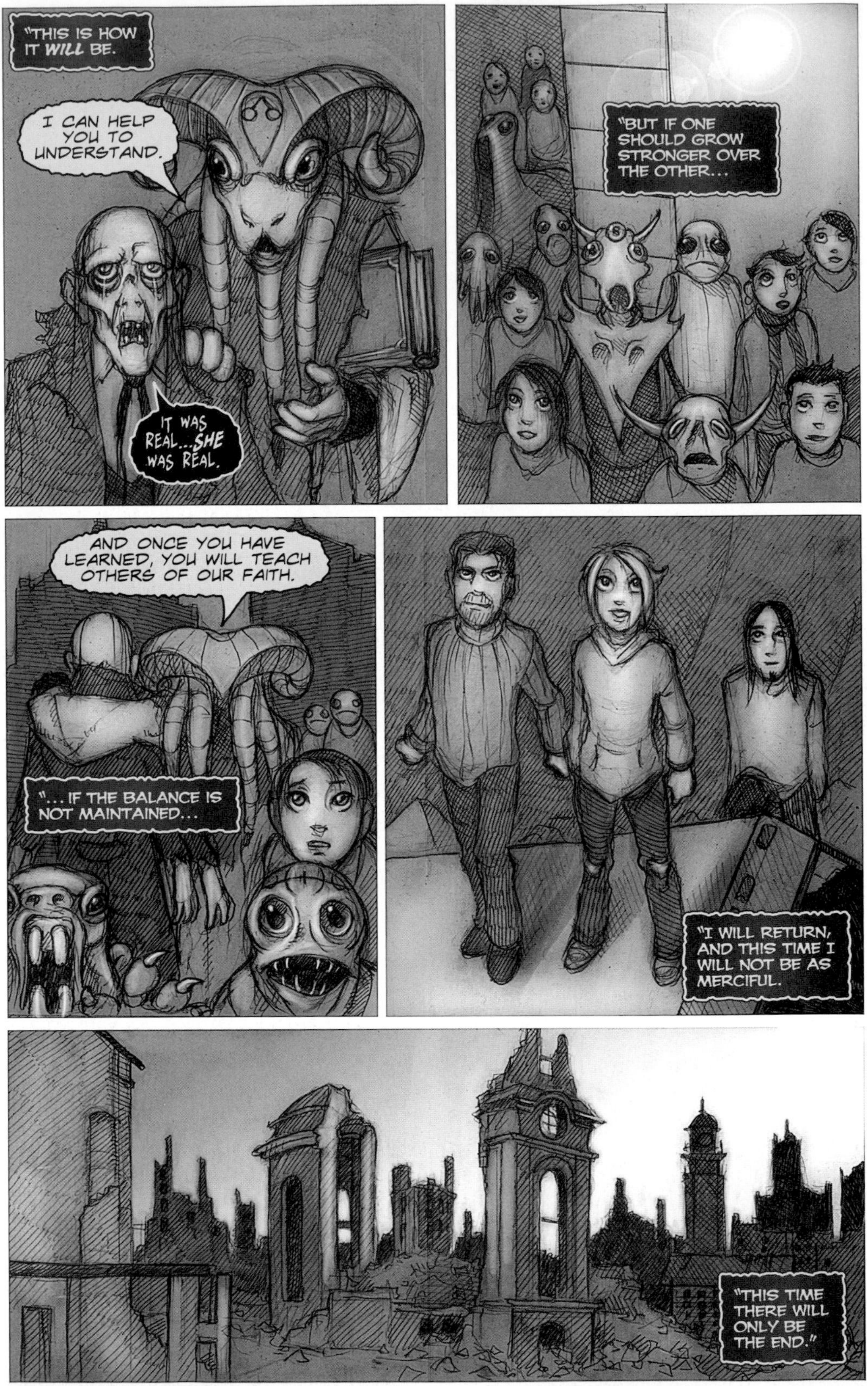
"THIS IS HOW IT WILL BE.
I CAN HELP YOU TO UNDERSTAND.
IT WAS REAL...SHE WAS REAL.
"BUT IF ONE SHOULD GROW STRONGER OVER THE OTHER...
AND ONCE YOU HAVE LEARNED, YOU WILL TEACH OTHERS OF OUR FAITH.
"...IF THE BALANCE IS NOT MAINTAINED...
"I WILL RETURN, AND THIS TIME I WILL NOT BE AS MERCIFUL.
"THIS TIME THERE WILL ONLY BE THE END."

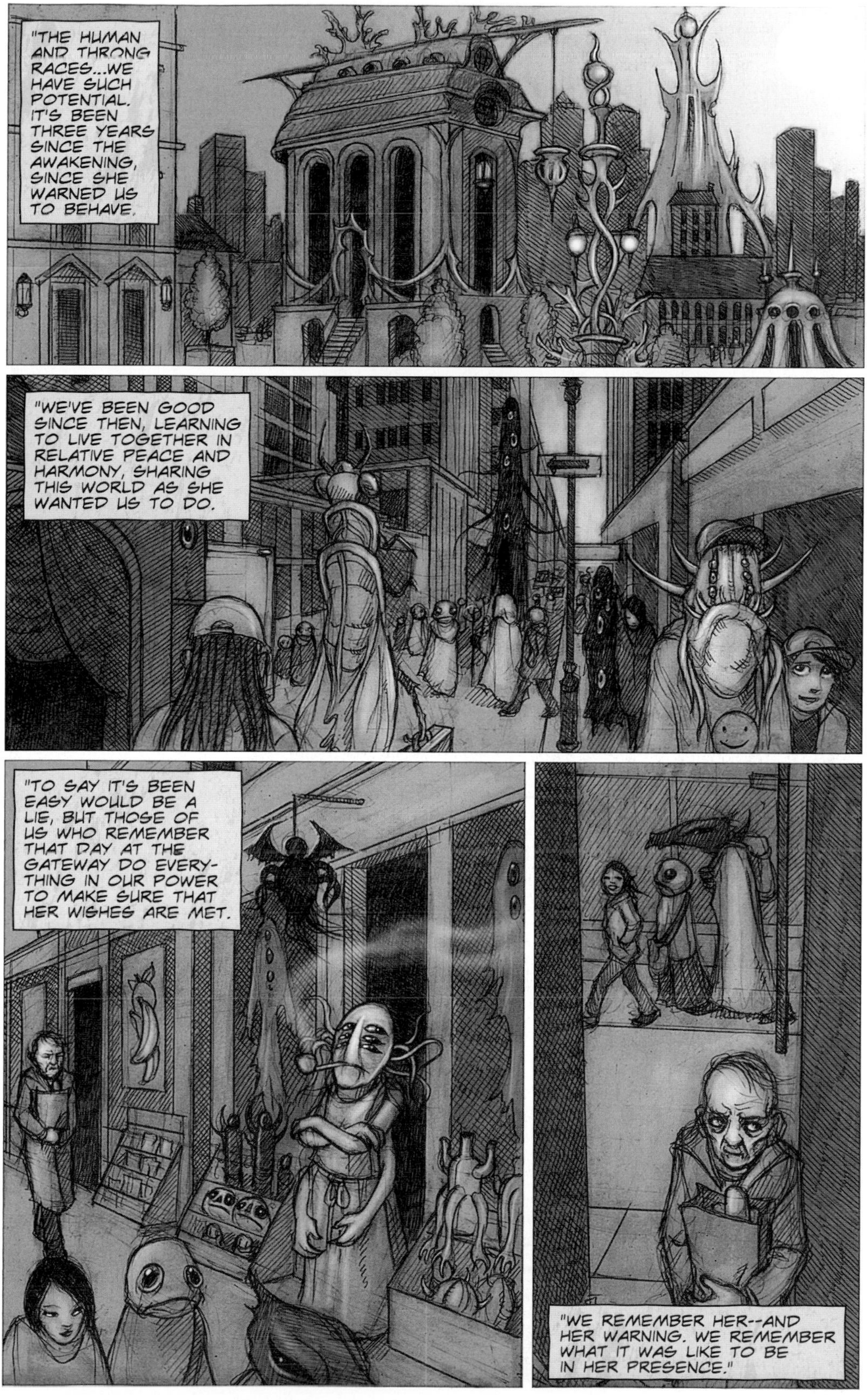
"THE HUMAN AND THRONG RACES...WE HAVE SUCH POTENTIAL. IT'S BEEN THREE YEARS SINCE THE AWAKENING, SINCE SHE WARNED US TO BEHAVE.
"WE'VE BEEN GOOD SINCE THEN, LEARNING TO LIVE TOGETHER IN RELATIVE PEACE AND HARMONY, SHARING THIS WORLD AS SHE WANTED US TO DO.
"TO SAY IT'S BEEN EASY WOULD BE A LIE, BUT THOSE OF US WHO REMEMBER THAT DAY AT THE GATEWAY DO EVERY-THING IN OUR POWER TO MAKE SURE THAT HER WISHES ARE MET.
"WE REMEMBER HER--AND HER WARNING. WE REMEMBER WHAT IT WAS LIKE TO BE IN HER PRESENCE."

"BUT THERE ARE THOSE OUT THERE WHO DON'T REMEMBER, OR DON'T CHOOSE TO. THOSE ARE THE ONES WHO WE NEED TO BE CONCERNED WITH.

"THOSE ARE THE ONES WHO NEED TO BE KEPT IN CHECK BEFORE THEY RUIN IT FOR US ALL."

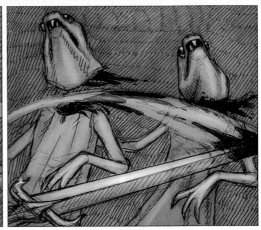

HERE, LET ME HELP YOU.

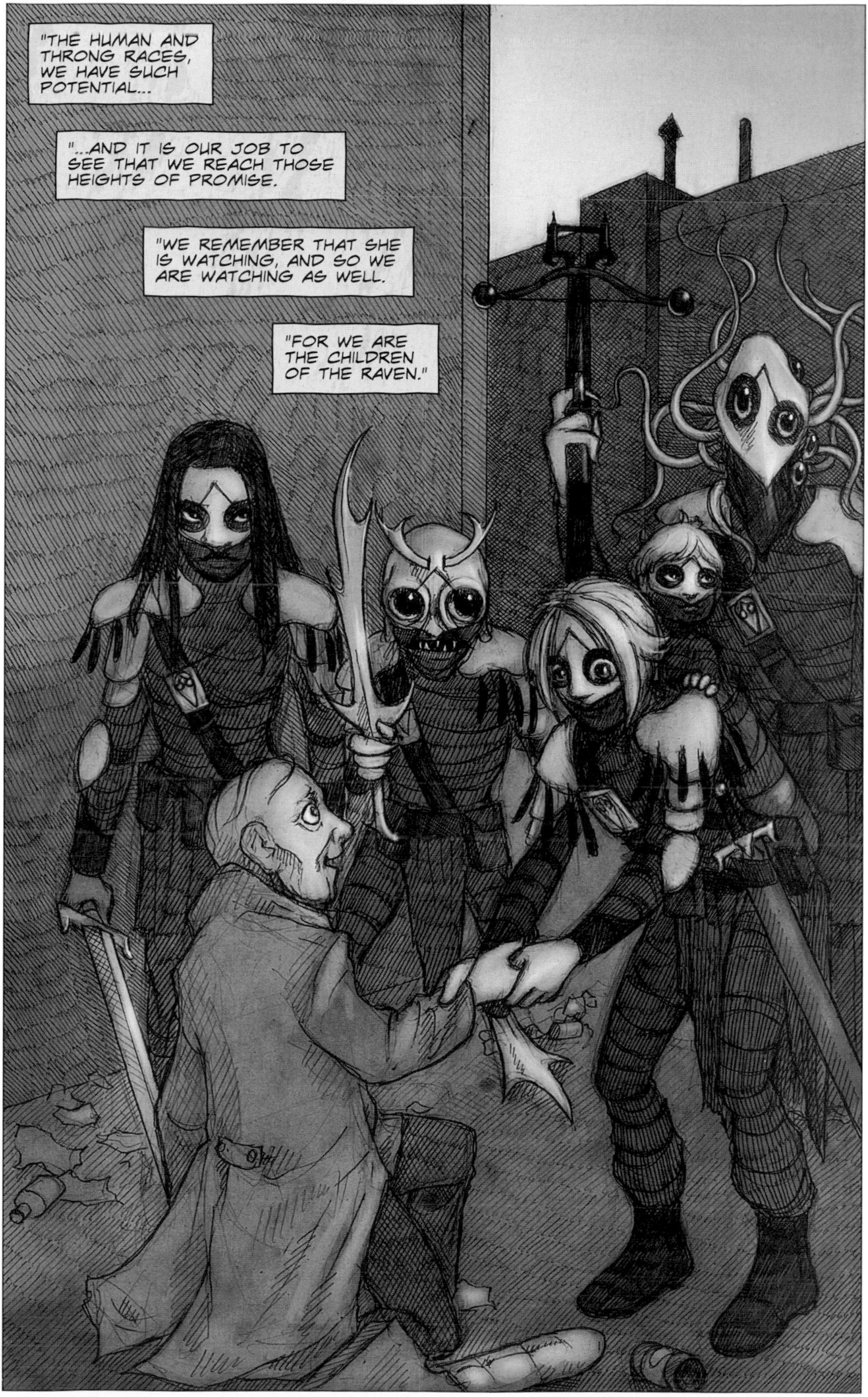
"THE HUMAN AND THRONG RACES, WE HAVE SUCH POTENTIAL...
"...AND IT IS OUR JOB TO SEE THAT WE REACH THOSE HEIGHTS OF PROMISE.
"WE REMEMBER THAT SHE IS WATCHING, AND SO WE ARE WATCHING AS WELL.
"FOR WE ARE THE CHILDREN OF THE RAVEN."

THOMAS E. SNIEGOSKI is a *New York Times* bestselling author who has written for children, young adults and adults, as well as for the comic book industry. As a comic book scripter, Tom has worked for nearly every major company in the comic book marketplace and has written such characters as Batman, the Punisher, Buffy the Vampire Slayer and Hellboy.

He is the only writer ever invited to work on Jeff Smith's international hit series BONE, collaborating with Smith on *BONE: Tall Tales* and the BONE: Quest for the Spark trilogy for Scholastic.

Tom is the author of the groundbreaking teen series The Fallen, which was transformed into three two-hour movies for the ABC Family channel in 2006 and 2007, earning stellar ratings for the cable network.

Sniegoski is also the author of the popular adult urban fantasy series featuring angel turned private eye Remy Chandler. The seventh book in the series, *A Deafening Silence in Heaven*, will be released in 2015.

Tom is currently working with Hellboy creator Mike Mignola on a new novel, *Grim Death & Bill the Electrocuted Criminal*, and with award-winning artist Frank Cho on an illustrated novel series called World of Payne. Both should be out sometime in 2016.

Tom was born and raised in the Boston area, where he still lives with his wife, LeeAnne, and their French bulldog, Kirby. Please visit him at sniegoski.com.

TOM BROWN is deeply uncomfortable referring to himself in the third person. He gets paper dirty (professionally) and has now done so for more years than he cares to admit to. Other examples of this compulsion can be found in the Hopeless, Maine, series, which he illustrates (and his wife and partner in crime, Nimue Brown, writes). When not imagining unspeakable monsters into being, Tom wanders the hills of Stroud (UK), digs (dirt), plays the tin whistle and drinks copious amounts of coffee (but not all at the same time).

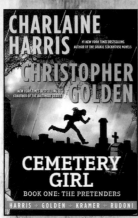

T344-0813